PLATE I

HIPPOCRATES

A composite portrait designed from a study of ancient medals and coins, by the Swiss artist, the late Albert Anker.

*Reproduced by the kind permission of Dr. Charles Du Bois, of Geneva*

[*front.*

# HISTORY OF MEDICINE

# HISTORY OF MEDICINE

**From the time of the Pharaohs to the end of the 18th Century**

**Charles Greene Cumston**

**GYAN PUBLISHING HOUSE**

**NEW DELHI-110002**

**HISTORY OF MEDICINE**

*(Medical)*

ISBN: 81-212-0673-1

Charles Greene Cumston



**1999**
Gyan Publishing House
5, Ansari Road
New Delhi-110 002

First Published London
Kegan Paul, Trench, Trubner & Co., Ltd.
New York: Alfred A. Knopf 1926

Laser typeseting: Gyan Publishing House
Printed at: Chawla Offest Printers

*THIS BOOK IS DEDICATED*
*WITH DEEP AFFECTION*
*TO MY WIFE AND MY SISTER.*

*C. G. C.*

# CONTENTS

# LIST OF ILLUSTRATIONS

# FOREWORD

> "*The little present must not be allowed wholly to elbow the great past out of view.*"
>
> ANDREW LANG.

THIS book has been written for the general reader and as an introduction for the student of medicine to the history of his chosen profession. The contents are a compilation of what the writer considers the most reliable and essential contributions to the subject, and, apart from some gleanings from his personal researches which are scattered throughout the pages, no claim is made to originality. Yet an attempt has been made to include matter not found in other works on the history of medicine in order that a clear concept may be obtained of the evolution of the healing art, while all unnecessary detail has been carefully avoided.

To save the reader trouble, only such references to literature as are considered necessary are made in the body of the text.

The author's deepest gratitude is due to his friend, F. G. Crookshank, M.D., F.R.C.P., of London, for revising the text, and his sincere thanks to Miss Bremner for her valuable help in the preparation of the manuscript.

And last, but not least, the author's profound thanks are due to Mr. M. R. Dobie for correcting the proofs and indexing the book.

GENEVA.

1*st May*, 1926.

# THE RELATION OF HISTORY AND PHILOSOPHY TO MEDICINE

## INTRODUCTORY ESSAY

By

F. G. CROOKSHANK, M.D. (Lond.), F.R.C.P.

*Physician to the Prince of Wales' General Hospital and to the French Hospital, London*

"J'étais dogmatique à vingt ans, observateur à trente ; à quarante je fus empirique ; je n'ai point de système à cinquante." Ainsi parlait un médecin qui passait sa vie dans l'étude de l'art. La matière que je traite exige d'abord quelques éclaircissements sur cette declaration d'un homme instruit.

—Théophile de Bordeu.

## THE RELATION OF HISTORY AND PHILOSOPHY TO MEDICINE

WHILST the successful, nay, the competent practice of Medicine—an Art which includes that of Surgery—may be, and often is, compatible with ignorance of the History of Medicine, he is the best physician in the classical and fullest sense of the word who unites a mastery of his Art to an intimate acquaintance with the great historical doctrines and the philosophies on which they are based.

In default of a Philosophy of Medicine there can indeed be no true Science of Medicine, and it is because the History of Medicine is now too often regarded as but a pleasant bypath, in which the amiable dilettante on whom practice makes no too exacting claim may stray, that Pathology—the true Science of Medicine—no longer exists, and that the word itself is accorded a significance by whose virtue is digged deeper, and ever deeper still, the gulf that separates the 'pathologist' from the bedside.

Since too, for Medicine, Philosophy and History are no less concretely united than Croce finds them to be for all other departments of knowledge, without History Medicine may only be scientific in the modern, or journalistic sense of the word—a sense imputing little beyond the possession of some attractive form of technical precision. That is to say, the art of the practitioner may be implemented by the exercise of technical procedures that have become more or less rationalized by appeal to what are called the auxiliary sciences—anatomy, physiology, chemistry, and physics—while, in default of proper first principles pertaining to Pathology, discussion may be assisted by reference to the principles of these sciences.

But this sort of thing, even if making Medicine 'scientific' from the point of view and for the purposes of journalism and subsidized 'research', does not constitute a "Science of Medicine."

And so it is that the modern but really uncultured, though not altogether untaught, student of Medicine leaves the study of biology, chemistry, physics, anatomy and physiology —disciplines relating to defined fields of knowledge by and in which facts are resumed in stated generalizations, and observations are interpreted in respect of certain first principles—to approach the study of Medicine itself without any enquiry into the foundations of Science, and without the slightest hint that the 'diseases' which he is about to learn to 'cure' or 'investigate' are other than natural objects of perception. Far less is he afforded any information as to the views once held—before the advent of the bacteriological dispensation now drawing to a close—in respect of the nature of disease and 'diseases'—unless in a sentence accompanied by the sneer of ignorance or the snigger of self-sufficiency. Small wonder, then, that the 'qualified man' enters upon the practical business of his life no less ill-equipped for profitable research, or for intellectual expansion and re-adjustment, than would be a taxi-driver, licensed for the Metropolitan area, competent to conduct an expedition across Central Arabia or the desert of Gobi.

It is by reason of this neglect, in official Medicine, of all study of History and Philosophy that, in presidential orations and the like exercises, it is still asked whether Medicine be a Science or an Art, and the dismal response is still given that the question may not profitably be discussed since it is one that cannot be answered. Nothing but the familiar reply could well be more fatuous than this familiar question!

Undoubtedly, there is an Art of Medicine: an Art, that is, in the sense of Sir Sidney Colvin's celebrated statement that "every regulated operation or dexterity by which organized beings pursue ends which they know beforehand, together with the rules and the result of every such operation or dexterity, constitutes an Art." Certes, there is such an Art of Medicine: one which, in Harvey's words, is a habit with reference to things *to be done*.

But on the other hand, Science, as Harvey said, is a habit in respect of things *to be known*. Truly, there is no reason at all why in Medicine we should not cultivate such an habit, in respect of things to be known; but, as we not only do not do so, and actually do refuse to do so, we cannot say that there we have ready to hand any such "ordered knowledge of the phenomena of disease and the relations between them" as would warrant us in claiming Modern Medicine to rank among the Sciences. Such ordered knowledge of the phenomena of disease and the relations between them as would, in the terms of another celebrated definition, "constitute a true Science of Medicine" is not to be furnished by mere empirical observation: by 'passive perceptions', that is, however ordered and recorded; but by that process of reasoning *concerning* the 'passive perceptions' in which alone, in the opinion of Plato, approved by Berkeley, does Science consist.

In other words, since our refusal to examine or even state the first principles of Pathology, there is not now any true Science of Medicine.

And so do we arrive at the paradox—true, as are all genuine paradoxes—that, when in the sixteenth century Medicine was, as we should say, less 'scientific' than to-day, Medicine was indeed, as it now is not, a Science in very truth.

For, in the sixteenth century, such "Institutes of Medicine" as that of Fernel (amongst others referred to by Dr. Cumston) did afford, as still, a valuable, orderly, ordered, and symmetrical presentation of the known facts then available in respect of the phenomena of health and disease, together with a rational and rationalized interpretation of them consistently with the philosophical and logical views of their exponent.

We are indeed justified in saying that not only has Fernel left us an admirable exposition of the Science of Medicine, as he saw it, but one that still influences profoundly the teaching of many who believe the true foundations of "Medical Science" to have been "discovered" since the Great Exhibition of 1851. But the twentieth century has as yet produced no such ordered and orderly presentation, as did the sixteenth, of the known facts concerning disease: duly set out and interpreted with respect to definitions, stated first principles, enunciated doctrines and terminal conclusions: embracing (as must any Science of Medicine) consideration of metaphysical problems of one kind or another, whether in relation to mental disease or to the understanding of the normal functioning of the body; and making, at any rate, some allusion to the epistemological and ontological questions which lie at the very base of the superstructure we call Science. We accumulate, and persist in accumulating *ad infinitum* records of our 'passive perceptions', and we surround ourselves with a vast assembly of material, some of which is here and there neatly docketed and sorted out. Hither and thither we may roam at our will, constructing, now with a Grecian capital, now with a Roman brick or two, and now with the fragments of a Gothic arch, some temporary shelter for ourselves against the desolating bleakness of instructed criticism. Some of us may even set up little composite altars at which we and a few special adherents may worship—for a time. But no Temple arises to take the place of those long since fallen in ruins. Our best efforts at syncretism have given us not a Pantheon but rather a Madame Tussaud's Wax Works, which, with the aid of modern journalism, serves to interest the public and sometimes to obtain 'Government Support.'

Architects of to-day, even though condemned to give ferro-concrete expression to the spiritual strivings of twentieth century post-war commercialism, still need must recognize the eternal principles bequeathed to us from Greece, from Rome, from Medieval Europe, and indeed from China and Peru. But the Modern Physician, prouder and more complacent than any Architect, while turning the weekly pages of the *British Medical Journal* and *Lancet*, feels he has nothing to learn from the philosophic physicians of Cos, of Alexandria, of Rome, of Baghdad and Cordova, and from the contemporaries—no lesser men than they—of Dante, of da Vinci, of Wren and of Newton.

A tolerant, and usually incorrectly verified allusion in the opening paragraph of an occasional address, that in itself gives renewed presentation to fallacies old before the Pyramids were built, is—too often—the sole tribute paid by Modern Physicians to the History of Medicine.

Were it otherwise, the Modern Scientist would recharge his fountain pen with less complacency than now, to prescribe for his best patient the latest nostrum forced upon his intelligence by the 'artistic' blotting paper calendars so benevolently and insistently sent him, in the name of Science, by Syndicalized Pharmacists.

How is it that the present state of affairs has come about? The History of Medicine itself supplies, in part, the answer.

* * * * *

Until perhaps a hundred or more years ago, it was not possible to become a Doctor of Physic (or of Medicine) without the acquisition of such knowledge of the History and Philosophy of Medicine as may still be obtained from the study of Hippocrates, of Galen, and of their ancient and modern commentators. The discipline was one of severity and of value. True, it was not always sufficiently implemented by clinical study; but is it therefore now reasonable to exclude from the curriculum all reference to what has been uttered by the greatest minds in interpretation of clincial observations? Unfortunately, and in increasing measure since the passage of the Medical Act, the classical and valuable distinction between the Practitioner, or Man of Art, and the Doctor, or Man learned in the Science of his Art, has become obliterated by the levelling down process which, in a democratic age, is considered to mark progress. Even the Royal College of Physicians of London has been compelled to avoid the reproach of medieval conservatism by sacrificing to the wolves of progress the last fragments of general learning till lately preserved for those seeking admission to Membership. Although the lamp of the History of Medicine, lighted in England by Freind in the eighteenth century, and jealously tended by Sir Norman Moore in the nineteenth, has never quite gone out, and though efforts have lately been made to cherish further the flame, yet, despite the encouraging appointment of a lecturer on the History of Medicine in the University of London, it cannot be said that, in Great Britain, there is either proper appreciation of the need, or proper provision of facilities, for the instruction of medical students and others in the History of Medicine. Nor is it probable that real advance will be made until the control of Medical Education and Medical Research is shared, at least in some measure, by those who love the history and principles of their Art and Science.

Now there is perhaps another reason for the neglect of the study of the History and Philosophy of Medicine in Great Britain. Medicine for some fifty years or so now has come, and properly, to ally herself with the various biological sciences. But this alliance was first effected under the influence and aegis of biologists and experimenters who, while making great contributions to the recorded sum of our 'passive perceptions,' were not always men of science in the fullest sense and who, indeed, though competent observers, sometimes lost their bearings in the field of thought. And so it is that the mid-Victorian and 'scientific' form of scholastic realism, with its profound belief in the 'reality' of causes, actions, forces and laws, and its staggering reliance on the something called Baconian or inductive logic (supposedly developed by the nominalist Mill, as an instrument for the precise discovery of Truth) has long exercised, and bids fair to exercise still longer in Medicine, an influence hardly credible to those aware of the present-day discussions between Science and Philosophy.

Our national distaste for hypotheses—when recognized as such, *bien entendu*—so long the object of gentle raillery from Continental thinkers, and our failure to absorb the teachings of our own great philosophers—Occam, Hobbes, Locke, Hume, and Bentham—whilst unintelligently lauding Bacon for what he never accomplished, has led us, in Medicine at any rate, to suppose that, if we only continue to go on observing and experimenting hard enough, and long enough, Truths, Laws and Eternal Verities will still continue to 'emerge' from the prison-house to which 'Aristotle' and the 'Scholastics' are supposed to have consigned them. And so, unless we pay timely heed to such writers as the authors of *The Meaning of Meaning* we fall into a pit we have digged for ourselves and, distrustful alike of reasoning and of hypothesis, assume as 'facts' the fancies which freely arise in our minds when considering phenomena—sc long, that is, as no discussion, definition, or theory of symbolization is embarked upon. Such fancies, when arising from the contemplation of experiments upon a guinea pig are, for modern 'scientists', 'scientific generalizations' *ex hypothesi*: reasoning conducted at the bedside, and in respect of clinical phenomena, is 'speculative,' unprofitable, and even 'metaphysical'! Indeed, such full reliance is placed by medical observers upon the experimental, or analogical, methods that some medical methods of research of to-day could only be paralleled were astronomers to study orreries rather than the heavens, and strategists to abandon all such purely 'literary" exercises as the study of the Caesarian and Napoleonic campaigns in favour of investigations of "what really does happen" during autumn manoeuvres on Salisbury Plain.

But, apart from all this, the fundamental error of confounding interpretations with perceptions, and of finding some expression of absolute Reality in agreeable interpretations—the error against which no one in recent times has fought more lucidly than Mach and his pupils—leads us, in Medicine, to see little value in former interpretations, and the only true light in those now fashionable. And this at the very moment when we reject the observations of our predecessors so far as they are inconsistent with our own interpretations, and select, for record, only those series of phenomena that support those of our interpretations which for the moment masquerade as 'facts'! Yet, properly used, not only the observations but the interpretations of Hippocrates, of Ballonius, and of Sydenham are even to-day as guides in our constant endeavours during the practice of our Art and in our patient gropings towards understanding the phenomena of Plague and Pestilence. The classical doctrines of Medicine should enter into the training, if not of every practitioner, yet of every *teacher* of Medicine, no less insistently than does acquaintance with the works of the Greeks, the Romans, the geniuses of the Renaissance—aye, of the Egyptians, Hindus and Chinese—become indispensable to the teacher and practitioner of Architecture. It is true that there is now a school, or the shadow of a school, which, dissatisfied with present trends, yet seeking a positive basis, is wishful to give a purely 'descriptive' account of the universe as seen to-day by them and others, and yet, withal, one which would avoid 'interpretations.' But so far as the accounts yet provided by this method are purely descriptive and free from implication of 'theory' or 'interpretation,' so far are the results of this method as sterile as would be the attempt to build a cathedral by forswearing design and arranging piles of material neatly on the site selected. So far as the accounts provided are useful, they are useful because 'interpretations' of temporary though undoubted value are put forward, even if in the guise of descriptions or as observed 'facts.' So, in Medicine, when we have waded through many pages of 'protocols' in some periodical 'Archives of Research'—dull pages in which experiments are lengthily set out in the duly approved manner—when we arrive at the final and professedly colourless 'Summary' we are bound to confess that, in a bald statement that X specimens of Y have been examined and found to be Z, there is little of profit *unless* we first know in what sense the author has used his symbols 'X,' 'Y,' and 'Z.'

But—God bless us—this is to admit in medical discussions the need for definitions—in John Hunter's opinion, of all things most damnable and, in the President of the Royal Society's—"notoriously difficult." Yet, once the need for definition is admitted the whole airy edifice of a purely descriptive account of the Universe—or any part of it—dissolves into the empyrean. For, the moment we begin to define our terms, we pass from the region of pure description, since, as Poincaré has clearly shown, the only definitions that do not involve a *circulus vitiosus* are those which are *predicative*, i.e., which are more than descriptive.

Now any account of any part of the Universe, however limited, that excludes metaphysical or philosophical discussion and that dispenses with the history of all previous accounts of that part of the Universe, is purely arbitrary and therefore unscientific—in terms of the only definitions of Science that command anything like general assent. The Aristotelian dictum that Science is concerned only with universals still holds. We admit, since Galileo, the necessity for proper selection and arrangement of the particulars, if useful and convenient universals are to be formed. But, the mere collection of particulars leads us no nearer to the proper formation of a universal than does a non-predicative 'definition' really 'define.'

Indeed, the formation of the 'universal' implies predication in respect of the particulars and therefore something more than description of them. This something more than description is Conception; and hence the importance of Conceptualism as more than a halfway house or *via media* between, as indeed an integration or reconciliation of, the Realist and Nominalist positions. In this respect perhaps no better statement of the methods of Science has yet been, or ever will be given than that of Harvey in the *Introduction* to his *De Generatione*. The compulsory study of this brief essay would alone justify the imposition, on every advanced student, of instruction in the History of Medicine.

It is only necessary to read again what Harvey—the contemporary of Lord Verulam—said concerning the place of the old methods beside the new, to realize how grotesque is the error involved in our favourite cliché—that, with Harvey *and* Bacon, Science entered upon a new birth that has since enabled Medicine to " free herself from the trammels of Metaphysic and Philosophy." It is no paradox to say that, just so far as Medicine has followed " the way pointed out by Bacon " and has freed herself from the 'taint' of metaphysics, so far indeed has she departed from the injunctions of Harvey and has ceased to remain a Science, despite the 'scientific' additions made to the exercise of our Art by the allied sciences.

Harvey's own great achievement in discovering the circulation of the blood did not, in very truth, constitute an 'induction' or establish any 'generalization.' It was rather an achievement of the same order as the conquest of England by William the Conqueror, the discovery of America by Columbus, or the building of Saint Paul's by Christopher Wren.

Harvey's further achievement—that of convincing the world of the truth of his statements—was a feat only to be accomplished by an intellectual giant who had the complete mastery of forms of thought and expression displayed in the *Introduction* just referred to. This is why an Englishman need not trouble to refute the claims made in favour of the prior discovery of the circulation by Cesalpinus or another.

Possible achievements such as Harvey's actual discovery are finitely limited, as are the discoverable continents or territories. But the wider prospects opened up to us if we attempt to obey Harvey's injunction and to " seek out the secrets of Nature by experiment " are, as Harvey's own work showed, prospects which require for their exploration all the intellectual weapons that the study of philosophy in the broadest sense places at our disposal. And Philosophy is History; and History, Philosophy. But the vain repetition of Harvey's advice to seek out the secrets of Nature by experiment—without any enquiry as to what he meant by experiment—is sometimes manifestly an excuse for neglecting the essential reasoning "upon our passive perceptions" that constitutes Science: just as Hunter's dictum—"Don't think, try"—is too often used to depreciate the value of those intellectual resources that Harvey himself loved to exercise. And so, in the belief that Bacon really did provide us with some machinery whereby Truth could be discovered, all attempts to codify the facts of medicine, to define our principles, and to elucidate the meanings of what we say, have been remorselessly put on one side, while logic, metaphysics, philosophy, and history, have been displaced from the curricula of candidates for even the Doctorate of Medicine and other special diplomas. The scrapping of these disciplines in the alleged interest of mental economy has, of course, resulted in the utter loss of that economy in thought which, as Mach insists, it is the mission of Science to secure. Parcimony is not economy; and economy in thought cannot be fully realized until and unless we recognize the value to thought of the teachings of the great English philosophers (other than Bacon) from Occam to Bentham, and of conceptualists of the schools of Kant, Mach, Vaihinger and Poincaré. Accepting the purely conceptual value of our universals, laws, and generalizations, as convenient interpretative expressions of what we perceive, and so *AS IF* true, we recognize the relative and related values of the interpretations of the past as well as of those of to-day. So perhaps, as Masson-Oursel would say, through analogically comparative or proportional methods, we may attain in some sense a notion of positive values. One hypothesis, says Poincaré, is not really more true, but only *plus commode* than another. And, when we realize that the differences between the various historical schools of Medicine, and those between their representatives to-day, mark differences in *milieu*, in perspective, in convenience, and perhaps in the personalities of the teachers, rather than in Truthfulness, we appreciate all the better the value of the study of the changes and progressions and regressions in medical thought and in practice that have occurred since the rival schools of Cos and of Cnidus first flourished. But when we thus regard the whole stream of medical history, we come to appreciate how, greatly as we have increased our perceptive range (and so our storehouse of facts) by the invention and application of modern instruments, appurtenances and methods, yet do the ancient schools and schisms in respect of interpretations of observed phenomena still persist. Still are there amongst us not only true Coans and obstinate Cnidians, but emphatic empirists and hardheaded dogmatists: inveterate methodists and worldly-wise eclectics: persistent iatro-chemists and no less determined iatro-mechanists: acrid humoralists and weighty solidists: eager vitalists and unyielding organicists; nay, enthusiastic mystics and doubting sceptics. But, just as—perhaps for the same reason—just as it has been said that all men are naturally either Aristotelians or Platonists, so may it be said and with truth that ever throughout the history of Occidental medicine, as still to-day, the line of cleavage between physicians and schools of medicine is fundamentally one of metaphysical attitude. First and foremost, consciously or unconsciously, physicians belong to one or other of two schools of thought, represented in the Middle Ages by the Scholastic Realists and the Scholastic Nominalists. Even when a professedly Conceptualist position is consciously adopted, as a *via media*—or better, as reconciling Realism and Nominalism—still, in the beginning and in practice, either Realism or Nominalism is naturally inclined to and, as a rule, is the final choice. The problem involved is, of course, the very central problem of metaphysics and logic—that of the nature and quality of universals. In medicine the name of 'a' disease—any disease, that is, that is *named*—is the name of a universal. The usual medical Realist is he who, transgressing even the idealism of Plato, assigns material value in his mind to the 'type' and so ultimately regards 'a' disease as an object in nature, an *entity*, that attacks a patient or invades his body, and is to be recognized by its natural characters. The medical Nominalist, on the other hand, concerns himself primarily with the state of his patient, and the signs and symptoms that he observes in him, and scoffingly refers to formal diagnosis—not for what it is, the identification of a particular with a generalized 'type'—but as the mere sticking on of a label signifying nothing save *flatus vocis*. The Coans were in this sense Nominalists: the Cnidian school was as undoubtedly made up of Realists or 'Platonic Idealists.' Never has medicine been without great representatives of one or other school of thought, though the greatest physicians of all have overtly or instinctively sometimes strayed from one camp into another in an effort to promote reconciliation, and so, like Sydenham, have exposed themselves to the trivial charge of oscillation and inconsistency from the mouths of petty men. Fundamentally then, the problem of the *nature of diseases* is one that is logical or ontological, and not medical, and must be faced as such. Hippocratic Nominalists—empirists with a *flair* for synthesis and induction—tend to give us an account of the phenomena with which Medicine is concerned, in the form of case-histories, annals, generalities and *consilia*, which serve us as *guides*. The Galenical Realists, on the other hand, —rationalizing systematists with a tendency to idolize Symbols—describe for us not *cases* but diseases. Not content otherwise than when naming and classifying these diseases, and giving real and permanent value to them as do the systematic botanists to their classes and species, they become case-hardened academics and close their eyes to fresh clinical phenomena. Now the problem shirked by all modern realists is this: How far is it necessary to adopt the purely mechanical device of a classification and description of clinical happenings in terms of *diseases* in order to resume the facts of Pathology in form convenient for the practical physician and the active teacher?

The fact is, of course, that Medicine *can* exist as a Science and can be—as in the past—practised successfully as an Art without any description of formal 'clinical entities,' or any belief in the real existence of such things. 'A' disease is, for all true followers of Hippocrates the Coan, not *ens* but *aliquid entis*, and the disease is peculiar to each sufferer. For Galen the Neo-Platonist 'a' disease is certainly *ens*, though not (as apparently for the majority of formal teachers of the modern schools) a material entity. It is, however, a Procrustean bed to which all 'cases' of it must be fitted. Safety and wisdom appear to lie in the middle course—the Conceptualism of William of Occam. A true Conceptualist may well appreciate the *convenience* of Realist systems in Medicine and may even hope to furnish the world one day with a working system as useful as was that of Galen until Realism made of it an article of faith, so sterilizing thought and rendering observation as impotent as superfluous. Systems are useful, and not harmful, for just so long as they are recognized as expedients—as viewing screens for the Reality, which must ever remain hidden to our eyes—and not as rendering visible Reality itself.

Now, if these and some allied problems are not again faced as they once were, in all their logical and metaphysical implications, our observed facts will never be coherently and usefully interpreted, while Medicine will remain, as at present, a mass of empiricism, partly leavened by realist rationalization ; a sort of mental conglomerate incorporating the relics of broken down and destroyed systems of the past. This is why the history of medical thought is indispensable to the establishment of a true Science of Pathology. As well discuss 'evolution'—as is too often done—in ignorance of what Thales of Miletus, Lucretius, Aristotle, Buffon, Cuvier and Lamarck thought, as proceed to write a text-book of Medicine in ignorance of the doctrines expounded by Hippocrates, Galen, Avicenna, Paracelsus, van Helmont, Sydenham, Haller, Bretonneau, Broussais, Hahnemann and a score of others !

Daremberg, in the famous preface to his *Histoire des Sciences Médicales*, has written of the divers and diverse manners in which the History of Medicine can be, and has been written. In England, at any rate, mere archæology, bibliography, biography, antiquarianism and curiosity-mongering has too often passed muster as the History of Medicine.

But, without any doubt, as Saucerotte showed (in a brilliant fragment curiously foreshadowing something of Benedetto Croce, and far too slightingly treated by Daremberg) the true History of Medicine—by which is meant something more than the History of the Medical Art—can only be written from the point of view of the Philosopher and Philosophy, since medical doctrine is, in the last resort, but the philosophy of nature.

* * * * * *

Since Occidental Medicine of to-day is derived mainly from Greek sources—if we leave on one side all question of Egyptian or other priority—the history of Occidental Medicine runs in parallel with that of Occidental Philosophy. But we would be in error in tracing Medical History in line of temporal extension only. Our survey must be œcumenical as well as secular, and the truest perspective is only obtained when, adopting such a truly comparative method as that of Masson-Oursel, we regard our own philosophy and practice no less objectively than do we those of other times and centres of culture, and when we institute analogies between diverse philosophies and practices only in terms of each relatively to the respective temporal and geographical—and therefore historical—*milieux*. Gross as they may appear to us, the beliefs and practices of Hindu and Chinese medicine flow as naturally and inevitably from the philosophies of the peoples concerned as did those of Hippocrates and Galen, while our own medical beliefs and practices are as incoherent and as conglomerate as are our own philosophies and religions, or what pass as such. Nay, Rivers, in his *Medicine, Magic and Religion*, has declared that even the medicine of Polynesian savages is a coherent and logical system deriving naturally and efficiently from an indigenous theory of life and nature. We must suppose such a philosophy to have become adopted after processes of real observation and thought, no less logical, and indeed no less scientific, than ours because disparate to ours and probably differently conditioned by the brain-patterns bred in a particular environment. So, for the Polynesian savage, until the white man introduces his religion, his diseases and his vices, there is little need for the white man's medicines and philosophies. Perhaps only in so far as our perceptive range is wider and our generalizations are more sweeping, may our systems be ultimately more 'true' than theirs. For the rest, their Art and Science, and ours alike, must be judged by their adequacy to the occasions that call for their exercise; for their fitness, and for the stability or equilibrium resultant from their use.

We sometimes forget that many of our own boasted 'advances' or 'discoveries' would not have been made, and would indeed never have been needed, had we not first retroceded from the way of physiological rectitude in our desire to press along the road of industrial progress at the expense of physical and moral degradation. Much more of which we boast ourselves is but a restatement in other languages—sometimes less truthful than before—of futile explanations which are acceptable because familiar by analogy. So, a dose of castor oil acts with equal efficiency whether given to expel a demon, to calm the vital spirits, to assuage the Archaeus, to evacuate morbific humours, to eliminate toxins, to restore endocrine balance, or to reduce blood-pressure!

But our reputation as doctors, now as in Molière's time, depends, not so much upon our results as upon the acceptability to the laymen of our 'explanations'. So men have the doctors they deserve: and so—in a very pregnant sense—*Similia similibus curantur.* The mission of History and Philosophy to Medicine is never more important than when assisting physicians to avoid the attribution of false values to doctrines that teach nothing new, to interpretations that do not really 'interpret', and to explanations that do not 'explain'. A true Science of Medicine will economize thought as did Galen's system and will give us opportunity for intellectual gain, as would have done Galen's had it not been accepted as expressive of 'reality.' But there is a not unimportant distinction between the *economy* of thought on the one hand and the neglect of thought on the other.

If we accept the conceptualist point of view of William of Occam, and regard our universals, our laws, our generalizations and our hypotheses as mental conveniences of advantage to us for mental traffic, for intellectual gain, for interchange of thought and for common stock-taking, and so as in no sense immutable, and insusceptible of modification, we may then systematize—or at least appreciate the advantages of systematization—without falling into the bonds of academic slavery. For the Academic, in the end, bows down and worships, not the ideal God whom he symbolizes verbally but the very symbol itself—the NAME or WORD which comes to be his Idol and so no longer the symbol which indicates the convenient Idea that resumes his experiences or perceptions. It is in the spirit of the Conceptualist, who puts in due relation the THING, the THOUGHT and the NAME, that the History of Medicine can be most usefully surveyed, for then will most easily be avoided the Scylla, on the one hand, of facile depreciation of the past and glib confidence in contemporary conventions, and the Charybdis, on the other, of obstinate adhesion to tradition and blindness to the present.

Our motto should be, in the words of Baglivi: *Novi veteribus: non opponendi, sed quoad fieri potest, perpetuo jungendi foedere.*

When we adopt this point of view, we cease, for example, to declare that diagnosis has only recently made progress and that our predecessors ignored many diseases known to us. To Hippocrates there was no need to summarize clinical experience in the staccato terms of Jones' Snappy Aids to Medicine or Smith's Bright Tips on Diagnosis. Yet many speak to-day as if the great figures of the past were surrounded by objects they had not the wit to perceive. They *thought* differently to us, truly. Did they think less adequately to their occasions than we do? The fact is that the false systematization in terms of definite 'diseases' with special signs, symptoms, etiology and morbid anatomy, so dear to the physicians of last century, shows everywhere evidence of breaking down under the self-imposed strain, whilst a reaction towards Hippocratic methods of diagnosis and description is once more clearly marked. Hippocratic medicine is in fact now being practised successfully by not a few who are guiltless of any acquaintance with the Hippocratic Collection. Those who practise thus are empirics of the best sort: modern students of Nature *as a whole.*

The whole history of Occidental Medicine may indeed be almost indifferently pictured as a swaying struggle between Nominalism and Realism, or between Aristotelianism and Platonism, or between the natural followers of Hippocrates and those of Galen; but most faithfully, perhaps, as between Hippocratic Cos and antagonistic Cnidus. At Cos men studied the organism, or *whole individual*, in health and in disease: at Cnidus, the *part* or organ: the disease, and the type, if not the *name*.

For Coans then and now, *disease* is a dissociation of the functional unity of the whole organism: their therapeusis is directed towards the re-establishment of functional integrity; their Art towards assisting the *Vis Medicatrix Naturae*. Each case was at Cos considered on its own merits: diagnosis was descriptive; and 'diseases' were 'accidents' of the body, the product of reaction between the body and the cosmos of which it formed part. But for Cnidians diseases were *affects*: situated in organs; classifiable; and possessing special characters, by which they were identified. Cnidian diagnosis is recognition of the name of the disease believed to be present; therapeutic efforts are directed against and adapted to the invading disease, rather than in favour of the sick person. Hence: specificity in therapeutics as in pathology, and the ultimate tendency towards Paracelsism, Magic, and even demonology. We recognize Coans to-day amongst our wisest and best-loved physicians: those whom we consult ourselves, as we would Hippocrates or Heberden. But our Cnidians and our Galens are amongst our most successful and renowned teachers; they are the 'eminent consultants' whose utterances, to borrow a delightful trans-Atlantic phrase, have such 'news-value'. In terms of Jung's dichotomy we should find introverts at Cos: but extraverts at Cnidus. And the same human and spiritual dichotomy may be traced in Dr. Cumston's pages, as having existed not only in Greece and Rome, but at Alexandria, at Baghdad, at Cordova, at Bologna, at Padua, at Montpellier, at Paris, at Oxford, and at Cambridge. If the glories of Coan medicine may be said to vanish sometimes in simple empiricism, or to degenerate into mere superstition and vague nature worship, so may the teachings and beliefs of Cnidus pass over into degenerate Neo-Platonism, into gnosticism, magic, Theosophy, and the like. Yet Hippocratic thought, if pursued, helps us to escape from empiricism, and sets us on the road towards fertile induction and reconciliatory synthesis, while the Roman systematization of Galen gives us a working machine that still functions, that still persists, as do the very Roman roads once trodden by the legionaries whose health was conserved by his pupils. Still, as has been said, the greatest masters, whatever the failings of their pupils, have ever been those who have sought to blend thesis and antithesis in one synthesis—who have sought to effect, not mere compromise, but true reconciliation.

Such efforts have always failed—as in a sense they must always fail—when attempt has been made to reduce them to writing: to communicate to others what, in a way, can be only experienced. But we feel that the greatest physicians—Hippocrates and Galen, Paracelsus and van Helmont, Sydenham and Haller alike—all shared at some time the vision of reconciliation expressed by the great scholastic poet when he saw:—

> "legato con amore in un volume
> sustanzia ed accidenti, e lor costume
> quasi conflati insieme per tal modo
> che ciò ch'io dico è un semplice lume."

* * * * *

The philosophic physician will not then demand with the cloistered St. Thomas à Kempis "Et quid curæ nobis de generibus et speciebus?" For, in the reconciliation of substance and accident, universal and particular, *genus* and *species*, we as philosophers see the attainment of that absolute which, by the physician, is pictured as the gift of divine healing—the performance of the miracle.

Perhaps this is the significance of the Hippocratic aphorism that the physician who is also philosopher is the most nearly divine.

# HISTORY OF MEDICINE

# INTRODUCTION

We can never be fully in possession of a science until we know the history of its development. This applies to medicine no less than to the philosophy of the sciences in general. It was not so very many years ago when the fevers existing along the coast of Greece were not understood, and naval surgeons who met with them supposed that they were dealing with either a new form of typhoid fever or some new pernicious febrile affection. Then Littré confronted the modern descriptions with those found in the Hippocratic Collection, thus giving them their true names and real signification. Researches conducted in recent years have shown the accuracy of the Hippocratic accounts, and we may say that to-day the diseases observed in these regions are those described by Hippocrates more than twenty-three centuries ago.

Then, too, the very best procedures for reducing dislocations are found in the Hippocratic Collection, and we know, according to the texts of Antyllus, that the operation for cataract was extensively practised by the ancients, while in the Hindu text of Susruta there is to be found a very precise and detailed description of lithotomy.

The medical profession of to-day lives too exclusively in the contemplation of the so-called modern discoveries, and neglects the work—we will not say of the ancients—but of our immediate predecessors. For example, the best editions of Laënnec are now entirely out of print and the modern publisher, who well knows the requirements of to-day, would never dream of reprinting more than a few passages culled from this classical work.

But the method in medicine has not changed. It is still the same as that followed by Hippocrates, and the disdain of our predecessors, as Leibnitz has rightly said, will expose us to the same mistakes and the same uncertainties as those which in the past have delayed the progress of science. They may be better avoided when one takes advantage of the experience of the past: "to neglect the past of a science," says Dezeimeris, "means in reality that it must be recommenced every day." We agree that well observed cases will always retain their value and should be received with respect, yet on the other hand doctrines are changeable and require an incessant revision. There are periods in which their transformation takes place with such suddenness that it almost assumes the shape of a revolution, and such great progress frequently leaves behind it a period of confusion which is propitious for marked reaction.

It is also quite true that an excessive and exclusive cult of medical history might lead to such a state of inertia as that which caused the physicians of the fifteenth century, who only searched for knowledge of truth in Greek, Arabian and Roman authorities, to fall into contempt among all. Such a state of affairs, however, could only be due to an abusive excess of learning, and the abuse of erudition certainly need not be feared in medicine at the present time.

In examining the history of medicine the question of the *history of disease* or *historical pathology* must not be overlooked. It is a vast field and certainly represents the most important part of the history of the healing art. Historical pathology gives us descriptions of disease in all ages that can be exactly applied to the diseases of to-day, thus showing that there are diseases of all time and all places. These maladies form the common property of human pathology; they are the inevitable result of the conflict of man with his surroundings and his struggle with the general forces of nature. Without speaking of those traumata to which man has been exposed in all places and for all time, one meets with morbid processes arising from the influence of heat, cold, dryness, and dampness. Again, we find those morbid processes which will afflict man to all eternity, of which the cause is a free rein to passions, excesses of all kinds, and the neglect of hygiene. Medical history also shows us other diseases which, although not occurring in all places, have existed in all times, and vice versa. For example may be mentioned seasonal diseases; febrile affections of a continued and intermittent type; affections produced by poverty; those which arise during great social upheavals; and those resulting from intoxication by food and drink.

Historical pathology also shows that diseases do unceasingly

PLATE II

GIOVANNI BAPTISTA MORGAGNI

A probably unique engraving. Collection of Dr. P. Capparoni, of Rome, and reproduced by his kind permission

[face p. 4

increase, and, although this may appear a paradoxical coincidence, it is really true that they increase in spite of the great progress in hygiene as we advance through the ages. The fact is, of course, that the majority of the diseases which successively appear in medical history are not " new diseases " ; they are but " diseases " which with the progress of science have been recognized as " types apart ". Thus, through the progress of diagnostic methods, many diseases of the heart and kidney have recently assumed importance, just as have special affections of the brain and spinal cord. Progress in these directions is historically recorded in connexion with the names of Corrigan, Bright, Rostan, and Duchenne. On the other hand historical pathology shows us that while some diseases described by the ancients are no longer recognized by us, being merged in other categories, some appear to be definitely extinct, and others again, though perhaps dormant for centuries, seem as it were to reappear from time to time.

Historical pathology is followed by the history of nosography. Firstly, symptomatology was developed and perfected. Disease having been studied from external signs, on the surface so to speak, the time finally came when each organ was individually examined, and perfected diagnostic methods have resulted in the perfecting of instruments for physical examination.

The prognosis and general aetiology of disease were the great glory of the ancient physicians, and it is not too much to say that little has been added in modern times. Yet modern medicine has marvellously perfected symptomatology and diagnosis, though in so doing it has only verified the truth of ancient acquisitions made in the domain of the aetiology and prognosis of disease. On the other hand pathological anatomy is a modern science founded by the great Italian physician, Morgagni, although all justice must be done to Theophilus Bonet of Geneva, who published at Geneva, in 1679, his *Sepulchretum, sive Anatomia practica ex cadaveribus morbo denatis*, which formed the foundation stone for the work of the physician of Bologna. By the more complete knowledge of the organic lesions accompanying disease and specifically characterizing it, pathological anatomy has tardily given us a more exact idea of the morbid species.

Yet history shows us that bygone physicians were not entirely without the information necessary to form a conception of the nature of morbid processes.

Therapeutics had at the beginning gone far beyond the other branches of medical science, and, in truth, even preceded the accurate observation of disease. The innate sentiment which forces man to alleviate pain in others made him, from the earliest times, search for the means of cure, but at the beginning he invoked the clemency of the higher powers and asked assistance from his familiar deities. Prayers, sacrifices, and incantations were amongst the first attempts at therapeutics. Such practices are found to-day among all primitive peoples and among those whose civilization has decayed.

Inversely from what is done to-day, man at a later period did not search for general indications for treatment, but asked of others who had had experience what plant was successful in controlling a given symptom; there was no *method* in therapeutics, there were only *remedies.* But the number of these increased daily, and to the use of plants was added that of metals, which in the Islamic school acquired a very great importance. It was not always a successful empirical trial which introduced a new drug into therapeutics; it was more often some futile consideration deduced from mythological attributes or gross analogy.

Hygiene, which is derived from physiology and aetiology, is contemporary with the study of the *causes* of disease, or perhaps it were better to say, was born from the terror, rather than the knowledge of disease. It had been an art before it became a science. In Egypt, and in all the Orient, Hygiene was a part of religious worship and the priests by their injunctions imposed upon the people and introduced into their customs many practices which are to-day applied in a modern form. With the Greeks Hygiene became a science and has progressed from their day on.

The amount of knowledge accumulated in the past is enormous, no matter what may be said to the contrary, and historical Nosography shows that it has bequeathed a large part of its treasure to modern medicine, because all that which is based upon observation is imperishable. But the ancients were not content merely to observe; they wished to rise to a conception of the nature of disease, yet could not resist the temptation to systematize prematurely. The history of medical doctrines is that part of the history of medicine in which the various systems are most unstable and fluctuate most in esteem. Although the facts have remained unshaken, all the older theories have crumbled away. This could not have been otherwise, because the essential foundation, namely physiology, did not exist, and the physical sciences were in their infancy. A modern can only appreciate these ambitious efforts impartially if he places himself in the intellectual environment of the time; and so the study of the history of medical doctrine can only be carried on properly by keeping strict count of the relationship of medicine with all the sciences, and with the philosophy of the times.

To-day the science of man in the normal state forms the basis of pathological research, but knowledge of anatomy and physiology was only acquired late in the development of the healing art. This, of course, is natural, because in early days the first requisites of the physician were to relieve suffering and to fight against death. At a later period he had more leisure to devote to study, and pathology should have been his first preoccupation, but he was not long in discovering that it was vain to discourse upon the disturbances of an organism, of whose structure he was ignorant; and the desire seized him to know what was beneath the skin, what was suffering and what had become diseased. Death, besides being, as it is to us to-day, the end of natural existence, had for him a solemn and mysterious character; religious terrors protected the remains of man who had lived. The dissection of human bodies exposed the physician to punishment by death down to the Middle Ages and even later, and was a foolhardy act in days when capital punishment was applied to generals who had left the bodies of their soldiers unburied.

Yet the physician could not be content with the anatomical data derived from the executioner or priest; inferences derived from the examination of animals' entrails were insufficient to satisfy the minds of learned men. It is, however, doubtful whether or not the first anatomists had any other means to information; neither Aristotle nor Hippocrates had ever opened a human body, and the teaching of human anatomy was first carried on at the School of Alexandria by Erasistratus and Herophilus.

As has already been said, physiology could only be developed at a late date and is necessarily far more recent than anatomy as a science. Unquestionably it had a beginning in the distant past but it did not form a *corpus* until modern times ; Harvey and Lavoisier are the two great names which mark the beginning of its vigorous growth. Therefore for many centuries medicine was deprived of this important branch, but it must not be supposed that physicians resisted the invincible temptation to explain the phenomena of life. In the absence of a positive physiology they created an imaginary one which was modified according to need and to the trend of the philosophy of the times.

We may therefore conclude that the utility of medical history resides in the fact, as Littré pointed out a century ago, that " there is nothing in the most advanced contemporary medicine whose embryo cannot be found in the medicine of the past ", and this statement is quite as true to-day as when uttered by the great French medical historian.

# CHAPTER I

## THE EVOLUTION OF MEDICINE

There is no subject which has given rise to more rational and irrational discussions than medicine. For the uncultured mind it is purely a procedure employed for the cure of disease. The physician is a kind of machine which furnishes remedies for human suffering; he has learned this trade and knows what curative means are applicable to a given disease. People who have no notion of the hierarchy and linking up of human knowledge of things, and who believe that an art, a science, or any kind of practical work can be learnt singly and without fundamental notions, are representative of the state of the human mind before anything was known and when all science could be summed up in a knowledge of the position of a few stars. For at this primitive epoch medicine existed, although in a very embryonic state, and as it certainly had the instinct of preservation for its origin, man tried to protect himself against hostile elements and to avoid unfavourable conditions respecting his health. This rudimentary hygiene was the first medicine known.

Therefore, uncultured minds aid us, by a sort of retrospective analogy, to surmise what primitive medicine really was. It must be understood that a total assimilation cannot be made between primitive and modern ignorant minds, but the method is the same in each case. The former were compelled, as the latter still do through intellectual inertia, to regard medicine as a collection of measures, discovered by mere chance or summary experience, which combats disease or rather the morbid symptom. This is because they do not know of the bonds uniting medicine with the sciences and cannot conceive that rational therapeutics can only be developed after scientific data of disease have been acquired. The mistake does not consist in believing that the object of medicine is the cure of disease and the preservation of health, but in the belief that it can do so from the very start and without knowledge of the various branches of learning upon which medicine depends. Hence the conception which the majority of the public have of modern medicine leads us to conceive what probably was the conception of primitive man.

These conceptions are merely suppositions and are referred to merely for the purpose of showing the popular opinions which, in fact, are more in conformity with the reality of things and must always be taken into account. Therefore from the point of view of the vulgar, therapeutics are confounded with medicine when they merely represent a part. Now, to disengage therapeutics from other medical knowledge is what the early healers did and what the village bone-setters do to-day, so that there actually exist at the present time representatives of rudimentary instinctive medicine, the medicine which even preceded theological medicine.

And here let it be said that in adopting four divisions—or epochs—in the evolution of medicine, namely, *instinctive, theological, metaphysical,* and *scientific*, we do not pretend that these divisions have a mathematical precision in respect of duration or nature, or that they regularly succeeded each other like the seasons of the year, but that, generally speaking, they are true.

Observation has legitimately been able to demonstrate three different tendencies in medicine for explaining everything: the first by supernatural powers, the second by forces or factitious entities, and the third by natural phenomena. These ways of thinking are mixed together in various proportions, the epochs merging into each other. Thus even to-day there are medical theologians and metaphysicians, as well as representatives of instinctive medicine —that which existed in the caves of Troglodytes, and will persist until the generalization of learning has attained a higher level than it has so far reached. In the pursuit of truth the human mind has not invariably passed from theology to metaphysics and from metaphysics to science; these have been modifying influences which have caused the laws to vary, but this is more nearly the truth than the supposition that the human mind passed through in succession spiritualism, sensualism, and mysticism, finally to end in eclecticism.

We have attempted to show that before the first theological

or fetishistic organization, that is to say, before the first civilization, a medicine derived from instinct existed, and this was the origin of the art of medicine. If, continuing the examination of reigning opinions with the object of comparing them with historic phases, we attempt to discover the continuers of the epochs when man believed in the perpetual intervention of a supernatural will in human affairs, we become suddenly impressed by the fact that in modern society there are people who—like the ancients—place the inventors of medicine in the heavens and make gods of them, and admit that there exists a relationship between God and disease. They look upon epidemics as being sent to chastise an epoch of impiety and unbelief and regard certain tangible phenomena, such as trances, mystic sleep, and other manifestations of a psychical order, as being due to divine power. The modern treatments by religious practices, by prayers, etc.—the prayer being thus transformed into a therapeutical procedure—sufficiently show that there are minds that will not detach even medicine from things belonging to their religious belief, which relates then to a superior power. And in this respect we think that there is a great similarity between persons thus disposed and physicians and patients in the days when oracles were consulted in case of disease and medicine was in the hands of priests, heroes, and kings, when diseases were regarded as signs of vengeance of the gods, when the Asclepiads, descendants of Æsculapius, were in exclusive possession of the practice of medicine, and there were protecting divinities for all cases of suffering and those ills to which man is heir.

Monotheism replaced the Pleiads of gods and semi-gods by a single will, but the method remained quite the same. To introduce an extra-human will or several component wills into the production or cure of disease, instead of perceiving that it was the result of certain atmospheric, tellurian, or other organic changes, was to be still in that period when man knew not his domain, himself, nor the physical, chemical, and biological composition of bodies, possessed—as mankind will never cease to be—with the intimate desire to explain things, but unable to do so for want of the necessary means for exploration, when man recognized an administering power. Herbert Spencer says that theology was born of a sentiment of the unknowable. In the Middle Ages, for example, in Italy, under Julius II, it was supposed during a great mortality among nurslings, that sorcerers sucked the blood of the infants.

But the present-day opinion of medicine among the public —the same as formerly reigned in the medical profession— is that which we qualify as metaphysical; this attitude towards medicine essentially consists, not in simply inquiring into the state of things, but in searching for their origin and end and everywhere looking for archetypes. Applying this definition to the subject under consideration, it is to be noted that a similar state of mind has resulted in what may be called *medical metaphysics* among physicians, that is, the search for the essences of diseases. Hence it is not to be wondered at that many persons adopt this way of thinking and strive to interpret, with only the resources of their intellect, the pathological phenomena or the use of drugs. Considering the art of medicine as similar to all other arts, they suppose that it can accept a certain dose of inspiration and personal ideas. In point of fact, this is what constituted the art of medicine before the great development of the medical sciences and, in our way of thinking, it corresponds to the metaphysical period of medicine. To-day a series of precise and positive data have changed the purely characteristic conditions of medicine as an art and have penetrated the doors of clinical medicine.

However, the current opinion of the public is not to be discovered here, and if we look about us we shall find ourselves in the midst of pure metaphysics. The notion of entities, forces, general and abstract causes, still predominates, having succeeded the notion of a peculiar regulating force governing all. Further on we shall consider historically the metaphysical or abstract phase which in turn was succeeded by the scientific phase, represented by Bichat, the true creator of modern biology. The scientific phase is superseding the preceding one unceasingly, and although this progress has only been rapid since the beginning of the XIXth century, it was begun long before by many important discoveries made. For is it not certain that the knowledge of the circulation resulted in enormous progress in the science of man, as well as in the explanation of disease and advance of the practice of medicine ? Without Harvey's discovery would rational blood-letting, blood transfusion, and intravenous injections ever have been added to therapeutic technique for the great good of humanity ? Thus, scientific elements have become superadded at every moment, changing or modifying both the art and the science of medicine —of empiricism and positive science. To-day, the general opinion looks upon medicine as an ordinary art, that is to say, a complicated collection of procedures for the cure of disease—curative measures varying considerably according to the physician. Men are loth to believe that there are positive elements in medicine, as for example a fundamental material lesion constituting a morbid state. This is because the public can only see two things, namely, a collection of symptoms or a symptom, a sign which strikes the imagination and for which there should be a remedy, which the physician will apply more or less appropriately according to the degree of his skill. Hence the criterion by which a physician is judged is the rapidity with which he causes an alarming symptom to disappear. In fact, it is necessity developing from the situation. When one is unable scientifically and hierarchically to connect facts one cannot conceive or admire other than those essentially and immediately practical results ; one necessarily commits the mistake of believing that science and practice are, if not antagonistic, at least mutually indifferent. There exists to-day a widespread prejudice violently separating the practitioner from the scientist. Is there need for combating this prejudice ? No. The profession at large keeps abreast with advances made in science. Is it necessary to show that every scientific discovery has its echo in practice, and that without those of Galvani and Volta, for example, we could not to-day attain the pedicle of a polypus with the galvano-cautery ?

Therefore, the various mundane appreciations of medicine which we have rapidly enumerated are entirely subjective. But where all this becomes clearer is to be found in attempts made to explain diseases themselves. Every medical man has met with examples of this ignorant research for the origin and cause of disease—bad blood or more or less acrid bile—humours that Molière called " peccant, crass, fuliginous, or feculent " are still invoked to-day as in the days of ancient humoralism, which has left deep imprints among the illiterate. All this is not serious in itself, but it is a sign of a vicious method, which consists in seeking an explanation of things by *a priori* theories, to which we shall refer when speaking of the evolution of medicine *per se*.

To admit, for explaining an illness, an hypothetical change in an organic liquid that is quite unknown is, it must be confessed, just a bit metaphysical, but this is above all the just decree of a long line of hypotheses and appeals to the supernatural, invoked as a general explanation of diseases and their remedies. It is in this way that forces, entities, and beings having only a subjective reality have been created, and by their aid it has seemed possible to give an easy interpretation of all phenomena, without verifying the value of an hypothesis that is positively admitted. Consequently for these theorists the words health and disease have not the positive signification that they have for us. Ignorance of anatomy and physiology leads to the conclusion that the pathologic state is quite independent of the normal state; disease is a being of new formation possessing a primary and individual existence. Now, it is known that a morbid state is intimately connected with the physiological state, and that perturbations of the organism are simply exaggerations or a decrease of one or several functions of the component parts of the body. Thus it becomes evident that more or less ingenious explanations are substituted for those derived from correct knowledge of the structure and functions of the body. To conceive a disease without knowledge of the affected organ, its functions and pathologic changes—that is to say, the lesion and its symptoms—naturally leads to very fantastic conclusions, and systems were developed in the past which built up a doctrinal corpus from these errors.

### *Science and Art of Medicine*

In what is to follow we do not pretend dogmatically to decide whether or not medicine is to be regarded as a science or an art. We believe that it is not possible precisely to distinguish what belongs to art and what belongs to science, for the reason that everything begins as an art, which in turn becomes a science. Before chemistry there was alchemy; before astronomy there was astrology; before the architecture of the present, founded on positive and concrete notions of geometry and mechanics, the art of building existed ; and the art of medicine was developed before medical science sprang up. In ordinary language these two words possess two very different meanings, but in reality they are synonymous when considered in the various phases of the development of medicine. What we wish to show is that medicine, after having been invaded by various elements foreign to its object (like the intervention of gods and other powers) little by little eliminated these elements and replaced them by other notions as knowledge increased.

In the blissful days of scholastics the thing would have been treated dogmatically, but, just as the strange subjects taken for theses for the M.D., such as : " Is woman an imperfect work of Nature ? " and others still more singular, would have been quite badly received, to treat a subject according to the procedures of Aristotle would have seemed somewhat original. This remark is necessary, because it might appear that we were losing sight of our object, which is to show what were the transformations undergone by medicine in its different phases, the various characters it assumed, and the philosophical manners in which it has been interpreted. This is why we have entitled this chapter " The Evolution of Medicine ", and this implicitly contains the study of the art and science of medicine, the forms that it has assumed, being artistic or scientific according to the various phases, theological, metaphysical, or positive.

All things considered, it may be said that the art existed less and less, and this qualification is all the more applicable to the theory and practice of medicine as one studies its remoter history. But there is nothing absolute in all this, because in all times there have been both artists and scientific men, and both qualities may be found combined in the same man.

In the XVIIIth century there would have been no hesitation or compromise. Voltaire—to invoke the most echoing voice of that century—expressly says : " Medicine, the art of operating with the head and hand, gives back life to a man about to lose it." And again he says : " Twenty physicians may be mistaken, but he who has the better understanding, who has the carpenter's eye, will guess the character of the disease; but in every art there are Virgils and Mæviuses."

There is no duality between art and science. Each art is dependent upon one or several sciences. Agriculture requires a knowledge of chemistry, physics, astronomy, and physiology, while medicine depends upon physics, chemistry, and biology. Reciprocally, each fundamental science lends its aid to a quantity of arts and to each art some of the six fundamental sciences belong. Thus the medical art is directly dependent upon biology. Hence the sciences are the foundations of the arts.

Now, although it is true that the arts rely on scientific truths, it is none the less true that the arts preceded the sciences, and that each science is derived from art; that is to say that practice preceded the theory or the law. This is because of human necessities. Then the sciences corresponding to the arts progressively developed, as man became more materially protected and thus was able to study the laws of phenomena. Then each science and its corresponding art developed parallelly, so that to-day it is the theory which has preceded practice in almost all branches of human knowledge.

What we have said may be summed up in the three following propositions. (1) There is no antagonism or radical difference between science and art; they are two sides of the same thing, not two different things. (2) Every art is directly related to one or several corresponding sciences. They develop simultaneously. (3) Every art, that is to say practice, has necessarily preceded both the theory and science related to it.

All this leads us to search for the most immediate causes for the delay of medical progress. We know that medicine is an application of biology, and since this abstract science was the last to be developed, it is clear that the medical sciences—anatomy, physiology, embryology, etc.—were the last to be developed, so that they remained in an imperfect state for a long period of time. There is a fact that history has noted, namely that admirable geometry existed in the days of Archimedes and Apollonius while in the middle of the XVIIth century, in Harvey's time, physiology was still in a detestable state. Auguste Comte has observed that biology "has been incessantly tossed about between metaphysics, which attempted to keep it back, and physics, which tried to absorb it, between the intellect of Stahl and the intellect of Boerhaave". In point of fact, the properties of living organized bodies being more complex and difficult to analyse, even great minds have been led to explain them by imaginary forces, while still others explained them by the simple chemical, physical, and mechanical actions, which are the indispensable condition of vital phenomena, but do not represent all of life, which consists of properties peculiar to organized substance or its component elements.

*Instinctive Medicine.*—All the ancient writers have said again and again that medicine was the gift of the gods and tradition says that Æsculapius was the son of Apollo. It is probable that diseases existed before the celestial powers thought of curing them; the gods were somewhat backward in sending the remedy. They perhaps might have done even better by not sending the ills which afflict man.

Let us now attempt to discover the cause for the appearance of medicine among primitive man. We are unable to ascertain what diseases were prevalent, but it is quite logical to suppose that a rudimentary practice of medicine existed from the time that mankind began to develop his instincts. The atmospheric changes—the heat of day and cold of night—must have developed instincts of preservation, ready to react against them, and these very conditions, which resulted in the building of primitive habitations, were also the cause of curative and hygienic practices.

However, as we possess no definite data on this subject, we can only offer hypotheses. To undertake to describe antediluvian medicine would be foolhardy, but it is permissible to reason by analogy, and to consider what medical practice among animals and certain savages consists of.

In the first place, have animals a practice of medicine of their own? Without becoming entangled in the hyperboles of Pliny, who pretends that animals practise the art of medicine, and without accepting the oft-told tales of the hippopotamus resorting to the art of blood-letting and the enema which the ibis skilfully projects into his large bowel, using his long beak for the purpose, we must admit that there may be a grain of truth in these assertions. Animals have no medicine of their own, strictly speaking, in that it is not perfectible like ours, and has for thousands of years remained purely instinctive. Yet although animals do not appear to have either the *beaux arts* or religion they are sensible to cold, heat, proper food, and the pleasures of love. They know how to protect their own existence, and that of their offspring. They are familiar with gymnastics and evince remarkable prudence in the selection of proper diets which, for some ancient physicians, represented all there was in medicine. These various practices among animals are probably the original rudiments of medicine, which at present becomes more and more complicated as the intellectual and material domains of man increase in extent. The basis of medicine is the instinct of preservation.

*Theological Medicine.*—We shall now show by historical examples that medicine has passed through the phases we have referred to, that it has had manners of being corresponding to manners of explaining things of this world, which still subsist. There is nothing astonishing that human thought should interpret differently—according to the epoch—the phenomena of nature and for this reason various currents of opinion developed until one absorbed all the others. It is essential that a general or theoretical idea shall bring together the notions acquired of the world and mankind and keep them under its dependence. Now, this dominating idea is the *cause* which the human mind attributes to the phenomena observed, and it has for origin the instinctive natural need to know and to explain. But this idea of all things—the cause—is not always identical At a given time "the inclination of man to suppose that in every cause there exists a will similar to his own" caused him to adopt the theological regimen, and he became a fetisher, polytheist, or monotheist; therefore it is clear that human affairs developed under the influence of various forms of theology which we shall examine from the view-point of medicine.

To believe that diseases are caused by the wrath of celestial powers, that cures are wrought by the clemency of the gods, is theological medicine. This phase of medicine in antiquity will be briefly considered. At this epoch medicine could hardly have assumed any other character. It is common knowledge that in the time of Grecian mythology there were titular divinities who exercised direct protection over the health of mankind. Then from the gods this mission passed into the hands of medical priests whose livelihood depended upon the altar and the annexed pharmaceutical shop or laboratory, although at the time therapeutics were in a very primitive state. We know of the temples of Apollo and Æsculapius—the Asclepieion of Cos and several others—cleverly erected in the most healthy surroundings and placed under the care of the Asclepiads. We are informed of the many fortunate recoveries obtained by these representatives of the divinity, collected and inscribed on votive tablets with the object of exciting the enthusiasm of the sick. It is perfectly clear that the art of medicine at this time was entirely contained in religious dogma and that there was an intimate relationship between the personality of the priest and that of the physician. Before Hippocrates, medical practice was confined to the Asclepiads, who were doubly revered, first because they distributed health, and secondly because they were mandatories of the divinity. Certain passages in the Hippocratic Collection throw a little light on this period of medicine, as for example: "a knowledge of the gods is inherent in medicine, because in the study of diseases and their symptoms there exists a multitude of reasons for honouring the gods. Physicians recognize the superiority of the gods, because the Omnipotent does not reside in medicine itself; it is true that physicians heal many diseases; but it is by the grace of the gods that a great many are recovered from." It should be added that Hippocrates himself, when speaking of diseases inflicted by the divinity, says: "It is thus with regard to the disease called Sacred; it appears to me to be nowise more divine nor more sacred than other diseases, but has a natural cause from which it originates like other affections."

Is it necessary to refer to the thousand or more male and female tutelary powers who, in the early days of Rome, presided over all diseases and functions as well as all needs? Some of these medical divinities have been admirably sketched by a contemporary writer: "Nona and Decima are nurses, the three Nixi are accoucheurs besides the wet-nurses Educa and Potina, and Carna the cradle-rocker, whose bunch of hawthorn wards off bad dreams from the infant," and again, "Mena who vexes the virgins, and the gentle Rumina who protects the breast of the nurse swollen with blue veins." These quotations are sufficient to give an idea of the Roman epoch. Cæsar, the conqueror of the Gauls, says: "The nation of the Gauls is given over to superstitions; those afflicted by serious disease immolate human victims or vow to do so, believing that, in order to appease the gods for the life of a man, one must give the life of another in exchange."

By what has been said, the eminently religious and theocratic character of antique medicine has been amply demonstrated.

In the Middle Ages the theological phase of medicine is still more accentuated. At this epoch, when the Catholic religion had complete sway and generally directed human evolution, all progress was not absolutely lacking, the filiation between pagan antiquity and positive modernity was not interrupted. To the Middle Ages is due the protection of the weak, who were recognized as equal to the strong, under the influence of Catholicism. A commencement of commercial and industrial wealth resulted from the security of serfhood, exonerated as it was from the anxiety of war, which had become defensive instead of being systematically offensive, as it had been. Although plunged in religious asceticism and an excess of superstitious faith, the Middle Ages brought eminence in the arts, Gothic architecture, glass-staining, church music; in commerce, the bill of exchange; in manufacture, clocks, paper, and mirrors; while scientific empiricism invented gunpowder, the printing-press, and the magnetic needle.

Nevertheless, the Middle Ages inflicted medicine with theological chemistry, the belief in the stars, sorcery, and demoniacal influences. One might have thought that the state of things would have been otherwise, since the theological regimen, although completely exhausted from the viewpoint of science, was full of life among the ignorant classes, as it was for better reason in the days to which we will now refer, that is to say, the end of the Middle Ages and the centuries immediately to follow.

Hippocratism and Galenism—doctrines that had held sway for centuries—had not become purged of theological conceptions, and the three souls of Plato and Aristotle, the theory of spirits, etc., invited the successors of these great Schools—the Galenists especially—to discover a means again to bear the yoke of supernatural medicine in alchemy and the Kabbala. Thus in the XVIth century, Jerome Fracastor, in his treatise on sympathy and antipathy, attributes these phenomena to the passage of invisible and indivisible atoms from one body into another, which is not so very different from the doctrines of modern magnetists and spiritualists. Then by analogy a relationship of the same kind was made between the constellations and the terrestrial world.

Along with these abstract phenomena, demoniacal or divine intelligent influences were evolved, because demons are simply changed products of the divinity and, as Sprengel says, "God again became the immediate effectual cause of all phenomena, and physics became transformed into true theosophy." Europe was overrun by sorcerers and travelling philosophers, associating with their pretensions some new secrets derived from Oriental magnetism and the doctrine of Zoroaster. They also made a point of using Hebrew words, in order that their formulæ might have more power from being written in the language employed by God when addressing angels and mankind. To these philosophers we owe the doctrine of signatures, in which the planets correspond to the various organs of the human body by certain signs, and herbs are identified with various anatomic systems by imaginary resemblances. For example, the spotted leaves of lungwort would cure or relieve affections of the pulmonary system, while the yellow juice of swallow-root was employed in diseases of the liver. The devil was attracted by the acrid humours of the melancholic subject, but God, by his exorcizers, caused the evil spirit to pack off more or less rapidly.

The demons presided over the planets upon which metals depended, hence it followed that a diabolical will could operate many wonders by variously manipulating these metals, and there was nothing to oppose the belief in their transmutation. All this prepared for Paracelsus the triumph of his illuminism, while it explained the functions of bodies by pretended harmonious relationship between the viscera and celestial intelligence, between the astral macrocosm and the visceral microcosm, so that the golden days of these theories were soon to come.

Singular happenings had already shown that in the popular mind there existed a true morbid predisposition ready to accept magic and kabbalistic doctrines. Thus in 1374, the epidemic of St. Vitus' dance made its appearance. Throngs composed of from two or three hundred to thousands of convulsionaries went from town to town, contaminating each with the contagion of the chorea with which they were afflicted. In 1458, in several parts of Germany, children were seized with a persistent desire to make a pilgrimage to Mont St. Michel, in Normandy, and those refused the permission to fulfil their desire invariably died from vexation at being frustrated in their plans. Following the black plague of the Middle Ages, bands of flagellants went about the country singing hymns of penitence and imposing mortifications upon themselves to appease the wrath of Heaven. They were everywhere received with ecstasy and not infrequently the same vertigo would suddenly remove from a town a large portion of its inhabitants.

Had such symptoms of theocratic domination only appeared among invalids or the vulgar masses without obtaining the confidence of the medical profession of the day, one might have some hesitation in placing them in the history of theological medicine, but we know that physicians regarded these morbid phenomena as having a supernatural origin. And these very physicians did not hesitate to interpret the hysterical anæsthesia of the skin as well as other disturbances of innervation and motility to the work of the devil. Continuing up to the XVIIIth century, these mental aberrations stamp medical practice with the seal of their dependence upon theology. In the reign of Louis XIV of France the inspired *Camisards* heard æolian harps, had angelic visions, and if, through Bossuet's intervention, they did not get the *dragonnade*, they no less experienced the pathological symptoms which the medical profession of the time regarded as unquestionably supernatural.

When later on the vineyard of St. Medard was the scene of an ever-celebrated epidemic of convulsions, it required a strong dose of religious Gallicanism to prevent the miracle from being repressed by the Royal police, because at the time philosophy was not in a position to offer any general opinion differing from that which was current in respect of the evolution of facts.

Before being reduced to a positive interpretation, these facts would have to have passed metaphysical explanations of which we shall soon speak, and which have always existed correlatively with theology, although in the Middle Ages they were in great part dominated by purely supernatural explanations, as we shall attempt to show when dealing with metaphysical medicine, where the same epochs will be studied from a different point of view.

In the period we are now speaking of, the Middle Ages, viewed in its consequences and at the moment when it is about to disappear, medicine was loaded with all kinds of elements foreign to its object—the inspection of the stars, alchemy, etc. The relative continuation of such conditions down to our day is not in contradiction to the historic *ensemble* of the three phases of the evolution of medicine which we adopt. To some *savants* religious faith has been regarded as compatible with the positive or scientific interpretation of the phenomena of this world ; but when they are not inclined to add their subjective appreciations in respect of the origin and end of things to the means of investigation at their disposal, these *savants* can collect the same experimental proofs, the same procedures of synthesis and of analysis as those who refute the supernatural in order to explain facts, but an insuperable abyss will separate them from those who exclusively accept scientific procedures, or, in other words, explanations within the scope of the ordinary human understanding. Perceiving that the foundations are beginning to be undermined by positive methods, the adherents of theological medicine are taking refuge in miracles.

Saint Chrysostom, in the IVth century, said that " formerly the extraordinary endowments of the mind were even bestowed upon the worthless, because the Church then had need of miracles, but to-day they are not even given to the deserving, because the Church no longer is in need of them ". But it would seem that the Church of to-day again feels the need of miracles, for many are constantly reported, and the remarkable point is that they all pertain to medical biology.

We would stress the fact that the theological phase of medicine is not confined to antiquity or the Middle Ages. Following the oath of the apothecaries of the XIIIth century : "First of all I swear to live and die in the Catholic faith . . . ; *item* : never to administer an abortive potion, etc.," we come upon Guy Patin in the XVIIth century, who maliciously or ingenuously writes : "What saved the King were three good blood-lettings and the prayers of good people like ourselves." Three centuries before, Guy de Chauliac energetically jeers at "the sect of women and many idiots who place patients afflicted with any disease in the hands of the saints, doing this because 'The Lord has given me what pleases Him,'" etc.

A regrettable remnant of the theological or supernatural regimen still existing, is present-day spiritualism, with table-turning, raps, mediums, and ectoplasm. All these are the remains of the magic and sorcery of the Middle Ages, and are of utmost interest to medicine, because there is an evident relationship between the phenomena of hallucination and ecstasy and the various neurological disturbances which accompany spiritualistic practices. The occult sciences of the olden days are still with us and take the place of alchemy and the Kabbala.

We have attempted to show the prolongations to our day of the theological period of medicine, with the object of again showing that our divisions are not absolute, only relative. This remark applies to the metaphysical phase which we shall now consider.

*Metaphysical Medicine.*—The metaphysical manner of interpreting things occupies the greatest place in the history of medicine. In the past it is complete and to-day it is comprised in a certain number of doctrines. Its long duration and expansion can be readily understood when one takes into consideration the human desire to know the first and last of things, as well as the ease of imagining abstract beings for explaining that which the human mind cannot understand. These fictitious entities are to be found not only in vitalistic, spiritualistic, and animistic medicine, but in various Greek and Latin schools. From the time when Hippocrates arbitrarily attributed diseases to the quality and varying mixtures of the four humours (blood, pituit, yellow, and black bile) down to Hahnemann, who said that "the cause of disease is a dynamic aberration of our spiritual life", medicine has been loaded with these more or less ingenious, but purely imaginary hypotheses. It is needless to say that in the days of the first attempts at medical organization they were legitimate and due to real ignorance or to anatomical and physiological errors upon which medical hypotheses and mistakes were built.

Diogenes of Apollonia, quoted by Aristotle, gives a description of the venous system, according to which "there are two large veins crossing the belly up to the spine, one on the right, the other on the left; each goes into the thigh corresponding to it", etc. For Hippocrates and his successors the arteries contained air; hence the conclusion that air was transported throughout the body in order to feed the innate heat. Anatomical and physiological errors were perpetuated down to Harvey and Haller, who established the fundamental truths. Metaphysical explanations were easy because positive discoveries were few and unimportant.

It is clear that it is useless to imagine that a "breath" animates the body when the structure of the central nervous system and its relations to the peripheral nerves are known. What use has one for vital or animal spirits when the phenomena of nutrition are understood?

Speaking in a general way, metaphysics applied to medicine is the search for the essence of the disease instead of its causative factors and nature. Hence humoralism, methodism, iatrochemistry, and other celebrated theories are metaphysical creations, in the sense that they are not founded on natural facts observed, but upon the intellectual faculties of their inventors, who developed their doctrinal systems according to their own light. A considerable number of medical systems, doctrines, and opinions present this character; it is essential to refer to some of them in order to show, by comparing them with modern ideas, what constitutes the metaphysical state. In what is to follow, mention will be made of a great many great names in medicine, and we will attempt to show that their metaphysical errors were inevitable, and intimately connected with the evolution of medicine.

According to Celsus, Pythagoras was the real author of

the doctrine of critical days, a doctrine whose theory was greatly developed by Hippocrates and Galen. There is a trace of experimental truth in this doctrine, but the mistake consists in supposing that an inevitable power determines the day for the development of the crisis, following a numerical order. Thus, according to Galen, crises arising on the sixth day (of the disease) are fatal; those on the seventh, on the contrary, are favourable.

The Dogmatists of the School of Cos, although recommending the study of anatomy and proclaiming the importance of facts observed, accorded to reasoning an importance that it cannot have in medicine, for discovering the cause and essence of disease. They pretended, with only the resources of the mind and only from the observation of certain facts, to be able to attain the notion of the primal reasons of the phenomena of life.

At a later date, the Pneumatic sect supposed that there was an aërial spirit governing the solids and liquids of the body.

Opposed to dogmatism and in contradiction with it, but less given to hypothesis, Empiricism not only rejected reasoning, but the study of anatomy as well. Facts were not to be interpreted, nor the cause to be sought for; no attempt was to be made to connect a functional morbid phenomenon with a disturbance of the humours or with any other trouble. The Empirics regarded all this as hypothesis, and in the end Empiricism was entrapped by the very dangers it tried to avoid. It only took note of the symptoms and the results obtained from remedies administered haphazard. Thus, after a sufficient number of case-histories had been collected, a mathematical table of diseases and their treatment could be compiled, which was the empirical theorem. Now all this is a kind of metaphysics, but there is nothing to prove that the succession of symptoms observed and constituted into a disease is invariable, and the mere fact that they have occurred a great number of times does not imply that they will be identically the same in future cases.

The ancient Empirics declared that reasoning was futile, that occult causes were not to be searched for, and they discarded the study of anatomy and physiology as "idle speculations useless for the art". Modern Empirics have pretended that it is by pure observation that great discoveries such as that of the circulation, irritability and contractility have been made. In the last century, Broussais justly remarked that discoveries are always guided by reasoning and induction. It is evident that those who make discoveries in any branch of knowledge are those who have been prepared by previous work, which has directed them in their researches.

Methodism offers a far more striking example of the pretension to explain pathological phenomenon by means of imaginary forces or modifiable factors. According to Asclepiades, who prepared his theories, which were later on taken up and developed, the tissues of the body are pierced with innumerable invisible pores incessantly traversed by atoms. When the course of these atoms is changed by dilatation or contraction of the pores, disease ensues ; thickened blood prevents free passage of the atoms by obstructing the pores, which results in pain. Hence all treatment consists in dilating or contracting the pores according to circumstances. All this is remarkably clear and of masterly simplicity. But the unfortunate point is that it is merely a subjective speculation.

Although we may anticipate what we shall say further on, a few lines may here be given portraying Asclepiades. Celsus remarks that " his maxim was that the physician should cure his patients *tuto, celeriter, et jucunde.* This would be the best practice were it not for the danger of going too quickly and too agreeably ". He made great use of hydrotherapy, but combined his treatments with " nonsensical magic ". As Broussais says, this artistic dogmatism was to exploit the fortunes of the rich of his day. Giving general metaphysical explanations of disease, ordering a mild and pleasant treatment in accordance with the wishes of his clients, with just a bit of mysticism and a suspicion of charlatanism, such was the practice of Asclepiades.

Themison, his disciple, was not so circumspect in his treatment, and with him Methodism appears in all its solemnity. There were for him three types of morbid states, namely, the *strictum*, the *laxum*, and the mixed, the last being a combination of the two first states. From this it is clearly evident that Methodism, by its exaggerated synthesis, resorted to metaphysics, as did empiricism, by forcing analysis and division to their extreme limits.

For the Pneumatic sect, represented by Aretæus, the spirit or *pneuma* is the cause of all diseases, when it is too hot, too dry or cold, too moist, subtle or thick, and thus are explained the various pathological conditions.

Humoralism again renews the theory of formation of diseases. It admits as an axiom the existence of the four cardinal humours whose changes produce disease. There is a perpetual struggle between living and gross bodies which are completely assimilated without any effort on the part of medicine. The humours are in a state of fermentation, ebullition, corruption, etc. All this is hypothesis, and although modern medicine studies the changes occurring in the fluids of the body it does so directly by laboratory methods.

It would be fruitless to search for metaphysics in the Middle Ages, for they were, as we have shown, above all occupied by theological and supernatural interpretations of things. As to Islamic medicine and Arabism, they simply reproduce the Greek theories and doctrines. Not until the XVIth century and those which follow will metaphysical medicine be found more flourishing than ever and even fortified by certain progress made in science.

At this epoch, issued from the Middle Ages, we first come upon Paracelsus, and later upon Van Helmont. These men really belonged to the Middle Ages, for they were both mystics and ontologists. Paracelsus believed in the influence of the constellations and the imprint of God on plants and other substances. Van Helmont, at the same time as he studied magic, attempted to obtain divine inspiration. But both these men admitted the existence of a spirit of life, an Archeus located in the stomach; in other words, they admitted a generally regulating supernatural power, as well as entities directly productive of vital phenomena.

Paracelsus maintained that the human body was composed of sulphur, mercury, and salt, and that disease resulted when the mercury became precipitated, distilled, or sublimated in the body, or the sulphur became coagulated or dissolved, or the salt underwent calcination or alkalified. Since they supposed that they knew so well the origin and nature of disease, all that was necessary for their cure was to employ chemical combinations and reactions.

For Van Helmont, disease resulted from a discord between the chief Archeus situated in the stomach and the secondary or subaltern Archeus seated in the kidneys and liver, and over all of them presided the great vital principle, the *duumvirate*, which resided both in the stomach and in the spleen.

In the XVIth century the most fantastic theories abounded. The Iatrochemists and the Iatromathematicians invented the most original subjective explanations; some thought life made up of physico-chemical phenomena, others of physico-mechanical acts. It was the faculty of imagination applied to the phenomena of life. It would be quite impossible to refer to all the metaphysical systems—all the monuments of ontology. Even Boerhaave admitted the existence and action of animal spirits, seated especially in the diaphragmatic region, while, so late as the end of the XVIIth century, the celebrated Stahl completed the edifice built up during the preceding centuries.

The doctrine of animism sums up in an authoritative way the efforts made by great minds to understand phenomena by hypothetical reasoning. Matter is passive, insensible, immobile; it requires an immaterial principle or being to animate it, and this principle is the soul. Stahl's influence extended during the XVIIIth century, and is not yet entirely extinguished. Theologians derived a new force from this medical doctrine; the idea of an absolute independence between matter and the soul or vital principle, fortified by both vitalists and animists, became fixed in the minds of many, and in the early part of the XIXth century Barthez gave it a new impulse, which lasted until the present scientific and positive dogma, which does not admit property or force without matter, or matter without property or force.

To sum up, it may be said that metaphysical medicine does not merely consist of forces, an Archeus and vital principles, which in reality do not exist; it also attributes to phenomena an importance that they do not exclusively possess or derives from others that which they have. It is from this point of view that mechanism and iatrochemistry should, it seems to us, be placed in medical metaphysics, because to attribute an exaggerated preponderance to physiological or pathological phenomena, chemical reactions and purely physical laws, and at the same time to disregard biological phenomena, is to create something which is not the expression of facts. Truth does not exist in one doctrine more than another, no matter how rational this doctrine may appear, unless it contains the whole truth. By the word metaphysics we understand that which is above sensible things as well as what is outside the realm of nature and reality.

These remarks on the evolution of medicine will, it is hoped, assist the reader in the understanding of what is to follow.

# CHAPTER II

## EGYPTIAN MEDICINE

It is evident that at the beginning of the world mankind was obliged to consider the question of Medicine, but centuries rolled by before Medicine became a profession. A person who had experimented upon himself or on others would repeat the experiment upon similar occasions, and communicate his results to friends and neighbours. Herodotus tells us that the Babylonians did this in his day, and that they placed patients in the public places (for they had no physicians) in order that the passers-by who saw them could give advice and encourage them to practise what they or others had successfully done in similar cases. Herodotus also adds that nobody could pass by these patients without inquiring into the nature of their disease. Strabo says the same thing of the Babylonians, Portuguese and Egyptians. The Portuguese, he says, following an ancient custom of the Egyptians, placed their patients in the streets or on the highways, in order that any passer-by, who had suffered from the same affection, might give advice.

If we reflect upon the antiquity of the Egyptians and Babylonians, who are the first peoples of whom we have any real knowledge, we may take what they did as an example of the oldest systematized methods of treating disease. As the number of diseases recognized increased, it became a necessity that their treatment should be undertaken by those who had given their time to their study and to the practice of the healing art. Consequently it is necessary to distinguish in the history of medicine between medicine that may be called natural—which we suppose to have been that of the early human races—and medicine considered as Science and Art.

Natural medicine commenced with mankind, and for all times has been in use among all nations from the beginning of the world, so that, as Pliny tells us, "If there have been people who did not employ physicians, these people nevertheless were not deprived of medical skill."

The difficulty one encounters is to discover the time when the second type, namely Medicine as Science and Art, became finally established, that is to say, the time when men had, or thought to have, a sufficiently large collection of cases, as well as some experimental data, in order that rules could be formulated regarding knowledge of disease, symptoms of the various morbid processes, and remedies suitable for cure or amelioration. Whether such rules were false or not, or the precepts good or bad, matters little to us : all that is necessary is to discover the epoch in which medicine was raised to the level of a science and an art. This epoch, as far as we know, begins with the first dynasty of the Pharaohs on the banks of the Nile.

Medicine indeed existed as a science and as an art centuries before the advent of Hippocrates. The Greeks and Romans extolled the antiquity, wisdom, and scientific knowledge of the Egyptians and even what they have written about them probably falls far short of the truth.

THE INVENTORS OF MEDICINE Thoth or Hermes was for the Egyptians the personification of the priesthood. According to Jablonski, the word Thoth, Theyt, Thayt or Thoyt, signifies in the Egyptian language an assembly of learned men, the sarcedotal college of a city or a temple. Consequently, the collective *sacerdos* of Egypt, personified and considered as a unity, was represented by one to whom was accredited the invention of language and writing, brought by him from the heavens and communicated to man. Thoth was the inventor of geometry, arithmetic, astronomy, medicine, music and rhythm, likewise of the institution of religion and its sacred ceremonies, as well as gymnastics and dancing, and, lastly, those arts, less necessary but still precious, architecture, sculpture and painting. So many volumes on all these subjects of human knowledge were attributed to this deity, Thoth, that no mortal could have been able to compose them all. Discoveries made long after the supposed epoch of the god's appearance upon earth were attributed to him. All the successive developments of astronomy and, generally speaking, the improvements acquired during each century became the property of this god and consequently added to his glory. Hence, the names of individuals were lost in the priesthood and the merit that each had acquired by his work was turned to the profit of the sacerdotal company and was regarded as that of the titular genius of this company.

In order that one may judge of the immensity of knowledge gathered by the learned of ancient Egypt, reference should be made to the forty-two volumes of the Hermetic Collection. The two first volumes contain the hymns to the gods and recount the duties of kings; the four following describe the arrangement of the fixed stars, the light of the sun and moon, the constellations and so forth. In ten other volumes is to be found the key of the hieroglyphics, likewise the description of the Nile, the topography of Egypt, the details composing the religious ceremonies and the places where they were consecrated, as well as the nature of all things necessary for sacrifices; then follow teachings regarding astronomy, cosmography, the course of the sun and moon, as well as that of the five planets. Ten other volumes are concerned with the art of preparing the victims, with religious ceremonies, feast-days and prayers, and, in short, with all that constituted Egyptian religion. These sacerdotal books were destined for the study of the laws, the knowledge of the gods, the discipline of the priests, as well as the way in which the revenues should be distributed.

The last six volumes were especially devoted to medicine, and what is to be particularly noted, is that these contained a complete theory of medicine. The first volume treated of anatomy, the second dealt with diseases in general, the third described instruments, the fourth drugs and medicines, the fifth diseases of the eye, and the sixth diseases of women. Assuredly it cannot be denied that this arrangement was very methodical! A description of the human body was first given, thus showing that one must begin with a knowledge of the subject upon which one must operate; afterwards, diseases were studied, then the instruments and medicaments necessary for their cure, and, as affections of the eyes and diseases of women are very numerous and require particular attention, they were treated by themselves as specialties.

As may be seen, medicine, reduced to theory, formed a body of teaching for the Egyptians and they endowed it with all the attributes of a true science. For that matter, it is easy to understand its advance and progress in a country where physicians were so necessary.

The overflow of the Nile has always been the source of various diseases and, in early centuries, its pernicious effects must have been felt superlatively, since the precautions necessary for facilitating the draining of the water had not been taken. On the other hand, the inhabitants living far from the banks of the Nile only drank brackish water, which was frequently corrupted. The water of the Nile, usually quite healthy in character, sometimes acquires, during the great heat, noxious qualities which communicate lethal disease. Also, during the early months of spring the disease-bearing wind, Khamsin, prevails. This hot wind is laden with a large amount of burning sand, to such an extent that the sky may become obscured and the sun become so shaded as to appear in eclipse. "When it blows from the south-west," says Denon, "it is terrible. It dries and inflames the blood, irritates the nerves and renders life painful. It oppresses the lungs to such an extent that involuntarily one looks for another place in order to breathe, and at the same time has the sensation of an ardent heat in the mouth; if the air is inhaled by the nose, the brain becomes affected and when one exhales the breath it is as if one gave issue to floods of blood." Prosper Alpinus tells us that this wind causes several kinds of epidemics, likewise certain lethal diseases, and above all very stubborn ophthalmia. Hence it is that with all these diseases the ancient Egyptians began early in their history to cultivate medicine. It may be added that Clement of Alexandria states that Moses learnt his medicine from the Egyptians, a remark indicating that medicine existed as a science in the earliest times among this people.

The god Osiris (or Apis) and his consort Isis are also supposed to have invented medicine, and, according to Diodorus Siculus, Isis taught the arts of medicine and divination to her son Horus, who rendered great service both by his remedies and by his oracles. Horus was a sun-god. The ancients regarded the sun as the principle of generation and corruption, consequently as the source of life health, disease and death. In his Greek form of Apollo he was a healing (and pestilence-bringing) god, who also presided over vaticination, poetry and music, because prognosis is a kind of prophecy, while poetry and music are two powerful calmatives for melancholia and pain. The priestesses of his temple called him Paeon in their hymns, this word being derived from the Greek word signifying to heal. Under the name of Belenus, the Celts adored him as the universal physician and had recourse to him in their diseases. But the true god of healing, the equivalent of the Greek Asclepius, or Aesculapius, was Imhotep.

For many centuries the Egyptians alone held the sceptre of the sciences and arts. When classical Greece and Rome began to come out of barbarism, Egypt had already experienced numerous vicissitudes and had traversed successive periods of greatness and decadence. Although much of Greek civilization, formerly ascribed to Egyptian and Phœnician influence, is now recognized to be salvage from the wreck of the Minoan civilization, the Greeks themselves regarded Egypt as the ancient source of art and knowledge.

The four principal medical papyri to be mentioned are treatises of medicine which have come down to us in a more or less complete state of preservation. The one that has suffered least from the marks of ages was found near Luxor in Upper Egypt by Ebers, who has translated it. The second, a part of which has been destroyed, is in the Museum of Berlin and is known as the Berlin medical papyrus. It was discovered enclosed in an earthen vase at Memphis (the capital of the first dynasties of ancient Egypt) not distant from the ruins of Saqqarah, a village not far from Cairo, and very probably belonged to the medical library of the temple of Ptah, referred to by Galen. An excellent translation of this papyrus has been made by Brugsch and Chabas. The third papyrus is at the British Museum and dates from the XVIIIth dynasty. The fourth papyrus was acquired by Edwin Smith, an American amateur Egyptologist, at Thebes in 1862, and after his death was given to the New York Historical Society. Although as yet incompletely deciphered, this papyrus throws most interesting light on Egyptian medicine.

The seventeen columns of writing which occupy the *recto* contain a treatise of medicine but are composed of case-histories and not merely prescriptions. The number of cases recorded amounts to forty-eight, systematically classified according to the organs from head to foot, and including all kinds of traumata affecting males. Each case-history is given on a definite plan ; a title, description of the symptoms, the diagnosis, prognosis and treatment, followed by a certain number of comments on the case. The fact that the Edwin Smith papyrus is a collection of case-histories and not of formulae is enough to distinguish it definitely from the three other papyri above mentioned. But what gives it its distinctive character as well as its value is the great number of comments—seventy in all—added to the case-histories, as well as a number of data they give us regarding the anatomical and physiological knowledge of the ancient Egyptians. In this papyrus, which dates from 1700 B.C., the oldest collection of case-histories is brought together for a didactic end and for therapeutical instruction.

Besides these medical treatises, the museums of Cairo and of Europe possess other interesting books on the medicine of the ancient Egyptians. Maspero refers to two lost works, of which one was written in the reigns of Hesepti and Send (Ist and IInd dynasties), and the other in the reign of Menkara (IVth dynasty). They unquestionably belonged to the library of Imhotep at Memphis, which was still in existence during the Roman epoch, and from which the Greek physicians derived much.

MEDICINE AND MAGIC. With our modern ideas it may seem astonishing to find medicine and magic united under the same heading. However, the ancient Egyptians thought otherwise and usually a single word designates both physician and magician. Unquestionably the Egyptians had faith in medicine, but a slight taint of the supernatural was not, in their minds, detrimental to the making of a formula. For example, the prescription of milk taken from a cow who had not yet calved was no surprise to them. Quite on the contrary, this specific advice appeared to them the proof of great care and profound science on the part of their physician. Moreover, the first thought that came to the mind of the patient was to consult a professional magician and, if he was not successful, the advice of a physician was then decided upon. But, generally speaking, remedies and incantations when combined were thought to increase the chances of recovery.

There exists a treatise on Egyptian medicine of over one hundred pages in-folio, including a preface, which may date from the time of Rameses I. The following lines are taken from the introduction with which the author presents his work to the public: "I have come out from the school of medicine at Heliopolis, where the venerable masters of the Great Temple have inculcated their remedies within me. I have come out from the Gynaecological School of Sais, where the divine Mothers have given me their prescriptions.

"I am in possession of the incantations composed by Osiris personally. My guide has always been the god Thoth, the inventor of speech and writing, the writer of infallible prescriptions, he who alone knows how to give reputation to magicians and physicians who follow his precepts.

"Incantations are excellent for remedies, and remedies are good for incantations."

The only fact that is to be retained from this preface is that an author of a scientific work is obliged to recommend himself by reference to the deity Thoth, in order that his book should be read.

It is therefore apparent that magic was extremely widespread in Egypt and practised above all for the help of physicians in every case where remedies indicated by science were fruitless of effect.

From what has been said the reader will perceive that medicine and magic were intimately united in ancient Egypt, one might even say intermingled, and in the study of their documents relating to medicine it soon becomes apparent that the study of magic must also be undertaken. It must, moreover, be remembered that the physician of the present day may be obliged to assume to a slight extent the part of a magician, especially when caring for persons with a nervous temperament, because it is not infrequently necessary to deal at the same time with both the mind and the body.

INCANTATIONS. Among the incantations that have been transmitted to us by the Egyptian documents, there are two of general application, and these should be quoted in the first place. Their power, so the papyrus tells us, is extremely extensive, since they are recommended for all kinds of disease. They are published in the preface of the Ebers papyrus as if they comprised within themselves the entire contents of the document. They are here given textually.

"Words to be said with exactitude and repeated as many times as possible when one applies remedies over a member of some one who is ill, in order to destroy all cause of disturbance residing within him.

"Isis has delivered Osiris, has delivered Horus from evil things which his brother Set had done him by killing his father Osiris. O Isis, great goddess of incantations, deliver me, free me from all bad, evil and cruel things, deliver me from the god of pain, from the goddess of pain, from a death, from the penetrating which penetrates me, in the same way as thy son Horus was delivered and freed. For I have entered into fire, I have come out of water, I have not fallen into the snare of to-day. I have said that I have been a child, that I have been small. O Sun, speak with your tongue! O Osiris, intercede by your intervention. Now thou hast delivered me from every bad, evil and cruel thing, from the god of pain, from the goddess of pain, from death."

As the title indicates, these incantations are especially to be used when employing external medication. The following is the incantation to be said when internal remedies are used:—"Come remedies, come and expel the things of my heart, of my limbs. Incantations are good for remedies and remedies are good for incantations. Do you not remember that Horus and Set were brought within the great temple of Heliopolis when the question of their legitimacy was being discussed? He is now prospering as he was when on earth, he does everything that he desires, like the gods among whom he now resides." These words were to be recited as exactly as possible and as many times as possible whenever the patient drank a potion.

In spite of the great importance that the Egyptians attributed to the use of these two incantations, they were frequently considered insufficient. They had the defect of being too general in character; therefore certain special formulae inspired a greater confidence. For this reason there were quite a large number which were pronounced in certain peculiar circumstances. For example the following incantation was used for the cure of specks of the cornea:—

"A clamour arises in the south of the sky as soon as night falls; the disturbance extends into the north of the heavens. The colonnades fall into the water. The sailors of the solar bark strike themselves with their oars in order to cause the head to fall into the water. My father comes, he brings it, he has found it. I, I bring it, I have found it. I have brought your heads, I replace them on your necks, I have reduced your wounds to their proper place. I have brought you to drive away the god of pain and death." This incantation was to be recited over tortoiseshell reduced to powder and mixed with honey, afterwards placed on the eye.

In order to give added power to a purgative medicine, it was quite sufficient to say: "O male hyena, female hyena, O destructor (male and female)."

In the case of tapeworm, the remedies used were accompanied by the following words:—"May these words expel the painful creeping progression traced in my belly by him who winds within! It is a god that has created this enemy! May he charm it and expel the affection that he has produced in my belly!"

As a last example of these incantations may be mentioned the following magic formula to be used when an emetic is taken:—"O demon who art within the abdomen of So-and-so, son of So-and-so, O thou whose father is surnamed He who causes heads to fall, whose name is death, whose name is the male of death, whose name is accursed to Eternity."

Many more medical incantations could be quoted, but those given are amply sufficient to give the reader an idea of the importance the ancient Egyptians attributed to this kind of magic. It is likewise probable that the reader has understood nothing of these incantations, but suffice it to say that in the minds of the patients they were efficacious. It is evident that when supernatural beings are addressed, likewise male and female hyenas, the gods of pain, and penetrants and destructors in general, one could not with decency employ the vulgar and intelligible language of simple mortals. These malevolent powers were thought to possess a language belonging to themselves only but known to the magicians, and this was transcribed for the great good of humanity in the medical magical papyri. The mere fact of speaking was not sufficient and the incantations were accompanied by gesticulations not used in daily life.

Physicians and Medical Schools. At the beginning of the treatise entitled "The Art and Mystery of the Physician who knows the Working of the Heart, who knows the Heart", which comprises several pages of the Ebers papyrus, will be found an enumeration of three kinds of practitioners to whom the work will be useful. The first class of practitioner is the ordinary physician, the third being the magician or charmer (*sa-u*). Maspero has indicated the second class of practitioner by the word 'exorcist', which literally means "a priest of Sekhet". Chabas and Diehl have translated the same word as "master purifier" and the latter authority, by the simple transcription of "a priest of Sekhet", without any attempt at interpretation. The goddess Sekhet was the goddess whose wrath produced the largest number of diseases, likewise the greatest mortality, and her priests were naturally designated for appeasing and exorcizing the disease that was supposed to be due to her anger. "For example, after a fracture, if the patient should have the luck to meet a skilful priest, the latter, acting by his own inspiration, could unite the fragments in such a way that the click of the bones could be heard when they joined together. If such a priest could not be found and if the patient was not afraid of death, then physicians with their books were brought, the latter containing drawings and shaded figures. When the injured limb had been dressed according to the lines of the figures contained in the books, bandages were applied and the patient continued to live after having regained his health. Man is never resigned to death even when a priest knowing how to unite fractures cannot be found." Berthelot, from whose book the above is taken, states that all this is the procedure of a bonesetter priest, who was regarded by the people as far superior to the physician whose science is contained in books.

It would seem that this text may serve to explain the classification of physicians mentioned in the Ebers papyrus. The physician was not included in the special priesthoods; he studied the make-up of the human body in books containing anatomical figures and he treated fractures according to the rules of art, by means of ligatures whose shape and use were to be found in the books, as indicated by the following passage: "The patient is treated (by the physician) in an inferior way but the patient nevertheless may recover. The priest does not possess this vulgar instruction. He acts following direct and entirely personal inspiration that he receives from God."

The work of an initiate was supposed to be far superior to that of the ordinary man, hence it may be readily understood why Zosimus places the priest far above the physician. On the contrary, the author of the treatise contained in the Ebers papyrus, who was a physician, places the medical profession upon a higher plane than the priests of Sekhet. He gives the following enumeration: 1. The Sa-unu, or physician who carries out his work according to the books; 2. the Uibu Sekhet, the priestess of the goddess Sekhet; 3. the Sa-u, the charmer, who possesses neither the acquired science of the first nor the divine inspiration of the second, but recites formulae, of the meaning of which he is ignorant, accompanied by ceremonies and gesticulations which usually he does not understand, and performs his cures following a routine which has been transmitted from other magicians quite as ignorant and quite as uninspired as himself.

If the classical authors are to be believed, physicians were very numerous in Egypt and greatly esteemed. Herodotus tells us that the practice of medicine was very wisely carried out in Egypt; that every physician adopted one particular specialty and did not treat several classes of disease. There were, for example, oculists, specialists for diseases of the head, dentists, and specialists for abdominal affections. Lastly there were those who specialized in internal diseases. The ophthalmologists were the most numerous of all in Egypt. They were supposed to be extremely skilful and their reputation was widespread. There were also many dentists, from which it may be supposed that dental affections were frequent.

The excellent reputation of the Egyptian physicians extended to foreign countries. Both Cyrus and Darius sent for Egyptian physicians in cases of severe illness, and in Pliny's correspondence with Trajan several letters are to be found in which he congratulates himself upon having been saved, when none of his countrymen had been able to cure him, by an Egyptian physician, practising at Rome, Harpocrates by name.

In military expeditions and during travel, everyone was cared for gratuitously, because the physicians received a stipend from the State. They determined the treatment of disease according to written precepts transmitted to them by a large number of celebrated physicians of the past. If by following the precepts of the sacred book they were unable to cure a patient, they were declared innocent and exempt from all reproach; if they acted contrary to the written precepts they could be condemned to death if the patient died, because the lawgivers of the time believed that few persons could devise curative methods better than those which had been followed for so long a time and had been established by the greatest minds of medicine. This extreme systematization in all things is very characteristic of the ancient Egyptians. Just as physicians should always treat their patients with the same remedies, so architects should always build the temples according to a single plan, while artists could only draw their personages according to fixed and immutable rules. Although Egypt, on account of this passion for stability, was deprived of progress which could have been made in art and science by the personal talent of her great men, she at least benefited in this remarkable respect, that during four thousand years she remained inviolably great, always preserving her special characteristics in spite of contact with other nations.

Medical Schools. From the very first dynasty medical schools, some of which are known to us, were founded in various parts of the kingdom. A college existed at Sais in which women were taught the profession of midwives, and these in turn gave instruction in gynaecology to physicians. At Heliopolis, a city where many learned Greeks went to study science, was a very large medical school placed under the protection of the solar god. At Memphis, the god Imhotep, the Egyptian Aesculapius, had a temple containing a medical library, the only extant book from it being the Berlin papyrus.

It is certain that the first Greeks assiduously frequented the Egyptian schools when Amasis, nearly six centuries before Christ, opened his country to foreigners. Only fragments of the works of these writers have come down to us, but many are the passages in the Hippocratic Collection, and in the works of Galen and Dioscorides, which represent almost literal translations of medical prescriptions that are to be found in the Egyptian papyri. It is, however, extremely doubtful if the priests of ancient Egypt communicated, even to initiated foreigners, all the knowledge in their possession. This doubt is based upon the following passage contained in Strabo. " They showed us," says the learned geographer, " the houses of priests as well as the places where Plato and Eudoxus had lived. These philosophers came together to Heliopolis and, according to some writers, they there passed thirteen years with the priests. After a time, and by many attentions and much politeness, they obtained from these priests, who were very learned in astronomy and medicine, but very mysterious and uncommunicative, the knowledge of certain problems ; but the priests hid from them the greater part of their knowledge."

ANATOMY. The knowledge of anatomy in Egypt must certainly extend back to a very remote time, because Manetho relates that Athothis, son and successor of Menes, the founder of the first dynasty, about four thousand years before the Christian era, was a physician and wrote books on medicine, the first of which treated of anatomy and dissection of the human body. This treatise, composed by the second of the Egyptian kings, would seem to indicate that at that time medicine was based upon anatomy. Undoubtedly at this epoch the fanatical respect for a body deprived of life did not as yet exist and to use a knife upon a corpse in order to search for the mystery of life in the secrets of death was not regarded as an impious act. According to the same writer (Manetho) Tosorthros, the second Pharaoh of the Third Dynasty, also applied himself to medicine and anatomy. If one should desire to form an idea as to what the first work by Athothis, referred to by Manetho as the first treatise on anatomy ever written, might have been, one has merely to read the following lines taken from the Berlin papyrus, which are supposed to be based on knowledge handed down from the time of Hesepti: " The head has twenty-two vessels which draw the breath from the heart and from there carry it to all parts of the body. There are two vessels in the breasts which conduct to the kidneys. There are two vessels in the legs, two in the arms, there are two vessels in the forehead, two in the neck, two in the throat, two in the eyelids, two in the nostrils; two in the right ear, through which the breath of ife enters, and two in the left ear, through which the breath of death enters."

Anatomy holds but a small place in the Ebers papyrus; all that relates to this subject is found in two small treatises at the end of the work written in a very ancient style and already sufficiently obscure at the time of the XVIIIth dynasty for the scribe to have considered it his duty to note the different interpretations of the various manuscripts which he used for composing his edition. One of these treatises claims to teach physicians the mechanism of cardiac action and a knowledge of the heart itself. Here are some extracts taken from this treatise. "There are in the heart vessels coming from all limbs. Every physician, every exorcist, and every charmer who places the fingers on the head, on the neck, on the hands, over the region of the heart, on the arms, or on the legs, will come upon the heart because the vessels of the heart are in all the limbs. There are four vessels in the nostrils, of which two give off mucus and two give off blood. There are four vessels inside the temples, which give off blood to both eyes and also produce the humours of both eyes. If tears fall from both eyes, it is the apple of both eyes which gives them."

A different interpretation:—"It is the circles which are formed by the iris and the pupil together which do this. There are four vessels in the middle of the head which give off branches into the occiput; the breath and the spirit enter the nose and go to the heart and lungs, which then distribute them to the entire intestinal cavity. The apertures which are found in the nose are two vessels which lead to the cavity of the eye." Another rendering: "These apertures which are in the nose are those which are in the head and in the neck of man for the purpose of respiration and through which he receives his vital spirit. If the heart hardens, it is the vessel called Skhep which causes this, because it is this vessel which brings water to the heart. If the aorta (literally, the opening of the orifice of its mouth) projects, all the limbs become brittle on account of the disturbance that the heart undergoes from this cause. If the aneurism develops, it represents a sac (pocket) developing near the stomach and liver; the orifices of the heart and vessels become prominent, and if they become inflamed the pocket bursts. There are four vessels for both ears, namely, two on the right and two on the left side; the breath of death enters by the left ear. There are six vessels leading to the limbs, three on the right and three on the left, which extend down to the soles of the feet. There are two vessels going to the testicles, which give rise to sperm; there are two vessels for the thighs, one going to one thigh, the other to the other. There are four vessels belonging to the liver, which supply it with water and breath, after which it (the liver) produces within its substance all the humours which the blood carries. There are four vessels belonging to the lungs and spleen, which also bring them water and breath. There are two vessels belonging to the kidneys, which give rise to urine. There are four vessels opening at the anus, which give it water and breath, because at the anus all the vessels of the right and left sides of the body open, the two vessels from the arms and the two vessels from the legs which carry the excretions (to the rectum)."

Lastly another theory, very similar to the preceding ones, is to be found in a treatise believed to have been written in the days of King Hesepti. "In man there are twelve vessels going from the heart to all the limbs and parts of the body. There are two vessels in the mammary region which produce inflammation of the anus. There are two vessels in the thigh. If he suffers from his thigh and if his feet are painful one should say: It is the crural region which has been taken ill. If he suffers in the neck and if the eyes become cloudy it is because the vessels of the neck have become involved by disease. There are two vessels in the arms. If he suffers from the arm and the fingers are painful, one should say: These are shooting pains. There are two vessels in the neck. There are two vessels for the forehead. There are two vessels for the eye. There are two vessels for the eyebrows. There are two vessels for the right ear through which the breath of life enters. There are two vessels for the left ear, through which the breath of death enters."

From what has been said the reader will at once perceive that the anatomy of the ancient Egyptians was extremely primitive. Nevertheless it should not be forgotten that the Ebers papyrus is based on works of the XVIIIth dynasty and the old dynasties of Memphis. It must also be recalled that the knowledge of the Egyptian physicians recorded herein dates back forty centuries before the Christian era and that, consequently, taking all things into consideration, they were fairly well advanced for their time. Dissection of the human body was forbidden, and experimental work in physiology could not be carried out. The horror of the ancient Egyptians for any person who would have violated the integrity of the human body after death was so great that the professional embalmers were always chosen from the lowest stratum of the population and were the object of universal hate. They were obliged to embalm the bodies with as little delay as possible, hence rendering an attentive examination of the interior of a body impossible and, as they never came in contact with physicians, these could not profit from their work as far as anatomy was concerned. Therefore this science remained in Egypt exactly as it was at the beginning of the first dynasty of the Pharaohs.

Semeiology and Pathology. The physicians of ancient Egypt were at an early period able to detect a certain number of diseases and make differential diagnoses with a certain amount of precision. As an example we will give the diagnosis of a certain type of inflammation, as given in the Berlin papyrus :—

" His abdomen is heavy, his stomach suffers. His heart is burning and beats with rapidity. His clothes hang heavy upon him as if he were covered with many garments. He is thirsty towards evening. The taste of his heart is perverted like that of a man who has eaten figs of the sycamore. His flesh is flabby, like that of a man about to die. When he crouches to urinate his thighs feel heavy and burn him. For this one should say : there is a swelling of the abdomen and the heart has tasted disease.

" To rid the patient (of his affection) it is necessary to obtain a contraction (of the abdomen). Thou shalt apply remedies for the swelling, namely fresh dates, juniper berries, honey, fruit of the sebesten-plumtree and so forth."

Here is another diagnosis taken from the Ebers papyrus :—

"If thou judgest that there is a thickening of the blood in all the members of a person, thou shouldst find them, taken singly or in groups, similar to the skin of an animal. The flesh will be found hard when palpated by thy fingers. The size of his limbs will be enlarged from the disease which is in the flesh. For this (affection) one says : It is a thickening of the blood."

Had the authors of the medical papyri that we possess taken the pains to describe their diagnoses of disease with the same care and detail that they have taken in the prescription of remedies, one would have been able to form a large collection of hieroglyphic medical terms. Unfortunately such is not the case, and in the majority of instances it is quite impossible to determine to what diseases the formulae apply; therefore one can only transcribe in the letters of the modern alphabet the Egyptian names of diseases.

Nevertheless, the *ensemble* of the prescriptions that has come down to us indicates in a general way the affections from which the ancient Egyptians most frequently suffered. Foremost among them, according to the Ebers papyrus, were abdominal affections ; secondly, come various types of ophthalmia—still frequent at the present time along the banks of the Nile ; next, retention of urine and intestinal parasites ; these are followed by diseases of the head, ears, and teeth, and lastly erysipelas, epilepsy and a certain number of swellings designated by a large number of special names. The Berlin papyrus refers to about the same number of diseases. As to the London papyrus, the only portion that has come down to us hardly treats of anything but burns. It is also to be pointed out that a number of the words frequently repeated by the scribe are very obscure.

The following passage taken from the Ebers papyrus describes diseases of the *rohet*, otherwise the stomach. "If thou comest upon a patient afflicted by an obstruction of the stomach, if he complains of heaviness after eating, if the abdomen is swollen, if the heart fails during walking, as in a patient who suffers from an inflammation of the rectum, examine him in the recumbent position, and if thou findest the abdomen hot and an obstruction of the stomach, say : This belongs to the liver. Give him the secret remedy composed of herbs that the physician himself should compound.

"The pulp of date stones; mix and dilute in water and give this to the patient upon four consecutive mornings in order to free the abdomen.

"If after having done this thou findest the right hypochondrium hot and the left cool, say for this: The internal juices combat the disease which gnaws them. If in examining the patient a second time thou findest the entire abdomen cool, say that his liver is cured, he is purified and has well taken his remedy."

The numerous means employed by the ancient Egyptians in order to ascertain if a woman will have children or not indicates the great desire on the part of the Egyptians in the days of the Pharaohs to have offspring. The following is a means for hastening delivery: "Burn turpentine resin close to the abdomen. If this means remains without effect, place a mixture of oil of saffron and sweet beer on the abdomen."

OPHTHALMOLOGY. Without going back to the Hindus, in whose sacred books traces of special practice are to be found, it is known that five centuries before our era it was the Egyptian priests who undertook the treatment of diseases of the eye and that the ophthalmic art was truly sacerdotal. The reputation of the Egyptian priests in this respect was known far and wide Herodotus says that Cyrus, king of Persia, caused a celebrated Egyptian oculist to come to him, and Woolhouse, in his comments, is of the opinion that Tobias' trip to Egypt had no other end than to study the diseases of the eye and the means of their cure. The great skill in the treatment of diseases of the eye acquired by the ancient Egyptians is readily explained when we consider their special experience.

In closing this chapter one remark should be made regarding anaesthesia in antiquity. We must go back to Pliny in order to find the earliest recorded notions regarding the various means for controlling pain. This celebrated naturalist stated that the ancient Egyptians employed a product called *memphitis*, which, when powdered and mixed with vinegar, anaesthetized the parts upon which it was applied to such a degree that they could be cut or cauterized without pain.

Dioscorides refers to the same fact, and says that the stone of *Memphis* which composed this powder was the size of a talent, was greasy to the touch and was found in various colours. However, this stone, once so greatly extolled, has long since been forgotten, and is nowhere else referred to.

Such an anaesthetic agent, although it may savour of the marvellous, can, however, be scientifically explained. In point of fact, modern science has shown that carbonic acid acts as a local anaesthetic. Now, marble is composed of carbonate of lime and decomposes under the influence of a powerful acid, such as acetic acid, which is, of course, present in vinegar. Hence in employing powdered marble of Memphis with the addition of vinegar a certain amount of carbonic acid is given off—which in the nascent state will act efficaciously as a local anaesthetic.

To conclude, it can be said that during the epoch of the Pharaohs the Egyptian physicians were celebrated. Theophrastus, Galen, and Dioscorides frequently quote prescriptions that they had learnt in the temple of Aesculapius at Memphis, and Pliny gives a prescription which would seem to have been taken from a Greek translation of a formula contained in the Ebers papyrus. The history of the origin of the healing art is certainly to be found in the various papyri mentioned in the foregoing pages.

# CHAPTER III

## HINDU MEDICINE. CHALDEAN AND PERSIAN MEDICINE

HINDU MEDICINE. The most ancient documents of the Indo-Aryan race are the Vedas, otherwise the "Books of Revealed Wisdom". The most ancient of these is the Rig Veda (or "Knowledge of Praise"), being composed of sacred songs written between one and two thousand years before the Christian era. Mention is there found of a special class of physicians. The book also contains passages praising the healing powers of herbs and waters It also mentions at least two diseases, namely phthisis and leprosy. But the fourth book, entitled the Atharda Veda (or "Science of Charms"), which was written seven hundred years before Christ, is, as might be expected, the one of these four great religious works possessing a medical character. Invocations of demons to cure or cause disease are to be found in great number. As an example, Takman, the demon of fever, is implored to strike the woman Sudra—a low-caste personage. The rarest remedies, however, seem to have been reserved for the use of princes. Thus the son of Bimbisara, king of Magadha, who reigned about 600 B.C., lost consciousness. In order to obtain a cure the patient was placed in six tubs of butter, one after the other, and lastly in a tub of sandalwood. It is interesting to know that the prince survived and succeeded his father on the throne.

Although the invocations given in the Atharda Veda were undoubtedly recited by Brahmins, it is especially to be noticed that the physicians of the Vedic age did not belong to this religious caste. In the ancient laws of Manu, physicians are placed among the impure individuals who are excluded from funeral feasts, and their origin is attributed, in the Brahmin writings, to marriage between men and women of different castes. However, it is probable that the great majority belonged to the middle Hindu caste—the Vaisyas—

comprising farmers and merchants ; at a later date physicians were permitted to have as students members of almost any caste, excepting a Sudra.

Beside the four great religious books, or Vedas, the Hindus possess books of less ancient date called the Upa Vedas, whose contents pertain to more mundane subjects, such as music, medicine, architecture and so forth. The first of these books is the Ayur Veda, or " Knowledge of Life ". This title applies to all these books, and comprises those in which the history of medicine has been supernaturally revealed. This is especially true of the writings of Charaka, which were revealed directly to him by Indra, so it is said, by the intermediary of a Rishi, or sage. The pages written by Susruta are said to have been dictated to him by the divine Dhanvantari, who became incarnate for this purpose.

The history of the birth of this Hindu Aesculapius is so curious that it should be recorded in these pages.

" A scourge fell upon the Universe and the disquieted gods came to their Vishnu, or father, to ask his advice. In reply, he declared that it was necessary to obtain Amrita, the drink of Immortality, and for this purpose the Ocean of Milk must be stirred up. Therefore, for the time being, the gods and demons forgot their quarrels and became united in the undertaking of this enormous work.

" The great serpent Vasuki coiled himself around the mountain Mandara and the gods and demons, seizing the monster by the head, made him turn the mountain on the back of Vishnu himself, who had become transformed into an enormous turtle and had sunk to the bottom of the Ocean of Milk.

" They laboured long, and the demons, who were nearest to the head of the serpent, were permanently blackened by the toxic vapours exhaled from the serpent's head. But finally the work was accomplished and then a moon, a wonderful tree, and a sacred cow came forth from the Ocean of Milk, representing the goddesses of Love, Wine, and Beauty, and last of all the physician Dhanvantari arose dressed in a white robe and holding in his hand the cup of Amrita."

On account of his pity for mortal ills, Dhanvantari became reincarnate on earth as a prince of Benares and, having etired into a forest as a hermit, according to the custom of the ancient Hindu princes, he dictated to Susruta, the son of the famous warrior and sage, Visvamitra, his book entitled the Ayur Veda. In the writings of Charaka and Susruta a large amount of medical and surgical knowledge is contained which can well bear comparison with that of the writers of the Hippocratic Collection. Such advanced knowledge of medicine was completely wanting in the more remote Vedic age. The most striking feature of these writings is the very high place given to surgery. This fact itself was held quite sufficient to show that these works possessed a divine origin, and Susruta says : " Surgery is first and highest in the healing art, it is pure in itself, its use can never die, it is a product of the heavens and a sure source of renown on earth (to those who practise it)."

At the same time he especially advises the unity of medicine, for he says : " He who only knows a single branch of his art, is like a bird with a single wing."

Both practical and theoretical knowledge must be combined : " He who is only versed in books will be both discomfited and cowardly when he finds himself in the presence of a patient, and he who rashly embarks upon the practice of medicine without first having studied the books of science, must not expect the respect of humanity, but rather merits punishment by the King.

" But he who combines the reading of books with experience can with surety undertake the treatment of disease."

Susruta also warns his students against too much reading, " . . . because the student who acquires his knowledge in this way is like an ass with a load of sandalwood on his back, for he feels the weight but knows not the value."

As a sample of the general style of the work and of Hindu military medicine, a few extracts from the thirty-fourth chapter of the first book may be given.

" When the king goes forth with his army to fight the enemy, or to punish them for their wickedness, he should take a learned physician with him who is a pious penitent, whose prayers will be heard.

" The physician should examine the food, water, woods, and the site of the encampment with the greatest care, because it is quite possible that poison has been spread on all these things by the enemy.

" If he finds poison he should remove it and thus he will save the army from death and destruction. He will find the means for doing this by reading the chapter on poisons.

" The pious penitent should remove all harmful influences by prayers and relieve the oppressed from their pain and the sinners from their shame.

" Should a disease develop in the army the physician should resort to every means for its control and especially he should give great attention to the person of the king, because he represents the entire people, and, as the proverb says: ' Where there is no king, the people will devour themselves.' The physician's tent should be near the king's and his medicaments and books should always be within his reach. A flag should fly over the physician's tent in order to show the wounded where he may be found."

At this point the author suddenly changes the subject :—

" The physician, the patient, the drugs, and the nurse represent the four pillars of medicine upon which recovery depends. When three of these pillars are as they should be, then with the aid of the fourth, which is the physician, recovery will be complete, and the physician will be able to cure a very severe disease in a very short time. But without the physician the three other pillars are quite useless, even if they are themselves all they should be—just like Brahmins who recite from the Rig and Sama Vedas when making a sacrifice without any Brahmin to recite the Ayur Veda.

" But a good physician may be able to cure his patient by himself alone, exactly as a pilot can guide a ship into a port without sailors. The physician who has been able to penetrate into the hidden meaning of medical works, who has seen and taken part in the operations (of medicine), who has a firm hand, an honest mind and a courageous heart, who has his instruments and his books always with him, who is possessed of presence of mind, judgment, resolution, and experience, and who values the truth above all things ; such a physician may be called a true pillar of medicine (*pada*). A patient worthy of the name should have vital force, and if he should not be very poor he should have sufficient control over himself not to indulge in harmful pleasures. All this if he has faith in his physician.

" A drug that can be considered as a pillar should grow in

excellent soil, should be plucked on a favourable day, and should be given in proper doses at the proper time. Also the plant should be fresh.

"Lastly a nurse is a pillar when he is good-hearted, when confidence can be placed in him, and when he exactly follows the physician's orders."

The greatest success of Hindu surgery was certainly in the plastic operations on the nose, and even at the present time the Indian technique is not infrequently resorted to. The great skill with which this operation was performed by the ancient Hindu surgeons was acquired by experience, since despotic governors and jealous husbands were accustomed to mutilate their subjects and their wives.

**Susruta** also mentions the section of the infra-orbital nerve in cases of neuralgia, as well as laparotomy and suture of the intestines in case of occlusion or other lesions of the intestine. He gives a description of more than a thousand instruments, but the first and best of these is the surgeon's hand. He also describes twelve kinds of leeches. This portion of his book was later on held in great esteem by the Arabian physicians who, as far back as the eighth century, translated certain portions of the works of the Hindu physicians.

All this leads us to a question of great importance, namely what was the date of this remarkable development of Hindu medicine, which appeared and disappeared in such a mysterious way. If we take the Arabian translations into consideration, the year A.D. 750 is the latest possible. The ancient writers, basing their arguments on the fact that Susruta and Charaka are mentioned in the great epic poem entitled *Mahabharata*, maintain that the works attributed to them must in all events be quite as ancient as the Homeric poems. Yet it should be pointed out that the *Mahabharata* has undergone revisions, and additions have been made down to quite an advanced date in the Christian era, while modern students of Sanscrit maintain that the language of these medical works is that of a period certainly much later than the invasion of Alexander, which took place in 367 B.C. Now, the dates 327 B.C. and A.D. 750 almost exactly mark the period of Buddhist domination in India, and it would seem more than probable that this Buddhist millennium was also the golden age of Hindu medicine.

The fraternal love and sympathetic pity which were taught by the Buddhist initiated were extremely favourable to the progress of the most sacred art which the prejudices of caste and the unending formalities of Brahminism restricted. And lastly we possess indubitable evidence proving that the physician was held in great honour by the Buddhists. Thus, one of the greatest misfortunes of poverty was that a poor man could not have a physician or medicines, and travellers were warned not to remain in a country where the following five things did not exist: a king, a river, rich men, teachers, and physicians.

When King Asoka—the Constantine of Buddhism—adopted this religion for himself and his empire in the year 250 B.C., he issued a series of proclamations, two of which relate to our subject. In the first it is said that a man with a kindly mind and well-beloved by the gods will never kill an animal, and perhaps this may be compared with some extraordinary passages to be found in the writings of Susruta, which prohibit any medical aid to be given to hunters and to all those who kill or trap animals. In the second proclamation Asoka says that he has established two "cures", one for men and another for animals. The word "cure" in all probability literally means an asylum, perhaps a hospital. Others have even seen in this word the equivalent of medical schools.

Not only in his own possessions but also in those of neighbouring monarchs, Asoka took every step that medicinal plants might be collected, and planted in places where they were not to be found.

The Buddhist pilgrims coming from China in the fifth, sixth, and seventh centuries, have left us their observations on houses for the sick that they found in various parts of India, and the well-known hospital for animals at Surat may very well have had its origin in Asoka's reign.

The *Mahavansa*, or Singalese Chronicle, affords also other striking evidence in respect of this question. When King Dutha Gamani was on his death-bed in the year 161 B.C., he ordered that a complete list of his acts should be read to him, and in this list it is said: "Daily I have maintained, in eighteen different places, hospitals supplied with food proper for patients and medicaments necessary to practitioners of medicine for the proper treatment of disease."

In the year A.D. 341 lived the King Buddhadisa, an excessively rich and very virtuous man. He was the patron of men of goodwill, disapproved of the wicked, and gave comfort to the sick by giving them medical aid. It is said that he himself wrought cures, but such tales as the following one are probably without foundation. "A herdsman drank some water very quickly. The water contained frogs' eggs; and one of these, entering a nostril, continued onward into the head. Within the skull the egg developed and a frog came forth, so that in rainy weather he would croak and gnaw the head of the herdsman. The Rajah split the head of the man and removed the frog, after which he brought the incised parts together and the wound healed very quickly."

However, there is no reason to doubt the veracity of the following tale: "By his kindness to the inhabitants of the island, the sovereign ordered hospitals to be erected, and he appointed physicians for all the villages. Having composed a work containing the elements of all the medical sciences, he distributed them to the physicians of the island that they might be used as a future guide in practice. He ordained that there should be a physician for every ten villages, he reserved twenty royal villages for the maintenance of these physicians, and he appointed other medical practitioners to care for elephants, horses, and the army. He erected asylums along the principal highways for the care of the blind and maimed in different parts of the country. It is also said that from his great compassion for mankind this kind King was accustomed to carry a case of surgical instruments with him and to proffer help to every afflicted person that he met."

The most important Singalese hospital was that founded by Parakrama the Great (A.D. 1164–89), and "this sovereign also had built a large hall which could contain several hundreds of patients, and he endowed it with everything necessary, as is stated further on.

"To each patient he assigned a male and female servant that he might be cared for night and day, and he prescribed the necessary diets, as well as various kinds of food. He also built many granaries which he filled, taking care to place therein everything requisite for physicians. He did everything in his power to support wise and learned physicians, well versed in all medical knowledge and skilled in the search for the hidden nature of disease. It was his habit to visit this great hall upon each of the four days of Uposotha of each month.

" And since he had a heart filled with kindness he looked upon the patient with eyes full of pity, and being eminently wise and skilful in the healing art he would call before him the physicians who were employed there and minutely question them as to their methods of treatment and, if he found that these were not good, the king, who was the best of masters, showed them where they were mistaken and clearly pointed out the road they should have followed according to the principles of science, while to some patients he offered medicaments with his own hands.

" He likewise enquired after the condition of those who were ill, as well as of those who were cured, and he ordered new clothes to be given to them. Hence this king, full of kindness and he himself absolutely healthy and free from all disease, cured patients of their divers ills.

" Yet there still remains a marvellous thing to relate, a similar story having never before been heard. A raven was afflicted with an ulcer on the face, from which he suffered intensely. The bird remained at the king's hospital and, as if he were under the spell of the king's great love for suffering creatures, he would not leave him and croaked most piteously. When the physicians had discovered the nature of the disease, upon the king's order the raven was admitted to the hospital for treatment. When recovery had taken place the king ordered that the bird should be carried into the city on the back of an elephant, after which he was to be freed. In truth such goodness is wonderfully great."

We will now give the legend of Jivaka, because it is one of the most curious documents of Indian medical history. The cases related show that the medical profession of the time was certainly first in surgical pathology. For example, volvulus of the intestine is clearly described, and the writer fancies that the case in which two worms were removed from the brain may very well refer to the removal of a thrombus from the lateral sinus. It is also evident that the operations of major surgery were at least known, and it is not at all improbable that they may have actually been carried out.

Jivaka's mother was Mango Flower. This poetic name was given her because she was not born as an ordinary human being, but after ninety-one kalpas—an immense period of time comprising millions of years—she finally developed as a mango flower. At her last birth she was plucked by a Brahmin, who discovered her in the following circumstances. He had a mango tree to which he gave all care, having it sprinkled with the milk of a cow which had drunk the milk of one hundred other cows. At last the mango tree blossomed to reward the Brahmin for all his care, and in the centre of an opened flower the Brahmin saw a young girl, whom he plucked and brought up. She became a celebrated courtesan, in fact the most celebrated of her time, and she was also known by the name of Amrapali.

Seven kings sought her hand at the same time, and as each wished to outdo the others the Brahmin, her adopted father, advised the kings to come together in order to decide which one possessed the greatest right to her hand. Bimbisara, one of the seven kings, being the slyest of them as well, slipped away from the council and, while the others continued their deliberations, he came to Amrapali and lay with her.

On the following day she spoke as follows: "Great king, you have deigned to lower yourself to my level. Now, however, you are to leave me; if I have a child he will be of royal blood. To whom shall I confide him?" The king replied: "If it is a son you will give him to me, if it is a girl I give her to you." The king then withdrew from his finger a golden ring and gave it to Flower of the Mango, so that later she could use it as a proof of the king's paternity. The king then went his way. Mango Flower became pregnant and this she hid for nine months from the sight of her admirers, and remained shut up in her palace. At term she gave birth to a son of great beauty, who held in his hand a bag containing acupuncture needles. The Brahmin, consulted in respect of this prodigy, declared: "This child is the son of a king; on the other hand he holds in his hand a surgical instrument, therefore he certainly will be a king-physician." Mango Flower ordered that her newly born child should be exposed in a public street. Abhaya, another son of Bimbisara, adopted him and gave him the name of K'iju (Jivaka).

According to the text of the Thibetan *Kandjur*, Bimbisara had two sons, one by a courtesan, whose name was Gjon-nu-Hjigs-Ned, and who became a carpenter, and another born of his adultery with the wife of a merchant, whose name was Hts'o-Byed-Gjon-Nus-Gsos, who studied medicine and who evidently was Jivaka.

According to Hardy, Abhaya was not the half-brother of Jivaka, but in reality his own brother, and this explains the readiness with which he adopted him and the tenderness that he showed him.

However this may be, from the age of eight years Jivaka gave evidences of a higher mental capacity than children of this age. Being called by his little friends a fatherless child, he asked his mother the secret of his birth, and in reply she gave him Bimbisara's ring and the child started out to find his father. The latter recognized him by the ring which he brought, and remembering his promise, appointed him his heir. At this declaration Jivaka declared that, since his father had another son older than himself born of another woman, he wished to renounce his title as prince and heir and give himself up to the study of medicine. To this the king gave his consent, and gave him as masters the best physicians of the kingdom.

But Jivaka followed their teachings so badly that these illustrious practitioners showed much vexation and reproached him in these somewhat servile words: "The art of medicine cannot be revealed (without study); in truth it should not be the study of a princely heir. However, the orders of the king cannot be opposed. It is now several months since we received his orders and yet, O Prince, you have not even remembered one-half of a single phrase of our formulae. If the king should question us as to your progress, what reply can we give him?" To this Jivaka quietly replied: "At my birth I held in my hand the sign that I should be a physican, and it is for this reason that I said to the great king that I would renounce all titles of glory and asked that I might study the art of medicine. Then why am I so neglectful in my studies that you are obliged to reprimand me? My conduct can be explained in a very simple way. All your science is quite insufficient and powerless to instruct me." Then seizing the books he asked questions of his masters to which they could not reply and in utmost confusion they kneeled before him and rendered him homage.

Jivaka desired a teacher truly able to give him learning in all the details of his art. Therefore he went to Taxacla, where dwelt Atri, surnamed Pingala, and renowned for his science.

When he arrived in the presence of this illustrious man the latter began by asking him how much he could pay for his tuition. Jivaka replied that he could not pay, that he had fled from his parents with the intent to learn, and he then offered Pingala to remain with him as a servant in exchange for his teaching. This arrangement was accepted and for seven years the master instructed his pupil. At the end of this time Jivaka asked when his instruction would be completed, but, without replying to the question, Pingala requested him to find, in a given region, all plants useless from the medicinal point of view. It is a question which should be more admired, the richness of Hindu therapeutics or the immense knowledge of Jivaka. It was an impossibility for Jivaka to find a single plant which, to his knowledge, did not possess a curative virtue, and when he told this to Pingala the latter said: "Go! You now have in your possession the science of medicine. I am the first among those in all Jambuddipa in possession of this art, and after my death you are my worthy successor." Thus commenced Jivaka's career. He cured all the patients that came to him and the legend says: "Sometimes with a single plant he treated all kinds of diseases, at others with all sorts of plants he treated a single affection. Of the herbs of this world there was not one which could not be employed by him; of the diseases of this world there was not one he could not cure."

When Jivaka died, after a well-filled life, all plants mourned him, saying that henceforth men would employ them without discernment and from their unsuccessful results they would accuse the plants of not being divine.

At the time when Jivaka began his memorable cures one must not overlook the marvellous legend of "Wood, the King Physician" of the illustrious practitioner. It runs as follows. "Jivaka went to the royal palace when, before the door, he met a small boy who was carrying two faggots of wood to his house. Now, as soon as Jivaka saw him he at once detected the stomach and the intestines through the body of the child, and he then said : ' In the book of plants the tree King Physician (Bhaisa Jyaraja) is referred to, which from the outside will illuminate the interior (of the body) so that the viscera within the abdomen may be seen. Are there not some bits of this tree in the dead wood carried by this child ? " He asked how much the boy would sell his faggots for, and in reply was told that six pieces of money would be their value. He paid this sum upon the spot, and just as the child placed the faggots on the ground his body became opaque.

" Jivaka then attempted to find among the bits of wood those which possessed the marvellous power. Taking one after the other, and placing each over the abdomen of the child, he obtained no illumination, but at last the two last bits of wood lighted up the interior of the child's body, and most joyously did Jivaka give the boy both his faggots of wood though retaining the two marvellous pieces."

When he had returned to the kingdom of Saketa, Jivaka treated the wife of a noted personage who had suffered for twelve years from fearful headache, which no physician had been able to cure. The text of the Trehitaka lengthily describes the perseverance that he was obliged to exercise in order to come in contact with the patient. She, being very greatly discouraged, would not see another physician and—a most delicious detail, quite worthy of modern times—Jivaka did not overcome her resistance until he assured her that payment should be made only after recovery ; in case of success the amount should be fixed by her. " Believing," says the text of the *sutra*, " that thus she would take no risks," she admitted him to her presence. At the same time she had little confidence as to the results that might be obtained by this young practitioner in a case where the greatest medical celebrities had failed.

Jivaka then questioned her as follows : " He asked the patient the nature of her suffering. She replied that she suffered in such-and-such a way. ' Then,' said he, ' how did your affection commence ? ' She replied that it commenced in such-and-such circumstances. He asked if it was of recent date or of long standing, and the patient replied giving the time at which her sufferings had begun. These data having been furnished, Jivaka poured a remedy fried in butter into the patient's nose. The butter came out at the patient's mouth mixed with saliva, with the result that all obstruction was removed and the patient cured."

Now, this woman collected the butter which had been ejected from the mouth and separating it from the saliva, said that it still could be used for fuel in a lamp. Seeing this Jivaka surmised that such avarice promised a very slender fee, and he repented that the amount of his honorarium had not been stipulated before treatment. But the patient, in whom a wise economy did not exclude generosity, gave him four hundred thousand ounces of gold, as well as slaves, servants, chariots, and horses.

Jivaka in turn was not ungrateful. After having been loaded with all these riches he returned to Abhaya and offered them to him as a souvenir of what he had formerly done for him.

The second cure mentioned in the legend is quite as marvellous as the one just related. The patient was a male whose intestines had become strangulated. He could not eat or drink because the occlusion was complete, so that emaciation was extreme. The cachexia was menacing the patient's life, and some even said that when Jivaka reached him he was thought to be dead and preparations were being made for the funeral. Nevertheless, Jivaka said that he could cure him, and immediately commenced preparations for an operation. He excluded everyone from the room excepting the patient's wife, and, after having locked the door, he rolled his patient in a sheet (the upper part of the body only, in all probability), covered his face with a pillow so that the patient could not see, and then, seizing a cutting instrument, split the integuments of the abdomen, brought out the intestines and showed the patient's wife how they had become knotted (a volvulus ?) and in a twinkling of an eye placed everything in proper position and sutured the abdominal incision. After that he rubbed the patient with an ointment, removed the pillow from the face and placed him back in bed. He then ordered a drink made with oatmeal, and three days later the patient was able to be up. The cicatrix was, as we say in modern surgery, so solid that the hair grew in the line of suture, which could not be distinguished from the surrounding skin.

For this case Jivaka received two hundred thousand ounces of gold, and, still showing his disinterestedness, he went this time to his former teacher, Pingala, to offer him this sum. The great man at first protested, but it may be believed that this was simply a matter of form, because, Jivaka insisting, he finally accepted the sum most gracefully, and at the same time he also took the more modest honorarium of five hundred ounces of gold that Jivaka offered him, the products of another case that he had cured. In receiving his fee from the latter patient, Jivaka spoke as follows: "If you absolutely insist in compensating me for the service rendered, give me five hundred ounces of gold, not that I wish to use this for myself, because this is why I ask it of you. Every man who has studied a doctrine should thank his teacher. *Although it was not my master who taught me what I know*, yet I am none the less his pupil, therefore when I have received your gold I shall give it him." Thus the transaction was concluded, and certainly money was never better merited, and never was there a more striking example demonstrated of the use of radioscopy! The patient of the five hundred ounces of gold was a young girl who, it is stated, was already dead when Jivaka undertook her cure. He came and, with his Bhaisa Jyaraja, he lighted up the inside of her head and there saw several hundred worms. He operated upon her and, what is not astonishing, he ordered that the patient should be kept in complete quiet for the ten days following the operation.

Again, by the use of his Bhaiśa Jyaraja, Jivaka cured the son of a Graphati who was performing gymnastics on a wooden horse. The boy fell, with the result that he displaced his liver so that the vital breath became stopped, as it could no longer pass through the organ. Here, again, using his knife—which seems to have composed his entire surgical outfit—Jivaka opened the abdomen and replaced the liver. This operation also earned him five hundred ounces of gold, which, this time, he gave to his mother.

Such are the four cures which won Jivaka his great renown.

Among the first cures he wrought, that of King Bimbisara is to be mentioned. The royal patient suffered from an anal fistula which soiled all his garments, rendering him ridiculous in the eyes of his queens. Jivaka applied an ointment, and, in payment for his recovery, the King ordered his five hundred wives to deliver up all their jewelry to the illustrious physician. But these Jivaka refused and on account of this he was raised to the dignity of physician to the harem and member of the congregation (of Buddha).

In another circumstance, although still quite young, he cured the king of Udeni, Canda Pradyota, who suffered from attacks of mania—according to Hardy it was jaundice—and who had caused to be killed a large number of physicians who had been unable to cure him.

When the king requested Jivaka to come to him, Bimbisara, who was also his father, hesitated to allow this most precious physician to leave. They therefore went together to the Buddha in order to consult him as to whether or not it was wise to go to this dangerous patient. If the truth were really told, the illustrious Jivaka, as will be seen a little later, did not always seem to be possessed of courage to meet every emergency and sometimes showed that his anxiety for his personal safety outweighed his professional duty.

The Buddha dictated the following conduct: " During a former existence you and I took oath to work together in order to give succour to the entire universe; I by caring for the diseases of the soul, you by caring for the diseases of the body. Now, I have become Buddha and this is why, in conformity with our former oath, you should bring together all beings before me, in order that I may cure them. This king is seriously ill, he has asked you to treat him; why do you not go to him? Go at once to succour him, invent some good procedure in order that he may be surely cured of his disease. This king will not kill you."

Jivaka therefore set off to Canda Pradyota, and with his Bhaisa Jyaraja he examined the viscera of the king and noted the disorder of the blood in his one hundred veins. He next wrung from the queen-mother her secret, namely that she had conceived her son by the agency of a serpent, measuring more than thirty feet in length, which fell upon her one day while she was asleep.

Jivaka discovered that in order to cure the king it would be necessary to give him melted butter, which was the antidote of the serpent's poison, which was contained in his body; this explained the king's horror for both melted butter and oil, which was such that their mere odour caused him to become furious. In complicity with the queen-mother, Jivaka caused the king to take the melted butter by deceit, but, fearing that once the butter had been swallowed the king would be nauseated and would detect the subterfuge, as actually happened, he considered it prudent to flee.

Now commences the story of the most fantastic journey which shows the unfortunate Jivaka, sure of the excellence of his treatment, but fearful of the violent reaction that it might produce in the king, flying at the greatest speed on the best royal elephant (which he, Jivâka, had stolen), followed by Kaka, the first minister, who had been ordered to pursue him, and who, into the bargain, had a violent personal dislike to him. But Kaka was fooled, because in order to stop pursuit, Jivaka, seeing that he was short of breath, offered to share with him a mango and a cup of water, and in Kaka's half of the mango he stealthily put a certain drug which caused the unfortunate minister to develop such a severe dysentery that he could not stop going to stool, and was seized with vertigo and such extreme weakness that he could not move.

The unfortunate Kaka implored Jivaka's help. The latter reassured him, telling him that he was in no danger and that the affliction was brought upon him merely with the intent to keep him immobile for three days. And so it was; at the end of this time, the poison having been entirely voided *per rectum*, the minister was restored to health.

While this episode was taking place the king also was cured, and although Jivaka was informed by a king's messenger that his treatment had been successful, he was still afraid to go back to his irascible client, so he again consulted the Buddha, who said: "Jivaka, in a former life, you made the vow to accomplish a meritorious action; how can you now stop half-way on the road? You must now set forth again and when you shall have cured the external disease of the king, I in my turn will cure his internal affection." Then Jivaka went to the king, refused all presents that the latter wished to shower upon him, and as compensation he only asked that the king would receive the Buddha into his presence and learn from him the sacred law. The king followed the physician's advice, and sent for the Buddha, who imparted to him both intelligence and wisdom.

We will not relate the memorable Caesarean operation performed by Jivaka, but there is another cure wrought by him which certainly is a great credit to his wisdom and shows that in all ages the physician has resorted to psychology in the treatment of his patients. Jivaka was summoned by a rich personage to whom the king, wishing to honour and thank him for services rendered, sent his own physician. The patient had suffered from violent headache for seven years, and after a careful examination Jivaka asked him this question: "If I cure you, what will you give me?" The patient promised all his worldly goods, and what was more he agreed to be the physician's slave. Without replying, Jivaka asked him if, in order to procure his recovery, he would be willing to remain in bed for seven successive months lying on the right side, on the left side for seven other months, and seven more months on the back. The patient agreed to this. The surgeon then made him lie down, and he was held upon the bed by attendants. Jivaka then deliberately opened the skull and extracted two animalculae, one large and one small, but history does not tell us to what species they belonged.

And here it should be pointed out that Jivaka, being anxious to follow the rules of medical deontology, agreed that both physicians who had attended the case before him were equally right although they had given diametrically opposed opinions in respect of the case. Jivaka declared that the physician who had said that the patient would surely die at the end of five days had only detected the presence of the larger animalcule, while the second who stated that the patient would die in a week had only suspected the presence of the smaller, which would have been unable to devour the patient's brain as quickly as the larger one, and therefore could not cause death in less than a week.

Having settled this question, Jivaka closed the skull of the patient, who was conscious all the time, sutured the skin and covered the incision with plaster. After a week the patient commenced to complain of lying on the same side, saying that he would rather die than continue in that position.

"Lie on the other side," said Jivaka. A week later the patient again complained: "Lie on your back," said Jivaka without any further remark. Another week having elapsed, the patient again complained. "Get up," said Jivaka, and then he addressed the patient as follows: "My dear sir, if I had not told you that you would be obliged to remain in bed for twenty-one months you would not have remained there for as many days, and for this reason I took my precautions, knowing you would be cured in three weeks." And he added: "You remember what you promised me in payment for my services?" The patient, faithful to his word, declared his readiness to fulfil his promise, but Jivaka said: "All that is a joke, simply give to the king, my master, one hundred thousand crowns, and as many for me, which will be quite sufficient."

But of all the cures wrought by Jivaka that in the case of the Tathagata, who suffered from constipation, was the most remarkable. The faithful disciple of the master, Amanda, consulted the illustrious physician and explained to him the affection from which the great man suffered. Jivaka ordered his body to be rubbed with oil for several days and after this preparatory treatment he went to the Tathagata and, believing that so great a personage could not be purged like everybody else, he resorted to the following rather original remedy. He took three handfuls of locust leaves, combined with a decoction of various herbs, and caused the patient to breathe the perfume. Now, Jivaka had calculated that each handful of locust leaves would cause ten evacuations of the bowels, consequently the master should have thirty stools in all. However, at the last minute he remembered that the case was particularly serious and said to himself that perhaps only twenty-nine stools would result, but continuing his reflections he consoled himself by remembering that the patient should purify himself by a bath which would give rise to the thirtieth necessary stool and consequently the result would be obtained. And in fact everything went well, and indeed the master, who knew everything that was taking place in the mind of the physician, had his bath prepared for him before Jivaka had returned to order it.

Far from accepting compensation in this case, Jivaka gave to his patient two marvellous pieces of cloth which he had received as a present from King Pradyota, and he begged him to allow the priests to wear simple lay clothes. This permission was given, and from this time on the inhabitants of the entire country rivalled each other in generosity in clothing the monks.

Such are the principal adventures that occurred to Jivaka, but in order to explain such wonderful success it is necessary to know what causes were at work. In a former existence on earth, Jivaka had belonged to a poor family. He swept for the Bhikshunis, and each time that his work was finished he said: "May I sweep away as quickly all diseases and impurities which are in the bodies of men of this world." Mango Flower, who at this time was a Bhikshuni in the convent, called her son, and he it was who summoned the physician when one of the sisters fell ill, and each time that the patient recovered Jivaka made the following vow: "In a later life I hope to be a great king's physician, and to treat all diseases of the four elements composing the body of all men and to cure them."

In concluding this chapter a few words are necessary with reference to Chaldean and Persian medicine. Information about this subject is necessarily vague, but Withington [1] has summed up the subject so concisely that we cannot do better than to give it in his own words.

In the opinion of Herodotus, the ancient Babylonians showed great wisdom in their treatment of the sick, for they had no physicians, but if any one was ill he was put out in the public square, and etiquette demanded that every passer-by should ask him to describe his symptoms. If the stranger had heard of a similar case, or had himself had the disease, he was expected to give advice as to treatment.

Modern discoveries confirm these statements in so far that it is very difficult to find a class of Chaldean physicians distinct from astrologers and soothsayers, and Prof. Sayce tells us that the same word was used to express "physician", "scribe", and "seer". But the state of medicine revealed by the cuneiform texts by no means justifies the good opinion of the historian, for it is probably the lowest form that ever existed in a civilized community. The Chaldeans appear to have contributed absolutely nothing to the general stock

[1] *History of Medicine*, London, 1894.

of medical knowledge, and we shall, therefore, notice them very briefly. Primitive theories predominate throughout: there are the usual demons causing disease, and the usual invocations against them, both of which the reader will find fully discussed in Lenormant's *Chaldean Magic*; but Prof. Sayce has recently translated fragments of a Babylonian work on medicine, which formed part of the library of Assurbanipal (Sardanapalus, 669–626 B.C.), and which appears to indicate some progress towards a more rational practice. In it the patient sometimes has his choice whether he will use charms or medicines, and the prescriptions given comprise a considerable variety of drugs, though their precise nature cannot often be determined.

The following are examples: "For a diseased gall-bladder, mix water and strong wine; drink quantities of calves' milk; calves' milk and bitters drink in palm wine; garlic and bitters drink in palm wine." As the translator observes, these prescriptions are in a sense homoeopathic, the "bitter" or gall bladder being cured by bitters. "For the attack of a demon, which after seizing a man cuts the top of his heart, for his preservation, the slice of a bird, sisi, siman, kharkar, bîmu, the very great snake, the seed of the bîmu, and the seed of the cedar must be drunk in palm wine."

It is also interesting to learn that the Babylonians were forbidden to use medicines on the sacred seventh day.

While, however, taking this unfavourable view of Chaldean medicine, it is well to remember that much yet remains to be discovered, and that the mounds of Mesopotamia may possibly still contain medical writings worthy to be compared with those of ancient Egypt.

The medicine of the Medes and Persians somewhat resembled the Chaldean, but had a still closer analogy to that of their near relatives, the Hindus, with the important difference that it produced no Susruta or Charaka. In place of the Vedas we have the Zend-Avesta, a work ascribed to Zoroaster, but of very doubtful date and authorship. It is said to have consisted of twenty-one books, containing no less than 2,000,000 verses, and to have been written upon 1,200 cowhides. The healing art seems to have been very frequently mentioned; for Pliny, who had seen a Greek abstract of the entire work, declares that the religion of the

Persians was evidently founded on medicine. Little of the Avesta has survived except the nineteenth book, the Vendidâd, or code of purifications—literally "The law against demons". Here we find the famous dualistic doctrine of the government of the world by a good and an evil deity, whom, until Orientalists are more agreed in their orthography, we may still venture to call Ormuzd and Ahriman.

Ahriman, according to the Vendidâd, created by his evil eye 99,999 diseases, apparently in the form of demons, whereupon Ormuzd appealed for aid to Aryaman, "the friend," a god of heavenly light, who is mentioned in the Vedas. Aryaman destroys diseases by reciting the Holy Word; but Ormuzd also took the 10,000 healing herbs which grew around the tree of everlasting life, and brought them to Thrita, an ancient sage and sacrificer (another Vedic personage), to whom also Kshathra-Vairya, Lord of the Metals, gave a knife, of which the point and the base were set in gold. Thrita thus became the Persian Aesculapius, and physicians are urged to follow in his footsteps, and, like him, to fight valiantly against the demons of impurity and disease. This story indicates the triple division of Persian medicine. "When physicians compete, O pure Zoroaster," says Ormuzd, in another passage, "knife-doctors, herb-doctors, and word-doctors, then shall the believer go to him who heals by the Holy Word, for he is a healer of healers, and benefits the soul also."

If a Persian wished to practise medicine, he must first experiment upon unbelievers; should three of these die under his hands he was for ever incapable; should he cure three, he was qualified to act as physician to the worshippers of Ormuzd "for ever and ever", says the Vendidâd, though some learned commentators held that the qualification might be lost.

The Vendidâd also fixes the amount of medical fees. A priest must be healed for his blessing; the head of a house, a village, or a town for the price of an ox, of low, average, or high value respectively; while the lord of a province must pay the price of a chariot and four. The physician is also to treat animals, especially the dog, for which he must receive the value of the animal next in rank, and in the case of a sheep, the lowest on the list, his payment is the price of a "good meal". Dogs must receive the same drugs as are given to rich men; and to Zoroaster's inquiry, what is to be done if the dog refuses to take medicine, Ormuzd replies that in such a case it shall be lawful to bind him, and force open his mouth with a stick.

One would have thought that a land where fees were fixed on so liberal a scale, and secured by the sanctions of religion, would have been a very paradise of physicians. But this was far from being the case. The medicine of the Medes and Persians seems to have been as conservative as their laws. The "word-doctor" long maintained his baleful pre-eminence, and the art of healing is probably as little indebted to the land of Iran as it is to the valleys of the Euphrates and the Tigris. The Persian kings, wisely enough, entrusted themselves neither to the Chaldeans nor to their own countrymen, but got their physicians first from Egypt and afterwards from Greece; and so valued were the latter that if a practitioner in the Asiatic colonies became at all distinguished for his skill he was liable to be kidnapped and carried off to the Persian Court.

In a later age, shortly before the faith of Zoroaster was driven from its ancient home by the sword of Islam, we find Persia the seat of an important development of medical science, but this also was mainly due to the labours, not of native but of foreign physicians.

# CHAPTER IV

## THE PHILOSOPHERS

Early Greek Medicine.—Of Minoan medicine we know almost nothing.[1] In the second millennium B.C. the sanitary arrangements of the palace of Cnossos were more hygienic than any built down to the eighteenth century of our era. An Egyptian book of medicine gives a formula for exorcising a malady in the Cretan language. The Cretans seem to have known certain drugs, *diktame*, which had miraculous virtues, *asplenum*, a remedy for affections of the spleen, and *daukos*, a fat-reducer. The names of these drugs, which are believed to be in the language spoken by the Minoans, existed in the dialects of Crete in later times. It is conceivable, but not provable, that some memory of Minoan medicine, whatever it may have been, survived, like other elements of culture, in classical Greece.

Homer gives us some little information about the medical knowledge and practice of his time. In the *Odyssey* the doctors form one of the few true professions. They are not priests, and the priests have no medical functions, but the few allusions do not permit us to say whether the doctor had any of the sacred character of the medicine-man. Of the other professionals, though the carpenter is altogether profane, the soothsayer and bard have something about them distinguishing them from other men. But in the *Iliad*,[2] Machaon and Podaleirius, the sons of Asclepius, the " good doctors ", command their ships, lead their men into action, have their *aristeia*, and get wounded like ordinary heroes. Asclepius himself is not a god, but a mortal king of Thessaly.

In an account of battles we naturally hear more of wounds than of disease, and since wounds, unlike disease, can be ascribed to manifest physical causes, it was natural that surgery should escape the influence of magic. Machaon is " a doctor worth many men, at cutting out arrows and laying

[1] See Glotz, *The Aegean Civilization*, pp. 139, 165, 385, 388.
[2] *Il.*, ii, 728, xi, 506, 828 ff.

on gentle drugs ".[1] Patroclus, certainly not a professional doctor, cut an arrow-head from the thigh of Eurypylus, washed away the blood, and " laid on a bitter root, rubbing it with his hands, a pain-killing root, which stopped all his pain ; and the wound dried, and the blood stopped ". This was the drug, which they said, Patroclus " learned from Achilles, whom Cheiron taught, most righteous of Centaurs ".[2]

In his accounts of wounds received in battle, Homer displays the anatomical knowledge of a man used to warfare. His description of the death of Diores and Peirous displays this. Diores " was struck on the right shin, near the ankle, by a sharp stone. . . . And the jagged stone destroyed both tendons and bones utterly. And he fell back in the dust, stretching out his two hands to his dear comrades, and breathing away his life. And Peirous, who had struck him, ran up, and stabbed him with his sword near the navel ; and all his inwards poured out on the ground, and darkness covered his eyes. But as Peirous fled Aetolian Thoas struck him with his spear in the breast above the nipple, and the bronze stuck in his lung." [3] When Meriones, chasing Phereclus, strikes him with his spear in the right buttock, the point goes through the bone and reaches the bladder.[4] Diomede strikes Aeneas with a stone on the thigh, at the point where the femur turns in the cotyloid cavity, and the stone, hitting the hip-joint, ruptures the two upper muscles and tears the skin.[5] A Trojan is slain by a wound which severs the vein, which, " running along the back, reaches the neck "—probably the inferior vena cava, since Homer can hardly have known the azygos, and severing that vein would not produce the instant death which he describes. In a description of decapitation Homer shows that he knows the muscles of the neck, as he also knows those of the chest, and, probably the difference between the cervical and dorsal vertebrae : " He was struck over the last vertebrae of the neck, and both muscles were severed."

So, too, Homer's account of the effects of wounds is accurate. Diomede's spear strikes Hector on the top of his helmet ; the helmet saves him, but he falls on his knees.

[1] *Il.*, xi, 514–5. [2] xi, 828 ff., 844 ff.
[3] *Il.*, iv, 517 ff. [4] *Il.*, v, 65 ff.
[5] *Il.*, v, 305 ff.

supporting himself with his hands, " and black night wrapped his eyes about "—undoubtedly a case of cerebral concussion.[1] There is an excellent description of the twitchings occurring when a mortal wound has been inflicted: Asios, pierced through the neck, falls to the ground and lies full length, grinding his teeth and plucking at the blood-stained dust.[2] Homer notes that one of the frequent complications of blows on the chest is haematemesis and haemoptysis. Hector, struck on his chest, near the neck, with a rock, falls, and when consciousness returns he vomits black blood and falls back to the ground. This is a case of traumatic haemetesis.[3] Lastly, we have a faithful description of fracture of the skull. " Idomeneus struck Erymas in the mouth with his spear and the bronze point went into the brain, breaking the white bones (the small bones of the base of the skull); all the teeth were loosened, and both eyes filled with blood, while blood gushed from the mouth and nostrils. And darkness fell upon his eyes." The symptomatology is here complete.[4]

Otherwise Homer tells us little of medicine. Helen dopes the wine with " nepenthe " from Egypt, a land which " bears many drugs, many fairly mixed and many baneful ", and is full of doctors.[5] Odysseus looks for a " man-killing " drug to put on his arrows.[6] A woman, too, has a reputation for knowing the virtues of healing plants.

There is no magic in all this; we only hear of a flow of blood being staunched with an incantation.[7] Yet it is hard to believe on this negative evidence that early Greek medicine was not mingled with magic. Stories like those of Medea and of the shirt of Nessus suggest the contrary, and the poisoning by sorceries, incantations, waxen images, etc., described by Plato in later times [8] need not all have been imported from abroad. There was a considerable element of magic and religion, even late in classical times, in the treatment in the health-temples at Epidaurus, Athens, and elsewhere.

THE SCHOOLS OF PHILOSOPHY. Theophrastus (370–285 B.C.) is the first writer who has treated the history of Greek

[1] *Il.*, xi, 349 ff. [2] *Il.*, xiii, 387 ff. [3] *Il.*, xiv, 409 ff., 436–7. [4] *Il.*, xvi, 345 ff. [5] *Od.*, iv, 220 ff. [6] *Od.*, i, 260. [7] *Od.*, xix, 457. [8] *Laws*, ii.

philosophy in a systematic way. He tells us that the first cosmologists formed regular associations composed of masters and pupils. This statement has been regarded by many modern writers as an anachronism and some have even gone so far as absolutely to deny the existence of schools of philosophy. Such a reaction against the older conception is quite justifiable if directed against the arbitrary classifications, such as "Ionian" and "Italian" schools derived from the Alexandrian authors of the age of the Successors through Diogenes Laërtius. But the express statements of Theophrastus must not be disregarded without serious motive, and since this point is of great importance, it is necessary to examine it somewhat closely. The modern view in reality rests on a mistaken conception of the route followed by civilization in its development. In nearly all domains of life it is to be noted that at the commencement the corporation was everything and the individual nothing. The peoples of the Orient hardly went beyond this degree of evolution; their science—or what they offer us as such—is anonymous; it was the inheritance of a caste or a guild, and it is clearly to be seen that in certain cases this may be applied to certain Greeks.

For example, medicine at its origin was confined to the mystery of the Aesclepiads, and there is every reason to suppose that all craftsmen, among whom Homer places the singers, were primarily organized in a similar way. What distinguishes the Hellenes from other peoples is that at a relatively ancient date these corporations fell under the influence of eminent individualities who gave them new directions of thought as well as a new impulse. At a later date the Asclepiads produced Hippocrates, and if we were better informed as to the early guilds it is probable that something very similar would be noted. But this fact does not eliminate the corporative character of the craft, and in truth it rather accentuates it. The guild became what we at present call a school and the disciple took the place of the apprentice. This was an important change. An exclusive guild, without other chiefs than its professional chiefs, is essentially conservative, while a band of disciples attached to a master whom they revere is the greatest factor of progress that we can imagine.

It is certain that the later Athenian schools were organized corporations, the most ancient being the Academy, and they remained as such for a period of nearly nine hundred years, so that the only question that we must decide is whether or not this was an innovation of the fourth century before Christ, or, rather, the continuation of an old tradition. Luckily we can rely upon the authority of Plato to affirm that the principal ancient systems were transmitted in the schools, for he makes Socrates say that "the men of Ephesus"—the followers of Heraclitus—in his day formed a large body; and nobody can doubt that the followers of Pythagoras formed a society. And in point of fact, there is hardly a school whose existence is not proven by authentic documents, unless it be the Milesian school, and even here we can invoke a significant fact, namely that Theophrastus refers to philosophers of a later date as having associated themselves with the philosophy of Anaximander of Miletus.

PYTHAGORAS (580–498 B.C.). There are few data of a positive nature in respect of the life of Pythagoras and our principal sources of information are the writings of Iamblichus, Porphyry, and Diogenes Laërtius. Iamblichus's writings are a miserable compilation, while those of Porphyry are far more reliable. We know that Pythagoras spent the first years of his life at Samos, that he was the son of Mnesarchus, and that he flourished during the reign of Polycrates. This date cannot be far from the truth because Heraclitus speaks of Pythagoras in the past tense. Pythagoras disliked the rule of Polycrates, who, in 532 B.C., became a tyrant, and he emigrated from Samos to Crotona in south Italy. Here he founded a religious brotherhood, which gradually became very powerful; there was definite teaching in connexion with it, and it seems to have been a school with an esoteric doctrine, into the full mysteries of which the novices were not initiated until after several years' service. The brotherhood established at Crotona became sufficiently powerful to get embroiled in political agitations, and it was owing to some contest between it and the democratic party at Crotona that Pythagoras had to flee the town and retire to Metapontum, where he died.

It has been questioned whether or not we should accept what writers as recent as Porphyry have to say about the abstinence of Pythagoras and his followers. Aristoxenes, who can be considered one of the most ancient authorities, can be cited to prove that the original Pythagoreans knew nothing about restrictions concerning the use of meat and beans. He states in an unequivocal manner that Pythagoras did not abstain from meat in general, but only from that of cattle and rams. He also says that Pythagoras preferred beans to any other vegetable on account of their laxative action, and that he had a great weakness for sucking-pig and young goat.

We know that Pythagoras taught that there was a kinship between men and beasts, and we may infer that abstinence from meat was based, not upon humanitarian and ascetic motives, but on a taboo.

The doctrine of numbers can be without doubt ascribed to Pythagoras himself, and has its importance in the history of medicine, because Hippocrates was unquestionably influenced by it in the fixing of his critical days. The doctrine of numbers is that according to which *things* are said to be *numbers*. It is a startling, if not an inconceivable doctrine, and there are many fanciful developments of it. For example, justice is defined as *four*, the first square number, because *four* so readily symbolizes the element of retribution which constitutes an essential part of the popular idea of justice. Similarly *three* is marriage, the union of the odd and the even (male and female). But all this is sheer symbolism and for further information the reader is referred to the works mentioned at the end of this chapter.

Heraclitus of Ephesus (about 500 B.C.). According to Heraclitus, man is subject to a certain oscillation in his "measures" of fire and water, and this gives rise to alternatives of sleeping and waking, of life and death. The classical passage on this subject is one to be found in the writings of Sextus Empiricus, who reproduces the analysis of the psychology of Heraclitus given by Aenesidemos, a sceptic who lived about 80–50 B.C. Here is the tenor of this analysis. The naturalistic philosopher is of the opinion that what surrounds us is rational and endowed with consciousness. According to Heraclitus, when we inhale this divine reason with the respiration we become reasoning beings. In sleep we forget, but when we awake we again become conscious, because in sleep, when the apertures of the senses are closed, the spirit which is in us is cut off from contact with all that surrounds us, and only the respiration preserves our connexion with it. When the spirit is thus separated from that which surrounds us it loses its faculty of memory, but when we awake the spirit looks through the apertures of the senses as through windows and, becoming united with the spirit which surrounds us, it recovers the faculty of reason.

We cannot refer to the theories of life and death as put forward by Heraclitus, as this would require too much space, and we must turn our attention to Parmenides.

Parmenides of Elea (450 B.C.) Parmenides wrote rather lengthily on questions of physiology. He believed that, like all things else, man was composed of heat and cold, and that death resulted from the disappearance of heat. He also formulated peculiar ideas related to generation. In the first place he taught that males came from the right side and females from the left side of the uterus.

Parmenides supposed that the female contained a greater quantity of heat and the male a greater amount of cold, an opinion which was refuted by Empedocles. It was simply the proportion of heat and cold contained in a man that determined the character of his thoughts, so that a corpse from which the heat had departed retained the perception of what was cold and dark.

These fragments of information imply little taken by themselves, but they are connected in a most interesting way with the history of medicine, in placing in evidence the fact that one of its principal schools was in close relationship with the Pythagorean association. We know that Crotona was celebrated for its physicians, even before the time of Pythagoras. Democedes of Crotona (500 B.C.) was a physician to the court of the King of Persia and married Milo's daughter. Moreover, we have some knowledge of a very distinguished medical writer who lived at Crotona during the interval separating Pythagoras and Parmenides, and some of the data regarding him lead us to look upon the physiological ideas expressed by Parmenides, not as mere curiosities but as landmarks by which we can trace the origin and the development of one of the most influential medical theories, that which explains health by the equilibrium of opposite factors.

ALCMAEON OF CROTONA (500 B.C.). Aristotle tells us that Alcmaeon was still a young man when Pythagoras was advanced in years, but he does not expressly affirm, as later writers have done, that Alcmaeon belonged to the school of Pythagoras. He, however, makes it clear that this physician derived his theory of opposites from the Pythagoreans, or else that the Pythagoreans borrowed it from Alcmaeon. At all events he was intimately connected with the brotherhood of Pythagoras, as is proved by one of the fragments of his work.

Alcmaeon was above all a biologist and physician, and we have very good reason to suppose that he dissected the human body, but what is most important of all is that he was the founder of experimental psychology. It is certain that he regarded the brain as the common sensorium, a most important discovery, and one accepted by Hippocrates and Plato, while Empedocles, Aristotle, and the Stoics returned to the more primitive idea that this function was fulfilled by the heart. There is no reason to doubt that Alcmaeon made this discovery by anatomical researches and that, as we have said, he practised dissection and, although the nerves were not at that time recognized as such, it was known that there were certain channels that could be prevented from communicating sensations to the brain when lesions developed in them. Alcmaeon also distinguished between sensation and intelligence, and his theories on the various senses are of the greatest interest. In his writings we find what is characteristic of the Greek theories of vision and the attempt to combine the opinion according to which vision is an act proceeding from the eye with that which attributes it to a reflected image in this organ. Alcmaeon knew the importance of air for the sense of hearing, but in respect of the other senses we have little information as to his theories. He represented health as an " insomnia ". He noted that the majority of things human were two in number, by which he meant that Man was composed of heat and cold, dampness and dryness, and the other contraries. For him disease was the " monarchy " of one or the other of these factors, while health was the reign of a free government in the body having equal laws for all. This was the directive doctrine which shortly after was developed by the Sicilian school, and, as we shall show, is closely connected with the theory of pores in later medical ideas.

Empedocles of Agrigentum (504–443 B.C.). Aristotle tells us that Empedocles was the inventor of rhetoric, while Galen regards him as the founder of the Italian school of medicine, which he considers quite equal to those of Cos and Cnidos. The influence of Empedocles on the development of medicine was certainly important, for it made itself felt not only in medicine itself, but through medicine in all the tendencies of scientific and philosophic thought. It is said that this philosopher had few successors, and this is quite true if it is applied strictly to philosophy. On the other hand the medical school that he founded was still existing in Plato's day and exercised considerable influence upon him and still more on Aristotle. The fundamental doctrine was the identification of the four elements with heat and cold, dampness and dryness. Empedocles also maintained that man breathed by all the pores of his body, and that the act of breathing was in close relationship with the movement of the blood. He thought that the heart and not the brain was the organ of consciousness. The physiology of Empedocles may be summed up as follows. He refutes the theory of Parmenides in the sense that, according to his way of thinking, the element of heat preponderates in the masculine sex and male offspring are conceived in the warmest part of the uterus. The foetus is formed in part by the male sperm and partly by that of the female, and for this very reason desire arises when the two sexes perceive each other, because they are composed of a mixture of the male and female. A certain symmetry of the pores in the male and female sperm is naturally necessary in order that procreation shall take place, and it was by its absence that Empedocles explained sterility in mules. The child resembles more closely the parent who has most contributed to its formation. As to the development of the foetus in the uterus, Empedocles taught that it was surrounded by a membrane, that its formation commenced on the thirty-sixth day and was complete on the forty-ninth. The heart is formed first of all, the nails and similar things last of all. Respiration only begins at birth after the fluids surrounding the foetus have passed away. Birth occurs at the ninth or the seventh month

Milk makes its appearance in the mother's breast on the tenth day of the eighth month.

The theory of vision is more complicated in Empedocles and, as Plato has adopted the major part, it is of the highest importance for the history of philosophy. Empedocles represented the eye as did Alcmaeon, that is to say, as composed of fire and water. As the flame in a lantern is protected from the wind by the horn, so the fire of the iris is protected from the water which surrounds it in the pupil by membranes possessed of very fine pores, so that the fire may go out without allowing water to enter. Vision is produced by the fire within the eye, which issues forth to meet the object. This theory may appear strange because we are used to the idea that images are impressed upon the retina, but to *look* at a thing certainly appears much more like an action proceeding from the eye than a purely passive state.

Theophrastus tells us that Empedocles made no distinction between thought and perception, a remark likewise made by Aristotle. For him the principal seat of perception was the blood, in which the four elements are more equally mixed, especially in the blood existing in the neighbourhood of the heart. This, however, does not preclude the idea that other parts of the body may also perceive, and in fact Empedocles maintains that all parts participate in thought. But the blood is particularly apt to feel because of its finer mixture, and from this it naturally results that Empedocles adopts the opinion put forward by Parmenides that our knowledge varies with the variable constitution of our bodies. This consideration becomes very important at a later date in respect of the foundations of scepticism, but Empedocles simply draws the conclusion that we should make the best possible use of our senses and control each sense by the others.

DIOGENES OF APOLLONIA (430 B.C.). Diogenes was principally interested in physiology, as is made clearly evident by his detailed study of the veins, which has been preserved by Aristotle. In point of fact, the physiological writings of Diogenes are essentially of the same character as the larger part of the pseudo-Hippocratic literature. And there is much to show that the writers of these curious treatises referred to them quite as much as they did to those of Anaxagoras and Heraclitus.

It was in Greece that Philosophy was first constituted as a synthesis of knowledge; the thinkers of Ionia attempted above all to explain visible things, and they certainly were entitled to be called physicists, a name given them by Aristotle. Now, in these early naturalistic speculations, man held a high place and among the subjects which presented themselves at this first awakening of scientific reflection there was nothing that had a more immediate or more pressing interest. Consequently the philosophical doctrines contain views on the great problem of life, which are frequently more ingenious than accurate, and some of these suppositions passed into the medical writings which form the Hippocratic Collection with hardly any change. The early philosophers and the early Greek physicians had a very great deal in common, and, although the Hippocratic school perhaps owe their constant clinical observation to the priests of Aesculapius, they are certainly indebted to the philosophers for the theories to which they appeal when they attempt to explain facts. This is particularly evident in the treatises pertaining to the diseases of women. In fact, there was no philosophical doctrine which was not appealed to by the disturbing problem of generation, and the Greek philosophers have left us many ideas on the nature of woman, on the significance of the various phases of genital life, and on gestation.

Although speculative, these theses were always inspired by facts; they are for the most part inadmissible hypotheses, but they are nearly all explanatory, and they exercised an unquestionable influence on the medical theories of the time. We know these opinions of the philosophers from the *Fragmenta* and the *Placita Philosophorum* of the Pseudo-Plutarch, and also from the *Dies Natalis* of Censorinus, although little reliance can be placed on the latter.

Among those questions which the philosophers were prone to discuss was that which dealt with the nature of the generative fluid and whether or not woman possessed it. According to the Pythagoreans, this fluid was the foam of the best part of the blood and flowed by drops from the brain. Diogenes of Apollonia regarded the generative fluid as a subtle air which escaped from the spermatic veins during coitus; for Democritus the fluid was derived from all parts of the body. Pythagoras, Democritus, and Epicurus admitted that the female possessed semen ; according to Parmenides a good constitution in children was the result of a proper mixture of the male and female genital fluid. The Pseudo-Plutarch goes further still, for he states that these thinkers admitted that the female formed semen in the ovaries. Now, it is evident that if these philosophers had known of the existence of the ovaries this fact would be found in the Hippocratic Collection, and it is not.

Hippon, who lived in the time of Pericles, supposed that women were possessed of semen, but believed that it was infertile since it escaped spontaneously, and he says : "This discharge takes place frequently apart from coitus, and is more common in widows than in other women." Hippon undoubtedly here is simply referring to leucorrhoea. This opinion is difficult to reconcile with other parts of his writings ; Hippon especially says that in the formation of the foetus it is the father who furnishes the bones, while the flesh is derived from the mother. It may be admitted that there were several persons by the name of Hippon and that each of these assertions may have been made by a different writer of the same name.

The ancients dissected the uteri of female animals, and it was from such anatomical data as they thus obtained that they deduced their knowledge of the uterus of women. Now, in most animals the uterus presents several sinuses and, applying this notion to woman, they admitted that her uterus was bifid. The prohibition of dissection resulted in the perpetuation of this erroneous conception down to the Middle Ages, and in the fifteenth century we find a distinguished professor of medicine at Pavia, by name Ferrari da Grado (1432–1472), writing that : "The shape of the womb is oblong, declivous, and almost round ; it is divided into two concave parts ending in a single neck to which they owe their origin. These two parts resemble two wombs, and are covered by a single tunic which binds them at a single point." It was to this notion of the bifid uterus that the ancient theory of generation was due. The Pythagorean school distinguished only two directions, namely the left side which represented the west, and darkness, while the right side represented the east, and therefore light. Hence, these cosmological data being applied to the bifid uterus, it was decided that the male foetus developed in the right uterus, while female offspring developed in the left. This theory is not to be found before Parmenides, but after him it was familiar to all thinkers and is frequently to be found in the Hippocratic Collection.

The philosophers often attempted to define the causes of sterility, but they seem to have only studied barrenness in mules, and to explain the barrenness they supposed that there were certain defects in the conformation of the womb. Democritus, like Empedocles, believed that sterility resulted from a malformation of the uterus, and he also tells us that this was the opinion of certain physicians whose names he does not give.

The ancient philosophers professed strange ideas in respect of the foetus and the Hippocratic Collection repeated them. According to Diogenes of Apollonia, the foetus was inanimate, and only commenced to live at the time of birth. Alcmaeon maintained that the foetus nourished itself throughout its body like a sponge, but it is perhaps better to accept the testimony of Rufus of Ephesus, who tells us that Alcmaeon taught that the foetus nourished itself by the mouth, and this is also the opinion professed by Democritus, Epicurus, Diogenes of Apollonia and Hippon, while Anaxagoras maintained that the foetus was nourished through the umbilical cord.

There are few fragments relating to menstruation. Parmenides admitted that woman was of a warmer nature than man, and thus he explained menstruation from the greater heat that she contained. Soranus of Ephesus criticises Empedocles for fixing the menstrual periods at the waning of the moon, and he points out that experience does not confirm this opinion.

Such vague and unverified affirmations make it difficult to form any precise opinion as to the theory of generation held by the philosophers, but a careful examination of the Hippocratic Collection shows us that the teachings of the philosophers, which were inspired by a gross empiricism and *a priori* doctrines, were often accepted by the Greek physicians, and it is for this reason that a rapid summary of their teachings has been given.

The scope of this book forbids a detailed account of the biology, medical theories and psychology of the pre-Socratic philosophers. The reader desirous of dipping more deeply into this most interesting subject is referred to John Burnet's *Early Greek Philosophy*, John I. Beare's *Greek Theories of Elementary Cognition*, and Gomperz's more extensive work, in four volumes, *Greek Thinkers*.

# CHAPTER V

## THE HIPPOCRATIC OATH

The Oath is one of the sixty books composing the Hippocratic Collection, or Corpus Hippocraticum, which was brought together and edited, at the commencement of the third century B.C., by a group of Alexandrian scholars at the request of Ptolemy. At the time when the collection was edited doubt existed as to which books were written by Hippocrates the Great himself; to-day it is generally accepted that he was the author of very few of them. Thus, of the sixty books, Grüner attributes ten, von Haller eleven, Littré twelve, and Daremberg two only, to the Father of Medicine. Be this as it may, whoever composed the Oath, it remains an historic document of the highest importance because it gives us all the data relating to the constitution and teachings of the mystery of the old Greek physicians, the Companions of Aesculapius. It likewise teaches us the moral obligations which the members of the medical body took upon themselves in their relationship with their patients, and among themselves, as well as with the community at large. As such it is a treatise on deontology of very great moral value, which has been the guide of the medical profession from the time of Hippocrates.

The authenticity of the Oath has been much discussed; many opinions have been emitted and perfect agreement has not yet been reached, but before discussing this point we will give the Oath.

"I swear by Apollo the physician, by Aesculapius, Hygeia, and Panacea, and I take to witness all the gods, all the goddesses, to keep according to my ability and my judgment the following Oath:—

"To consider dear to me as my parents him who taught me this art; to live in common with him and if necessary to share my goods with him; to look upon his children as my own brothers, to teach them this art if they so desire without fee or written promise; to impart to my sons and the sons of the master who taught me and the disciples who have enrolled themselves and have agreed to the rules of the profession, but to these alone, the precepts and the instruction. I will prescribe regimen for the good of my patients according to my ability and my judgment and never do harm to anyone. To please no one will I prescribe a deadly drug, nor give advice which may cause his death. Nor will I give a woman a pessary to procure abortion. But I will preserve the purity of my life and my art. I will not cut for stone, even for patients in whom the disease is manifest; I will leave this operation to be performed by practitioners (specialists in this art). In every house where I come I will enter only for the good of my patients, keeping myself far from all intentional ill-doing and all seduction, and especially from the pleasures of love with women or with men, be they free or slaves. All that may come to my knowledge in the exercise of my profession or outside of my profession or in daily commerce with men, which ought not to be spread abroad, I will keep secret and will never reveal. If I keep this oath faithfully, may I enjoy my life and practise my art, respected by all men and in all times; but if I swerve from it or violate it, may the reverse be my lot."

As we have already pointed out, from the day that it was realized that the large collection of writings supposed to be due to Hippocrates, far from forming a homogeneous body, was probably not all by the same writer, but derived from different schools and written in different periods, the origin of the Oath has been discussed. According to some, the Oath was written before Hippocrates, while for others it dates from the time of Alexander. The most valid arguments seem to be those which maintain that the Oath dates from the Hippocratic period. Such is Littré's opinion, who says: "If one is satisfied with a great probability, one cannot refuse to admit that it was drawn up, if not by Hippocrates himself, at least for the period and the uses which were really the period and the uses of Hippocrates." And in point of fact the Oath is in conformity with the usages of the time of Hippocrates. The best testimony to this is to be found in Plato, who speaks of Hippocrates, and tells us that he was from the Island of Cos and belonged to the family of Asclepiads, and that he taught his art without accepting a salary. In the Oath there is a promise to accept none from the sons of one's masters, but the physician has a right to receive a fee for tuition from other students, and according to Plato Hippocrates followed this rule.

Moreover, in the other works of Hippocrates are to be found many counsels and phrases similar to those in the Oath, and some of the best Hippocratic writings are entirely composed of them, such, for example, as the work entitled *The Law*. It therefore would seem that the Oath belongs to the same period as those works written in a similar manner and treating the same subjects, and not at the period of Alexander because the books of this period are decidedly different, and do not contain rules for the moral conduct of the profession.

Those who maintain that the Oath dates from the period of Alexander base their arguments on the division of the healing art into dietetics, pharmaceutics and surgery, a division which is found in the Oath and also in the works supposed to have been written in the time of Alexander. But for the majority of critics this argument is of little value.

If we do not consider the invocation of the Oath and its conclusion or imprecation, the Oath may be conveniently divided into two parts. The first shows us the organization of medicine in the days of Hippocrates, as well as the object of the mystery into which he who takes the Oath is entering. The second—a splendid page of medical deontology—contains the promise of a stern moral conduct in the practice of the art.

The mystery of physicians under Hippocrates was an independent but very exclusive society. It was composed only of its members and sons of members, but it would admit those who had undertaken to keep the Oath. It also united its members for life in mutual aid and support. The principal duty of its members was the teaching of medicine. This consisted of three parts: general precepts, moral or professional, given in oral lectures; medical doctrines (Plato refers to Hippocrates giving lectures); and the study of books and the pursuit of clinical and pharmacological instruction.

The sons of the masters were members of the mystery by right. Those who did not belong to the families of the

Asclepiads could join after taking the Oath, but were obliged to pay certain fees. The teaching of the Asclepiads was not secret, as has often been maintained, but everything tends to prove that they were extremely jealous of their mystery and wished to keep away all those who were not capable of becoming proficient in the art. The doctrine contained in the Hippocratic Collection was intended to be made public, and the Periodeutae, who went from town to town in the practice of their profession, largely contributed to this publicity. Moreover, there is nothing in the Oath, as some have maintained, to show that the mystery of the Asclepiads was a priesthood or that there was a school dependent upon the temple of Aesculapius. It is quite true that the members of this mystery pretended to be the descendants of Aesculapius or his ancestor, Apollo, and that they invoked them in their prayers, but for all that they were not priests.

The Oath is not a religious oath. It is a lay oath. We know from many researches that there was a difference between the medicine of the priests belonging to the temples of Aesculapius and medicine as practised by the Asclepiads. The former was treatment by suggestion in a kind of sanatorium situated in the country in a very mild climate, with every facility for sports and attendance at theatres. The priests were supposed to explain dreams. All this was far different from the medicine of the Asclepiads, which was solidly based on clinical observation and experience. Plato assures us that Hippocrates was an Asclepiad, and not a priest of Aesculapius or of Apollo, and all attempts to make out a connexion between the Hippocratic writings and the practice of medicine in the temples have been failures. What is very possible is that the Asclepiads may have established their schools near the temples and, as Meyer Steineg has pointed out, they had need to be near them, because in the work entitled *On Decorum*, belonging to the Hippocratic Collection, is to be found the following sentence : " Physicians should bow before the gods because their art is not provided with means of cure in abundance."

The famous school of Salerno is, at a later date, an example of how in the same place lay medicine and the medicine of the priests can prosper side by side. This school was so famous throughout the world that pupils came from all over

Europe to learn the healing art. And it is an undoubted fact that this school was a lay school and in no way dependent upon ecclesiastical medicine. At the same time medicine as practised by the priests was in a flourishing condition. The works of Hippocrates were studied and commented on by the professors of this school, and they followed the Asclepiads in that they formed a mystery which united professors and students.

In conclusion it may be said that, contrary to the theory that university life began with the School of Salerno, the Oath clearly shows that it began with the schools of the Asclepiads.

The second part of the oath consists in the promise made by the physician to lead an exemplary life during his entire medical career. It is an account of the different duties of the physician. For convenience sake this part may be divided into five sections, as follows :—

" I will prescribe regimen for the good of my patients according to my ability and my judgment and never do harm to anyone."

It is to be noted that the word δίαιτα has not the limited sense that it has in English. Beside diet, it includes baths, massage, and gymnastics, all of which were in high repute, and might perhaps be well translated by " treatment ". The oath goes on to say that the physician should overcome all opposition shown him in the patient's family circle. He should prescribe for his patient but at the same time should avoid all danger for him, or anything detrimental to him.

" To please no one will I prescribe a deadly drug, nor give advice which may cause his death. Nor will I give a woman a pessary to procure abortion. But I will preserve the purity of my life and my art."

This implies that the physician should protect his patients when they wish to end their days, that he should comfort them and prevent them from carrying out their project. The supreme duty of the physician is to cure ; his greatest crime would be to co-operate in the destruction of life by murder, suicide, or abortion. It is to be remembered that in the days of Hippocrates the moral attitude in respect of abortion was not very high, and Aristotle himself advised abortion even when there is no medical indication for it, his only reservation being that the embryo should not yet have received life. Littré says that this prohibition shows that the practice of abortion was not generally approved, and that the physicians of those days would no more lend their help to this detestable practice than those of to-day.

"I will not cut for stone, even for patients in whom the disease is manifest ; I will leave this operation to be performed by practitioners."

This sentence implies that the physician will never perform lithotomy. The Asclepiads were perfectly familiar with vesical calculus, which was frequent in the Mediterranean countries and Egypt. They were perfectly conversant with the symptoms and made a perfectly correct diagnosis by introducing a metallic sound into the bladder, as is done to-day. But they did not operate, because, as the Oath states, there were specialists for this operation. These specialists were the lithotomists that Herodotus refers to when speaking of the specialists in Egypt. But all Greek medical literature is silent as to the technique of the operation. It is Celsus who at a much later date tells us that Ammonius, of Alexandria, invented an instrument for crushing the stone and removing the pieces. The only thing which is certain is that the operation was performed at a very ancient date, but no document exists which tells us when it was first done.

It has often been questioned why the Asclepiads, who had raised surgery to such a high level, did not practise lithotomy, and it has been supposed by some that this prohibition was not directed against the operation of lithotomy but against castration. That eunuchs existed in antiquity is well known, and that castration was at that time practised for various motives, as in the Orient at a much later date. One has merely to refer to the severe edicts promulgated by Hadrian and Constantine against this mutilation, whereby the physician who practised it was condemned to death. It is, however, difficult to understand why this operation should have been performed in the days of the Asclepiads.

Some modern translators have given the following version : "I will leave the cutting for stone to my subordinates." This incorrect rendering can be explained by the fact that in mediaeval times surgery had sunk to a very low level, having fallen entirely into the hands of ignorant barbers, who were looked down upon by physicians. The translators argued that the Asclepiads took the same attitude as the physicians of the Middle Ages, considering that cutting for stone was beneath them, and therefore had it done by their subordinates. But in this explanation the fact is overlooked that in the days of Hippocrates there was no division among the members of the medical corps. The Asclepiads performed all operations and they certainly would not have a low order of practitioner operate for stone. They were far too conversant with surgery; they simply took oath that they would not do it but rather would turn over such cases to specialists in this branch of surgery who possessed all necessary skill. A free translation should be: "I will never cut for stone, but will send these patients to specialists versed in this operation." The Asclepiads maintained that a physician should recognize the limitations of his knowledge and should have the courage to admit that he was ignorant of certain parts of his art. If his own science was insufficient for the cure of a patient, he then should have recourse to the opinion of a more experienced physician. This idea is to be found in another passage from the Hippocratic writings: "When a physician is uncertain as to the condition of a patient and is disturbed by the novelty of an affection that he has never seen before, he should never be ashamed to call in other physicians to examine the patient with him . . ." Thus understood, this part of the Oath will always increase in importance as medical science progresses, because it becomes more and more impossible for a physician to be versed in all branches of the art.

"In every house where I come I will enter only for the good of my patients, keeping myself far from all intentional ill-doing and all seduction, and especially from the pleasures of love with women or with men, be they free or slaves."

This fourth paragraph of the Oath is so clear that no explanation is required. As in other passages in the works of Hippocrates, a very high standard of personal conduct is required of the physician who would be worthy of the name.

"All that may come to my knowledge in the exercise of my profession or outside of my profession, or in daily commerce with men, which ought not to be spread abroad, I will keep secret and will never reveal."

This fifth and last part of the Oath is the promise made by the physician never to reveal any information that he may have obtained in the practice of his profession and is so clearly set out that no comments are necessary.

The Oath remains and will always remain. The physician of to-day should possess the same qualities as the physician in the days of Hippocrates. His duty remains the same, and in our days of speculation and medical specialization the Oath is more useful than ever.

# CHAPTER VI

## HIPPOCRATES, AND THE HIPPOCRATIC COLLECTION

A wit once remarked on the Homeric question, that the poems were not written by Homer but by another man of the same name, and this may likewise apply to some of the Hippocratic writings. There were seven physicians bearing the name of Hippocrates, who lived during the period when this collection was being written. But it is generally conceded that the Father of Medicine was the second of these. He was born in the year 460 B.C. and was supposed to be descended in a direct line from Aesculapius and Hercules.

The biography of Hippocrates may be said to be entirely apocryphal and so no allusion will be made to it. He has always been known, and quite rightly so, as the founder of modern medicine, and all writers who have dealt with Hippocrates and his writings have always spoken of him with the highest praise. For example, Galen says that Hippocrates was always his guide in his search for the greatest truth; he also says that the divine Hippocrates was the greatest of physicians and the first among philosophers. In his *Histoire des Systèmes Philosophiques*, de Gérando says that Hippocrates gave in all branches of medical science the foremost and most wonderful example of how to proceed in these sciences; of all the ancients it was he who best knew, best developed and best applied the experimental method, and who considered Nature as a philosopher. All the natural sciences felt the influence of his genius and in several of his writings Aristotle has borrowed much from him. Hippocrates combined judgment with experience to a very high degree. Haviland, quoted by Littré, passes the following judgment on the work and character of the Father of Medicine. "Hippocrates was an original observer and in all his works he is careful to communicate the full result of his experiments without much theorizing. Consequently, when studying his works, comparison should be made between what was written more than two thousand years ago and what happens to-day. With the Hippocratic writings before him the student should determine the connexions which subsist between the results of modern investigations and these ancient books. By so doing he will be able to form a just estimate of Hippocrates and the school of Cos, and the really great development of clinical medicine two thousand four hundred years ago."

There is no doubt but that Hippocrates travelled extensively, and during his travels he acquired great knowledge of peoples, places and things. Thus he noted the changes that climate produces in the human race; he saw that disease varies in type under varied conditions. Everything related to life inspired him with the most intense interest, but his profession was always before him and during his long life he worked in order to perfect it as far as possible. To do good unto mankind was his clear duty and he never remained indifferent to any phenomenon of Nature which could enlighten him in any way with respect to disease.

In the perusal of the Hippocratic writings one is struck by the fact that infectious diseases, such as puerperal fever, pyaemia and suppurating wounds, are extremely well described with a profusion of detail of the symptoms.

Hippocrates frequently accuses Air of giving rise to disease and suppuration. In fact he gives it an all-important part in this respect. Speaking of this element in the book entitled *On Winds*, he says: "According to all appearance the cause of disease should there be found (in the air), when it enters the body in excess or in insufficient quantity or too much at a time or when tainted by morbid miasmas." At another place, entering into more detail, he adds that Air is the cause of fever, especially when the latter is accompanied by inflammation, for example after a contusion of the feet. According to his way of thinking, inflammation may develop after a contusion and this inflammation is accompanied by a rise of temperature.

For the school of Cos, Air is the immediate agent of inflammation in wounds and it is stated that "sporadic fevers have the same cause". In the book on *Humours* the following sentence is to be found: "Diseases develop from odours exhaled from mire and marshes," and in the book entitled

*On the Nature of Man* the same idea is expressed when it is stated that the cause of epidemic diseases resides " in the air from which escapes a morbid exhalation contained within it ". The entrance of air into a wound cavity or air coming in contact with some internal viscus or the focus of a fracture is a very unfortunate complication. In abscesses opening internally, the least serious are those which have no communication with the outside.

In the *Aphorisms* it is stated that if the omentum extrudes from a wound it will of necessity decay. In the work entitled *On the Articulations* the statement is made that when one or several ribs are fractured without any depression of the splinters inwardly, and in cases of exposure of bones, fever rarely ensues. It is only when a denuded bone comes in contact with the air that suppuration and fever occur, because in these cases there is contusion of the flesh and these lesions often give rise to cough, tubercles, empyema and suppurating wounds.

The physicians of antiquity were fearful of contact of air with wounds for the very good reason that they had observed many cases of death following these injuries, and they were fully conversant with septicaemia and pyaemia, as is proved by the following passage in the book entitled *On the Articulations*, where dislocation with the exit of the bone through the integuments is described. " In cases where the bones . . . have become dislocated and, having caused a wound in the integuments, protrude completely through them . . . reduction should not be attempted . . . it is well known that these patients will die if the bones are reduced . . . it is a spasm that kills them (tetanus). . . . The dressing should consist of a pitch cirate and compresses soaked in wine." The text then goes on to say that if a spasm occurs after reduction the dislocation should be at once reproduced and affusions of hot water frequently made.

It is unnecessary to multiply these quotations ; air, tainted with morbid miasmas, is, according to Hippocrates, the cause of many diseases, but we had to wait for the advent of Pasteur to give the experimental proof of what the physician of Cos suspected.

A very important point in the teachings of Hippocrates is the great stress he lays upon the individual predisposition of the patient, which in modern medicine we call the soil, and also on the greater or lesser resistance of the various organs. And it is stated: " He who would know in cases of ulcers how each will end should in the first place determine which individual disposition is the best and which the worst for wounds."

In the book on *Ancient Medicine* will be found the following: " But flatus (air), when it obtains admission, increases and becomes stronger, and rushes towards any resisting object; but owing to its tenderness, and the quantity of blood which it (the liver) contains, it cannot be without uneasiness; and for these reasons the most acute and frequent pains occur in the region of it, along with suppurations and chronic tumours (phymata). These symptoms also occur in the site of the diaphragm, but much less frequently; for the diaphragm is a broad, expanded, and resisting substance, of a nervous and strong nature, and therefore less susceptible of pain; and yet pains and chronic abscesses do occur about it." This paragraph may be summarized (leaving aside the rather peculiar explanations that it contains) as follows: the flatus when it rushes in (the infectious agent) reaches an organ such as the liver where it finds the necessary conditions (morbid receptivity); it there produces inflammation, suppuration and abscesses (infection).

The part played by drinking water in the genesis of disease was well known by Hippocrates. In his immortal treatise entitled *On Airs, Waters and Places*, he says: " I now wish to set out what there is to say on waters, and to show which are unhealthy and which are healthy, what disadvantages and what advantages result from the waters we use, because they have a very great influence upon health." He then reviews the various waters, examines their respective qualities and ends with the following conclusions: " The still and stagnant waters of marshes are the cause of diarrhoea, dysentery and intermittent fever Those cities which are favourably placed for the sun and the winds, and where the waters are of good quality, are less touched by these disadvantages. But those where stagnant and marshy waters are used, and whose site is bad, suffer more from them."

According to Hippocrates rain water is the best, but it should be boiled in order to prevent its going bad, and here again the soil and predisposition of the patient again play an important part, for it is stated that "a strong, healthy man need make no choice, as he can always drink any water, but he who suffers from a delicate condition has need of the best water obtainable."

From what has been said it is evident that Hippocrates possessed very precise ideas as to infection from water, since he gives it as a cause for diarrhoea, dysentery and malaria. He also advises boiling water just as we do to-day, in other words sterilizing it.

It would also seem that Hippocrates suspected that surgeons sometimes infected wounds with their instruments and hands, because in the book entitled *On the Use of Liquids* the antiputrefactive qualities of sea-water are extolled, and it is pointed out that when fishermen are wounded their wounds do not suppurate unless meddled with.

The general infectious processes following wounds, such as pyaemia, tetanus, and erysipelas, were well known to the school of Cos, as well as those arising after labour or miscarriage. The latter have been remarkably described, but the scope of this book will not permit of quoting passages from the two books entitled *On the Nature of Women* and *Diseases of Women*, although they abound in cases of these infections. Let it be briefly stated that injury during labour was especially feared, therefore obstetricians were advised to pare the nails carefully before performing version or embryotomy and to use blunt-ended knives. "If the womb is ulcerated, blood, pus and ichorous fluid are discharged . . . the belly becomes distended . . . and it is painful to touch as is a wound. Fever, grinding of the teeth, acute and continued pain in the genital parts, pubis, lower abdomen, flanks and lumbar region, ensue; this disease is especially prone to occur after a labour when something putrefies in the womb; it also occurs after abortion."

Passing now into the domain of surgery, we would refer to a few passages relating to purulent infection following wounds in general. In one of the cases related in the books of the *Epidemics* it is stated "pus formed; on the eighth day a chill followed by fever, the patient's condition was not satisfactory; at times when the patient had no fever his condition was as on the preceding days." These symptoms are reported in a case of a wound of the skull with splinters of bone which required trephining. Hippocrates points out that the fever and chills were due to the pus and that the only means of saving the patient was an operation which would allow the surgeon to cleanse the wound completely. In the same book he also refers to a case of abdominal suppuration which was treated by cauterization which caused the discharge of pus to subside; but on account of a mistake in the diet during very warm weather fever and diarrhoea ensued and the patient died.

These remarks are interesting from several points of view. In the first place the use of heat was resorted to for destroying the focus of pus, while at the same time Hippocrates points out that he attached great importance to the amount of resistance that the patient offered against infection, because, in spite of the good that might be derived from operating, having committed an imprudence in diet, he succumbed to the infection. Moreover the part played by pus in the pathogenesis of fever is clearly shown, when Hippocrates says that "the majority of patients who have suppurative processes are seized with chills and fever" and so "when suppuration occurs chills and fever develop in the majority of cases".

Passages relating to tetanus are very numerous in the Hippocratic writings. For example: "He who was injured by a sharp lance . . . was seized with contractions behind, similar to those occurring in opisthotonos; the jaws became locked . . . the accidents became more serious and death took place on the second." And again: "He had the index finger crushed by an anchor, inflammation ensued, with sloughing and fever; he was purged . . . finally the jaws were fixed one against the other; then the neck became involved; on the third day the patient was contracted in the back; on the sixth day he died."

Erysipelas is well treated of in the Hippocratic writings. For example: "The bone was exposed and erysipelas developed; with the erysipelas sloughing and suppuration occurred."

And what is more, not only was Hippocrates conversant with purulent infection, but he also suspected that the blood vessels and the blood were not without their influence in the infection of the economy by pathogenic agencies from the air. In spite of the fantastic explanations that he offers in respect of the genesis of chill preceding fever, he nevertheless concludes by saying that "the blood co-operates with it (the air) in the febrile process." And again: "As to the foci from which chills develop, for example wounds, these are to be found in the blood vessels."

Hippocrates was not ignorant of the part played by blood in the formation of pus, for in the book on *Wounds* it is stated: "Wounds become inflamed when suppuration is to take place and suppuration is derived from the blood, which becomes changed and heated up to the point when, becoming putrefied, it is transformed into pus."

We will now examine the principal characteristics of medical science as understood by the Hippocratic school. According to Hippocrates the general causes of disease were heredity, climate, seasons, and the epidemical constitution. Heredity is dependent upon the morbid disposition of the sperm, from which all parts of the body are formed. Hippocrates, as a true son of Greece, was sensible of the harmony in all things. Hence anything which disturbs the state of normal equilibrium of the body is the principal cause of disease, and morbid processes are of relatively little import, the physiological state being all.

The morbid causes act by changing the humours, which are the blood, the phlegm, the black, and the yellow bile. These four elements act by increasing or decreasing certain normal arrangements in their mixture—for example, the mixture of phlegm which is cold with bile which is essentially hot. Fever results from a heating of the bile and a chill indicates that phlegm has become mixed with the blood. But another theory of fever is to be found in the Hippocratic Collection, according to which the rise in temperature is due to an exaggerated production of phlegm, which causes the tissues to swell, thereby interfering with the secretions. Catarrh, which plays an important part in Hippocratic pathology, results from an exaggerated secretion of phlegm in the brain and this phlegm is conveyed to some given point in the body. Thus the flux may be carried to the eyes, the ears, the lungs, and so forth; the heart itself may become involved and then palpitations and dyspnoea may arise. The mixture of the four elements is the source of severe disease, notably the development of suppuration, because pus, as has already been pointed out, is merely corrupted blood or liquefied flesh.

Abscesses are either simple, metastatic or congested; they are frequently surrounded by a pseudo-membrane, especially when a fistula exists.

Critical days are of the greatest importance, and this theory of critical days was manifestly connected with the number seven. The numbers 3, 5, 7, 9, 11, 17, 21, 27 and 31 are the critical days; that is to say those on which the crisis takes place, indicating that recovery is to ensue, and all treatment consists in keeping up the patient's strength and especially in awaiting and regulating the crisis.

Hippocrates thoroughly understood the great importance of prognosis, and this depends on a state of repose of the body, the nutrition, the vital forces, the temperature, the colour of the skin and the character of sleep. When the patient continually lies upon his back, or his movements are slow and difficult, the prognosis is bad. The examination of every secretion was a constant care of the Hippocratic school and regarded by them as of the greatest importance.

The semeiology was based on signs and subjective symptoms, but particular importance was given to symptoms by which the general state of the patient could be judged. The body heat was estimated by placing the hands on the chest. What Hippocrates studied above all was the condition of the skin and exudates, tympanism, sleep, and the state of wakefulness, restlessness and uneasiness, chills, diarrhoea, cough and sputum, hiccough, the urine, the tears, hunger and thirst, plethora, pain, memory, the condition of the mucosa of the nose and throat, the eyes and the patient's mental condition, including dreams. Palpation of the right and left hypochondria was never omitted.

The diagnosis was also based on anatomy. For example, in the fifth book of the *Epidemics* a case of penetrating wound of the abdomen is given wherein diagnosis of injury to the intestine with intra-abdominal haemorrhage was made.

Among the intermittent fevers, *causos* plays an important part; the patient appears frozen, although he is burning with fever internally. This affection easily transforms into pneumonia. There are also certain descriptions of a disease which appears to be typhoid fever, while mumps with testicular metastasis is described. The eruptive fevers and diphtheria are not described.

Amongst local affections may be mentioned diarrhoea, dysentery, tonsilitis, and tumefactions of the spleen and liver, and it is pointed out that when the spleen is enlarged epistaxis frequently occurs. Various forms of ulcers, nasal polypi, acute and chronic laryngitis, bronchitis, pneumonia, pleurisy and hemiplegia are described. It is stated that hydrothorax is common in cattle. Erysipelas is frequently described and pulmonary phthisis also. Renal lithiasis, as well as haematuria are accorded much space in the books, as well as abscess of the kidney and wounds of the bladder, which are regarded as fatal. Vesical calculi, tumours of the testicle, and varicocele are described; but dislocations and fractures and wounds of the head were the branches of surgery in which the Hippocratic school excelled, into the details of which we unfortunately cannot enter.

As to nervous diseases, phrensy is described, represented as a disturbance of the understanding accompanied by fever. Undoubtedly the ancients confounded this condition with typhoid fever or serious cases of pneumonia, and they explained it by an obstruction of the vessels by phlegm. Apoplexy, lethargy and various forms of palsy are described but not clearly.

Having now considered the essentially clinical aspect of the Hippocratic writings, we should make reference to the medical system of Hippocrates and the School of Cos. Although Galen gave the name of dogmatism to the Hippocratic system and although the term humoralism may also very properly be used, we prefer to call his system *naturalism*. This medical system has as principal directive the medicative powers of Nature. In order thoroughly to understand this system one must realize the idea that Hippocrates had of Nature in general and the nature of man in particular. By the word Nature Hippocrates implied a force penetrating the entire economy and presiding over all the phenomena present in the state of health or in the state of disease. In other words, the nature of man is man himself; man feeling, acting, and reacting. Viewed as a whole, Nature consists of those forces which govern all beings by their own immutable laws. It is the constantly active power directing and maintaining all the physiological and pathological functions.

The following are the principal tenets of naturalism, and they represent all the consequences of this doctrinal system.

1. There is a principle, simple in nature and multiple in its effects, which presides over the economy of all living bodies and which, by pre-established laws, therein produces all the phenomena seen in them. This principle is Nature as understood by Hippocrates, and he says in substance that Nature gives life to everything, and in all things it is sufficient to the animal creation. Nature knows, without ever having learned, all that is necessary or unnecessary for animal life. In fact, Nature is a primal faculty or principle; but there are many others which are dependent upon her and these govern the living body. It is by them that Nature attracts all that is proper for each species and it is also by them that she separates and rejects all that is useless or harmful, because Nature is essentially providential in her action. Lastly, according to the case, Nature is formative, conservative or medicative.

2. Nature reveals herself in man by crises and by symptoms. The internal crises, that is to say these phenomena and these symptoms, will indicate in certain cases that she is quite sufficient in herself and will triumph over the morbid cause. In other cases they show that Nature is too weak and has need of assistance. And lastly, other cases by their irregularity and lack of order will cause her efforts at cure to be of no avail and will show that she needs to be ruled and directed.

3. Nature has as stimulators and supporters of her action the good or the evil done by modifying agents acting upon reasoning and sentient beings.

4. In the state of health, Nature is simply formative and conservative; in disease she becomes medicative. In all circumstances her co-operation is always of the utmost necessity, because as soon as she repudiates her goodwill nothing useful or good can be obtained from her.

5. No absolute rules can be formulated for therapeutics, because Nature differs just as age differs, and what one day may be used with advantage may often have the contrary effect on the next day.

6. Properly speaking, disease should be regarded as a

combat between medicative Nature and the morbid cause. The welfare of the patient depends upon the strength and wisdom of Nature.

7. The supreme object of Nature is the preservation of man, whom she formed, and the placing him in a position where he may perfect his soul.

The theory of coction, crises and critical days is the inevitable consequence of what has been said concerning the conservative and medicative power of Nature, and is to be found in all the Hippocratic writings. It may be found combined with other theories, and in particular permeates the doctrine of the four elements and the four humours. In common with the ancient Asclepiads, Hippocrates believed that a large number of diseases had as a cause the presence of a morbid agent within the body. Therefore, combining this theory with his idea of medicative Nature, he demonstrated that man's nature, on account of the properties with which Nature had endowed it, would attract this morbid agent—whether this agent came from within or without—and after coction had taken place would be thrown out of the body through one of the several emunctories that she might choose according to the needs of the given case.

Thus Hippocrates was led to develop the theory of coction, which he afterwards perfected by the theories of crises and critical days. That coction is about to take place will be heralded by an intensity of the symptoms. While it is under preparation fever increases and the patient will be either in a state of extreme excitability, or in a state of extreme collapse. There are symptoms preceding, accompanying and following the process of coction, with all of which the physician must be thoroughly cognizant. He must be able to distinguish between those which are good and those which are bad, so that he may correctly predict the outcome of the disease.

The critical period is the lapse of time necessary for coction of the morbid matter to take place. Those crises are regarded as salutary which take place on the third, fourth and seventh day, and it is the duty of the physician to leave this critical period untroubled by the exhibition of useless or untimely remedies. His line of action is to favour the work of Nature, bringing her aid when necessary.

When coction has taken place, Nature will usually free the body of the morbid agent by expelling it in the sweat, urine or stools, and it is at this time that the physician should be particularly attentive as to what is taking place. He should study all the tendencies of Nature and ascertain the emunctory that she seems to be choosing for the elimination of the morbid agent. By so doing he will be able to help this important work by administering sudorifics, diuretics or laxative remedies, according as to whether Nature herself wishes to free the body of the morbid agent by the sweat, the urine, or the faeces. On the other hand, when coction is effected incompletely or badly, medical help must be given by those recognized means which will aid Nature when she is weak. It is quite true that coction and the crises do not always take place on the days indicated by Hippocrates, but this is exceptional.

From the point of view of treatment, naturalism expressly recommends us to do exactly the opposite of that which the disease produces, that is to say to oppose cold to heat, heat to cold, dampness to dryness and so forth, according to the general axiom—which is not absolute—laid down by Hippocrates: *Contraria contrariis curantur.*

To sum up, it may be said that naturalism was created from the time when Hippocrates discovered the one great fact which governs all other facts in the operations or the functions of life; the fact which contains *in parvo* all medical science and practice:—of the existence of a formative, conservative and medicative power inherent in the organism, by which it feels, reacts and develops, preserves itself and combats all morbid causes and the effects produced by them.

However simple this discovery may seem to us at present, it is without question the most important of any that has ever been made in the science of the human body.

# CHAPTER VII

## THE DIRECT SUCCESSORS OF HIPPOCRATES. THE SCHOOL OF ALEXANDRIA. ERASISTRATUS AND HEROPHILUS

After the death of Hippocrates the Great, the science of medicine was still further perfected by his son-in-law, Polybus, one of the most renowned practitioners of the School of Cos. Galen was loud in praise of the skill and experience of Polybus, as well as of the fidelity with which he followed the precepts and conduct of his illustrious father-in-law. Little is known about him and the books that have been attributed to him—*The Means of Preserving Health* and *The Diseases and Nature of the Sperm*—are in all probability apocryphal. It is, however, likely that Polybus was the author of the book entitled *De Natura Pueri*, which is to be found in the Hippocratic Collection.

Aristotle and his disciple, Theophrastus, contributed indirectly to the progress of medicine by their extensive studies on natural history. Diogenes Laërtius mentions, among more than two hundred works written by Theophrastus, a history of plants, fragments of which have come down to us and which appears to have been a very important work. A description of the medicinal properties of the simples is there to be found. Dioxippus of Cos (370 B.C.), a disciple of Hippocrates, if we are to believe Suidas, is supposed to have written a treatise on medicine and two books on prognosis, while Petronius is known to us from the writings of Celsus, who affirms that he lived before Erasistratus and Herophilus. Celsus remarks that he smothered his fever patients under heavy coverings in order to cause sweating and to stimulate thirst. After the fever decreased he ordered the patient to drink cold water. If sweating did not occur he doubled the dose of water and induced vomiting. When improvement in the patient's condition had become sufficiently evident, he ordered him to eat roast pork and goose, and to drink wine. Then, if the patient did not recover as quickly as desirable, he again ordered an emetic, and for this purpose he used sea water. Petronius was not a believer in dietetic methods and Galen, after having condemned the method of those who brought the strength of their patients very low by too long fasting, blames him for having erred by giving his patients too much food.

Diocles, of Carystos (350 B.C.), whom Galen held in very high esteem, appears to have made considerable progress in medicine and may be considered, with Empedocles and Democritus, as one of those who first studied anatomy scientifically and, although his gross dissections brought forth sarcasm from Galen, they certainly rendered the greatest service to this science. It is to be noted that in point of fact Diocles had studied the adnexa so thoroughly that Soranus (A.D. 98–117) and even Galen went to the trouble of speaking of the Fallopian tubes which Diocles was the first to compare to horns of cattle. He was unquestionably a very skilful practitioner and the Athenians appreciated his talent to such extent that they called him the second Hippocrates on account of the numerous recoveries he wrought, as well as for his great attachment to the doctrines of the School of Cos.

Caelius Aurelianus has given us some interesting data as to the way in which Diocles treated his patients. In cases of haemoptysis he ordered a potion composed of glue boiled in water with flour and bramble, while in intestinal occlusion he ordered the patient to swallow a leaden ring.

Praxagoras of Cos (340–320 B.C.) was one of the last of the Asclepiads whose name has been preserved in history. Although, according to Galen, he was a rather poor anatomist, he nevertheless wrote some works on medicine which enjoyed very great reputation. A determined humoralist, he attributed all diseases to changes arising in the fluids of the body and he even multiplied the number of those that are to be found in the Hippocratic writings to such an extent that he described ten kinds of humour without counting the blood.

Caelius Aurelianus has given some details as to the way he treated disease. Thus, in intestinal occlusion, if repeated exhibition of emetics had remained fruitless, he dilated the rectum with injections of gas, and if this remained ineffective he opened the abdomen and attempted to remove the cause of the obstruction. In the treatment of epilepsy Praxagoras was also very radical in his procedures. He caused the head of the patient to be shaved, and cauterized the scalp thoroughly, filling the patient with disgusting remedies.

The famous school of Cnidos, about which we know so little, but which played such an important part in the history of medicine, also had, at the period of which we are now speaking, some very illustrious representatives at medicine. The physician Euryphon, of Cnidos, who lived at the time of Aristophanes, was represented on the stage by Plato the comic poet, when he showed Cinsias the son of Evagoras, reduced to the state of a skeleton after a pleurisy, the chest full of pus and the body covered with sloughs, the result of treatment inflicted upon him with the cautery by Euryphon.

Contrary to the School of Cos, the School of Cnidos completely neglected general pathology and studied particular diseases. Chrysippus, the master of Erasistratus, is one of the better known of this School. He was strong in his condemnation of the abusive use of blood-letting and purgation, as Galen tells us. The same authority states that his writings were already very rare in his time. None of them have come down to us, but the name of Chrysippus is mentioned with great respect by Caelius Aurelianus, Plutarch and Macrobius. Pliny reproaches him for changing the old prescriptions, but it is a well known fact that the Roman writer detested this innovator. Chrysippus, according to Pliny, wrote a treatise on plants in which he particularly extolled the curative virtues of cabbage, and he is especially important in medical history because of his student Erasistratus, who embraced many of his opinions and, like his master, had a very poor opinion of many of the aphorisms of Hippocrates.

THE SCHOOL OF ALEXANDRIA. This School, so celebrated for its anatomical discoveries, exercised a tremendous influence upon ancient medicine. Caelius Aurelianus, Aretaeus (A.D. 30–90) and above all Galen, are unanimous on this point. It is, however, probable that the School of Alexandria did not make use of the medical doctrines of the Egyptian physicians of the period of the Pharaohs. We have already pointed out that anatomical knowledge was very rudimentary among the Egyptian physicians; their symptomatology was extremely vague and their therapeutics meagre and combined with the practice of magic. Recent studies have shown that Erasistratus and Herophilus derived their medical knowledge exclusively from Greece:—a notable fact is that the Schools of Cnidos and Cos both had representatives at Alexandria, because Praxagoras, one of the last of the Asclepiads, was the teacher of Herophilus, while Erasistratus was the disciple of Chrysippus.

Erasistratus (300–225 b.c.). As we have just pointed out, Erasistratus, the rival of Herophilus, and, like him, one of the founders of the famous School of Alexandria, belonged much more to the School of Cnidos, on account of his master Chrysippus, than to the School of Cos, of which Herophilus remained the representative in spite of certain changes he made in its doctrine, while the ideas of Erasistratus inclined towards *Methodism.*

The doctrines of Erasistratus are quite as difficult to grasp as those of his rival and for the same reason. Of the numerous works that he wrote, none has come down to us, so that we can only form an opinion of them from the undigested fragments that various later writers have given in their works. In his book entitled *De Venae Sectione adversus Erasistratum* Galen tells us that this physician was not an advocate of blood-letting and it would seem, according to the same authority, that in all his writings he only mentions it once—when speaking of vomiting of blood—and then only to say that it is useless. However, the disciples of Erasistratus who lived in the time of Galen maintained that their master did not absolutely proscribe the letting of blood, and that they resorted to it occasionally, although much less frequently than other practitioners. On the other hand, Caelius Aurelianus assures us that Erasistratus bled in cases of loss of blood and that it was some of his followers who, at a later date, completely rejected this practice.

Erasistratus had likewise a poor opinion of purgative medication. He certainly had recourse to enemata as well as emetics, as did his master Chrysippus, although with greater prudence and discretion. For example, in respect of enemata, he ordered that they should be composed of mild ingredients, and he rejected those which were irritating and astringent. He considered that purgation had the same action as blood-letting, that is to say, that it decreased plethora, but he maintained that morbid humours could be eliminated by other means than purging and blood-letting, and that these two methods were quite capable of corrupting them still further.

His disciples rejected the theory of *attraction* that is to be found in the Hippocratic Collection; the thinnest and most dilute humours came away the first, while the grosser were the last to be eliminated, and this elimination could only be obtained by the use of the more violent remedies.

Instead of purgatives and blood-letting, Erasistratus had recourse to fasting and abstinence (as the Methodist school did later on), and when these were not sufficient to reduce the plethora of the body he advised exercise. He pointed out that the action of plethora was to cause a transfusion of the venous blood into the arteries, thus giving rise to fever and inflammation. It is thus that Galen gives us the theory of Erasistratus on exercise: "Those who are accustomed to exercise should indulge in it somewhat more when they feel plethoric and thus they will avoid illness. When one has taken sufficient exercise he should take a hot bath in order to cause sweating. Afterwards, if he finds himself over-heated, he should take cold baths for several days, after which he should keep quiet and observe strict abstinence. Should one take food it should be very simple, such as herbs. Those who are not accustomed to exercise should not resort to it, although it is an excellent means for diminishing plethora."

Erasistratus points out that plethora should not always be treated in the same way. If it makes itself known by epilepsy or expectoration of blood, the treatment is quite different; the epileptic patient should move about constantly, while the phthisical patient should on the contrary avoid both fatigue and work. Plethoric patients should take as food only melon, cucumber, herbs (of which chicory is particularly excellent) and vegetable marrow. He was a warm advocate of simple medicaments and was very much opposed to the complicated formulae to which the physicians of his day gave the name of "antidotes of the gods". He was likewise opposed to mixing minerals, plants and animal substances together. He also decried abstract reasoning. Galen tells us that both Erasistratus and Herophilus were only partially dogmatic in their theory; only diseases of the organic parts were they inclined to treat by reasoning but, nevertheless, they were not inclined to adopt the ideas later developed by those Empirics who denied the importance of the causes of disease. Dioscorides tells us that Erasistratus wrote a book on this subject and in order to show the importance of the aetiology of disease he mentioned poisoning by bites of venomous animals. "If the *specific* cause of disease cannot always be ascertained, one should at least discover the *apparent* cause, which will often furnish very excellent indications for treatment."

Erasistratus had many disciples, of whom Galen mentions quite a number, but their fame was unequal. Among them may be enumerated Straton of Lampsacos, Xenophon of Cos, Ptolemaeus of Alexandria (A.D. 150), a certain Chrysippus (not Chrysippus of Cnidos), Charidemus, Hermogenes, Artemidorus, Athenion, Apollonius of Memphis. Strabo, who lived during the reigns of the three first Caesars, tells us that Hicesius of Smyrna (A.D. 60), a very celebrated physician in his day, founded a school in that city and there taught the doctrines of Erasistratus. It would also appear that the treatise on dietetics written by Hicesius was very popular.

Celsus refers to a famous surgeon, Philoxenus (A.D. 50), who was a fervent disciple of the teachings of Erasistratus. And lastly Galen refers to a number of disciples whom he knew during his own day and who remained extremely attached to the teachings of their master. It would seem, however, that they considerably exaggerated his doctrine, especially in respect of blood-letting, and, what is most extraordinary and very unlike their master, they, with the Empirics, despised the knowledge that one can obtain from anatomy and the practice of searching for the causes of disease. One among them, however, by name Martial, a contemporary of Galen, did cultivate anatomy with much success.

HEROPHILUS (300 B.C.). Herophilus seems to have been quite as successful as a practitioner of medicine as he was as a teacher of anatomy. He defined the science of medicine as the perfect knowledge of what takes place during health, of the changes caused by disease and lastly, of indifferent things not pertaining to the condition either of health or of disease. Among these " indifferent things " he included precautions that should be taken for preserving health and for curing disease. Celsus tells us that he was an ardent advocate of medication and that he resorted to the use of drugs far more than the physicians of the dogmatic school who had preceded him.

Herophilus studied the pulse with great care, a thing which had not been done up to his time, but unfortunately he carried this study too far. Pliny says " One needs be a musician and even a mathematician in order to understand the pulse according to Herophilus, to detect the exact harmony and measure according to the age and the disease ", but adds that this great subtlety was not to the taste of everybody and the Empiric school was especially opposed to it. According to Galen, Herophilus wrote in condemnation of the *Prognostics* of Hippocrates, which, however, as we know, is a very remarkable work. Caelius Aurelianus also states that Herophilus wrote nothing of the cure of very common diseases such as pleurisy and quinsy, in spite of the fact that he states that it is the lungs that are the seat of the disease in pneumonia and that the latter only differs from pleurisy because in this disease the entire lung suffers at the same time. He also referred to paralysis of the heart according to the teachings of his master Praxagoras and pointed out that it is the cause of many sudden deaths. He had great faith in white hemlock as a drug and compared it to a valiant captain who first enters into a city after having inspired all his soldiers with his own zeal.

It has been a moot question whether Erasistratus or Herophilus had the greater following, but this question need not detain us here. However, in looking over the chronological tables published by Daremberg, it would seem as if the disciples of Herophilus were far more numerous, and even more noted, than those of Erasistratus. Then, too, Galen's statements would seem to confirm this opinion. The followers of Herophilus, quite contrary to their master, seem to have neglected the study of anatomy. But there is one among them, by name Eudemus (290 B.C.), who was a celebrated anatomist and was probably his master's equal in this science. Callimachus, a disciple and relative of Herophilus, was one of the first to write commentaries on the works of Hippocrates; Callianax, another follower, celebrated for his knowledge, was likewise famous for his brutality towards his patients. Baccheius of Tanagra also wrote commentaries on the Hippocratic writings. He admitted four types of haemorrhage, namely: from rupture, exosmosis, sloughing and transudation, and he also wrote a treatise on the pulse. Cratevas and Mantias wrote a very excellent treatise on materia medica that Galen declares to have been the best of those which preceded the great treatise of Dioscorides. Chrysermus and Cydias were also followers of Herophilus, whilst another, Demetrius of Apameia (250 B.C.), wrote a treatise on therapeutics which is referred to by the ancient writers with much praise.

A certain Zeno wrote a voluminous work on the *Epidemics* of Hippocrates. Dioscorides is loud in his praise of a certain Andreas of Carystos as a pharmacologist.

When Ptolemy Physcon had expelled many physicians and learned men from Alexandria because he thought that they were in league with his brother, a school was founded under the direction of Zeno at Laodicea, in which the doctrines of Herophilus were taught, and among the teachers are found the names of Alexander Philalethes and Cleophantus the master of Asclepiades, who extolled the virtues of wine.

And lastly, Caelius Aurelianus frequently quotes with great praise a certain Apollophanes who was physician to Antiochus the Great, and we know by Galen that he was a follower of Herophilus. Galen also speaks of a certain Heracleides, whom he regarded as an excellent physician and who lived during the first century after Christ. One of Galen's contemporaries, by name Apollonius Mys (30 B.C.) who belonged to the same sect and must not be confused with Apollonius of Cition (an Empiric) also wrote some books on medicine, while Demosthenes Philalethes was celebrated for his knowledge of diseases of the eye to such an extent that his fame extended down to the Middle Ages. Soranus also mentions favourably a Demosthenes when writing on the diseases of children, but it is a question whether or not this is the same Demosthenes as he to whom we have just alluded. And lastly, another follower of Herophilus, Gaius of Neapolis, was a gynaecologist who lived about the same time as Soranus, and is frequently quoted by Caelius Aurelianus.

# CHAPTER VIII

## THE SCHOOL OF EMPIRICS. ASCLEPIADES: HIS MEDICAL SYSTEM

Until now we have merely spoken of a more or less mild dogmatism which gradually became modified by time. That is to say, those physicians to whom we have referred still remained to a certain extent faithful to the teachings of the School of Cos. The same cannot be said of the Empirics, and Daremberg has pointed out that while the physicians of Cos and Cnidos did not differ as to the main principles of the healing *art*, it was at Alexandria, and from the very beginning of that school, that the medical profession became unruly and divided into two great factions, namely, the Dogmatics and Empirics. The former took as a basis a multitude of systems for their reasoning, while the latter rejected all kind of abstract reasoning. Haeser inclines to the opinion that the Empirics were composed of the followers both of Herophilus and of Erasistratus. The disciples of the Empiric School regarded Acron of Agrigentum (400 B.C.) as the founder of their sect, and we know that he lived in the time of Hippocrates. However, a certain disciple of Herophilus, namely, Philinus of Cos (250 B.C.) who wrote six books against the teachings of the celebrated Baccheius, should in all probability be considered as the first recognized professor of Empiricism, though Caelius Aurelianus mentions a work by his disciple Serapion which was far better known than the books of the master, Philinus himself.

In order to judge of the Empirics we have only the writings of Celsus, Galen and Caelius Aurelianus, and, unfortunately for the disciples of Philinus and Serapion, Galen, in whose works we obtain the greatest knowledge of them, is far from favourable.

The basis of the doctrine of the Empirics was that in medicine reasoning was useless and experience alone was necessary. Now, according to them, experience was of three kinds: it could be the result of mere chance; for example, a man having a severe headache falls, cutting his forehead, and by the loss of blood from the wound he finds himself better. Next, there is experience obtained on purpose, as, for example, when a man with fever drinks as much water as he can in order to find out whether he may thus obtain relief. Thirdly: experience may be repeated and verified by reproducing what chance or intention has demonstrated. It was the last form of experience, to which they gave the name of observation or autopsy, that they considered the basis of medical art. In those instances where the data obtained by experience were wanting and yet it was urgent to act, they considered it proper to proceed by analogy from experience of some similar condition. This was, according to their own definition, "the substitution of a similar thing." For example, in diseases of the skin they employed remedies used in erysipelas, while in affections of the upper limbs they resorted to treatment which had been found effectual in affections of the lower limbs.

Their horror of formal or deductive reasoning was so intense that they claimed that one should observe treatment at the same time as the disease. To observe a case of pleurisy was merely to observe the blood-letting which should cure the patient, so that instead of using the word *indication* they used the phrase *observation of phenomena*. Now, in what did their observation of pleurisy consist? In simply adding up the sum total of the characteristic symptoms, which they called a concurrence of symptoms. The Empirics were careful to avoid searching for the aetiology of disease, consequently for them anatomy was superfluous and several among them wrote books to demonstrate its uselessness. On the other hand they were careful to search for "second causes", that is to say, those conditions in which disease develops.

Daremberg is very severe in his criticism of the Empiric school, while Haeser is certainly more just and admits that it rendered considerable service to the practice of medicine. Thus, its practitioners remarked that diseases were composed of a series of symptoms—a concurrence of symptoms—which distinguished them from simple discomforts such as heat, swelling, pain, cough and so forth. And, as has already been pointed out, they were careful to take into particular consideration those symptoms which to them appeared the most important.

The Empirics did not change the nomenclature of diseases and retained that of the Dogmatic school; they more particularly based their practice on observations carefully written and for this reason they principally studied those which had been published by renowned practitioners. For example, they greatly appreciated the clinical observations that are to be found in the Hippocratic Collection. Observations made by several physicians together appeared to them better than the case-history reported by a single physician, and they did not trouble themselves much as to who the physicians were, a fact which gives evidence of their impartiality.

Among the most celebrated Empirics, Zeuxis, and more especially Heracleides of Tarentum, are to be mentioned. The latter wrote a treatise on pharmacology which was greatly appreciated at the time; he is said to have been a pupil of Glaucias and was dubbed the Prince of the Empirics. He was likewise skilled in surgical science. Celsus and Caelius Aurelianus have preserved some of his precepts, notably the way in which opium should be administered. Caelius Aurelianus also describes the treatment that Heracleides followed in cases of phrenitis, intestinal occlusion and so forth, and also diseases of the eye, in which he was very skilful. Caelius Aurelianus also tells us that he wrote a commentary on Hippocrates in four books, in which a number of obscure terms employed by the Father of Medicine were explained. Another book by Heracleides referred to by Caelius Aurelianus was entitled *De Internis Passionibus*, and it is known that he also wrote a treatise on the pulse contradicting the book of Herophilus on the same subject.

Among other members of the Empiric school should be mentioned Apollonius, a contemporary of Zeno; Apollonius Biblas (180–160 B.C.), who wrote a treatise on intestinal parasites; and Zopyrus, a contemporary of King Mithridates, whose pupil Poseidonius wrote a commentary on Hippocrates' book on the *Articulations*, a book on epilepsy and a large work in twenty-nine books against the teachings of Herophilus. This may perhaps be the same referred to by Rufus in his book on the plague. Another noted Empiric was Aelius Promotus, who wrote a book on pharmacology, of which a few fragments have come down to us. During the first century of the Christian era the most noted Empirics were Heras, of Cappadocia; Menodotus, of Nicomedia, against whom Galen wrote several works which are lost; and lastly Theodas, of Laodicea. Haeser is of the opinion that Marinus and his pupil Quintus, the celebrated anatomist, may also be regarded as members of the Empiric school, as well as Satyrus Pelops of Smyrna, who was also distinguished in the science of anatomy. And Sextus Empiricus who lived during the fifth century also belonged to this sect.

ASCLEPIADES (100 B.C.). HIS MEDICAL SYSTEM. After having reached a great development under the first Lagids, the School of Alexandria was not long in breaking up under King Ptolemy Physcon, whose tyranny caused a great number of distinguished physicians and other learned men to flee. The Greek genius whose light began to become dim in Egypt was then about to change to a new field and to search, far from the Nile, a more fertile soil for its development. But, what is remarkable, it was no longer Asia Minor, the kingdom of the Ptolemies, nor even Great Greece, the country of the Hellenes, that was to be the scene of a new blossoming of science and thought. This was to take place in an enemy country, at Rome, which had subjugated Greece and now began to be conquered by its high civilization. And in point of fact, although the Roman people spoke Latin, the aristocracy were perfectly conversant with Homer's tongue, which was as familiar to them as their maternal idiom. The patricians and the rich plebeians were already fully aware of the advantages to be derived from a more refined culture. Then too, the Latin race was very closely allied to the Hellenic race and for a long time had been subjected to the influence of such Greek colonies as Tarentum, Cumae, Naples, and so forth. The ancient Roman pride revolted from time to time against these innovations, and physicians and rhetoricians had once been banished from the Eternal City. But this had occurred during a temporary storm, and Cato the Elder occupied himself during the last years of his green old age in learning the language of the men whom his austerity denounced.

Asclepiades was the founder of the movement with which we are about to deal. It is evident that in every respect he was no ordinary man, and Daniel Le Clerc points out that the testimony of antiquity was very favourable to him. Pliny, that most scathing censor of physicians, is compelled to recognize—in spite of the bitter criticisms he makes—that Asclepiades was possessed of great eloquence and in many ways happily reformed the practice of medicine of his contemporaries.

Asclepiades was born in Asia Minor, a country which furnished the majority of the eminent physicians of the Graeco-Roman period. He saw the light of day at Prusa, a city of Bithynia, and studied medicine under Cleophantus who, besides teaching him the systems of Herophilus and the Dogmatic school, pointed out the great benefits which may be derived in disease from the exhibition of wine suitably used. Asclepiades, like nearly all the great practitioners of antiquity, was also well versed in the study of *belles-lettres*, so much so that he could occasionally resort to the oratorical art. If we are to believe Pliny, he only took up medicine at Rome because he found that his original profession was not sufficiently lucrative. Hear what the Latin writer has to say on the subject. "Asclepiades came to Rome, as a great many of his compatriots did, in order to accumulate a larger fortune than he could in his own country, and upon his arrival he began to teach rhetoric, but, not finding he could make enough money, he decided to try the practice of medicine. At this time he had no medical knowledge whatsoever, but he thought that his eloquence, combined with some study, would enable him to impose himself upon the Roman public and that the best means of doing this and to enhance his reputation was to oppose the practice of Archagathus, who was a prominent practitioner at the time. But the prestige of Archagathus was on the wane because of his cruel methods of treatment. Asclepiades also rejected many treatments employed by other physicians which he considered as more harmful than useful."

According to Pliny, the practices condemned by Asclepiades were as follows. Firstly, certain physicians literally suffocated their patients under heavy bedclothing in order to produce sweating at all costs, or else actually roasted them near a hot fire or broiled them in the full rays of the midday sun. Secondly, he condemned a very ancient method for curing quinsy by introducing a certain instrument into the throat in order to dilate this passage, an operation requiring much skill and time. Thirdly, he condemned astringent emetics and purgatives, which injured the stomach without doing any real good to the patient. If he did resort to emetics he usually gave them after supper, and for opening the bowels he usually made use of enemata. Lastly, Asclepiades did not believe that there were any specific medications for the liver, kidneys or lungs; in other words that there were any specific remedies for the various organs of the body.

Galen, who has given us the ideas of Asclepiades in great detail, points out that the system of this physician was entirely based on the teachings of Epicurus. This means, according to his way of thinking, that the human body, like any other matter, is composed of small unchangeable and indivisible atoms. Galen also tells us that, according to Asclepiades, the soul itself is made up of these small bodies, but in a very subtle state. From all this it is evident that his doctrines ended in pure mechanism. He ridiculed the vital properties that were admitted by the Dogmatic school; that is to say, the power of living bodies to discriminate between what was useful to them and what was harmful, appropriating the useful and rejecting the harmful. In short, Asclepiades wished to explain everything and simplify everything, and he thus rejected the important discovery, according to which the tissues of the human body select only such foods as suit them. However paradoxical this teaching may appear, it nevertheless existed, as well as the theory of the curative virtue of Nature, which called forth the sneers of the Methodists. It is to be noted that this period of medical history is one of those which clearly show the danger of trying to explain everything simply and rejecting all that seems vague or indefinite.

A very curious passage is to be found in Caelius Aurelianus, giving us more detail than does Galen concerning the bases upon which the system of Asclepiades rested. It is evident that the ideas of this physician were taken in their entirety from Epicurus, but with the difference that atoms were called molecules. The qualities of bodies depended, according to him, on the arrangement, shape and size of the atoms, and as a comparison he took silver, which is white when in a block and black when it is in filings. Nature was merely the *ensemble* of atoms, to which movement must be added; Nature is blind and Asclepiades says that one will be deceived in believing that good will be derived from what one calls Nature, because often she will be harmful. He absolutely denied the critical days of Hippocrates, and did not believe that diseases had a regular evolution. And he added that time—meaning a given number of days for a disease to undergo its evolution—had no power in itself, nor had the will of the gods; it was the physician who by his skill and address should make himself master of the situation. Since Asclepiades did not believe in the regular course of diseases he was of opinion that the physician should intervene energetically, and he ridiculed the passiveness of Hippocrates and the Dogmatic school, saying " the practice of the ancient physicians was merely a meditation on death ".

And now comes his theory of the causes of health and disease! Asclepiades states that the human body remains in its natural state as long as matter is freely absorbed between the pores—the interatomic spaces—so that health results from a correct proportion of pores in relation to the matter which they should absorb and allow to pass. Death is the result of a disproportion between the pores and matter. The most common accident is obstruction of these pores, which, according to Asclepiades, produces phrensy, lethargy, pleurisy, high fever and pain. If the pores are too oblique, the result will be the production of fainting, languor, exhaustion and so forth, while extreme emaciation and hydropsy are the result of extreme dilatation of the pores. Hunger is engendered by opening of the large pores of the stomach and abdomen, while thirst is due to opening of the smaller ones. Finally, from a rather obscure passage in Caelius Aurelianus, it would appear that Asclepiades admitted a third cause of disease, namely a disturbance or confusion of the body juices, or the mixture of liquid matter with the spirits. But this was an *antecedent* cause and not a *conjoint*, that is to say, a *near* cause. He explained intermittent fever as follows. The quotidian is produced by the retention of the largest of all the atoms, the tertian by that of the medium atoms and the quartan by that of the smallest.

Asclepiades' therapeutics were not as original as he maintained, for other physicians had already shown the excellent results obtained by gymnastics, massage, and hydrotherapy. As to the good effects of wine, Pliny tells us he derived this from the teaching of his master Cleophantus. In his writings he considers the three principal means of cure that he speaks of as gestation, friction, and wine. Friction included massage as it was practised by the ancients ; gestation consisted in the patient being transported in a boat, carriage, litter and so forth; the use of wine needs no explanation.

Instead of using gestation at the end of a disease, he employed it even during the most marked pyrexia and from the very onset of the disease, because his maxim was to cure fever by fever and by exhausting the patient's strength. As to friction, it should be recalled that Asclepiades used it for dropsy and even pretended that insane patients could be made to sleep by massage. Asclepiades wrote much on this method, but, what is most extraordinary and not in accordance with the knowledge he had obtained from the gymnasts, he did not recommend exercise for people in health, saying that it was quite unnecessary. This absurd idea seems to have been taken from Erasistratus. He gave wine in febrile cases (providing that the temperature had lowered slightly) and filled his insane patients with it to the point of drunkenness, claiming that by this means he could produce sleep. In cases of lethargy, he gave wine for a different motive, in order to excite and awaken the senses, while at the same time he used strong odoriferous substances such as vinegar, castoreum and rue. He often added sea water to wine, believing that this mixture would be more diffusible on account of the salt it contained, and ordered large quantities of wine to be taken in cases of catarrh.

In diarrhoea he prescribed the use of cold water, probably in order to constrict the pores ; as to food, it would seem from a passage in Celsus and another in Caelius Aurelianus, that he allowed his patients to eat freely after he had thoroughly exhausted them and as soon as the temperature showed a tendency to drop.

Since Asclepiades banished from his practice the use of many of the medicaments used by his colleagues, many of these latter maintained that he used no drugs at all, but Scribonius Largus calls them liars and says that this was only true in the case of acute diseases and not for chronic affections.

# CHAPTER IX

## THE METHODIC SECT. THEMISON AND THESSALUS. THE PNEUMATIC SECT. THE ECLECTICS AND COMPILERS

Methodism was founded by Themison of Laodicea (123–43 B.C.), who practised medicine at Rome during the reign of Augustus, and from the time of this physician it has borne the name which characterizes it, because its creator thought to have discovered a method by which medicine was made easier to understand and practise; perhaps also because in this system everything was much more regularly ordered than in Dogmatism.

Themison paid little attention to the causes of disease; what concerned him most was what diseases had in common with each other. Having decided this, he maintained that all morbid processes had two special causes, namely the constriction and the relaxation of the pores of the organism, which in reality were merely the *laxum* and *strictum* renewed from Greek teaching. There was also a third, or mixed, kind, which was derived partially from the *laxum* and partially from the *strictum*. Another very important change made by him was the division of diseases into two classes, namely acute and chronic. Themison distinguished three periods in the evolution of disease, which are the same as those given by Hippocrates, namely a period of increase, a period of full development, and a period of decline. Now, it was thought quite enough to know whether the affection was acute or chronic, and in what period it was, in order to treat it, and so Themison gave as a definition of medicine "a method which leads to the knowledge of what diseases have in common".

Themison had the greatest contempt for all obscure questions pertaining to the art of medicine, whose importance had been anticipated by the Dogmatics, although they were unable to understand and explain it. His system certainly was akin to that of the Empirics, but he separated from them inasmuch as he admitted the value of reasoning. In other words, the system of the Methodics was nothing else than a rational system founded on theory and on a basis that reason alone could furnish. Themison differed from the Dogmatics in therapeutics principally in that he derived his indications for treatment entirely from the type of disease present, and he systematically neglected the aetiological treatment which played so large a part in the Hippocratic writings. The age of the patient, his nationality and mode of life, and the season, troubled him little, and the same may be said of the region of the body afflicted by disease. Although Themison was the pupil of Asclepiades and derived inspiration from him, there was some difference between the two, as may be seen by reading Caelius Aurelianus and Galen. While Asclepiades admitted that the pores were inter-atomic spaces, Themison paid no attention to their nature or their arrangement; he said that the pores were not evident, though he was obliged to admit their existence in order to explain the production of sweat. On the other hand, although Asclepiades had admitted that in principle all diseases are due to a disproportion between the pores, he nevertheless did not fail to base his theory, as did Hippocrates and the Dogmatics, on the properties properly belonging to each disease, because he did not believe that it was possible to found all treatment on a single principle. Themison, with his coarser intellect, dared to take this bold step, and from his time on the Methodics only concerned themselves with what diseases had in common, without taking their differences into consideration.

In spite of these dissimilarities of doctrine, Themison's medical conduct towards his patients was practically the same as that of his master, Asclepiades. Caelius Aurelianus admits this, and gives the following reasons: "Themison was still entangled in the errors of Asclepiades and the Methodic sect was at the time in its infancy or perhaps not even yet formed." It is to be recalled that Themison founded Methodism rather late in life, and that he did not have the time to introduce those changes in his therapeutics that his doctrine required. Caelius Aurelianus reproaches him for having given cold water as a drink to his patients after having bled them, which in reality, in accordance with the principles of the sect, was employing two medicinal procedures having a contrary action. Caelius also reproaches Themison for purging with senna in cases of asthma, and with aloes dissolved in water in lethargy. Themison also purged with senna in catalepsy, and to this drug he also added castoreum. His practice also differed from that of the other Methodics in respect of food, exercise, baths and the use of bleeding, leeches and cupping. Dioscorides gives us a rather interesting anecdote of this physician. It would appear that, having been bitten by a supposedly rabid dog, he cured himself with considerable difficulty and after much suffering, and Caelius also tells us that on account of his former sad experience he would develop attacks of hydrophobia as soon as he attempted to write about this affection.

If we are to believe Juvenal, who says : "*Quot Themison aegros autumno occiderit uno*," the medical system of Themison did not prevent him from killing a good many patients. However, Themison certainly enjoyed a very great reputation, as we know from Pliny, who calls him *summus auctor*. As immediate disciples Caelius mentions Proculus and Eudemus. According to him Eudemus administered enemata of cold water to patients suffering from the so-called cardiac disease. Tacitus also mentions a certain Eudemus, physician to the famous Messalina, who composed a number of secret remedies in order to impress his patients with his skill.

THESSALUS (A.D. 60). Thessalus, who lived some fifty years after Themison, introduced many more changes in the system invented by Asclepiades. He enjoyed great reputation in his day, according to Pliny the Elder, but his extraordinary vanity and self-satisfaction spoiled the real talent with which he was endowed. He said that the *Aphorisms* of Hippocrates were a tissue of lies, and stated that all physicians who had lived before him had done nothing useful, and he ordered that upon his tomb should be engraved the words "the conqueror of physicians".

Though in reality he had only distorted the teachings of his master Themison, he boasted that he had created an entirely new medical system. Galen is very severe in his judgment on Thessalus, and tells us that he was of low extraction, that his father was a wool-carder at Tralles, the place of his birth, and that he was brought up by women. Galen also states that he retained, on account of this humble origin, a servile character, for he was humble before the great while with his colleagues he was insolent to the highest degree. He obtained a practice among the rich patricians by the accommodating way in which he treated them, and Galen contrasts his behaviour with the proud independence of the ancient physicians, saying that they commanded their patients as a general commanded his soldiers, while Thessalus obeyed his as a slave his master. If the patient wanted a bath Thessalus acquiesced ; if he wished to take cold drinks, ice was ordered. However, Galen makes the very just remark that Thessalus had many imitators.

When Thessalus went abroad in the streets of Rome he was always accompanied by numerous disciples and patients whom he had cured. Pliny says that " there never was a mountebank appearing in public with a larger company than that which usually followed Thessalus ". The number of his disciples was all the greater from the fact that he promised to teach them medicine in six months ! In reality, Methodism had greatly simplified medicine, at least in appearance, and had dissipated the belief that this science was the most difficult of all. Hence it had a great success among the slothful and mediocre minds which always form the majority in any profession.

The following are the changes that Thessalus introduced into Methodism, according to Galen : " Thessalus," he says, " changed some things in the system of Themison and Asclepiades, because these practitioners believed that health resulted from symmetry of proportion of the pores, and re-establishment of health after sickness was due to the return to symmetry of pores which had become disproportioned. Thessalus believed that in order to cure a disease the condition of the pores in the diseased part should be entirely changed, and from this theory is derived the word ' metasyncrisis ' which signifies a change in the pores." Thessalus regarded mustard and in general all the acrid and hot simples as metasyncritic drugs. Dioscorides also gave them this name, because, he said, they possess powerful properties of attraction or for changing the condition of the pores. For that matter this term is used by Galen and Aëtius, although they were not Methodists. Thessalus also was the first distinctly to adopt the three days' abstinence with which the cure of all diseases was begun, and this was followed by all the later Methodists. Thessalus absolutely condemned the use of purgatives, and this proscription became an article of faith in the Dogmatic creed. As a reason for this he gives the following explanation : " Let us take an athlete, that is to say the strongest and the healthiest man that can be found, and let a purgative be given him. Now, in spite of the fact that all the parts of the body are healthy, we will see that what is expelled by the medicament will be corrupted. Hence the medicament has changed into a corrupted matter that which in the first place was not corrupted." And he adds : " The physicians of the Hippocratic sect are foolish not to see that when they wish to purge the patient of his bile, they purge him of his pituit, and as soon as they attempt to evacuate the pituit they cause bile to be expelled ; therefore purgatives can only be harmful since their effect is exactly contrary to what is desired." We shall again refer to the doctrines of Thessalus when giving a summary of the *De Morbis Acutis et Chronicis* of Caelius.

After Thessalus, the ancient writers refer to a Methodist of great note, Philumenus, fragments of whose writings have been handed down to us by Caelius, Aëtius of Amida (A.D. 502–75), and Alexander of Tralles (A.D. 525–605). Other followers of Methodism were Aelius Promotus, Magnus, Mnaseas, Proculus, Antipater, Eudemus, Olympiacus, Apollonius, Attalus, and so forth, but their names alone have come down to us.

In order better to concentrate on the study of the Methodists living during the first century of our era, we have not yet referred to other sects which developed towards the end of the first century in opposition to the theories of Themison and his disciples. Although these movements were unsuccessful they nevertheless are of considerable importance, because Methodism, on account of its simplicity and the ease with which it was acquired, resulted, as we have already pointed out, in a very large following. But its gross mechanism and all that was adventurous and false in its theories could not long escape thoughtful minds. On the other hand, the ideas of Hippocrates had lost too much for them to be re-adopted in their original form. In these circumstances it was to philosophy that the new sects turned for their guide, but instead of Epicureanism they adopted the teachings of the Stoics. Zeno's theories had been accepted by all, and Seneca by his writings had popularized them in Rome and they enjoyed a consideration that was usually refused to the conceptions of Epicurus. The tendency was not yet towards monism, nor especially to materialism. Man had hardly come out of barbarism and reduced everything to terms of himself, that is, to a rather childish anthropomorphism, and was therefore not disposed to be long content with a doctrine which was far ahead of the time. It is true that Epicureanism had as followers many persons without principle and without morals, but the enterprising and bold minds, those that put an inert mass in motion and force it to follow a given direction, stood (with a few brilliant exceptions, such as Lucretius and Favorinus) for Stoicism and the rival sect. The theory of the Pneuma, the igneous spirit which animates alike the universe and each particular body—that which is called the universal soul—furnished an excellent means for avoiding collision with Solidism or Humorism, and it was this theory that gave the name of the Pneumatic School to the partisans of Athenaeus (69 B.C.), of Cilicia.

Athenaeus appears to have been a very distinguished physician whose knowledge, according to Galen, embraced almost the entire field of medical science. He believed that the pneuma put in motion the formative elements, namely cold and heat, and the plastic elements, namely cold and dampness. Its normal or abnormal action created physiological or morbid phenomena. This conception reminds us singularly of the teachings of Barthez and his disciples of the school of Montpellier, in the latter part of the XVIIIth and the beginning of the XIXth century. Although it sharply opposed what was too absolute in the Methodists, yet it conceded so much to the doctrines of this sect that Athenaeus has often been regarded as a disciple of Themison.

Those fragments that have been preserved by Aëtius and especially by Oribasius, although greatly mutilated, nevertheless show that Athenaeus was possessed of a brilliant mind and was an excellent practitioner. As a disciple of Athenaeus,

Galen refers to Magnus of Ephesus who was the Palace Archiater during the reign of Hadrian. Magnus wrote a book the loss of which is most regrettable because he therein set forth the changes and discoveries made in medicine from the time of Themison.

The disciples of Athenaeus were very greatly attached to the doctrine of their master, and Galen, in a jesting way, says that they would have betrayed their country sooner than they would have given up the principles of their sect. Yet it is to be pointed out that Agathinus of Sparta (A.D. 90) gave the lie to this assertion by founding a new medical school, that of the Eclectics, which, as the name indicates, was attached to no sect and adopted every good theory, no matter where found. There is in existence a very important fragment on diseases of the skin by one of these Eclectics, by name Herodotus. Rufus of Ephesus (A.D. 100) was the most celebrated of the time. Unfortunately we know but little concerning this great physician, almost all of whose writings have perished. His treatise on the pulse is about the only one that has come down to us, and is based on the doctrines of Herophilus and Erasistratus. Without wasting time in idle generalizations, Rufus gives the position of the heart, its movements, and the variations of the pulse according to the patients, and so forth. The pulse of the newly born is composed of two short beats, that is to say a short systole followed by a short diastole; the pulse in older children is a smoothly running stream; in the adult it is like a spondee, while in elderly people the systole is twice as long as the diastole. At the beginning of a fever the pulse is small and depressed; at the onset of disease the diastole is longer than the systole; at the phase of full development the systole and diastole are equal, while at the phase of decline the systole is much longer than the diastole. In phrensy the pulse is small but strong, while on the contrary in lethargy it is full; in cardiac disease the pulse is even smaller than in phrensy, but is stronger; at the same time it is irregular because the pneuma which, according to the disciples of Athenaeus, produces dilation of the arteries, distends the pulse in an irregular way. Rufus also refers to slow pulse, frequent pulse, and so forth. In speaking of apostemata (tumours) Rufus remarks that some of them are happily modified by the occurrence of fever, and he regrets that the physician is unable to cause fever for this reason. It is possible that he observed the favourable influence of erysipelas on certain malignant neoplasms, as has been done of late years in case of sarcoma.

Archigenes of Apameia (A.D. 48–117) frequently referred to by Caelius Aurelianus, belonged to the same sect, and, like Rufus, he enjoyed a great reputation. Galen says that he was endowed with great talent and had a fine mind, but that he was too much given to subtlety.

Alexander of Tralles (A.D. 525–605) also speaks highly of him. Archigenes wrote a treatise on the pulse upon which Galen made commentaries, but both of these works have been lost. Archigenes also made a great distinction between diseases, which was of capital importance, admitting that they were either primary or secondary. We also know that he gave much attention to febrile affections, the various phases of diseases, and that he wrote upon the effects of castoreum and hemlock, but by a study of the fragments of his writings that have been handed down to us by Aëtius it becomes evident that Archigenes frequently copied from the writings of Aretaeus (A.D. 30–90) without mentioning his name.

At this point mention should be made of Aretaeus, that distinguished physician whose renown at the present time is so great, which was not the case in antiquity. His independent mind prevented him from belonging to any one of the numerous medical coteries which flourished in his day, and consequently his works were neglected by the members of these, that is by practically the entire medical profession of the time. We know very little of him, excepting that he was born in Cappadocia. Caelius Aurelianus does not speak of him and Galen, who is so prolix in his details about the adversaries of Dogmatism, passes him by in silence. It seems probable that he lived in the time of Vespasian, and perhaps even of Nero also. He wrote a very remarkable work in eight books on acute and chronic diseases, which is all the more important to us because it is almost intact. The doctrines therein set forth are extremely mixed, but the influence of Methodism and Pneumatism is marked. His treatment was active and he was prone to exhibit drastic purgatives.

The first four books are given up to the discussion of acute diseases and their description is very remarkable, especially that of pulmonary phthisis, but taken as a whole there is no fundamental difference from those found in Caelius Aurelianus. It should be remembered that Aretaeus was the first to refer to diphtheria of the pharynx and larynx under the name of syriac ulcer.

Dioscorides (A.D. 40–90) wrote on pharmacology. His work, which gave him his great reputation, has fortunately come down to us intact. He was born at Anazarba near Tarsus, the capital of Cilicia, a city essentially learned and possessed of a medical school. He may be regarded as the father of pharmacy. He seems to have lived during the time of Nero and Vespasian, and for many years followed the Roman armies as an army surgeon. These long trips at least had the advantage of familiarizing him with a large number of rare drugs. It is very probable that he published his work in the year 77 or 78 of our era, that is to say, shortly before Pliny, who does not quote Dioscorides, probably because they were contemporaries. Dioscorides' work consists of five books, in which are described very methodically remedies taken from the animal, vegetable, and mineral kingdoms; practically all drugs used by the ancients are found therein.

But it is true that Dioscorides was preceded in the description of drugs by a number of physicians whose writings have been lost, for example Cratevas, Andreas, and so forth, without counting Theophrastus (370–285 B.C.), the most ancient of them all. Dioscorides is simple in style, but without elegance, and from time to time one finds barbarous words taken, for example, from the Celtic or from the Thracian. The following is a summary of the work: (1) Aromatics, oils, ointments, balsams and extracts. (2) Animals, honey, milk, fat, wheat, vegetables, mustard and so forth. (3) and (4) Roots and seeds. (5) Wine and minerals. He gives the synonyms of the drugs and the country where they are found and it has been said that his botanical descriptions are so exact that the great botanist Tournefort, during his travels in the Orient, was able to recognize a large number of plants described by Dioscorides.

# CHAPTER X

## SORANUS. CAELIUS AURELIANUS AND HIS *DE MORBIS ACUTIS ET CHRONICIS* LIBRI VIII

Methodism, in spite of such opposition, continued, however, to be the most important of the medical sects. During the IInd century its followers included the greater number of medical practitioners, at least at Rome, and the reaction started against it by Galen bore no fruit until a long time after the death of this illustrious restorer of the humoral doctrines. During the IInd century Methodism was fortunate enough to have a champion of great value in Soranus of Ephesus, as well as Caelius Aurelianus, whose works are merely an abbreviation of the writings of the physician of Ephesus.

SORANUS (A.D. 98–117). This learned physician came from Asia Minor, a country which gave birth to the greater number of the illustrious physicians of antiquity, as has already been said. Galen tells us that he was born at Ephesus, and it would appear from various passages of his works that he studied medicine at Alexandria at a time when this city still had the most celebrated school of medicine. He went to Rome because this offered the best centre for his activities and talent, but it must not be forgotten that, as we shall show in the chapter devoted to the practice of medicine at Rome, the then capital of the world was far from being a centre of scientific thought. In this respect the large cities of Gaul and Spain were far better endowed.

Soranus became famous during the reigns of Trajan and Hadrian; not only was he considered by the Methodists as the most illustrious representative of their sect, but he was held in great esteem by his colleagues in general. Galen, the most violent enemy of Methodism, is obliged to render justice to Soranus and excepts him from the outrageous epithets which he showers upon Thessalus and Themison. In certain parts of his works he even lauds treatments that Soranus used in various diseases, and he contributed not a little to the glorification of his rival to posterity. The celebrity of Soranus lasted for many centuries, and existed even in the time of Suidas, and as late as the XIth century; Gariopontus, one of the famous physicians of the school of Salerno, appears to have been inspired by different passages from his works. "Endowed," says Hahn, "with an unprejudiced and judicious mind, with good sense, and an impartiality such as no other physician of antiquity displays, excepting perhaps Celsus, and with all this the possession of a great talent of observation, Soranus was able to take advantage of the observations and ideas of his predecessors, as well as of those of his adversaries. And he showed himself also an excellent clinician."

From all we are able to ascertain, Soranus was the greatest gynaecologist of antiquity, and his practice of obstetrics was very remarkable. He was also celebrated as a surgeon, and this reputation was well deserved, as is shown by his excellent little treatise on fractures and dislocations that has been handed down to us by Nicetas. On the other hand it should be recalled that Aëtius and Paulus Aeginata borrowed much from his writings. But antiquity praised him above all for his talents as a physician, and, although unfortunately his most celebrated work is lost to us, yet we can obtain an idea of it from the bad Latin translation made by Caelius Aurelianus—a physician about whom we know for certain neither the time when he lived nor from what country he came. What does seem perfectly clear is that, whatever his status as physician, he was at any rate a translator of not only one but of several works of Soranus.

Caelius Aurelianus appears to have been born at Sicca, in Numidia, a supposition derived from the appellation of Siccensis given him by both the Leyden manuscript and Lorsch's Codex. It is probable that he was a contemporary of Galen, or came soon after him. Haeser is of the opinion that he practised medicine for some time at Rome, and Caelius himself tells us that he professed medicine and that the work which we shall consider was dedicated to Bellicus, one of his pupils, whom he calls the most brilliant of his disciples. It is evident that Caelius was a poor Greek scholar, and for this reason his Latin translation of Soranus's writings is a miserable literary production. It is very probable that the writings of Soranus were much more complete and possessed of a greater clinical sense than the translations of Caelius would lead us to suppose. The latter probably took it upon himself to exclude many interesting passages and important discussions for fear of making his book too long.

On the other hand, although Soranus was the principal inspirer of Caehus, we do not believe that he was the only one, for the Latin writer refers to Thessalus, Themison, and other physicians belonging to their sect (such as Asclepiades, Praxagoras, Erasistratus, Herophilus, Heracleides and others), whose ideas on many points of pathology he has preserved. From this point of view the undigested compilation of Caelius Aurelianus is of the greatest importance for those wishing to obtain an exact idea of medicine in antiquity. The Latin of Caelius is deplorable, to such an extent that Daremberg believed him to be a contemporary of Cassiodorus ; but Guardia and Haeser are not of this opinion, and point out various passages in which Sextus Empiricus speaks of the Pseudo-Pliny who borrowed from Caelius. Hence it may be supposed that he lived in the IVth, and not the Vth century after Christ.

Caelius divides his work into two parts, the first being composed of three books. The first part treats of acute diseases, the second of chronic affections. The Methodists appear to have given the best description of the latter processes. Diseases are divided into those produced by constriction of the pores, secondly those produced by relaxation, and thirdly diseases of a mixed kind, that is to say, those in which certain parts of the body are relaxed and others contracted. In what is to follow we have carefully summarized the principal types of acute diseases comprised in these three classes, namely phrensy (ataxic fever), lethargy (adynamic fever), the result of constriction of the pores, next the famous cardiac disease, a very vague affection, which Caelius, like Soranus, considers due to relaxation of the pores ; as to pneumonia and pleurisy, they are comprised in the mixed type. Among the chronic affections due to constriction of the pores Caelius places paroxysmal cephalagia, vertigo, asthma, epilepsy, mania, melancholia, jaundice, amenorrhoea, paralysis, catarrhs, phthisis, colics, dysentery. Hydropsy belongs to the mixed type. Diarrhoea and haemorrhagic and menstrual flux, when excessive, are all due to relaxation of the pores.

In the *strictum* type of disease the evacuations are suppressed and the diseased parts become swollen and hard. On the other hand, in the case of flux the diseased regions become softer, more relaxed and thinner. When these symptoms were very marked the Methodists were easily able to get out of their difficulties, but when the clinical picture was less accentuated, they " saved face " by hair-splitting discussions in which they appealed to secondary symptoms. Their description of diseases is generally short, but the principal symptoms are given with sufficient distinctness although many important data are given merely in a few lines or words. Prognosis and diagnosis are in general good, and in spite of the errors inherent in the Methodist doctrine there is less subtlety and more clinical reasoning than might have been hoped for.

Like all the disciples of Themison, Caelius lays special stress on the points in common between diseases. Being an enemy of subtleties, he avoids the definition of diseases, although in certain passages he gives those of Soranus, Themison and Thessalus, as well as those that had been given by celebrated physicians of other sects. In the case of the latter, however, it is rather to oppose them, persuaded as he is that no local disease properly speaking exists, and that the entire organism is diseased at the same time. Many times he points out that search for the organ principally diseased is a fruitless task. Thus, in speaking of phrensy, he says that some writers believe that the brain is involved, others the meninges, others again the heart or diaphragm, and that we must not tire our brains in this search. Then, too, he considers it useless to bother about all this, since the same treatment is quite proper in all diseases of the *strictum* type, no matter what part of the body is the seat of the disease.

In reality the Methodists had a fairly good therapeutical principle, in that they attempted to cure patients by the simplest means, especially those that are used in the state of health. The bedroom played a highly important part with them. The Methodists concerned themselves greatly with the air that the patient should breathe, and, since they considered all diseases as resulting either from constriction or relaxation of the pores, they attempted to procure a relaxing or constricting air according to the case. For example, in cases of phrensy, in which the pores are contracted, they placed the patient in a large and well-lighted and fairly well-heated room. In the cardiac disease, in which the pores are dilated, they placed the patient in very cool and darkened rooms, and from this point of view Caelius claims that the Egyptian *hypogea* would be excellent. When these were wanting the patient was often placed in a grotto. They covered the floor with branches of mastic tree, grape leaves, myrtle, willow and pomegranate, and from time to time sprinkled them with cool water. The patient was fanned with large palm leaves in order to keep the air around him fresh, for they said that more care should be taken of the air to be breathed than of the food to be eaten, because eating only takes place at intervals, while air is breathed unceasingly, and at the same time the subtle atoms of the air penetrate more easily between the pores than the grosser atoms of food.

Following the practice of Asclepiades, the Methodists took the greatest care of the kind of bed the patient had to lie on, at times prescribing a feather mattress, at others (when the pores were relaxed) a hard one. The amount of bed covering was fixed exactly according to the nature of the disease, and they even went so far as to prescribe the size of the bed.

We have already referred to the three days' fasting with which Thessalus commenced the treatment of any and every disease. The disciples of Themison, and Soranus himself, were meticulous in their classification of food and drinks according to their relaxing or constricting effect. Asclepiades, the real founder of Methodism, denied that there were any drugs having a particular action on a given organ, as hepatic, nephritic, etc.—in other words specifics. The writings of Caelius clearly show that Soranus fully agreed with this theory, which was accepted by the larger number of the Methodist sect. "These specific remedies have never been discovered by reasoning or attempting to penetrate what one calls occult causes," says Caelius, and he further remarks that no one can say that he has by chance found remedies which have given such results, as the Empirics maintained. Those they have professed to have found are so abominable and so far removed from those usually employed that it is difficult to see how their use can be recommended. And if they maintain that their remedies are the result of the experience of ancient physicians it is surprising that these therapeutists have recourse to these remedies instead of employing those general means of cure, such as air, sleep, waking, food, and so forth. Further on, referring again to these so-called specifics, Caelius says that many people have great confidence in them, although they are worthless, because they are often contrary to those that science prescribes. Nevertheless, Caelius himself recommends specific remedies in the case of intestinal parasites, but escapes the appearance of inconsistency by saying that the parasites form part of the body.

As has already been pointed out, Asclepiades, Thessalus and Themison were very much opposed to the use of purgatives, and Caelius, in referring to this question, when speaking of phrensy, reproaches Heracleides, the Empiric, for purging phrenetic patients with scammony. According to the Methodists, purgatives can only replace one disease by another, that is to say they replace constriction of the pores by dilation. But in hydropsy it would seem that Soranus employed purgative medication. Hence Caelius is obliged to admit its use, although regretting this concession to experience. He speaks of it with constraint and says that the true way of treating hydropsy should be to avoid drugs given by mouth, because they upset the bladder or else inflame and ulcerate the intestine; they spoil the stomach and are only good to cause anorexia and to increase thirst. For this reason hydrotherapy is to be preferred, and is to be employed in cases of severe anasarca, while one should try to prevent the body from again swelling. It is to be observed, however, that in this affection Caelius prescribes diuretics, which he usually discountenances, but here, again, it is clear that clinical observation had furnished irrefutable evidence of their value.

Caelius was no advocate of narcotics, and he says that if they are given in small doses they cause headache, while large ones produce death. However, from time to time he advises their use, principally that of a preparation made with syrup of poppies or of opium. This he prescribes in hemiplegia, but only as a constricting agent, to cause the bleeding vessel to contract.

He disapproved of the use of the cautery and regarded escharotics as both cruel and useless, stating that they upset the phase of full development of a disease and are quite useless when relaxation occurs. Among the relaxing treatments, diet and blood-letting are the most important, and it is to be remembered that the Methodists did not abuse the use of bleeding. When Caelius speaks of it he seems to mean that it should only be employed once during a disease, excepting in the case of mania. The Methodists resorted to wet cupping frequently. Their cups were usually made of copper and sometimes of glass, earthenware, or horn, and the opening was always small.

As constricting remedies Caelius especially recommends water, cold oil, vinegar, and decoctions of plaintain, myrtle, roses, poplar, and so forth. Severe sweating he treated with powdered chalk or calcinated alum. In diseases resulting from dilatation of the pores he ordered barley flour boiled in water, toasted bread dipped in vinegar, and small quantities of cold water.

By carefully reading Caelius one will be able to understand the famous *metasyncrisis* of Thessalus, a confused description of which is given by Galen. *Metasyncrisis* simply consists in renovating the pores of the organism, and its process is composed of several periods, which together form a cycle. This conception is to be found in part in the writings of the Hippocratic Collection. The first period was the reconstructive, consisting above all in the use of stimulating substances, such as pepper, mustard, cloves, wines, baths, gymnastics, massage, and the application of sinapisms. The second period consisted in the re-establishment of the strength that had been exhausted by the first. According to circumstances, either period might be first employed.

We know of no better way in which to make the Methodist doctrines understood than briefly to summarize the five principal acute diseases described by Caelius Aurelianus, namely phrensy and lethargy (which belong to the *strictum* type of disease), the cardiac disease due to *laxum*, and pneumonia and pleurisy which result from the mixed type. Phrensy, according to the ancient Greek physicians, was any febrile phenomenon accompanying ataxic manifestations. As Haeser points out, it certainly must have entered into many serious forms of typhoid fever, but this was not the only disease, for pneumonia and various other pyrexias accompanied by delirium, convulsions, and restlessness, must have been included under the name. Its chief characteristic was disturbance of the intelligence: *nomen igitur sumpsit a difficultate mentis.* The word phrensy is derived from the Greek *phren*, which signifies the diaphragm, and, in fact, this muscle was for a long time regarded as the seat of the intelligence, although Hippocrates had attempted to correct this error and attributed to the brain the function wrongly given to the diaphragm. The following is the definition given by Herophilus according to Demetrius: *nam Demetrius*, *Herophilum sequens*, *libro sexto quem de passionibus scripsit, hanc definiens, delirationem dixit vehementem, cum alienatione atque febre desinentem in interfectionem celerem aliquando et insanitatem.* What differentiated it from mania was the accompanying fever. Lastly, Caelius insists upon its essentially rapid progress. Asclepiades attributed it to a constriction of the pores of the membranes of the brain: *Asclepiades*, *primo libro de celeribus scribens passionibus*, *phrenitis*, *inquit*, *est corpusculorum statio sine obtrusione in cerebri membranis*, *frequenter sine sensu*, *cum alienatione et febribus.*

Caelius insists upon the intense constriction of the pores as Asclepiades had taught, and remarks that it is this intensity that makes the difference between disease and the slight constriction that may occasionally be observed in the healthy state. According to the Methodists, this very great change arising in the pores produces fever by disturbing the entire body. According to Asclepiades, constriction of the pores produced *sopor*, and it was thus that he explained the somniferous action of poppy. The symptoms of phrensy, as described by various writers of the Methodist sect, are as follows. In the first place there were the premonitory phenomena according to Asclepiades and the majority of the physicians of the other sects, but these hardly fitted in with the system of the Methodists, so that Thessalus and his disciples denied their existence, saying that in this so-called premonitory phase the disease was already constituted.

Neither did they believe that phrensy only occurred at certain determined periods of the year, for example, in autumn.

Those who admitted premonitory phenomena mention insomnia, headache, painful sensitiveness of the neck of the bladder during micturition, with a redness and a special look of the eyes. For Caelius all these simply signified that the meninges were the seat of disease, and consequently these morbid phenomena could be met with in other diseases than phrensy. However this may be, the disease when once declared offers the following clinical picture: a violent fever which reaches the surface of the skin with difficulty and a small, hard and rapid pulse. Nose-bleeding is frequent, sleep is disturbed, insomnia frequent, with a mild delirium. The patient remains on the back, the face is congested, and the urine scant and high-coloured; the patient frequently experiences dizziness and tinnitus aurium; occasionally there is praecordial distress, and palpitations occur without any cause. Caelius also mentions the possibility of intestinal disturbances. He indicates how to make the diagnosis of phrensy and to do this all the symptoms presented by the patient must be taken into consideration: *intelligimus phrenitim ex toto signorum concursu. Unum etenim singulare quicquam, ut est alienatio, vel febricula, non designat phreneticum, sed si multa concurrerint, quae nihil aliud quam passionem designent.* In order that there shall be phrensy a mental disturbance is not the only thing necessary; there must be fever, a small and rapid pulse, and carphology. After this, Caelius carefully explains each one of these terms, especially the last. He then refers to those affections which may simulate phrensy, namely mania, melancholia, pleurisy and pneumonia, and also poisoning from belladonna. Mania and melancholia are never accompanied by fever, while their progress is very much slower, and lastly they present phenomena peculiar to themselves which are not met with in phrensy. Thus the sadness of the patient is a peculiar trait of melancholia, as is the care with which he avoids others, his earthy complexion and so forth.

Yet one must not mistake for phrensy those fevers which may at times be accompanied by restlessness and delirium, though from the point of view of practice this is of little importance, because in all acute diseases with constriction of the pores treatment is the same. The distinction may be made by the local phenomena : *nam phreneticis atque furiosis caput magis, melancholicis stomachus patitur.* The hard, small and rapid pulse of phrensy is quite characteristic. Lethargy offers many points in common with phrensy and Caelius is absolutely categorical in this respect, namely that the ataxic phenomena are frequently replaced by adynamic phenomena and *vice versa*, but the face is paler, and more earthen in colour in lethargy. Lethargic patients look as if they were sleeping and they are not restless, but their respiration is not regular as it is in real sleep ; the pulse is more compressible and weaker than in phrensy.

For a long time physicians had been at a loss to know which organ was involved in phrensy, and opinions varied according to the writers as well as the sects. The Methodists did not admit local diseases and always resorted to the same treatment in acute diseases with constriction of the pores, hence they were not particularly interested in this question, as Caelius frankly states. He, however, does give the principal theories which were current on the subject. Some supposed that the disease was in the brain, either at the base or the convex part, while others upheld that the meninges were involved ; others still believed that the seat of the disease was in the heart or the pericardium, while yet others believed that phrensy was seated in the diaphragm : *aliqui igitur cerebrum pati dixerunt, alii ejus fundum sive basim . . . alii membranam, quae cor circumtegit ; alii arteriarum eam quam Graeci aorten appellant ; alii venam crassam . . . alii diaphragma.* And Caelius adds lightly : *nos igitur communiter totum corpus pati accipimus, etenim totum febre jactatur.*

These general remarks in respect of the therapeutics of the Methodists will show the reader the outline of their treatment in cases of phrensy. The patient was placed in a large, well-lighted, quiet room, moderately heated and well-aired, the walls bare of pictures and statues, while all bright colours were eliminated in order not to disturb the patient's imagination. The mattress was to be hard, so that the patient might keep quiet ; relaxation of the pores was to be obtained by keeping the patient awake and, of course, commencing the treatment with the three days' diet, while, should the pain be violent and the breathing difficult, the patient was to be bled according to the prescription of Thessalus, but more frequently recourse was had to cupping, preceded or not by scarification. The entire body was gently anointed ; and liquid food given on certain days of the week in order to maintain the patient's strength ; but wine was absolutely prohibited. In these acute diseases produced by constriction of the pores, a point was made not to overfeed the patient. Animals' brains and fresh-water fish were particularly indicated, but food was only given every other day. As may be seen, the Methodists adopted an expectant treatment in acute disease, which was just the opposite of the one adopted in the chronic maladies.

This was not always the plan followed by other sects, and on this point Caelius gives us some very important data. He says that Hippocrates is silent on the treatment of phrensy Praxagoras ordered active purgation when the patient was strong and if plethoric he resorted to blood-letting, choosing either a vein in the arm or one in the tongue. Caelius severely condemns this violent purgation and the acrid enemata prescribed by Praxagoras, and he believes that this treatment could only result in a relaxation of the pores. Erasistratus, in the fifth book of his treatise on *Fevers*, advises giving wine to which honey has been added, and he also resorted to intestinal derivation. In his treatise on *Acute Diseases*, Asclepiades condemns purgatives, enemata, and the application of vinegar and sinapisms to the head ; should the pain be violent he let blood, but he remarked that, although this was successful at Athens, at Rome it was more likely to be injurious, because the Romans were worn out with debauchery. Soranus ridicules this statement of Asclepiades, saying that what is useful in one place will be useful everywhere else.

Lethargy is treated in the second book of Caelius, and under this very vague name very different diseases were included, but all of them had this in common at a given stage, namely abolition of the functions of relation. Caelius points out that phrensy transforms into lethargy and that this may occur inversely. Lethargy is far more serious than phrensy.

The dulling of the senses in lethargy had been noted by all

the Dogmatics and Empirics. Caelius says that if, in phrensy, constriction of the pores becomes intense, the disease changes into lethargy, but if the pores become relaxed the contrary takes place. Soranus had noticed that drowsiness was never a good sign, so he opposed Asclepiades' opinion, which in this circumstance was often too optimistic, saying that this drowsiness is not beneficial to the patient and is a result of a depression of nervous force which is very apt to end in death. What shows this state of general weakness is the pulse, and, if it becomes depressed in cases of phrensy, this disease will change into lethargy.

Lethargy has been defined differently by other physicians; for them it was a general disturbance of the senses accompanied by high fever terminating in a very serious condition. This was the opinion of Herophilus, according to Demetrius. It would appear that Asclepiades did not trouble himself about the definition of lethargy, but Alexander of Laodicea did: *sed Alexander Laodicensis ex Asia secundum ipsum ait lethargiam esse subitam vel recentem passionem cum febribus et pressura atque sensuum jugi difficultate.* According to Athenaeus, it was a delirium accompanied by mental depression. In comparing phrensy with lethargy Asclepiades had indeed pointed out that in the former the patient was excited, while in the latter the mental disturbance was accompanied by sleep and mental depression. Briefly put, one was an upheaval of the cerebral functions, while in the other they became depressed or even entirely suppressed. In lethargy there is fever, which differentiates it from epilepsy.

Soranus says that lethargy is more frequently encountered in elderly people than in others, and he also notes the dilatation of the arteries from vaso-motor paralysis which he detected in the radial pulse, and is acute enough to describe the principal characters of the pulse, that is to say fullness, the loss of resistance to pressure and slowness of the cardiac beats.

In lethargy there is a known element—the result of a general disposition of the organism—namely the idiosyncrasy offered by certain phrenetic patients for lethargy. And there was a peculiar element, for example a very high fever which could only with difficulty rise to the surface of the body and thus escape.

The following are the symptoms differentiating lethargy

from other diseases. As we have said, fever, drowsiness, and a full but slow and compressible pulse, were the principal symptoms, and we have likewise given the definitions which distinguished epilepsy from phrensy. In poisoning from belladonna, the pulse was found very slow, but full; in cases of drowsiness produced by intestinal worms the pulse was thought to be hard and rapid, while peculiar gastric and intestinal disturbances were present.

The disciples of Asclepiades taught that lethargy could be either acute or chronic, and that it was due either to contraction or to dilatation of the pores. With other Methodists, Soranus supposed that lethargy, like phrensy, resulted from a disturbance of the entire body which made itself known by mental manifestations.

Caelius says that in lethargy it is difficult to begin the treatment by *diatrition*—the famous three-day diet—with which the treatment of all other diseases was begun, but it can be advantageously resorted to as soon as the lethargic condition is on the wane. The patient should be placed in a light room, moderately heated, and from time to time an attempt should be made to rouse him by calling his name into his ear, tickling or pricking him, and gently massaging the limbs. Fomentations of sweet oil should be applied to the head, while the bed coverings should be soft. One should not omit to give the patient drink. If the fever continues, blood should be let on the first day of *diatrition* or even during the three days. As soon as *diatrition* is begun, water or water slightly thickened is to be given, fomentations are to be placed all over the body, and when the three days of *diatrition* have passed liquid food is to be given. The patients are then allowed to sleep a little so that they may regain sufficient strength for *metasyncrisis* to take place. For constipation, enemata consisting of water with a little oil are to be given and, as in cases of phrensy, the head is to be shaved and scarified. The use of leeches on the head is also recommended if the scalp becomes tumified.

Caelius tells us that Diocles prescribed very violent medication in lethargy, as well as rough massage and sternutation. He also employed large amounts of vinegar. This practice was displeasing to the Methodists because among these medicaments some dilated the pores while others constricted them, and sternutation was supposed to cause violent perturbation to all the molecules of the body.

Praxagoras lauded liquid feeding, but according to the Methodists this was a mistake. Asclepiades maintained that many remedies given in phrensy were also proper in lethargy ; he resorted to sternutation by the use of strong odours in order to cause vibration of the meninges ; he applied sinapisms to the scalp to which vinegar had been added, while the patients were given drink three or four times a day.

Caelius next refers to a disease which the Greek authors call catalepsy : *Vicina atque similis est lethargiae passio, quam Graeci catalepsin appelant.* Its principal symptoms are an acute fever with aphonia, a dullness of all the senses, immobility of the entire body with the eyes open and fixed. He says that Hippocrates and Diocles called this affection aphonia, while Praxagoras named it the comatous affection, but, according to Caelius, this was not a new word, because Hippocrates had also employed it. Caelius points out that the majority of physicians had confused lethargy with catalepsy, but Asclepiades and his disciple, Chrysippus, had separated the two diseases. Magnus, Agathinus and Archigenes had also given excellent descriptions of catalepsy, according to Caelius, and it may be recalled that these physicians belonged to the Methodic sect. Briefly put, the symptoms given by Caelius show that catalepsy was a similar condition to lethargy, but that it was a symptom of various morbid processes.

Caelius tells us that *pleurisy* derives its name from the part of the organism which is the most diseased : *pleuritis a parte corporis quae magis patitur nomen sumpsit.* Its causes are many : *fit autem ex variis antecedentibus causis ut coetera passiones.* Nevertheless, traumata, drunkenness and violent bodily exercises are the most frequent causes. Caelius recalls the definition of pleurisy given by Aristotle, namely that it is a coction of liquids without condensation, but he does not accept this definition and gives the opinion held by Apollonius Mys, who belonged to the sect of Herophilus :—*pleuritis est communiter passio temporalis, atque celeris, secundum laterum membranas, quas hypezocotas vocant, atque inter earum carnem.* Asclepiades defined it as an efflux of humour occurring in a very short time within the thorax, accompanied by fever and 'vaulting' of the ribs. Caelius stresses this 'vaulting' produced by pleurisy. According to Soranus the disease is characterized by a severe pain in the side, a short, dry cough, high fever and a fluid collection in the pleura. The collection varies in nature from one case to another. According to Soranus this disease is more frequent in men and in elderly persons: *tussiculosa enim atque frigida senilis est aetas, quo intelligimus profecto hanc passionem pueros difficulter incurrere.*

It was found more frequent in cold than in warm seasons, and in respect of the pain, Caelius states that it may extend into the side of the neck and even down the arm on the diseased side. It may be fixed or mobile, and makes breathing difficult; the patient cannot lie on the back on account of the pain. Other symptoms given by Caelius are insomnia, restlessness, thirst and loss of appetite, all of which become exaggerated if the illness grows worse. Caelius states:—*mentis alienatiō, gutturis stridor, et sonitus interius resonans aut sibilans in ea parte quae patitur.* From this it is evident that Laënnec was not the first to listen to the chest in cases of pleurisy.

Caelius describes the sputum characteristic of empyema, when the contents of the pleura are emptied through the bronchial tubes. In a short paragraph he gives the symptoms indicating that the disease is turning to peri-pneumonia, or that a 'vomica' is to take place. In the first case the face changes, becoming manifestly injected, especially over the cheek bones, and this is followed by the development of nervous disturbances. When a vomica takes place in empyema, the pain persists, the patient loses strength, breathing becomes difficult and the pulse feeble. Caelius tells us that Herophilus maintained that it was the lung that was diseased in pleurisy, while Asclepiades, Diocles, Erasistratus and his disciples taught that the site of the disease was the pleura. Those who shared the opinion of Herophilus pointed out that there was nothing to show that an inflammatory tumour existed, as there was neither redness nor induration nor pulsation; the cough was due, they believed, to irritation of the pulmonary fibres. But Caelius is not of this opinion, for he says that tumefaction on the diseased side really exists, while the pain of pleurisy cannot be explained by a disease of the lung since this organ is without sensation. This is not true of the thoracic walls because their lining membranes are sensitive.

Empyema closely resembles pleurisy, but there is no fever, and breathing is simply interfered with without being superficial and difficult, as it is in pleurisy. If there is nasal catarrh with difficulty in breathing, thoracic pain and fever, these phenomena taken together quite closely simulate pleurisy. Since in the days of Caelius physicians did not possess the necessary instruments for the detection of physical signs, diagnosis was of course a difficult matter, but for all that Caelius gives certain differential signs, such as a severe and persistent pain on the diseased side, while the nature of the cough and of the sputum is not the same as in pneumonia.

Caelius recalls that Hippocrates controlled the pain by inhalations, but, if everything fails to relieve it and if it extends to the neck and down the arm, blood is to be let from the arm, while if pain remains localized in the chest emollient applications will suffice. Diocles resorted to blood-letting also and the exhibition of cathartics. He allowed young subjects to eat from the eleventh day on ; in summer he ordered cold food, and in winter hot. Praxagoras ordered an emulsion of pepper to which vinegar and occasionally wormwood were added. He waited until the fifth day before bleeding, provided that the weather was not cold, but he never resorted to this practice in elderly subjects or in those who had been weakened by the disease. Asclepiades also bled, but noted that this practice, which gave good results at Athens, often failed in Rome, especially in cases of pleurisy, and in his treatise on *Acute Diseases* he states that purgatives should not be resorted to, but rather enemata should be used. He allowed his patients to drink freely and to take food on the second and fourth day. In respect of this treatment Soranus remarks that the patient should always be bled when the affection is due to constriction of the pores, whether it be at Rome or anywhere else.

Peripneumonia (pneumonia) is, like pleurisy and lethargy, a disease of the entire organism,[1] but has a very marked

[1] This opinion is accepted to-day and is looked upon as the ultra-modern conception of this disease.

localization in the lung. It has the same aetiology as pleurisy: *perficiunt hanc passionem causae quae etiam pleuriticam faciunt.* It often occurs during pleurisy and sometimes develops during a severe cold or sore throat.

The Methodists do not seem to have been capable of giving a definition of pneumonia. According to Asclepiades and his disciples it was an effluxion with fever with an acute development, accompanied by tumefaction of the chest. Soranus states that it is a violent and acute constriction of the pores in the lungs, with sputum, thirst, and temporary fever. Other symptoms are anorexia, pain in the side with difficulty in lying on the affected side, congested eyes and cheek bones, dyspnoea with superficial and distressed breathing and rusty-coloured sputum. As is to be seen, little can be added to this symptomatology. The nervous disturbances of pneumonia, according to Caelius, are restlessness, insomnia and carphology. In those cases where recovery is to take place, these symptoms progressively subside, while, if death is to ensue, they increase in intensity.

As to the seat of the disease, Diocles placed it in the pulmonary veins, while, according to Erasistratus, it was in the arteries, and Praxagoras maintained that it was the posterior part of the lung that was involved. Herophilus believed that the entire lung was diseased. Asclepiades supposed that the site of the trouble was in the bronchial tubes, and lastly Apollonius maintained that the affection arose in both the arteries and the veins. But to Soranus is due the credit of maintaining that it was a general disease with a pulmonary localization. Caelius points out that in a disease in which the entire economy is involved it is useless to consider the localization from the point of view of treatment.

We conclude these remarks by mentioning a few other diseases, but first of all a word of explanation in respect of the word tumefaction, which frequently appears in the description of pleurisy and pneumonia. This tumefaction indicated contraction and, as it was the principal phenomenon, it was considered as of greater importance than effluxion, which, however, made these two diseases belong to the mixed type, that is to say, in certain parts of the body there was constriction, in others dilatation of the pores.

All the diseases so far studied are accompanied by

fever, but this is not the case in the cardiac disease, apoplexy, convulsions, ileus, hydrophobia and tetanus, which are described at the end of the second book and throughout the third. The term cardiac disease appears to have comprised the most varied affections; it includes anaemia, syncope and palpitations. According to the writers of the Graeco-Roman period, the disease would seem to have been rather more of a gastric affection, but quite as ill-defined and quite as confused in so far as the principal symptoms are concerned. According to Asclepiades, the two affections which were comprised in the term of the cardiac disease consisted of violent cardiac beats, a wretchedly small pulse and dyspnoea.

In speaking of sore throat (which also included laryngitis), Caelius makes an interesting allusion to tracheotomy as practised by Asclepiades in urgent cases: *ac si major, inquit, passio fuerit, dividendae sunt fauces, hoc est tonsillae et partes supra uvam constitutae; etenim summa est in his aequalis sive par incisura, quam appellavit bronchotomiam. Dehinc a veteribus probatam approbat arteriae divisuram ob respirationem faciendam, quam laryngotomiam vocant.* Unfortunately it would seem from this passage that this practice had already fallen into disuse.

Caelius carefully and very exactly describes hydrophobia, and asks whether it is a disease of the body or of the mind, though personally he holds that it is both; the mind is diseased because the patient cannot bear the sight of water, while the body is diseased because, although thirsty, he refuses drink and has hiccough and other serious symptoms. He also points out that the chief seat of the disease must, from the symptomatology, be in the stomach or the belly. It also would appear that many supposed it to be a new disease, but Caelius is not of this opinion, and says that, supposing this were true, it is useless to regard it as a new kind of morbid process, since all general diseases are comprised in those due to contraction or dilation of the pores. Artemidorus and Eudemus believed that the affection was new, because the ancient physicians, who were so exact in all matters, did not refer to it, and found in its incurability another proof that it was a new disease, because "had it been known in ancient times, physicians would have found a remedy for its cure." But another writer states that

Democritus had spoken of it and Hippocrates had discoursed upon it in his writings on phrensy, when he said that certain patients drink little and the slightest noise frightens them. Caelius is unable to understand why this disease should be regarded as a new one, since dogs have existed in all times; he believes that the incurability signifies nothing, because this likewise applies to cancer, which is far from being a new disease.

By the term of *morbus cardiacus* Caelius and Soranus did not refer to the heart but to a gastric affection accompanied by distinctly cardiac phenomena. In this they were in conformity with the opinion of Hippocrates and Erasistratus. Caelius, who considers it as an affection particularly characterized by loss of strength, distinctly states that its seat is in the cardia and in the stomach. However, he adds that some physicians believed it to be an inflammation of the heart, and for this reason they called it syncope, and it is under the latter name that he describes *morbus cardiacus*; *cardiacam passionem aiunt quidam duplici significatione nuncupari, communi et propria. Sed communem dicunt eam, quae substantiam in stomacho atque ore ventris habuerit, ubi etiam mordicatio sequitur supradictarum partium, ut Hippocrates primo et secundo libro Epidemion commemorat, et Erasistratus libris quos de ventre scripsit. Propriam autem dicunt eam, quae cum sudore fuerit atque pulsu imbecillo, de qua nunc dicere suscepimus. Nomen autem haec sumpsit passio, ut quidam volunt, a parte corporis quae patitur.*

It would seem that Soranus made no definition of *morbus cardiacus*, but, according to Asclepiades and his disciples, the heart was the organ involved, there being a contraction of its pores. Soranus was not of this opinion, believing that on the contrary there was an acute and temporary dilation of all the pores of the body, which was more prone to occur in elderly subjects, and in men rather than in women. The process was due to very numerous and varied causes; those referred to by Caelius are gastric disturbances, severe emotions and excessive fatigue. There is a larvate form of fever with a rapid and depressible pulse, which may also be irregular; there are also oppression, insomnia, hallucinations and drowsiness. The limbs are cold. As to an increase of the secretions, Soranus thought this was not always present. Later on the body became swollen and livid, speech was interfered with, the lips became white, while the eyes were sunken in their sockets. At the end of the disease diarrhoea developed, likewise a very marked dyspnoea. Lacrymation was a very bad prognostic element and so likewise was anorexia. On the other hand, if the patient was to recover, the normal characters of the pulse returned, the skin became warm, the dyspnoea decreased, the patient became mentally better, while sleep and appetite returned. Caelius states that in his day there was much discussion as to whether patients afflicted with *morbus cardiacus* had fever, and he says that most of the physicians before Asclepiades maintained that they had not, and Asclepiades himself thought that fever was absent in most of the cases. Themison, Thessalus and Demetrius stated that fever was present in some subjects, especially at the beginning and end of the disease, and Soranus admitted that fever might occur from relaxation of the pores.

As to treatment, Soranus states that it is not an incurable disease, as some have maintained. The patient should be placed in a cool and dark room, and above all the sun's rays should be excluded. It should not be forgotten that the disease was produced by dilatation of the pores, and therefore the contrary condition was to be brought about by cold and darkness. If sweating continued the body surface should be sprinkled with cold water. Internally, various astringent preparations were given.

From what has been said in the foregoing pages, the reader will have been able to form some idea of the progress made in medicine from Hippocrates to the advent of Galen, to whom we shall direct attention in the following chapter.

# CHAPTER XI

## GALEN

Galen flourished from A.D. 130 to A.D. 200, and with him Hippocratic medicine was restored ; nay, he even made it shine as it never had before. Nevertheless, it must be admitted that through him medicine acquired a new dress rather than was enriched, and the dogmas of Hippocrates really lost force and purity in the hands of Galen, although assuming a more attractive and perhaps a more systematic character.

Claudius Galenus, the most illustrious of ancient physicians after Hippocrates, was the son of Nicon, a celebrated architect, as well as a learned and very rich man. Galen was physician, surgeon and pharmacist, since in his book on antidotes he tells us that he had a shop for the sale of drugs (*officina*) situated on the Via Sacra. This shop was burnt in the reign of the Emperor Commodus, in that great conflagration which reduced the Temple of Peace and several other buildings to ashes.

Brought up and educated by his father, Galen developed a pronounced inclination for science, a great love for study, and a profound respect for the great masters, especially for Aristotle. He first gave himself up to the study of the sciences, the cultivation of letters, mathematics, and philosophy and, when in a position to appreciate and judge the teachings of the various sects, adopted the severe principles of Zeno and the Stoics, and the philosophy of Aristotle. It was then that his taste for medicine showed itself, and his one idea was to become a physician. To this end he visited the schools of Greece and Egypt, so as to study science at its source. He stayed at Alexandria, which was then the sanctuary of the sciences and the meeting-place of all learned men. He studied and commented on all the writers and, when he had formed a doctrine of his own based upon theirs, feeling that he was worthy to practise medicine successfully, returned to Pergamus, his native city, where he practised for about two years. Then a very terrible revolution occurred, and he withdrew to Rome, where celebrity and fortune as well as discouragements and injustice awaited him.

Galen was hardly thirty years of age when he came to Rome, but he soon rose in the esteem and affection of the patricians. He obtained favour with the Consul Boethus, the Praetor Sergius Paulus and even the Emperor Severus. But, as we have already said, cruel experiences awaited him. His great superiority as a man, as well as his good fortune, made him many enemies among his colleagues, who misrepresented and libelled him. At last, after long struggling courageously against his detractors, and full of bitterness, he set out again on his travels.

Galen passed five years in wanderings, until at length, at the solicitation of his friends, and the urgent persuasions of Marcus Aurelius and Lucius Verus, he returned to Rome.

At this time physicians, as we have already pointed out, were divided into several sects, namely Dogmatics, Empirics, Methodists, Pneumatics and Eclectics. Galen declared himself hostile to all of them and treated all with an equal contempt. Faithful to Nature's lesson, he accepted the dogmas and followed the precepts of one master alone—Hippocrates. He commented on the writings of the Father of Medicine, and in this great work made use of all the resources which his enlightened mind, prodigious erudition and keen imagination placed at his disposal. Galen was profoundly learned, but he desired to explain everything, and, attempting so much, was unfortunately led beyond the limits of wisdom, and it is regrettable that he developed many hypotheses which spoiled his doctrine almost to the extent of compromising his reputation. So, if Galen began well, he finished badly. But it is only just to say that he promulgated wise theories on the curative powers of nature, on morbid affinities and on the nature of disease and the crises in disease. His works, which for centuries were regarded as oracles, contain truths of the highest kind. Galen had yet another virtue, that of employing the power of his mind and the authority of his name to lead the medical profession back into a better road, and to show them the great superiority of the Hippocratic writings over those which came from the then popular sects. It must be frankly admitted that Galen would certainly have equalled Hippocrates if he had had less imagination and independence of character, and also if he had been uninfluenced by the philosophy of Aristotle. In fact, had Galen had a less enthusiastic and unrestrained mind he would have been content to annotate the Hippocratic writings and to perfect his system, but, drawn by his ardent imagination, he could not make up his mind to play a part which he wrongly regarded as secondary.

Some fanatical supporters of Galen have gone so far as to make him the rival of Hippocrates, but this is a mistake, for Hippocrates has no rival, and Galen himself would certainly have rejected such a comparison. In praise of him, it may be said that he always showed an admiration for the Father of Medicine which was almost a religious veneration.

If we compare these two illustrious men, due credit may be given to each. Hippocrates possessed to the highest degree the genius of patient observation, methodical reasoning and prudent generalization. He first observed, afterwards reasoned and then wisely generalized. Galen, on the contrary, with his brilliant but audacious mind, impatient and quick, generalized without waiting to observe, and built castles in the air. His theories and systems, based on few, or even incompletely observed facts, lacked a solid foundation. Attentive and judicious, Hippocrates followed step by step the processes of nature, verifying them by observation. Galen proceeded more boldly; impatient of restraint, he could not bear opposition. Having formed an idea, if he found on investigation that the facts did not tally, he rejected them. Briefly put, Galen explained facts by hypotheses, while Hippocrates was content to observe the phenomena of nature without explaining them. Both were animated with the most ardent zeal and the purest intentions, and both wished to enlarge the horizon of science, but this noble ambition was in Hippocrates expressed by love of his art and the greater good of humanity, while in Galen it seemed to be subordinated to a need for glory and to a thirst for renown. Centuries have respected the doctrine of Hippocrates, but have completely destroyed Galen's system of medicine.

But now let us admit that Galen added to the resources of an extremely keen mind a very large store of varied knowledge, and that he so to speak deepened the encyclopaedic system of his time.

With the exception of physics and chemistry there was no part of medicine of which he did not treat. He wrote on materia medica, on the composition of remedies and on anatomy, and his works offer us the most complete picture of the human body and its functions that antiquity has handed down. He described the bones, ligaments, cartilages, and muscles; the skin, brain, heart, nerves, and their membranes; the stomach, the intestines, the liver, the gall bladder, the spleen, kidneys, pancreas, the bladder, and the generative organs of both sexes.

In physiology Galen dealt with the movements of the heart—systole and diastole—and he seems to have had some idea of the pulmonary circulation. His works, which for the most part were destroyed in the burning of the Temple of Peace, gave to him an immense and really merited reputation. As to his doctrine, it may unhesitatingly be said that it reigned supreme up to the end of the XVIth century.

A fact to be noted is that writers, who pretended to ignore or to underestimate Galen's writings, frequently expressed in other terms the teachings which they derived from the dissertations of the great physician of Pergamus.

To summarize, it may be said that Galen often made too many definitions and divisions and for this reason his works are often difficult to read, while his verbosity is notorious. But, as a matter of fact, if it be admitted, and everyone seems to agree on this point, that great men should only be judged by the standard of their time, it must be frankly admitted that much injustice has been done to Galen. In truth most of his views are sublime, and it may be said that if they did not have the same success as those of Bacon, this was because mankind had not yet acquired the maturity due to sixteen centuries of development.

After having honourably practised medicine during the reigns of Antoninus, Marcus Aurelius, Commodus and Pertinax, Galen returned to his native country during the reign of Caracalla and there died during that of Septimius Severus.

Imbued with the philosophy of Aristotle, Galen maintained

that organized bodies, like the bodies of nature, were composed of four elements or principles, themselves possessing four principal qualities. The four elements were fire, water, earth and air, while the four qualities of these four elements were heat, moisture, dryness and cold. And lastly the four elements and their qualities constituted the primary basis of all parts of the body or of the animal economy. According to Galen, the body is composed of three distinct parts, namely the solid and liquid parts and the spirits. In this respect Galen was in perfect agreement with Hippocrates, who had admitted that there were solid parts, or containers ; liquid parts, or contents ; and lastly spirits, or forces. What we call solids, Galen calls parts, and he divides the parts into similar and organic parts. The similar parts are peculiar in that they are always and in every way similar to each other, down to their very last molecules. They comprise the bones, ligaments, membranes, veins and arteries, nerves, fat, glands and flesh. The organic or composite parts are formed by the combination of all or nearly all the similar parts. Galen called them organic (instrumental) parts because he looked upon them as the machinery, or instruments, destined to carry out the movements and the functions of life. The ear, eye, hand, foot, heart, intestines, stomach and other viscera, belonged to the organic or instrumental parts.

Galen admitted four principal humours, namely the blood, pituit (or lymph), and yellow and black bile. The blood is the liquid *par excellence*, and the source of all the humours, the pituit includes all the serous and mucous fluids. In each of these humours such or such of the primal qualities of the elements predominates. For example, the blood is a hot and moist humour ; yellow bile is a hot and dry humour ; the pituit is cold and moist, while the black bile or *airabile* is cold and dry. And lastly the majority of diseases, primarily or indirectly, arise from an excess, a deficiency, or a change in these four fundamental humours and their specific qualities.

Galen admitted three kinds of spirits, namely the natural, the vital and the animal. The *natural spirits* consisted of a subtle vapour which arose from the blood (which itself was formed in the liver), then went to the heart and there combined with air, thus giving rise to the *vital spirits*, which in turn became transformed into *animal spirits* in the brain. These three kinds of spirits are the source of three corresponding faculties which exist in the organs where they are formed and which afterwards become the motive of their action. These three faculties are the natural, vital and animal; they produce natural actions, vital actions and animal actions.

The natural faculty is seated in the liver; the liver presides over digestion, nutrition and generation. The vital faculty resides in the heart, which, by way of the arteries, supplies the entire body with heat and light. And lastly the animal faculty, the most important of the three, is seated in the brain; it is the source of sentiment and movement and is present everywhere in the economy, being carried by the nerves. It governs all.

Galen further divided the *actions* of each faculty—natural, animal, and vital—into internal and external. The internal actions of the natural faculty effect sanguification and digestion; the external actions of the faculty give rise to the venous circulation as well as to the supply of blood to all points of the economy, and thus to the growth of the individual and the propagation of the species.

The internal actions of the vital faculty give rise to the violent passions and these are seated in the viscera; the external actions of the vital faculty produce movement and pulsation of the arteries, and the distribution of arterial blood to all the parts.

Lastly, the external actions of the animal faculty preside over sensation and muscular movements, while the internal actions of this faculty produce the exercise of the intellectual functions which results in imagination, judgment and reasoning.

Then, above all these primordial faculties, and a series of secondary faculties which represent the vital properties of the various parts of the body, Galen admitted a primal force which is the source and soul of all the faculties, and, as life itself in its essence and principle, this power or force dominates all the others. This was in other words, Nature, according to the teachings of Hippocrates.

Galen's anatomical knowledge was very extensive relatively to the time when he lived, and in this respect he went far beyond Erasistratus and Herophilus. He was the first to dissect the muscles and to describe their shape, situation and direction. He probably only dissected apes and other animals, because the Roman laws did not allow the dissection of human bodies, and it was only exceptionally or surreptitiously that physicians could procure the bodies of bandits who had been killed on the highways, or of soldiers who had fallen on the battlefield. Even at Alexandria, all parts of anatomy other than osteology were demonstrated on animals, particularly apes.

Galen's knowledge of physiology, pathology, and semeiology was very limited and frequently full of subtleties and errors. But we must admit that even these errors excited the curiosity of observers, and in this respect they were useful and even indirectly served science. Continuing the work of Erasistratus and Archigenes, Galen studied the pulse with much care and detail, and pointed out that it is from a profound knowledge of the pulse that the best indications of disease are to be had, so that it should always be used as a guide. He teaches that the pulse is at times simple, at others composite, long, broad, high, or frequent; again it may be vehement or slow, weak or soft, hard, unequal or intermittent, and finally it may be dicrotic, wavy, trembling or convulsive. All these variations represent just so many signs and sources or indications in disease; they are dependent upon various causes, such as age, sex, the temperament and changes occurring in the six *non-naturals*, which play a very important part. To give an idea of the extent of Galen's researches on the pulse it is enough to say that he wrote sixteen books on the subject.

Galen was very minute in his description of the various conditions and changes taking place in the urine, and he gives the indications and prognostics that may be derived from examination of this excretion during the progress of various diseases.

According to Galen health depends upon the harmony and temperament of the four humours and the four qualities properly belonging to them. As long as the humours are in proper ratio, one to the other, and the natural proportion of the similar parts is maintained; as long as the humours possess the right temperature and mild qualities, the economy enjoys a perfect condition of health. In other words, all the organic functions are being carried out according to the laws of their normal constitution; but, on the other hand, as soon as any disorder arises among the elements, and the qualities of these elements undergo a change, or as soon as a humour or humours become defective either by excess or insufficiency, or from their quality or proportion, the equilibrium of the bodily functions becomes upset and by passing from the similar parts to the organic parts the vitiated humour necessarily brings about disturbances of the functions, so that disease either develops gradually or suddenly makes its appearance, as the case may be. Perfect health exists only when complete equilibrium is maintained between the elements, the elementary qualities, the humours, the spirits, the similar solids and the organic solids.

It was starting from these principles that Galen established the series of *temperaments*, of which he admits four principal, namely the sanguine, the phlegmatic, the bilious and the melancholic. Each of these temperaments is either hot or cold, dry or moist, according to the elementary quality that predominates over the three others. Galen next divides these temperaments—which in a way may be called primary—into other more composite temperaments, which result from the combination of two elementary qualities. Thus, for example, he admitted dry and warm, hot and moist, cold and moist, and cold and dry temperaments. And lastly, he admitted that besides the normal, simple or composite temperaments, a person might possess a peculiar type of temperament properly belonging to him. This particular type of temperament was designated by the name idiosyncrasy, and Galen maintained that it was the result of a change arising in ordinary temperaments, produced by certain peculiar dispositions belonging properly to the individual. However, the difference between the temperaments and their divergence from the natural type did not constitute a *disease* but merely a predisposition to disease, and any individual in this state was regarded as healthy in spite of this change of temperament just as long as its force was not sufficient to prevent the proper functioning of the body.

Galen also admitted a *neutral* constitution; this was an intermediary state between health and disease; a transition state between the state of flourishing health and the interference with the parts which is the commencement of disease.

Disease, according to Galen, is a *contra-natural* state, whose principal condition is to injure the proper exercise of the functions. It is an abnormal condition of the body which primarily, by itself alone, prevents the parts from carrying out their functions and fulfilling their action. This is the general definition, but it is not the only one that Galen gives. In the *Treatise on the Difference of Symptoms* he says that disease consists in a superabundance, scarcity, or change taking place in the humours, which all contribute to disordering the elements and their parts. Now, in this respect, Galen completely adopted the ideas of Aristotle, his master, who defined disease as the disorder of the elements whose harmony constitutes health. Considered from this point of view, diseases are for Galen either sanguine, bilious, pituitous, or atrabilious, according to whether one or the other of these humours acts as cause of the disease by excess, scarcity, or quality or by a defect of their circulation or movement. Hence each disease requires different curative means. At times one must attenuate the humours or dilute them, at others their quantity must be increased or they must be thickened, cooled or warmed, purified or evacuated from the body, according to the case. For this there are two different sorts of medications, namely remedies endowed with the power of purifying the humours and of bringing them back to the normal state without provoking evacuations, and measures which evacuate in order to remove the superabundant or vitiated humours.

Galen advises making a fundamental distinction between the *affection* and the disease. The affection consists of an intimate, general and direct vitiation of the animal economy, which is, so to speak, saturated by a morbid humoral principle which *affects* the entire solid and liquid animal mass. Disease, on the other hand, is the manifestation of this occult vitiation which undermines and destroys the economy. In other words disease is a particular, local and phenomenal aspect of the *affection* which fundamentally constitutes a general morbid state. Cancer, for example, presents a general and a local state ; the general state is the vitiation of the humours —the general cancerous *state*, or *affection*. The local state, on the other hand, or the manifest cancer, the cancer in evidence, is the disease. Finally, the *affection* often remains hidden within the economy without giving any objective manifestation of its presence ; but from the time that it produces a group of reactions it constitutes what Galen calls the *disease.*

In this respect Galen imitates Hippocrates and divides diseases into epidemic, endemic, sporadic, acute, chronic, benign and malignant. He admits three groups of diseases; the first comprises diseases of similar parts, the second diseases of organic parts, while the third embraces those diseases which are common to both the similar and the organic parts. The diseases of the first group are due to a disturbance of the similar parts, and this disturbance exists with or without matter. A disturbance with matter arises when the natural heat increased or diminished is kept up by a morbid humour; the disturbance without matter exists when the normal temperature of a part is altered independently of the presence of a morbid humour.

The second group of diseases comprises all those irregularities in which the organic parts may be involved, either in respect of their shape, size or number, or in respect of their situation, union or abnormal separation.

Finally, the third group includes all wounds and injuries produced by physical or chemical agents, such as steel or fire. Galen placed in this category solutions of continuity due either to an incision, a bite, or rupture.

Galen admitted a simple and a composite disturbance, as well as an equal and an unequal disturbance, but it is useless for us to follow him in these subtleties, which are the result of his adventurous imagination and dialectical propensities.

Galen attached the greatest importance to the study of the morbid causes. They are, he says, those which reveal to us the true and, so to speak, individual nature of each disease, because every morbid process is necessarily contained in its cause, just as each effect is contained in its principle.

Galen divided the causes of disease into external and internal, manifest or evident and non-evident or occult. Among the external causes he places six things which he calls non-naturals; these are those which preside over the preservation of health, when one leads a healthy life, but on the other hand produce disease when one abuses one's health or when these non-naturals are of bad quality. These six things are to-day comprised in what we call hygiene and are air, food, and drink; rest and movement; sleep and waking;

the retentions and excretions of the body; the passions of the soul and the movements of thought.

Galen admitted two kinds of internal causes: the antecedent and the conjoint. The *antecedent* cause can only be recognized by reasoning; it almost always consists of a vitiation of the humours by excess or insufficiency or by cacochymy. The *conjoint* cause can be estimated by the strength of the patient.

The condition of the humours is an important source for the cause of disease. All the humours of the body are subject to plethora, which may be either general or local. Plethora is general when all the humours are involved in it; it is local when it merely consists of the excess of a single humour. There are two sorts of plethora, namely, plethora in respect of the vessels, and plethora in respect of the forces. Plethora of the vessels takes place when the arteries or veins, and ducts or reservoirs, appear to be unable to contain the liquids which flow through them. Plethora of the forces ensues when the patient, on account of his constitution, cannot bear a small quantity of liquids or humours. There is this difference between the sanguineous and the other—bilious, pituitous or melancholic—kinds of plethora, that the blood constituting sanguineous plethora may be found in superabundance in the economy without causing any change in the quality of the other humours; while "pituit" and atrabile or bile, when exceeding the other humours in quantity, infect all the liquids and even the blood, which, thus changed, may produce a general cacochymy.

The humours may be in a state of cacochymy simply from degeneration of their primary qualities, and cacochymy may result from the fact that under the action of certain morbid causes, the humours become either warmer or colder, drier or moister, sweeter or salter, more acrid or more bitter, than in the normal state. Each primary affection of the humours possesses peculiar characteristics by which it may be detected. Warm or cold sanguineous plethora may be recognized by the following signs: the patient looks warm and animated, the pulse is strong, the respiration laboured and short, the head is hot and the body corpulent; the patient easily falls into a condition of drowsiness and is tormented by dreams in which he sees lights or fires. These symptoms assume greater consistency if the subject has led a sedentary life, if he overeats or drinks, if he is very sanguineous and if he is suffering from the suppression of some ordinary evacuation.

Hot and moist or bilious cacochymy is diagnosed by the colour of the skin and eyes, the ochre-coloured coating of the tongue, a bitter taste in the mouth, a continual desire to drink cold liquids, nausea and distaste for food, irascibility of temper and above all by bilious evacuations taking place from the stomach and bowels. The causes predisposing to this state are a dry and warm temperament, late nights, passions, and the continued action of a very high temperature.

Moist and cold pituitous cacochymy may be diagnosed by the general exhaustion of the patient, who is generally very sensitive to cold; while the skin is pale and cold, the pulse weak, slow and soft, the urine is pale and voided in large quantities and there are serous discharges, various forms of catarrh and oedematous tumefactions.

The symptoms which indicate cold and dry or melancholic cacochymy are borborygmi, a permanent state of constipation or diarrhoea, an insatiable and depraved appetite, insomnia or a sleep interrupted by fearful dreams. Sorrows, passions, excesses of all kinds and poor food especially predispose the patient to this condition. Galen also mentions as *material* causes of disease a change in the position, size and shape of the organic parts, and (like Hippocrates) says that the introduction of air into the blood vessels is the most common cause of nervous affections.

By the term *conjoint* cause Galen meant that one which is the most intimately connected with the disease, which directly produces it.

Galen defines *symptom* as a morbid manifestation which is dependent upon the disease and follows it as the shadow follows the body. He admits three kinds of symptoms: those which are derived from a vitiation of the secretion, those resulting from disturbances of the excretions and, lastly, those which are dependent upon a poor functioning of the parts. According to him the sign is that which allows one to recognize an unknown affection when the latter is completely enveloped in the symptoms. There are two kinds of signs, the diagnostic and the prognostic. The former are those which characterize the disease and are divided into pathognomonic signs and adjunct or uncertain signs. The pathognomonic signs are those which exactly characterize the disease and inevitably denote it. The uncertain or adjunct signs are those met with in an infinity of diseases and are not absolute. The diagnostic signs according to Galen are derived, firstly from the very essence of the disease, secondly from the causes of the disease, thirdly from the symptoms and lastly from the peculiar disposition of each patient.

The prognostic signs are those which indicate the duration and probable outcome of the disease. They are derived firstly from the form and nature of the morbid process, secondly from the reigning constitution of the season, thirdly from the state of the season, and lastly from the patient himself, the condition of his strength, his age, temperament, habits and physical and moral constitution.

Galen in all his writings stresses the necessity of localizing disease. He says that there is nothing more important than to know which organ is diseased—in other words, the *seat* of the *affection*. Faithful to the precepts of Hippocrates in respect of *sympathies*, Galen advises the minute analysis of all that composes the morbid state before one pronounces upon the nature of the state. He especially advises the delay of treatment until one has anatomically established the part played by the *idiopathic* state and the concomitant or *sympathetic* state. The knowledge possessed of the different functions of the body in the normal state is the very source of diagnosis, and the disturbance of the functions indicates the morbid condition of the disturbed organ. Thus a difficult and laborious digestion indicates that the stomach is affected ; when there is great difficulty in micturition an obstruction in the bladder or some lesion of the urinary apparatus is indicated. A persistent change in the pulse is frequently the sign of heart disease, while defective movement of certain parts of the body often indicates an affection of the nerves. On the other hand the functions may be disturbed by the sympathy which exists between certain organs ; thus, for example, vomiting often depends upon an affection of the kidneys, in which case it is *sympathetic*. Now, this should cause the physician to be attentive, for those remedies which would be used in a supposed case of stomach trouble would be useless or even dangerous when in reality the kidneys are the seat of the disease.

In spite of the too lightly repeated proverb that Hippocrates says Yes and Galen says No, we are of the opinion that Galen's therapeutics are in the majority of cases in perfect conformity with those of Hippocrates. Galen admits the Hippocratic doctrine of crises and critical days, and points out that health should be preserved by that which is in relation to it, and that disease, which in reality is something contrary to nature, should be dealt with by that which is contrary to it. Therefore, as we have just said, Galen completely adopted the views of Hippocrates who had formulated the axiom: *Contraria contrariis curantur.* Nor did Galen neglect *prevention.*

The first duty of the physician is to prevent disease, and his first effort should be its cure when it has declared itself in spite of all hygienic means. In order to prevent disease one must either escape from or destroy the causes which produce it. This is the first dogma—the dogma *par excellence.*

Galen wrote several books on diet, and the various changes that are to be made in food according to the patient's age, the season of the year and the state of health or disease. The works of Galen on this subject, together with those of Hippocrates, should be considered the true source of the most modern books on hygiene.

Galen wrote lengthily concerning the preservation of health by exercise, the ordinary use of baths, massage and the means of promoting excretion. He recommended riding in carriages or in litters, boating, exercising the voice by declamation or singing. He gave excellent instructions on the way in which we should regulate the various exercises and above all he stressed the indications and contra-indications for their use. Galen says that after long study one should be very moderate in eating and drinking, should walk in the open, use baths rather cool than hot, eat food that is easily digested, keep the bowels open, take frequent foot baths and, if all these means are insufficient, resort to blood-letting.

Before undertaking the treatment of a disease one should examine and, so to speak, carefully weigh the various circumstances in which the disease has developed; afterwards the indications for treatment can be deduced. These are to be found in an attentive consideration of the age, sex, and temperament of the patient, and especially an examination of the condition of his strength and his habits. One must not overlook the importance of the organ involved, because we have the noble organs and the secondary organs. The brain, heart and lung are the three most important. In any circumstance it is the disease, itself the cause of all the symptoms, which should first of all hold the attention of the physician ; it is against the disease and then above all against the cause which has produced it that the treatment should be directed. The entire art of medicine is contained in this precept.

Next the physician should attempt to control the *indication*. Now, according to Galen, the indication is that which suggests what should be done in respect of a thing, existing either in the thing or outside it. For example, in respect of diseases, Galen derived the indication from the very nature of the affection itself, as well as from the condition of the patient. In respect of the affection, he examined its cause and symptoms with the minutest care. In respect of the patient he examined his constitution, temperament and strength, which he considered from all points of view.

Galen was a great advocate of blood-letting, and employed it frequently, sometimes to the extent of almost depleting the patient. However, he never ordered it until he had carefully considered all the indications as well as all the contra-indications. He bled in plethora and for the complications arising therefrom, but rarely resorted to it in children under the age of fifteen years, and the amount let was always in proportion to the patient's temperament and strength. He said that it was better to err on the side of insufficient blood-letting than by excess. Galen also used leeches, scarifications and wet cupping. He opened the jugular veins and even performed arteriotomy in serious and urgent cases.

With the exception of theriacum and opium (which he prescribed for inducing sleep, calming pain, and controlling excessive diarrhoea), Galen used few internal remedies. According to him, all the properties of drugs depended upon their elementary qualities : namely, heat, cold, dampness and dryness. There were also degrees for each of these qualities, so that a food or a drug might be cold or hot in the first, second or third degree, and thus would be related to the cold or hot qualities of the disease. Hence it results that for a cold or a hot disease in one of these four degrees one should employ a drug endowed with opposite qualities of heat or cold in the same degree.

Such is an outline of Galen's system, which, without any doubt, is one of the most famous which have ever been produced, and was for centuries almost the only one to be employed. The honour for this he must share with Hippocrates, whose work he continued and developed, and it is this fact that explains the favour that the Galenic system enjoyed in Europe, Asia, and Africa for thirteen hundred years.

# CHAPTER XII

## THE PRACTICE OF MEDICINE AT ROME

During antiquity the medical profession does not appear to have submitted to any test as to the capacity of the physician or of his studies. Greece had its celebrated medical schools, but they conferred no diploma of any sort. In consequence of this the Romans were compelled to follow the traditions of their first masters, those who really initiated them into the science of medicine, so that the practice of the art was completely unfettered. "At Rome, during the Empire as well as the Republic," says Révillout, "medical diplomas did not exist. Medicine was practised whenever and however one wished, without obligation to follow studies or submit oneself for examination in the art." This assertion is confirmed by *Cod.*, vii. 7. 1, § 5, *De comm. serv. manum.* In fact, this text shows that in Roman law any individual, male or female, was considered a physician if he or she professed to be one.

For that matter the generic term of *medicus* comprised all those who gave themselves up to the various branches of the healing art and to everything related to the science of diseases and their treatment. As we shall see, at the commencement of the practice of medicine the various branches of this science were confused with each other and the art of preparing medicaments (of pharmacy, as we call it to-day), was practised by physicians in the strict sense of the word. As knowledge increased and the domain of pharmacy enlarged, necessitating greater study in this particular branch, it became necessary to specialize. However, the name *medicus*, without any other particular denomination, always included those who occupied themselves with the cure or treatment of patients, and, save for certain restrictions which will be referred to, it will be in this broad sense that this term will be employed, as stated in *Dig.*, l. 13. 1, § 3, *De variis et extraord. conditionibus: Medicos fortassis quis accipiet etiam eos qui alicujus partis corporis vel certi doloris sanitatem pollicentur : ut puta si auricularius, si fistulae vel dentium.* Thus also it was said : *medici sunt hi qui medicamenta conficiunt, vulnera curant, cucurbitas admovent, item qui circumcidunt aut castrant.*

This absolute freedom in the exercise of the profession, the social condition of those who exercised it, and the frequently criminal use that they made of their science, naturally gave rise to great abuses and helped to lower the standard of the profession. Medical practice requires great independence, and all the qualities of the free man. Now, in reality, it was principally slaves or freedmen belonging to the great houses, or foreigners without scruple, who practised the art, all docile instruments and only too often the accomplices of corruption, debauchery, immorality, and crime.

In principle, then, at Rome anyone could practise the art without qualification; but in practice, before exercising it, the novice was obliged to follow the teachings of a master, with whom he visited patients in order to acquire the necessary experience. This teaching was purely practical and clinical, as the following epigram of Martial would lead us to suppose :—

> *Languebam, sed tu comitatus protinus ad me*
> *Venisti centum, Symmache, discipulis.*
> *Centum me teligere manus aquilone gelatae.*
> *Non habui febrem, Symmache, nunc habeo.*

Among the novices some more particularly studied dietetics—the art of curing by diet—others gave themselves up to surgery, and some studied pharmacy or the art of curing by drugs. At the beginning these three branches were mingled together and probably were very elementary, but with the progress of medical science they became divided without complete separation of the bonds which necessarily united them to each other. Some physicians specialized in one only of these branches, and it is thus that pharmacy (which we will now consider) assumed a greater importance and extension, though it never as in our day became an absolutely distinct profession.

Those who gave themselves up to the study of disease were necessarily obliged themselves to prepare the remedies that they prescribed for their patients. They did not possess the knowledge necessary to guide them, and therefore pharmacy had no really scientific character; chemistry did not exist as a science and, although the art of mixing certain efficacious drugs was known, it was only learned by chance or by completely empirical knowledge.

In a commentary on Papinian's *Responsa*, Book VIII, it is shown that at this epoch medicines were prepared by the physicians themselves, and this assertion is based on the text of Paulus the Jurisconsult. *Medicus olim conficiebat medicamenta, non, ut fit hodie, ab alio confici imperabat. Quamobrem Paulus, lib. III Sent., tit. De instrumento medici legato: Legato cedere omnem apparatum conficiendorum medicamentorum.*

In fact, Paulus states that in legacies composed of objects used in the profession of a physician one must include *apparatus omnis conficiendorum medicamentorum* : all objects serving for the preparation of medicaments.

Paulus the Jurisconsult, who gives us this information in respect of the physician compounding his remedies, lived about the second century of our era, and this was also the period during which Galen flourished. Galen, himself a very accomplished pharmacist, may as a matter of fact be regarded as the father of pharmacy. But before him there were those who specialized in this branch, as he himself states, for he mentions Asclepiades as called the Pharmacist, and praises him for the progress he made in the preparation of remedies and the art of applying them. In the preceding chapter we pointed out that Galen had a pharmacy (*officina*) at Rome, and his numerous works contain a great number of formulae, some of which are used even to-day. For that matter Galen was not the first physician who had opened an *officina*, which in reality was a kind of public pharmacy. Pliny tells us that the city of Rome received Archagathus (219 B.C.), and after having granted him the freedom of the city, bought him a shop at the expense of the Treasury, situated on the square of Acilius, where he practised his profession. Several other physicians of Rome also had their shops, where patients consulted them when they had need of their services. These shops, where medicine and pharmacy were practised, at length developed in all the cities of the Roman Empire, when they offered sufficient pecuniary inducement and there was a large enough population.

According to Galen (*Comm. prim. in libr. Hippocr. de medic. officin., cap. VIII*) the cities which maintained public physicians were obliged to give them *officinae*, which in Latin countries were also called *medicatrinae* or *medicinae*. Galen has also left us three books of commentaries explaining the purposes and management of *officinae*, and Briau points out that these apothecaries' shops contained, besides instruments and dressings, all simple and compound medicaments that the physicians themselves gave on the spot, or that were sold to the public to take away. Consequently these shops were regular pharmacies, furnished with all the mineral, vegetable, and animal remedies employed at the time. In one of his comedies Plautus makes one of his characters say that when needed poison could be obtained in these *officinae* :—

> *Cur ego vivo ? Cur non morior ? Quid mihi est in vita boni ?*
> *Certum est : ibo ad medicum atque me ibi toxico morti dabo.*

*Dig.*, xviii. 1. 3, § 2, *De contrahenda emptione*, also deals with the preparation of medicaments and their sale, as well as with poisons, confirming Plautus : *Veneni mali quidem putant non contrahi emptionem, quia nec societas aut mandatum flagitiosae rei ullas vires habet ; quae sententia potest sane vera videri de his quae nullo modo adjectione alterius materiae usu nobis esse possunt : de his vero quae mixta aliis materiis adeo nocendi naturam deponunt, ut ex his antidoti et alia quaedam salubria medicamenta conficiantur, aliud dici potest.*

From these quotations it will be seen that the art of pharmacy played a very important part, perhaps more definite than might generally be supposed, even in very early Roman medicine, and that usually the physician in the strict sense of the word was a pharmacist as well, and only too often during the days of despotic emperors he may have been a poisoner at the service of those who paid the largest fees !

However, in the second century of our era, quite a number of physicians relied upon others for the preparation of their medicaments. Those who devoted themselves to this branch at this period were called *seplasiarii*. This term was derived from the fact that at Capua the public place where the merchants dealing in simple drugs pursued their trade was called Seplasia. The seplasiarii, who were far from honest, cheated as best they could in the quality and the quantity of the products they sold. They lived in a quarter of Rome not far from the Capitoline Hill, designated by the name of *vicus thurarius* or *vicus unguentarius.* These merchants not only sold medicinal drugs, but they also dealt in materials used by perfumers and dyers. Galen calls them *pharmacopolae* or *migmatopolae.* To furnish their *officinae*, physicians also dealt with the *herbarii* or herb-gatherers.

These dealers in simple drugs were in a way, in respect of their relationship to those who prepared the more composite medicaments, what in our day the herbalists are to the pharmacists. They competed somewhat with the physicians since the healing art could be exercised in full liberty, but their clients were from the lower classes, and as a matter of fact they were the physicians of the poor.

This is a brief summary of the general characteristics of those who exercised the healing art at Rome, but, as Quintilian says, among the *herbarii* one should really include men who wished to be physicians in the strict sense of the word. In these preliminary remarks they have been considered without distinction as following a profession, but the same legal principles cannot be applied to them if they are considered as *personae*, that is to say, in respect of their position in society and in the Roman family, according as they were slaves or free, freedmen or free men, citizens or aliens, fathers of families or sons of families. Hence we must consider first the slaves practising medicine or pharmacy.

Slavery was one of the principal sources of strength of the ancient civilizations. It is particularly bound up with the ideas of the Romans in political, economic, and civil matters, so that a study of the professions exercised at Rome must almost always take slaves into consideration, because they could practise almost any of them.

In order to understand what slavery was at Rome, and how slaves exercised the liberal professions and often possessed a considerable influence over their masters—as physicians or teachers—it must not be forgotten that the slaves at Rome were of the same colour and often of the same race as their masters, while their learning was often very much superior and when they were of a cultured race, such as the Grecian, their habits and inclinations were more refined. They thus were able to dominate their masters by their immense intellectual superiority. Hence one must not take the texts in a rigorous sense and suppose that in practice, as in principle, the situation of the slave-physicians was that of slaves in general. Roman writers tell us that certain slaves in the Roman family were held in high consideration and might even have *vicarii* in their service.

Thus, although servile, they nevertheless enjoyed a privileged position, because from the very nature of their functions they were placed above the *vulgum pecus* or the *familia.* Among them was the physician, and, according to his aptitude and special knowledge, he might be at the same time the surgeon of the master and of the familia. This function was sometimes fulfilled by women, as we shall show later. In an inscription discovered in 1825 these words are to be found : *Metilia Dona Medica.*

As to the principles governing the condition of slaves in general, the Digest states that there was no difference in the conditions of slavery : *in servorum conditione nulla differentia.* If this rule was rigorously applied the following would be the situation of these slaves practising medicine or pharmacy from the viewpoint of Roman law.

Firstly, in relation to his master, the position of the slave-physician is summed up in the idea that the former is his owner. Certain consequences ensue from this ownership of his person and his possessions.

The power of the master over the person of the slave underwent many important changes during the development of Roman law, the causes and effects of which are interesting. At the beginning the power of the master was absolute, he had the right of life and death. But the early Romans did not abuse this formidable right. In the epochs of the great conquests, slaves were recruited among despised and distant nations, so that the masters, becoming more and more corrupt and capricious, were unlimited in their cruelties, and could even send slaves to torture or crucify them, saying : *hoc volo, sic jubeo, sic pro ratione voluntas.*

From the second viewpoint, namely that of property, the

slave-physician could not acquire any patrimony, any more than could other slaves. Consequently, if he accomplished an act which by its nature resulted in the acquisition of the right of property or credit—if, for example, the slave-physician professionally attended foreigners—any reward that he might acquire was for the profit of his master, and when the latter could not profit by it, the acquisition did not accrue. Therefore the slave was merely the organ or instrument of his master and only for the purpose of acquiring.

However, in spite of the principle that the slave had no personality properly speaking, his relationship with a third person manifested a certain personal capacity in fact, rather than in law, that could not be denied him. Thus, if a slave-physician in the exercise of his profession committed a mistake to the prejudice of the health of his patient—as, for example, by voluntarily poisoning a patient—there arose from this mistake or misdemeanour a civil obligation, as from his contract it became a natural obligation. In both cases the obligatory lien did not become practically effective against the slave until after he had been made a freedman, which condition would allow him to acquire a patrimony. But it frequently happened that the effect of such a contract and of such a misdemeanour fell upon the master, before manumission in civil or praetorian jurisprudence had occurred. Several inscriptions have been found which confirm the supposition that there were public slave-physicians. Freedmen are frequently distinguished by the letters *L. P.* (*Libertus publicus*) *medicus*.

Briau observes that the exercise of the medical art began with domestic medicine practised within the house of the master, and that therefore the first physicians at Rome evidently were slaves. This opinion may be accepted, but only if this domestic medicine be confined to the very ancient epochs. In fact, until the Romans had developed constant relationship with Greece, that is to say, for a very long time, one can hardly surmise what the medical art may have been in the land of Romulus.

It was only when the Greek physicians arrived at Rome, either as slaves or as freedmen, that Roman medicine and pharmacy really developed. At this time rich Romans wished above all to be in possession of slave-physicians who had been taught their profession by great masters. They were always accompanied by them in their travels and during their stay at their country places, and they placed the care of their health in the hands of these servants with complete confidence, the latter becoming fully conversant with the temperament and, consequently, the diseases of the master and the family, while they were even lent as a special favour to friends who were ill.

In his *Histoire de l'Esclavage dans l'Antiquité*, Wallon says that at Rome medicine experienced the same vicissitudes as grammar. On account of the gross ignorance of the Roman it was at first despised, but soon was sought after by all the rich families. Physicians were wanted for the care of the body, as grammarians for the instruction or amusement of the mind.

For that matter, we find in the Code of Justinian ample proof that slave-physicians were valued very highly, for this Emperor allowed for slaves of either sex skilful in this art the maximum slave price—sixty pieces of gold; while the price for eunuchs (who were very much sought after) was limited to fifty pieces.

Of the slave-physicians and pharmacists to whom reference has just been made, those who had acquired some knowledge of the healing art or had merely learnt it by contact with Greek slaves who had practised medicine in their own country, could by the kindness of their masters or of the State become freedmen. Then, if they continued to practise their profession on their own account, they constituted the class of freedmen-physicians which we now come to consider.

The status of freedmen was *one* in ancient law and again under Justinian, but in the classical period three classes were recognized: the freedmen issued from a regular manumission, the *dediticii* from whom nothing could remove the stigma of slavery, and the *Latini Juniani* whose quality was derived from a manumission applied to minor slaves of thirty years of age or from masters who did not possess the power of full ownership of a Roman citizen.

Like other freedmen, those who gave themselves up to the practice of medicine were placed in a rather peculiar situation in respect of the duties which they had to fulfil towards their patron and also towards the society which had received them into its midst. Considered in his social relations, the freedman was placed amongst the *homines humiles* (or lower class) in distinction to *homines honesti* (or upper class); his *existimatio* was not intact and, down to the end of the Republic, the slavery that he had undergone prevented him from being equal to the free man.

Among the three classes of freedmen above enumerated, which existed during the classical period, the *dediticii* were lowest, being deprived for ever of all public rights, of *connubium* and *commercium*; they could only make contracts under *jus gentium.* The law prohibited them from appearing in Rome, or within one hundred miles of the city. An infraction of this law had as penalty the return to slavery. The worst of their situation was that it was impossible to get out of it and they never could become citizens. However, their condition was not hereditary and their children, treated as ordinary aliens, could become citizens. We have simply mentioned this fact because physicians may have been comprised in this class.

The freed *Latini Juniani* were excluded from any political legislation and among the private rights the *connubium* did not belong to them; as to the *commercium,* they enjoyed it, but with important restrictions. In the first place, if they inherited anything, such as a legacy, this faculty was often illusory, because they were obliged to obtain the citizenship during the life of the testator or within one hundred days after his death, in order to be able to benefit by the bequest. Their patrimony would be turned over to the master or his heirs as slave's earnings, but they could acquire the citizenship by a regular process of manumission or by the will of the Emperor, and it is probable that when physicians who were freed *Latini Juniani* had rendered valuable services to distinguished personages or to towns this favour was granted them.

Finally there remains a third class of freedmen, in which there were a number of physicians, namely, that of the citizen freedmen. Under the Empire the freedmen were raised from their inferiority and some of them were accorded the *jus aureorum anulorum,* or the right to wear the gold ring, or even the *restitutio natalium,* or relief from their condition, the effect of which was to place the freedman on the same level as the free man. Certain freedmen made scandalous fortunes ; for example, the freedman of Augustus by name Licinus whose marble mausoleum, near the Via Salaria, inspired the following epigram :

> *Marmoreo Licinus tumulo jacet, at Cato parvo,*
> *Pompeius nullo. Quis putat esse deos?*

Among them were many physicians.

A great many inscriptions show that they held all kinds of employment at this time at the imperial court and in the houses of the great. They married the daughters of the most noble houses and even relatives of the imperial family. Felix, the brother of the freedman Pallas, married the grand-daughter of Antony and Cleopatra.

The freedmen-physicians also profited by imperial favour. Antonius Musa, physician to Augustus, was honoured by the dignity of equerry and was loaded by riches given him by the prince and the Senate ; he had an annual salary of 250,000 sesterces. All physicians belonging to the imperial house did not, it is true, occupy so high a situation, and it is probable that many freedmen were employed as subordinate assistants to the freemen-physicians, foreigners or Roman citizens, because a very old inscription refers to a physician-in-chief—*supra medicos*—and a *decurio medicus*. It was during the Empire that the largest number of foreign physicians made their appearance, and of these we shall now speak.

At the time when Rome had conquered the greater part of the known world, when the city had become the centre into which the conquered peoples sent their riches and their manufactures, their science and arts, foreign physicians and pharmacists became very numerous, and such constituted the larger number of free physicians, on whom Julius Caesar conferred the citizenship when they established themselves there. The most capable among them were selected for this honour ; especially those that were considered sufficiently learned to teach pupils. Many came from Greece where, under the impulsion of Hippocrates and his descendants, the art of medicine had progressed, and among the Latin writers and historians many physicians are referred to, whose names we already know.

Among these foreign physicians are to be found several

Orientals, particularly Egyptians, who were expressly called to Rome to treat certain endemic diseases common in their country, such as a contagious affection which, in the reign of Tiberius, came from Asia and spread over Rome. Lucian also speaks of a physician from Damascus, who pretended to have a sovereign remedy for gout, and Pliny tells us that generally patients had more confidence in foreign physicians.

The compounders of pharmaceutical products, who, as we have already pointed out, had a tendency to withdraw from the practice of medicine properly so-called and to make their art a distinct profession, were to be found among the foreign empirics. The sale of medicaments was for them a very lucrative occupation, all the more profitable because in the common opinion the most expensive remedies were the most efficacious. Many foreigners entered upon the profession of *pharmacopola*, which any person could practise. However, not all had the same success and certain of these charlatans had their clientèle among the poor and were content with selling ointments, love philters and even poisons to those who would pay the price. The plebeians, says Thomas, had neither the time nor the money to consult physicians who had been trained in the Greek schools; therefore they consulted those foreigners who were quite as capable of applying a bandage as of rapidly satisfying an avid heir. L. Claudius, the *pharmacopola* of Ancona, has remained celebrated through centuries on account of Cicero's speech for Cluentius. It was he who furnished the poison with which Oppianicus poisoned Dinaea.

This unwarrantable interference of foreigners, dishonestly and unscrupulously seeking in the pharmaceutical art only the opportunity of making unlimited wealth, resulted in many disadvantages, and it soon became impossible to obtain properly prepared remedies. Even Pliny the Elder complains that the preparation of remedies began to be neglected by physicians, who found it a simpler matter to buy their plasters and ointments all ready compounded by these pharmacists, who in turn had often been cheated by dealers in drugs of bad quality. Galen makes the same complaint.

As legislation did not suppress the abuse, measures were at length taken to put a stop to these frauds. In Syria, Egypt,

Cappadocia and Pontus, as well as Africa, drugs were collected under the supervision of the governor. In Crete there was an officer specially appointed to collect medicinal herbs. They were enclosed in bales or baskets on which the name of the plant and its place of origin were inscribed; some of these were stored in the imperial warehouses, others were sent to Rome and sold. Such were the necessary precautions that had to be taken by Rome in order to protect as far as possible the public health against those aliens who, conquered by the Roman armies, took their revenge by living upon their conquerors. For that matter they were not the only ones to benefit by the practice of the healing art, and we shall show that even Romans, although not in such numbers, practised medicine, but before referring to them we will consider the legal situation of these foreign physicians and pharmacists.

In reality this did not differ essentially from that of other aliens who did not have the full Roman citizenship—*jus Quiritium, jus civitatis, jus civile.* Such were the principal elements of this *jus civitatis* which was not enjoyed by foreign physicians, who could neither wear the toga nor take the name of a Roman family; severe penalties were inflicted upon them if they misrepresented themselves or if they usurped the rights of the Roman citizen. Under the Emperors, the condition of the foreigners in general and the *medici* in particular was improved, and, as we shall see, a number of them acquired the citizenship, thus increasing the number of free Roman citizens who gave themselves up to the practice of medicine. And of these we shall now speak.

As already said, the practice of medicine required no diploma, and, as it was a lucrative profession, the lower classes especially gave up their trades and became physicians, thus deteriorating the profession. They were accused of poisoning and adultery, as Pliny tells us and as the following epigram of Martial shows:—

*Uxorem, Charideme, tuam scis ipse sinisque*
*A medico futui; vis sine febre mori.*

To these imputations other subjects of reproach were added, such as avidity and even rapacity, ignorance and charlatanism. This discredit of the medical profession explains why the Romans, especially during the first centuries of the Republic, when customs were more severe, generally did not resort to it, and Pliny says: *Solam hanc artium Graecarum nondum exercet Romana gravitas, in tanto fructu paucissimi Quiritium attigere, et ipsi statim ad Graecos transfugae.* But this repugnance weakened as soon as morals became more relaxed and the sole thought of everyone was to become rich by any means whatever. Hence the conditions altered more and more, and Cicero, distinguishing the learned and liberal from the servile professions, places medicine in the foremost rank. Then other advantages were conceded to those who practised this profession, and Julius Caesar gave the citizenship to all who exercised the healing art at Rome. These favours were continued under Augustus; hence there were freemen physicians and Roman citizens practising medicine, especially at the court, during the early days of the Empire, and they were held in high esteem, some of them coming from good families. During the early days of the Empire, Vettius Valens, one of the physicians to Claudius, was even an equerry, a rank to which other physicians had been admitted, as we have said.

We have now considered the principal *personae*, that is to say, the various parts that physicians and pharmacists played in Roman society. We will leave aside the influence that their quality of *filius* or of *paterfamilias* might exercise on their legal status, but we believe it meet to complete this chapter by some brief considerations on the part played by women in the practice of medicine and pharmacy at Rome. Women enjoyed a greater liberty and far more consideration at Rome than in Greece, and it is unquestionable that some female slaves gave themselves up to the study of disease. Among these privileged slaves, who by the nature of their functions were superior to other slaves of the familia, some of them were physicians and pharmacists of the master and his household. These women physicians occasionally studied the science of poisons and their antidotes, for during the epoch of imperial corruption, poisoning was of frequent occurrence at Rome and the skilfulness of servants who could counteract poisoning by enemies was as greatly appreciated as was their skill in poisoning the enemies in turn.

The famous example of the slave Locusta, who by her detestable services was for a long time spared and, according to Tacitus, was maintained as an instrument of the government, is well known. As her price for the poisoning of Britannicus, Locusta received immunity and considerable domains, and even had disciples ; but, in the reign of Galba, she was put to death with others.

It was not only among the slaves that female physicians were found, because freedwomen, Roman citizens, and aliens also practised medicine. From the very first year of our era, Scribonius Largus speaks of an *honesta matrona* who had cured several patients afflicted with epilepsy by the use of a certain preparation of her own. Pliny speaks of alien women practitioners, among others a certain Olympias, who was supposed to produce abortion with a mixture of goose's grease and mallow. He also gives several formulae of a female physician named Salpe, who practised the art of obstetrics, and of another known as Lais. Galen speaks of one Elephantis, who wrote a treatise on the cure of alopecia. This personage is perhaps she who, according to Martial, composed obscene poetry. And lastly mention is made among the *medicae* of a Cleopatra and an Aspasia. Among the women physicians mentioned during this period (whose origin was for the most part Greek) there are a certain number whose votive inscriptions give purely Latin names, and among these are to be found slaves, freedwomen or women of free condition, bearing the epithet of *medica.* This qualification was admitted at Rome during the first centuries of the Empire. Ulpian, the jurisconsult, in his commentary on the Praetorian Edict, considers the professional status of midwives in the case of a divorced woman who affirms or denies pregnancy. For that matter, at Rome the art of obstetrics was generally exercised by *obstetrices,* who were also called *medicae.* These midwives evidently played quite an important part, because quite delicate expert work was given them and it is certain that in many circumstances they gave their care to women who from prudery did not wish to consult a physician.

The texts clearly show that the *medicae* attended patients for diseases which did not necessarily result from pregnancy and labour. In the Digest there is a passage from Ulpian which leaves no doubt that the *medicae* and *obstetrices* really practised medicine in general :—*Sed obstetricem audiant quae utique medicinam exhibere videtur.* It was a matter of fixing the salary due to them. Justinian, in his Code, fixing the price of slave physicians, refers without distinction to both men and women exercising this profession.

From what has been said it is evident that Roman women played an important part in the practice of the healing art. Their legal status must have been the same as that of other women at Rome, and varied according as they were slaves, freedwomen, aliens or Roman citizens, *sui juris* or *alieni juris*.

A great number of individuals practised various branches of medicine, such as surgery, pharmacy and so forth, and lived at the court of the Emperors. History has preserved the names of five physicians at the court of Augustus, among whom was Antonius Musa (already mentioned) while there were two physicians of the name of Andromachus, who lived at Nero's court. Gaul also sent physicians to the palaces of the Roman sovereigns; Crinas of Marseilles had the most aristocratic clientèle at Rome in the early part of the first century of our era; while we know of Charmis and Demosthenes (also of Marseilles) as well as Julius Ausonius of Bordeaux. Pharmacy was especially represented by Galen, who may be called the Father of Pharmacy.

It is probable that all these court physicians received honours, privileges and prerogatives attached to their position, and they were given a special title expressing the dignity enjoyed by them. Galen, when he calls Andromachus, Nero's physician, by the title of Archiater, is the first author known to us who employs this title, which has given rise to interminable disputes, some inferring that it means "physician of the prince", others "prince of physicians". But it appears that no attention has been paid to a passage in the writings of Gregory of Tours, in which the two titles of Archiater and *Primus Medicorum* are applied to the same personage, thus evidently indicating a single position, that of first physician to the house of the ruler. However this may be, it is clear that under the Roman emperors the *medici Palatini* were given this title. But it was hardly, if ever, employed until after Alexander Severus, who was the first to regulate the service of the Archiaters, as the following passage from Lampridius shows: *Medicus sub eo unus*

*Palatinus salarium accepit; caeteri omnes, qui usque ad sex fuerunt, annonas binas aut ternas accipiebant.*

The title of Archiater was also given to the public physicians in the pay of certain cities, and there is a decree of Antoninus Pius, who appointed public physicians in certain towns. Antoninus says that the least of cities may have five physicians who shall enjoy immunity, while more important towns may have seven and the larger cities ten, although this latter number shall not be exceeded. This decree did not confer the title of Archiater, which was given to public physicians for the first time by Constantine.

It has been maintained, upon the authority of various texts and epigraphic monuments, that there were still other physicians or Archiaters besides those who were physicians to the emperors and public physicians of cities. Briau has mentioned physicians especially attached to the service of the portico called the *xystus* in public gymnasiums, and those of the Vestal Virgins. The Archiater of the *xystus* (which was a place for the practice of gymnastics during bad weather and where the athletes exercised) no doubt gave his care to the many accidents requiring the services of a skilled physician, while the Archiater of the Vestal Virgins gave his skill to this important and respected college of the Romans.

## CHAPTER XIII

### ISLAMIC MEDICINE

For a long time it was maintained that the Arabs were merely servile copyists of the Greeks, and even that they caused a delay in the evolution of medical science. This is a mistaken opinion. At the time when the Arabs appeared in the Orient, Greek science was in complete decadence, and the practice of magic reigned supreme. Not only did the Arabs save the Greek treasures from the irredeemable loss to which but for them they had been doomed, but they developed the taste for scientific studies, both in the East and in the West, by popularizing and commenting upon the Greek works. Had they merely been content with collecting Greek science and transmitting it to Europeans, that would alone have been a great glory to them. But they did better still, for in the arts, as in the sciences, they did original work.

It is perfectly true that at the base of Arabian civilization we find Graeco-Byzantine civilization, but very soon the Arabian character asserted itself and all Arabian works showed an originality which distinguishes them from the productions of former civilizations. " The Arabs," says Humboldt, " drove back the barbarism which had already existed in Europe for two centuries . . . ; they went back to the eternal sources of Greek philosophy ; they did not stop at saving the treasure of acquired knowledge ; they increased it and opened up new routes for the study of nature."

Up to the last twenty-five years Islamic medicine and the Arabian physicians were only known by Latin translations of their works which, according to the opinion of all historians, are very defective. The studies of Dr. Lucien Leclerc in the history of Islamic medicine are, however, epoch-making, and others, without particularly concerning themselves with medicine, have shown the great merit of the Arabian physicists and have proved that their civilization was not plagiarism. Among these should be mentioned Dr. Gustave Lebon, who has written a remarkable work on Arabian civilization, while of recent years Professor G. Colin has written a number of very interesting works and made several translations, especially of Avenzoar; Professor Guibues has recently translated the book entitled *The Art of Treatment*, by Najm ed-Din Mahmud; nor should the important contributions by Dr. H. Renaud and Prof. E. G. Browne's *Arabian Medicine* be overlooked.

After having achieved their conquest the Arabs, whose empire extended from the Indus to the Atlantic Ocean, were quite as active and offered proof of the same qualities in the domain of science as they had shown in the art of war. Adapting themselves rapidly to the teaching of the Greeks, they soon went beyond their masters.

Without going back into the too remote past to enquire into the civilization and the mode of life of the Arabs in the pre-Islamic period, we may believe that they had possessed for long intellectual qualities and aptitudes which the nomad life of the desert had kept in abeyance. Then, obedient to the voice of their prophet, the Arabs went forth to conquer the world for Mahometanism, and when they came in contact with the débris of ancient civilizations they showed their aptitude by putting into practice the beautiful precepts of their prophet, who said to his followers: "Teach science which teaches fear of God; he who desires knowledge adores God; when he spreads it he is giving alms; he who has it becomes an object of veneration and goodwill. Science protects from error and sin; it lights the road to paradise; it guides us through the pleasures and pains of life; it is an ornament among our friends and a shield against the enemy. The memorials of the wise alone endure because their great deeds serve as models and are repeated by the great minds who follow them.

"Science is the remedy for the infirmities of ignorance, a comforting beacon in the night of injustice. The study of the sciences has the value of a fast; the teaching of them has the value of prayer; in a noble heart they inspire the highest feelings and they correct and humanize the perverted."

The *Hadith* have the force of law among Mahometans and it therefore results that it is an obligation for them to study.

Unfortunately, during the centuries of decadence the heads of the religious brotherhoods limited this obligation to purely religious studies.

As to medicine, the influence of the precepts of the Prophet was considerable. It has been said that the Arabs are fatalists; hence they should neglect the care of the body. But this is an error and the majority of Mahometans follow the example of the Prophet who attached such great importance to the care of the body, cleanliness and health. Mahomet unceasingly repeated: "God has not inflicted diseases upon us without at the same time giving us the remedy." And the Arabians started out on the search for these remedies. The Koran itself sanctions the zeal that the Arabs have always displayed in the study of medicine and says: "He who has restored life to a man shall be accounted as if he had restored life to humanity." (Koran, Chap. V, v. 35.)

These and other precepts explain the eagerness and jealous care with which the Mahometan rulers protected and encouraged the learned. For them this was a work of piety. It is to the Khalif al-Mamun of the Abbasid dynasty that belongs the credit for having created and assisted the growth of this intense intellectual movement which was to reveal the riches of Greek science to the Arabs. And it was, in fact, during his reign that the work of translation attained its height. The presence at Bagdad (whither he had been summoned by the Khalif) of the Nestorian physician, George Bachtichou, was the spark which was to light the sacred fire. As a matter of fact the Nestorians played a very large part in initiating the Arabs into the Greek sciences by giving them the first translations made. Never shall the world see again so marvellous a sight as the Arabs afforded during the IXth century. These pastoral people, whom religious enthusiasm had suddenly made masters of half the civilized world, immediately set to work to study science. During this time the Germanic hordes prided themselves upon their brutal ignorance, and it took them several centuries to link up the chain of tradition, while the Arabians accomplished it in one century.

At the start it was the Christians who were the initiators of the Arabs and presided over the early work of translating.

Among the great translators of Greek into Arabic should be mentioned Honein ibn Ishaq, who went to Greece and, staying there two years in order to learn the language, returned to Bagdad with a large number of manuscripts. His literary activity was prodigious. He commented upon Hippocrates, translated a large part of Galen's writings, as well as those of Oribasius and Paulus Aegineta and portions of Aristotle and Plato. These translations were made directly from the Greek into Arabic. Another celebrated translator was a Greek, called "Qusta ibn Luqa", who knew Arabic quite as well as his own tongue. It is probable that later on the Arabs were able to read the Greek authors in the original, just as they learned Latin and the Castilian tongue in Spain. The library of the Escurial contains Arab-Greek, Arab-Latin and Arab-Spanish dictionaries compiled by Mahometans.

Although full credit must be given to the Abbasid dynasty for setting on foot this intellectual movement of the IXth century, it is not to be forgotten that the people also had a large share in it. In all the large cities the rich paid their weight in gold for translations and vied with one another in the possession of libraries and the rarest works.

While the Arabs were raising civilization to the highest degree, the Greek nation slowly but surely continued towards the most complete decadence. Theological disputes filled all minds and those who did not share the dominant ideas were ruthlessly persecuted. Forgetting the rational principles of Hippocrates and Galen, the Greek physicians sank into empiricism, mysticism and the strangest superstitions. As early as the VIth century Aëtius of Amida advised the use of a certain ointment, and while applying it the patient had to utter these words: "May the God of Abraham, of Isaac and of Jacob give virtue to this medication." This quotation will suffice to show the real psychological state of the physicians of the time. History does not mention a single Greek physician worthy of the name during the entire Islamic period, while the sovereigns at Constantinople were obliged to seek Arabian physicians for their medical advisers. Indeed, it may be said that Greek medicine was non-existent when the Arabs appeared upon the scene and that this state of affairs continued from the IXth to the XIVth century. As soon as a city was taken the first care of the Arabs was to found a mosque and a school. Independently of the ordinary schools for general instruction, the large cities, such as Bagdad, Cairo, Toledo and Cordova, possessed universities having laboratories, observatories and rich libraries. Spain alone had seventy public libraries. The library of Khalif el-Hakim II at Cordova contained six hundred thousand volumes, forty-four of which were catalogues.

On the subject of this ruler, and in order to give an idea how these sovereigns protected learned men, we can do no better than quote Louis Viardot (*Essai sur l'Histoire des Arabes d'Espagne*, 2 vol., Paris, 1833).

" El-Hakim was the most zealous, generous, and enthusiastic protector that letters, sciences and arts had ever known. His father, Abdu'r-Rahman, had given him the most learned masters that he could obtain from the Orient, foremost among whom was the famous Ismail ibn Qasim Abu Ali el-Kali, born at Diar el-Bekir, whom the Khalifs of Bagdad were in the habit of consulting.

" In his youth el-Hakim took upon himself the cost of publishing the poem Al Ikd-al-farid (The Only Necklace) by the celebrated poet of Cordova, Ibn Abd el-Rabbihi. When he became Khalif he developed an intense interest in human knowledge and did everything for its advancement. In all countries where the Arabian language was spoken (that is to say to the furthest limits of Asia), he sent envoys with copyists whose only business it was to transmit all kinds of writings they could find, and he thus tremendously increased the collection of manuscripts formed by his ancestors.

" The great munificence and the unlimited friendliness with which he rewarded merit and the talents of the learned, increased twofold the company of illustrious persons brought together by his father, among whom were highly talented women."

The majority of Orientalists who have studied the works of the Arabs admit that long before Roger Bacon they were in possession of that method which later on led to so many discoveries, the result of the perfecting of physical instruments. Speaking of the school of Bagdad, Sédillot (*Histoire des Arabes*, Paris, 1854) says : " What especially characterized the Bagdad school at its beginning was the truly scientific spirit which presided over all. To go from the known to the unknown, then from effects to causes, and only to admit as true what had been demonstrated by experimental work; such were the principles taught by the masters. During the IXth century the Arabs were in possession of this fruitful method, which a long time afterwards was to be, in the hands of modern investigators, the instrument of their finest discoveries."

It is clear that one cannot expect to find in the Islamic writings the results which have been attained by modern experimental medicine, but those obtained by the Arabs by the method of observation were often far superior to those of their forerunners and even of Galen himself. This method, which enabled the Arabs to make such interesting discoveries in astronomy and chemistry, was unfortunately limited in medicine by religious scruples. The prohibition of dissection and autopsies prevented them from anticipating the important anatomical discoveries of the XVIth, XVIIth and XVIIIth centuries.

The philosophical and medical doctrines of the Islamic physicians need not concern us; taken as a whole they were those of Galen and Hippocrates, in other words, the humoral theory, which exercised its influence throughout Europe until the advent of the great Pasteur, the Father of Modern Medicine, who revealed the true causes of so many diseases. One cannot reproach the Islamic physicians of the IXth, Xth and XIth centuries for being content with the Greek theory of humoral medicine, especially since recent researches are again leading us to this theory, although it wears a different dress.

Even in the realm of pure theory one meets with more than one manifestation of the philosophical spirit which inspired the learned men of Islam. They made more than one attempt to place in doubt the ideas then current, but they were timid attempts and had no result. When one reads such reflections as those of the Arabian physician Najm ed-Din ibn el-Lobudi to the effect that the existence of the body and its preservation depend exclusively upon the blood and not upon the four humours, as was generally maintained by physicians and philosophers; when we consider the aphorism of the learned Arabian alchemist Geber, that "the various bodies are composed of the same elements, but in different proportions", one is tempted to believe that the great thinkers of this period foresaw many truths that modern discoveries have revealed.

Rhazes, whose true name was Abu Bakr Muhammad ibn Zakariya, was born at Ray (hence his name ar-Razi, or, in Europe, Rhazes, under which he is most generally known), and saw the light of day in the second half of the IXth century, dying at an advanced age in about the year A.D. 923. His principal medical works are the *Hawi* or *Continens*, the *Mansuri*, and a treatise on eruptive fevers. Rhazes held a very surprising opinion for the period, namely that, properly speaking, fever did not represent a disease, but only showed that nature was working to bring about a solution of the disease (*Continens*, Book XXIII, p. 347).

From the point of view of pathology the Islamic physicians made three important advances; they methodically classified the scattered elements of Greek medicine; they created clinical medicine, and lastly they enriched pathology with a knowledge of new diseases. "It appears to us," says Leclerc, "that scientific genius is produced in two ways and is known by two signs, namely the methodical classification of a number of given facts and secondly, the culture of abstract sciences. The Arabs followed both paths. As to the first, they early undertook the classification of notions of medicines and facts leading to them."

Ali Abbas, whose right name was Ali ibnu'l-Abbas al-Majusi, was an Arabian physician of the Xth century, the author of the *Maliki*, and of a treatise on dietetics, which may be considered a masterpiece of the time. It was in the above spirit that he wrote the *Maliki*, and Avicenna his *Canon*. So, if we consider them only from this point of view, the Islamic physicians have the merit of having well analysed the Greek writings, which were often tiresome to read and difficult to understand. They extracted the most important matter from them and placed it in relief, leaving aside everything that was superfluous. One has merely to read Galen and afterwards Avicenna in order to see the difference. The former is obscure, the latter perfectly clear; order and method reign in the latter, which in Galen we seek in vain. The *Maliki* and the *Canon* are to the highest degree didactic and this explains the popularity they enjoyed in the faculties of Europe down to the beginning of the XVIIIth century. The following passage is extracted from the preface to the *Maliki*: "The science of medical art being the foremost of all sciences and the most important for its power and its dangers, as well as the most useful of all, since everyone has need of it, it has been my desire to include all of it in a complete book on medical art containing all that is necessary for the physician, as well as for everybody to know, for preserving health in those who already possess it and for restoring it to the sick, because I have not found in any of the ancient or modern physicians a complete book which contains all that is related to the practice and science of medicine." Then Ali ibnu'l Abbas reviews the list of celebrated physicians from the time of Hippocrates to Rhazes and points out that they all lacked method and conciseness. "The *Maliki* of Ali Abbas," says Leclerc, "marks a great advance in the medicine of the Orient. An Arab dares to do what he could not discover in the ancient Greeks, namely, to comprise in a single work the whole field of medicine. This work is not, as is the *Continens* of Rhazes, an inventory of all the facts left to medicine by the ancients and the moderns. The science is embraced as a whole, all its parts are co-ordinated, the data that each writer has claimed are submitted to a critical examination."

The *Canon* of Avicenna, conceived according to a larger plan and a more rigorous method, included all branches of science, and had a tremendous influence on the fate of medicine in the Orient and among the European nations. Avicenna—rightly Ibn Sina—was the most celebrated Islamic physician of the XIth century, and may be said to have been an intellectual prodigy. It is perhaps possible that never before or since has there been so precocious, so facile and so wide an intelligence united with such extended and indefatigable energy.

Although the Islamic physicians were preoccupied with theory, they did not lose sight of the practical side of medicine. In point of fact it was in medical practice that they most distinguished themselves. The masters trained students in their own ideas, and, although attending to private practice, still gave their help to patients in hospital, as will be shown later on. The greatest Islamic physicians—Rhazes, Avicenna, and Avenzoar—were all at the head of hospitals. Thus they had all the time necessary to study patients and to follow the complete evolution of disease. They made case-histories and their hospitals, like that at Bagdad, kept registers of these, in proof of which we have the collection of hospital observations frequently referred to by Rhazes in the *Continens*.

The Arabian physicians also wrote works on clinical medicine, such, for example, as the collection of case-histories by Mohammed et-Temimi, which may be regarded as the first book on the subject. In the clinical study of disease they showed themselves keen observers and their description of symptoms shows a precision and an originality that could only be obtained by a direct study of disease. In diagnosis and prognosis they excelled.

Up to the time of the Islamic physicians, meningitis had been confused with acute affections accompanied by delirium. After having outlined the symptomatology of this disease, Avicenna defines it as follows: "Acute *sersâm* is an inflammation or tumour of the envelopes of the brain. The prodromata of this disease consist of headache, disturbed sleep and mental depression without cause. As soon as the process becomes localized in the meninges, the first symptoms developing are restlessness, violent headache and pain in the neck. Occasionally there is epistaxis and slight incontinence of urine. When the disease has fully developed all hope of cure is vain. There is intense fever and mental depression and the patient remains perfectly silent and indifferent to what is said to him. Respiration is rapid and irregular; the thoracic movements are, however, ample and deep; localized or generalized convulsions occur; sleep is disturbed and accompanied by extreme restlessness and hallucinations, the patient cries out and is unable to bear light.

"At the terminal phase of the disease, the tongue becomes paralysed and insensibility is general; if the patient be touched with a (pointed?) instrument, even with considerable pressure, he feels nothing; finally the limbs become cold and the patient dies from asphyxia."

Little has been added in modern time to this symptomatic picture of meningitis, and little change has been made in the prognosis. Avicenna's diagnosis is quite satisfactory, as he makes a distinction between primary meningitis and the phenomena of secondary meningism of other acute affections. This is what he calls *sersâm ettabii* or secondary *sersâm*, or even pseudo-*sersâm*. He also mentions that pleurisy and pneumonia may give rise to the symptomatology of *sersâm* and that in such circumstances inflammation of the meninges may be real, when death inevitably occurs on the second or third day after the onset of the meningeal phenomena.

Many other quotations could be taken from Avicenna's chapter on nervous diseases, particularly the aetiology and diagnosis of various types of hemiplegia and paralysis. However, we will merely refer to the diagnosis of facial paralysis (*leqaonâ*). Avicenna distinguishes two types, one of central origin, the other the result of a local lesion of the nerve itself. The latter is the more frequent. As to differential diagnosis, Avicenna states that in the central type sensibility is disturbed and the eyelid droops, while the skin becomes deviated to the healthy side, likewise the tongue. In the peripheral type there is, on the contrary, no disturbance of the sensibility, but the skin of the forehead on the affected side is tense, the wrinkles disappear and there is a decrease of the secretion of saliva.

Avicenna has given a good description of affections of the respiratory apparatus. Pleurisy, he says, must be differentiated from simple inflammation of the intercostal muscles, inflammation of the mediastinum, and abscess of the upper surface of the liver. He points out that there are cases in which a differential diagnosis is impossible because an inflammatory process of the liver may extend to the pleura.

Avenzoar, whose real name is Abu Merwan Abd al-Malik ibn Abu'l-Ala Zuhr (A.D. 1094–1160), was one of the most celebrated physicians of Mahometan Spain in the XIIth century. He belonged to the celebrated family of the Zuhr, which during more than a century produced so many great physicians.

Avenzoar was the first author to describe cancer of the stomach, saying: "At the time when the miserable Ali confined me in prison, I saw a man who could not digest his food and was the subject of a remittent fever, which was at times severe and at others mild. There was a slight diarrhoea and it was impossible to determine the cause of the symptoms complained of by the patient." And he adds that the patient was in a state of marked emaciation while palpation revealed the presence of an indolent tumour, which, however, was tender when pressed upon.

Avicenna describes the symptoms of pyloric stenosis and gastric ulcer. Of the latter affection he says that, whenever pain in the stomach lasts for some time and is rebellious to all forms of medication, the question of ulcer must be considered. Among the symptoms of this affection, he especially insists on acute pain which varies in site and time in relation to eating and is dependent upon the localization of the lesion ; a burning sensation, intense thirst and irregular febrile manifestations are noted.

The semeiology of the liver is particularly well studied by Avicenna. The condition of the organ can be ascertained by palpation, which reveals hardness or enlargement of the gland, likewise the presence of a tumour. A deep-seated pain accompanied by a feeling of weight indicates that there is a tumour of the liver or a swelling of its parenchyma. When the pain is acute it is due to an inflammation of the envelopes of the liver. Important data are furnished by the condition of the hepatic functions, such as the condition of the digestion and the stools, occurrence of haemorrhage, and the condition of the gall bladder and spleen, whose function, he says, is intimately connected with that of the liver. He also refers to information that may be obtained from the condition of other organs which are secondarily involved in diseases of the liver—the heart, stomach and kidney—as well as the condition of the tongue and quantity of urine voided. Also the presence of icterus, emaciation, fever and pruritus.

In the aetiology of hepatic diseases, Avicenna appears to have known the harmful effects of alcohol on the liver, because he says that wine induces diarrhoea of hepatic origin which is extremely difficult to control.

The diagnosis of icterus (jaundice) is particularly well described. He distinguishes icterus by retention, icterus caused by corruption of the composition of the blood (which to-day we call haemolytic icterus), and toxic icterus, due to bites of insects or snakes, the ingestion of poisons or drugs. The description of the symptoms and pathology of the various forms of icterus that follows is extremely up-to-date, but space forbids further quotation.

Generally speaking the subjects dealt with by the Islamic physicians are especially treated from a clinical standpoint and reveal a personal experience which is often lacking in the works of the ancient writers. Thus, in speaking of tumours in general, Avicenna affirms that, contrary to the opinion of the ancients, the brain and the bones may be the seat of tumours.

Galen maintained that apoplexy was rarely produced by true plethora. Avicenna, on the contrary, declares this to be a most frequent cause and defines apoplexy thus: " It is the loss of sensibility and movement following an *occlusion* seated within the brain in those places traversed by the nervous influx of sensibility and motricity." A detailed discussion of this definition then follows. The occlusion and arrest in the continuity of the cerebral substance can be produced in three different ways. Firstly: by plethora, the congestion invading the brain, especially the ventricles; but it may also be seated in the meninges and produce the syndrome of meningitis. Plethoric subjects with a red face and congested eyes are predisposed to this type. Secondly: a thick substance may reach the brain—by way of the circulation—and produce an occlusion, just as this may result from intense cold. Just what this occluding substance may be, autopsy alone could reveal, but we know to-day that it is a blood clot carried by the circulation which causes embolus of a cerebral artery followed by apoplexy. The third form is that in which the brain, reacting against morbid matter, contracts the blood vessels likewise, thus giving rise to cerebral anaemia.

In the plethoric type, Avicenna advises copious blood-letting as both prophylactic and curative treatment, and he affirms that he has obtained really marvellous results by resorting to it, but that usually the patient will be hemiplegic.

A few words will now be said of certain diseases first described by the Islamic physicians. Avenzoar was the first to describe pericarditis. " A fluid collection similar to urine arises in the pericardium. When this affection has developed, the patient loses strength and becomes markedly emaciated and dies cachetic. The treatment of this affection—as to myself I know none that is effective—consists in giving solvent and desiccating remedies, and these should be so subtle that their action may reach the pericardium."

Avenzoar also speaks of the dry form of pericarditis, which, he says, is a condition in which the pericardium becomes covered with successive layers of matter, making it very thick. "The humour of the pericardium has a tendency to become compact and to coagulate. The patient suffers from dyspnoea."

This is what he has to say about abscess of the pericardium. "The pericardium may be the seat of an acute tumour. If from the onset of the disease the physician lets blood, he may perhaps be able to arrest the disease. He should also prescribe drugs for controlling the heat and also those which fortify the heart. The slightest delay in treatment may be fatal because this abscess is very serious."

Avenzoar made the earliest mention known to us of abscess of the mediastinum, which, he says, becomes evident by a sharp and continuous cough, and a tensive pain felt behind the sternum. "Respiration is short, difficult and frequent; fever is irregular and high, and chills occur. The patient complains of severe thirst; the pulse is hard and unequal."

Among the Arabs of Spain who developed medical science to the highest degree in the Middle Ages, the imposing figure of Abu'l-Ala Zuhr, the father of Abenzoar, stands out. Among his writings is to be mentioned a little tract entitled the *Ted Kira,* which has been translated by Professor G. Colin. In this is to be found the following description of pneumothorax. "When cough results from a dyscrasia it is persistent and cachexia develops. The cough frequently causes perforation into the lung and the condition becomes incurable. This is why one should hasten to adopt a treatment and to attenuate the accidents by all means possible, at the same time dealing with the pathogenic element."

Avenzoar speaks of the *naa'lat,* which, according to Colin, is a senile verruca undergoing malignant transformation. "*Naa'lats* may develop on the surface of the body; they are tumours, usually seated under the shoulder, and have a tendency to reach the deeper structures. They may be seated on the right or the left side. They only occur in persons of advanced years and usually in those who have met with adversity, or have given themselves up to intellectual work, or have been greatly preoccupied in other matters. This was the case of my father, on whom God have mercy."

To Rhazes we owe the first description of the specific eruptive fevers, namely smallpox, measles and scarlet fever, and herein the eminent physician is fully revealed. For the first time Rhazes, and after him Avicenna, discussed an absolutely new conception in the aetiology of these diseases, namely congenital contagion. This contagion is effected by a kind of leaven existing in the blood of the mother, which reaches the foetus through the placenta. This leaven ferments and the blood, trying to purify itself, rejects the peccant matter from the body through the openings of the glands in the skin. For this reason Rhazes states that everyone is subject to this disease. This is a theory which even to-day might appear seductive if the word leaven be replaced by that of bacteria. It remains true that its consequences, from the viewpoint of the prognosis of the various clinical types of smallpox, exactly coincide with our present-day knowledge.

Avicenna states that variola is most contagious in the spring-time and autumn, and is also more frequent in these seasons. Children are more frequently taken with it than adults, while elderly people are rarely attacked unless the existing season is excessively contagious. One can have variola only once in a lifetime.

The disease makes itself known by pain in the back, violent headache, general asthenia and tingling throughout the body and itching of the nose; the eyes are red and watery; the respiration is difficult, the voice hoarse and sleep disturbed by fearful dreams. All these symptoms will be accompanied by fever. The eruption begins in the form of raised red spots which change into papules filled with purulent fluid. The vesicles then burst and rid themselves of their contents, becoming transformed into pustules which desquamate and give rise to severe itching.

If the eruption breaks out easily it will suppurate nicely; the temperature will drop after suppuration has become established, and the patient will recover. If, on the contrary, the fever persists the prognosis is bad. When the papules are in great number and are confluent, and when they do not contain pus, we are dealing with a very malignant form of the disease. The haemorrhagic type is also extremely serious. When the papules or vesicles are small, hard, violet in colour or dark red or black, and when they are accompanied with pain and very high fever, early death is to be expected.

Rhazes regarded the eruption as an unimportant epiphenonomenon—a kind of crisis, the symptoms indicating the condition of the vital forces and the gravity of the patient's condition obtaining his more particular attention.

Avicenna included measles and scarlet fever in one description, because in the Middle Ages the two diseases were regarded as one under the name of *morbilli*. Morbilli, Avicenna tells us, are a kind of bilious variola ; there is hardly any difference between the two affections other than that the morbilli are derived from the bile and a lesser quantity of morbid matter comes to the surface of the skin, while variola at once produces pustules on the cutaneous surface. The prodromal signs are about the same, although the general symptoms, such as fever, dyspnoea, and lassitude are more intense in the morbilli. Also the latter are less serious than variola, but there are cases that are more serious and even fatal, especially when accompanied by cough and intense dyspnoea. The eruption in variola takes place gradually, commencing on the face, while in the morbilli on the contrary it suddenly appears upon the entire body surface. Nasal catarrh and watering of the eyes are more marked in the latter affections.

As to treatment, in ordinary cases dietetic means are quite sufficient without fatiguing the patient with medication. During the first phase of the disease cold water should be given internally, vapour baths are to be ordered and purgatives should be used with great circumspection, and only when constipation really exists.

As has already been pointed out, the Mahometans were prevented from performing autopsies by religious scruples, with the consequence that neither anatomy nor surgery could make any real progress. The Islamic physicians used Galen's anatomical works, from which they derived sufficient knowledge to enable them to perform operations, occasionally of an audacious nature. They knew the human skeleton well, and some of their descriptions (like that of Avicenna) are sometimes far more complete than Galen's.

Moreover, in view of certain details in the description of organs, as well as certain new anatomical observations attributed to them, it is not at all unlikely that some of them dissected animals, especially monkeys.

According to Portal, Avicenna possessed an exact knowledge of the pupil and the movements of dilatation and contraction of the iris. The same author supposes that he discovered the insertion of the muscles of the eye, the Greek writers being entirely silent on the subject. As a matter of fact Avicenna speaks of six motor muscles for the globe, four of which are inserted by a common band in the fundus of the orbit, a discovery that several later anatomists attributed to themselves. The other two muscles are the small and the great oblique, which, Avicenna says, are for the purpose of holding the globe, and are attached on its posterior aspect. Avicenna was conversant with the lacrymal ducts, which are intended, he says, to carry the tears into the inside of the nose.

In speaking of the operation for lacrymal fistula, Rhazes pointed out that one must be careful not to injure what we call the external or anterior branch of the nasal branch of the opthalmic nerve of Willis. No mention is made of this by any Greek surgeon. Rhazes also described the laryngeal branch of the recurrent nerve, which he says arises near the trachea. This nerve, he notes, is sometimes double on the right side, and all due honour should be given him for this discovery which has long been considered as modern. The muscle which opens the glottis attracted him, particularly in respect of his theory of aphonia and of suffocation.

Avicenna's physiological reason for the different convolutions of the intestine is interesting. " It is," he says " to have the food remain the proper time in the gut in order that the nutritive material may have sufficient time to become separated from the useless matter. If a man had but a single intestine the food would be ejected too quickly and he would be obliged to take food all the time ".

There is no question then but that the Islamic physicians beneficially influenced the progress of surgery and of medicine.

A MEDIEVAL SURGERY (XVth CENTURY)

Enlarged by A. Mittendorff from Petrus Hispanus (*Author's Collection*)

[*face p. 200*

Abulcasis, whose real name was Abu'l-Qasim Khalef ibn Abbas az-Zahrawi, was born at Zahra, near Cordova, and died, it is said, in 1013, at the age of 101 years. Abulcasis was the medical authority most frequently consulted by surgeons of mediaeval times. His larger work on medicine bears the name of *al-Tasrif*, and is divided into thirty books. His most original work, however, is the *Liber Servitoris* or *Book of Simples*.

To Abulcasis alone among the great Islamic physicians belongs the credit of having restored surgery to its former glory. Undoubtedly from time to time we find some operative indication buried in the large treatises of other Islamic writers. But Abulcasis certainly should be credited as having summed up all the surgical knowledge of the times in a single treatise, the thirtieth of his large medical encyclopaedia. Although this book is not the most original of his writings, it nevertheless became a classic in the mediaeval schools of Europe. What probably contributed largely to the success of this book were the illustrations of instruments which it contains. This book might have disappeared completely, for the other Islamic physicians paid no attention to surgery, and, in his preface, Abulcasis says that surgery was not in repute in his country and that it had practically disappeared without leaving a trace behind. Some remnants of the writings of the ancients still remained but transcription had corrupted them so that they were often unintelligible and useless, and for this reason he wished to revive this science by writing a work upon it.

Abulcasis goes on to say that "the reason why skilful operators do not exist to-day is that the art of medicine requires time (to learn); he who would practise (surgery) should first study anatomy as given by Galen, in order to know the functions of the organs, their shape, their temperament, their relationship (to other organs), and to know the bones, tendons and muscles, their number and position, also that of the veins and arteries, as well as the regions through which they pass.

"If anatomical knowledge be ignored, mistakes will be made and the patient will be killed."

Abulcasis, in common with Islamic physicians in general,

has been reproached as being an audacious compiler and a plagiarist of the Greeks. It is certainly true that the foundations of the surgery of Abulcasis are made up of the surgery of Paulus Aegineta: at least such is the impression given by a hasty comparison of the two books. But if Abulcasis is read carefully it will be seen that the important operations he describes include also a very precise operative technique which does not exist in Paulus. It may be said that these are merely details, but in the case of surgery, details, especially operative, are of the highest importance.

The personal observations that he gives, and the care with which he warns the reader of the dangers incurred in operating, are sufficient proof that Abulcasis was not a mere compiler, but rather that he was a very skilful surgeon.

Abulcasis considers the cautery an excellent means of treatment and refers to more than forty affections in which it is applicable. He is the first to give the precise indications for its use and at the same time to point out its dangers in certain cases. Thus in abscess of the liver he resorts to the cautery, but at the same time he indicates its contra-indications. In order that this operation shall be successful Abulcasis points out that adhesions between the liver and the peritoneum should have taken place, otherwise the patient is exposed to the danger of certain death by the entrance of pus into the abdominal cavity—a perfectly modern surgical aphorism. In cases of abscess of the liver, spleen or kidney, Hippocrates resorted to incision, and for this reason it has been maintained that with Abulcasis surgery declined. But, on the contrary, with our modern surgical technique, we should rather praise the prudence of the Arabian surgeon living in a period when neither asepsis nor antisepsis was known.

In cases of hydrocephalus Abulcasis rejected incision, and he stated that in all the children in whom he resorted to it death rapidly followed. Let it here be remarked that within the last few years attempts have been made to cure hydrocephalus by surgery and surgeons have obtained the same results as those recorded by Abulcasis.

Avicenna and Avenzoar had already advised tracheotomy in angina. Avenzoar never performed the operation on man, but he did on sheep, and in one case the animal recovered with very simple treatment.

Abulcasis performed transversal tracheotomy between the third and fourth rings of the trachea, and to prove the innocuity of this operation he relates the case-history of a slave under his care who cut her trachea without involving the large blood vessels of the neck. She rapidly recovered. He says that the operation is useless when the angina (i.e., the diphtheritic membranes) extends downwards to the ramifications of the trachea.

Abulcasis deals more thoroughly with goitre than any of his predecessors and clearly defines the difference between ordinary goitre and cancer of the thyroid. He remarks that while cancer of the thyroid is incurable, ordinary goitre should only be operated upon when it is a small, soft tumour, forming a single cyst.

He knew Pott's disease thoroughly and his description of it is excellent; he even, as also Avenzoar, described the nervous complications encountered in this disease. He points out that death in these cases frequently results from asphyxia.

Abulcasis is brief in his remarks upon abdominal surgery, but his technique of lithotomy is far ahead of that of any of his predecessors, and, according to Friend, he was the first to describe vaginal lithotomy in the female.

Lithotrity has always been looked upon as a modern discovery, but the writer is of the opinion that it was performed by Abulcasis, for, as Leclerc points out, the following passage occurs in the twenty-first treatise of the book on practice: *Et si cum hoc regimine non exierit, studeat implere ipsam (vesicam) cum instrumento quod nominatur* alnul, *apud viam transitus, vel accipiatur instrumentum subtile quod nominatur* mashabarebilia, *et suaviter intromittatur in virgam, et volvi lapidem in medio vesicae, et si fuerit mollis frangetur et exibit; si vero non exiverit, oportet incidi, ut in cirurgia determinatur.*

Much more could be said of various surgical lesions described by Abulcasis, as well as his operative technique, but what has been given will be quite sufficient for a clear understanding of the real service rendered to surgery by this skilful surgeon.

Abulcasis also wrote on obstetrics and gynaecology. He performed craniotomy when the foetal head was large, and in his chapter on the treatment of uterine abscess the use of the speculum is thoroughly described. He also reports a case of a female who was pregnant in which the foetus died without being expelled. She became pregnant a second time and again the foetus died. Some time afterwards an abscess developed at the umbilicus, which opened spontaneously, giving issue to a large number of small bones. The patient recovered and lived for several years, although a fistula remained.

Avenzoar also wrote upon some diseases of the uterus. Thus he speaks of very short and very long uteri (probably referring to the cervix) and declares that nothing can be done for this malformation.

Avicenna writes lengthily and with much detail on elongation and induration of the uterus (cervix), of flexion, of prolapses and of uterine tumours. He points out that cancer of the cervix is extremely grave.

Arib ibn Said el-Khateb, towards the end of the Xth century, wrote a complete treatise on the generation of the foetus and the treatment of pregnant women and the newly born. The writer makes this statement on the authority of Leclerc, who had the manuscript, and who also says that this author entered into much detail on abnormal presentations and the technique of version.

The practice of Islamic ophthalmology need not be considered here. Suffice it to say that the operative technique was extremely advanced.

Islamic pharmacology and therapeutics do not offer a single example of specific medication as we understand it to-day. Treatment was purely symptomatic, and it cannot be denied that the starting-point of the discoveries of the Mahometan physicians in therapeutics was entirely empirical. Yet, though usually ignorant of the active principle of a drug, the lack of this knowledge, which the progress of chemistry and experimental work has alone made possible, did not prevent them from attaining therapeutic success. When they wished to experiment with a new drug they followed the rules laid down by "Aben Guefit", and the animal used was the monkey. It was thus that Rhazes, wishing to study the effects of mercury, which was reputed to be very toxic, administered it to a monkey, and he gives the results of his experiment as follows : " As to pure mercury, I believe it not to be very pernicious ; it gives rise to intense abdominal and intestinal pain, but afterwards leaves the body as it entered it, especially if the subject takes exercise. I gave it to a monkey that I had at my house and things passed as I have said. I noted that he twisted himself about, clenched his teeth, and pressed upon his belly with his hands. Calomel, and especially sublimate, are very dangerous and very active poisons. They cause very sharp abdominal pains, colic and bloody stools. The emanations of mercury give rise to paralysis."

The experimental method enabled the Islamic physicians to introduce a large number of new drugs and to determine the exact therapeutic indications of old ones derived from the Greeks and, into the bargain, to find new properties in them. For example, the Greeks regarded opium as very dangerous and rarely employed it. The Arabs developed its indications and regarded it as *the* specific for pain, while they frequently prescribed it in potions for cough and diarrhoea and in an electuary to produce sleep.

Modern writers on opotherapy and organotherapy are simply walking in the tracks of the Arabs, for the latter were perfectly familiar with these methods. They gave dried fox's lung in asthma, because they considered it of value as the fox does not get out of breath in running. In cases of anaemia they ordered their patients to drink the blood of animals just slaughtered and also to eat fresh bone marrow. Avenzoar gave fox's brain in epilepsy. Credit should also be given to the Arabian physicians who have always given an important place in treatment to hygiene and dietetics. Both Rhazes and Avenzoar unceasingly repeat that the abusive use of drugs does not preserve health but, on the contrary, places the body in a state of lessened resistance.

The study of medicinal substances found in Dioscorides is, in its scientific form, an Islamic creation. It was especially from the XIIIth century onwards that the study of botany was carefully carried out by the Arabian physicians. Their botanists broke away from Greek tradition and travelled in order directly to study nature. Ibnu's-Suri, a Syrian sage, always took an artist with him in order to make paintings of his specimens. Abu'l-Abbas, better known by the name of Ibnu'l-Baytar, one of the greatest Arabian botanists, travelled throughout the Orient and Northern Africa for his botanical researches. His best known work is the *Jami'l Mufridat*, or *Collection of Simples*, in which he treats of foods and simple medicaments derived from the three kingdoms in alphabetical order.

The Islamic pharmacopoeia contained two hundred new plants, a great many of which are still used at the present time, and it may be well here to mention a few of the most important. Among laxatives, the Arabs added rhubarb, senna, cassia and manna, and so forth. As stimulants they were the first to use nux vomica and camphor. Among their medicaments having a preponderant action on the nervous system may be mentioned aconite, Indian hemp, and amber. They introduced colocynth as a diuretic and drastic aperient as well as santal, and they well knew the effects of ergot concerning which Ibnu'l-Baytar states that "it is a violent poison and when ingested produces bloody urine, a black tongue and disturbances of the intelligence." The Arabs recounted the various forms of a given medicament, its absorption and doses, their contra-indications and their antidotes in cases of poisoning.

But of all the advances made by the Islamic physicians, those in chemistry and pharmacy were the most important. Geber (whose real name was Abu Musa Jaber ibn Hayyan al-Kufi) was an Arabian chemist of the IXth century; he understood the composition of sulphuric and nitric acid, as well as of *aqua regis*. The Islamic physician used for external application silver nitrate, sulphate of copper and iron, realgar and numerous metallic oxides. It should, however, be added that the learned French chemist, Berthelot, denies him the credit of having discovered these bodies, after having studied certain works on alchemy attributed to Geber. The work on alchemy entitled the *Summa* mentions the composition of these bodies, it is true, but, according to Berthelot, it was not written either by Geber or by any other Islamic physician, but by a learned alchemist of the Middle Ages. It is a book of the

XIIIth century and can in no way be attributed to an Islamic author of the VIIIth and IXth centuries, and Berthelot believes the most probable hypothesis to be that an unknown writer of the latter half of the XIIIth century wrote the book and issued it under the patronage of the revered name of Geber. However, as long as we have no sounder proofs than those advanced by Berthelot we may accept the general belief that the discovery of these bodies was made by the Islamic physicians. As a matter of fact there is nothing which prevents us from believing that the Latin translations were made from original Islamic texts which were the inspiration of the Latin alchemists of the Middle Ages, but have now disappeared, having been lost in the destruction of the Moorish libraries in Spain. At all events, even if the *Summa* was not actually written by Geber, it would be difficult to contest its Islamic origin.

The Arabs were the first to introduce chemical preparations into pharmacy. By using sugar instead of honey in the composition of potions and syrups they made a great advance. They obtained alcohol—the word itself is Arabian—from distillation of feculents and fermented sugars. In virtue of their discovery of sugar and alcohol and their application of chemistry to pharmacy, it may safely be said that the Islamic physicians created the latter important branch of medicine as we know it.

From another point of view also were they creators; for they made pharmacy a speciality, so that the physician no longer compounded his own remedies. The practice of pharmacy became an institution which was placed under governmental control and, in fact, the pharmacists were held responsible for the quality and just prices of all medicines. Ibnu'l-Baytar was appointed inspector of pharmacists and herbalists in Egypt.

The Islamic Codex, otherwise known as the *Krabadin*, is divided into two parts. The first comprises compound medicines, and these are sometimes arranged in alphabetical order, and sometimes by therapeutical or pharmacological analogies. The second part comprises medicines properly belonging to each organ or part of the body. In this case the order followed is that of taking man from head to foot, and a series of recipes are given for the treatment of diseases of each part of the body. In other words the first part of the pharmacopoeia is for the dispenser's while the second is for the physician's use.

By taking hygiene as one of the foundation stones of its moral code, Islam gave a great impetus to the study of this branch of medicine. Unlike some other religions, Islam as it were codified the precepts of hygiene and made them binding upon all. The Prophet says: "Cleanliness is piety," and again: "Science is twofold: the science of the body and the science of the soul."

The use of baths and ablutions, the prohibition of fermented drinks, the search for paternity, the obligation of marriage in case of seduction—hence the protection of women against the caprice of men—all these ordinances imposed by Islamism result in a social hygiene of the highest order.

From the IXth to the XVth century the teaching of medicine was very well organized in the schools of Bagdad, Damascus, Cairo and Cordova, which were usually connected with a hospital so that theoretical teaching was completed by clinical instruction at the bedside. After a certain time a kind of diploma (*Ijaza*) was given to students as a certificate of complete study.

In A.D. 931 an event occurred which shows how much medicine had developed in Bagdad, and also that it gave rise to medico-legal enactments. A patient had died from the carelessness of his physician. The Khalif decided that from that time on nobody should practise medicine unless he had been examined by Sinan ibn Thabit, physician-in-chief at the Bagdad hospital.

The Islamic physicians were among the first to develop clinical teaching in hospitals, indeed, the first hospitals worthy of the name really date from the Islamic period. The Adudi Hospital built at Bagdad by Adudu'd-Dawla had a staff of twenty-four physicians. The medical services were already specialized. There were an accident department and sections for fever cases and for diseases of the eye, the attending physicians being assigned to these services according to their special knowledge.

In the Xth century many hospitals sprang up in the

great city and each was placed under the direction of the most famous physicians, while at the same time hospital inspectors were appointed. The following passage, taken from the biography of Sinan, the son of the famous translator Thabit ibn Qurra, which has been translated by Leclerc, may here be given to show hospital organization at this time.

"The Vizir Ali ibn Isa was given the general superintendence of the hospitals, while the service had been confided to my father by the order of the Khalif Muqtadir. One year the patients were so numerous that the Vizir wrote to my father (as follows): 'I think that the condition of the troops is bad on account of their number and the nature of their lodgings; it has appeared to me that the sick must lack necessities. The staff of physicians must also be insufficient. It is essential that physicians should be especially attached to them, that they visit them each day, that they treat them and distribute food and medicaments among them.' My father carried out these orders."

It may therefore be seen that at this time physicians were attached to the army.

The Bagdad hospitals kept a good record of case-histories and as a proof of this we have a collection of hospital cases frequently referred to by Rhazes in the *Continens*.

At Damascus there were several hospitals, among them the Great Hospital which was founded by Nuru'd-Din. In the *Abdellatif* (an account of Egypt) we find the following remark: "At Damascus," says Khatib Dhahin, "is the Bimaristan (hospital), an institution unequalled in the world." Then a curious anecdote is given. "In the year 831 (A.D. 1427) I came to Damascus. With me was a gentleman of Persian origin, a man of talent and taste, and of great intelligence. This year he made a pilgrimage to Mecca. . . . When he entered this hospital and saw the food distributed there, as well as all the conveniences and luxuries that were there enjoyed by the patients, he conceived the idea of remaining there, pretending that he was sick, and he did remain for three days. The physician, having come to him in order to ascertain the nature of his disease, and having felt his pulse, at once recognized the real condition of affairs and ordered him to eat the foods that give him the most pleasure, such as tender chickens, jams, sherbets, and all kinds of choice fruit. The three days having elapsed he (the physician) wrote out a prescription to the effect that a guest should not remain longer with a host who had accorded him three days' hospitality.'

Hospital organization and the work of the sanitary police were very advanced in Egypt. One of the most celebrated hospitals of Cairo was el-Nasiri, named after its founder, its staff including very famous physicians. Each category of disease had its particular section, and was attended by specialists. The large endowment enabled the patients to be kept in every comfort, while the physicians were paid a large salary. Musicians and singers came to entertain convalescent patients. Lastly, when patients who had recovered left the hospital they were given five gold pieces which enabled them to live for some time without having to do any heavy work.[1] It may be added that there was also a special hospital for women.

One of the greatest minds of the Middle Ages was Gerbert of Aurillac (930–1003), who afterwards became the head of Christendom under the name of Pope Sylvester II (A.D. 999). He crossed the Pyrenees to go to Toledo to obtain from the Arabs knowledge which was lacking in Gothic Europe. After his return to France he spread the scientific and medical knowledge he had acquired in Spain, and taught at Rheims with great success. It may be said of him that he was, in France and Germany, the Savioni of science in the monasteries and cathedrals at the end of the Xth century, and that he prepared the religious, literary and scientific renaissance of the XIth century. Now, Gerbert was well versed in things medical, and his sojourn in Spain had deeply initiated him into mathematics, astronomy and the medical sciences. It may therefore be said that Gerbert transported Islamic science into Germany and France and finally into Italy when he became Pope.

Gerbert and Constantine the African (1010–1087), were but the forerunners of the great translators. The true period of the Latin translations began in the XIIth century with Archbishop Raymond. It was not by the Crusades—as is generally supposed—but through Spain, Sicily, and Italy, that Science penetrated Europe. In 1130 a college of translators was established at Toledo, which was in Spanish hands at this time, and under the patronage of Archbishop Raymond it commenced Latin translations of the most celebrated Islamic writers. The success of these translations was considerable, and opened up a new world to Western Europe, and during the XIIth, XIIIth, and XIVth centuries this work was not relinquished.

The most active and prolific translator was certainly Gerard of Cremona (1114–1187). He made over seventy-one translations, twenty-one of which were medical works. Among these we may mention the *Canon* of Avicenna, the *Surgery* of Abulcasis, the *Mansuri* of Rhazes, and some fragments from the *Continens*. He also translated into Latin such Greek writers as Galen, Hippocrates, Plato, Aristotle and Euclid, who had been translated by the Islamic physicians into their own tongue. It is largely owing to such translations that teachings of the ancient authors, whose original works are lost, have been preserved to us. Not only did Europe derive its science from the Arabs but it also obtained a greater and far more intimate knowledge of Greek science from them, so that, as Leclerc says: "the Arabs thus repaid to the Christians of the western world the services that had formerly been rendered to them by the Christians of the East."

# CHAPTER XIV

## THE MEDICAL SCHOOLS OF SALERNO AND MONTPELLIER. THE ARABISTS

When the mediaeval schools of medicine began to rise, about the XIth century, scientific medicine had made practically no progress since Galen. The best work that had been done in the intervening period was the preservation of old knowledge in encyclopaedias. But the prevailing treatments had been the blind application of drugs of the most fantastic kind and magic imported from the East. When Christianity became the State religion, though it had opposed Pagan magic and superstition, it had stifled medicine and all science. The belief in possession by devils made priestly laying-on of hands, prayer, and exorcism the usual cures. Most of the Fathers rejected earthly means of healing. Medicine was a mixture of old medical tradition, Christian mysticism, and magical charms. During the Dark Ages, the monasteries of the West copied and translated recipe-books, herbals, and dietaries, in which scraps from classical writers were mingled with magical lore and grotesque pharmaceutics.

The School of Salerno.—As the medical schools of Salerno and Montpellier represent two of the principal links in the chain of medical history, some little attention must be given them. Without discussing the origin of the School of Salerno, we believe that the hypothesis long ago emitted by de Renzi may be accepted, namely that this school was not founded by Constantine the African, by the Lombard princes, or by the Benedictine monks, but by the physicians of the city itself, who were sufficiently numerous and learned to attract to their lectures those who were desirous of acquiring the art of medicine otherwise than by following the teachings of a single master. The first teachers at Salerno never dreamed of founding a school; they merely wished to impart their knowledge to others less learned than themselves, but little by little the reputation of these masters extended far beyond the city, and students became numerous on account of their reputation for remarkable cures as well as for the quality of their teaching. It is a question whether these masters were laymen or ecclesiastics. Thomas believes we may presume that, about the XIth century, the masters of Salerno studied theology and took orders. Puccinotti states that the founders of the school were Benedictines, while Mayer believes that, in principle, the establishment was united by a sort of medical freemasonry. It is, however, probable that the origin and constitution of the school were laic, because, as Daremberg points out, there is no theological doctrine in the ancient writings of its members.

It is not impossible that the School of Salerno was founded about the time of the fall of the Roman Empire. The first record relating to it is an indirect mention made in the year 924 by the monk Richer, who says that Louis d'Outremer had a physician of Salerno attached to his court, and that the latter was the rival of another physician by the name of Derold. Secondly, we have the account of a trip made by Adalberon to Salerno in the year 984. He came at this time to Salerno to seek relief from disease, as is stated in the chronicles of the Bishops of Verdun. These documents prove that as early as the Xth century the reputation of the School of Salerno had reached Northern Gaul. But since the archives of the Kingdom of Naples give the names of the physicians at Salerno from the year 846, it is clear that the school was already in existence about the middle of the IXth century.

In respect of the history of the school, we have little information before the year 1000 and none of the writings of the masters before this epoch have come down to us. Ragenifrid, who flourished towards the end of the IXth century, Pietro III, who was both physician and bishop, Grimoald, and the physicians who took care of Adalberon in 984, are among those of whom we know little or nothing. But from the year 1000 to 1075—the time of the arrival of Constantine in Italy—names become numerous and documents abound, while the works of this period which have been handed down to us, clearly testify to the rapid development taken on by the School of Salerno at the very commencement of the XIth century. At this time the practice of medicine at Salerno was absolutely independent; it had as yet borrowed nothing from Islamic medicine, and was based upon Greek and Latin works, while its theories were those of Galen or of the Methodist sect. The physicians of whom we know something are: Alphanus, Gariopontus, John Platearius the Elder, Cophon the Elder, Constantine the African, Archimathoeus, Musandinus, Gerard, Roger, and last, but not least, the famous 'lady doctor' Trotula.

We know nothing about the writings of Alphanus II (A.D. 1040), and very little about him personally. He belonged to an illustrious family of Salerno, studied medicine in that city, became archbishop and afterwards cardinal, and died at a very advanced age. Two very short quotations from Leo of Ostia and Peter the Deacon indicate that he was a skilful physician. The former tells us that Desiderius, Abbot of Monte Cassino, who later on became pope under the name of Victor III, came to Salerno to consult Alphanus for a very severe illness that he had contracted by observing excessive abstinence and prolonged vigils. Leo calls him *prudentissimus et nobilissimus clericus* and also says that he was well versed in things medical. Peter the Deacon tells us that he was the author of a book entitled: *De quator humoribus corporis humani*, which dealt with physiology and pathology. This book has not come down to us, unless it is the one that de Renzi published in his Collectio Salernitana, under the title of *Quator humoribus ex quibus constat humanum corpus.*

Gariopontus is one of the oldest and most illustrious masters of the School of Salerno, of whose works we know something. He seems to have attained the height of his fame about the year 1040. Although his writings are unquestionably compilations, yet he had ideas of his own. His favourite writer, whom he follows step by step, so to speak, was Theodore Prisciani, but he also did not neglect the Greek and Latin authors, such as Alexander of Tralles, Paulus Aeginata, and, above all, Galen. He studied profoundly the writings of the latter, and thoroughly assimilated his ideas.

In respect of his doctrines, Gariopontus does not blindly follow Galen's teaching, and frequently adopts the heterodox doctrines of the Methodists, which Galen detested. There were three schools or sects, as we know, namely Empiricism, which was based entirely on observation, and neglected the study of anatomy, Methodism, the doctrine of Themison, which sought for the cause of all disease in the *strictum* and *laxum*, and lastly Dogmatism, the outcome of the doctrines of Hippocrates and Galen, and based on the theory of the four fundamental humours, their elementary qualities and natural forces. Now, in the works of Gariopontus, we find a combination of the doctrines of Methodism and of Galen.

The title of his work, *Passionarium, seu practicam morborum Galeni, Th. Prisciani, Alexandri et Pauli, quem Gariopontus quidam Salernitanus redegit*, shows that he cannot be accused of plagiarism, because he states that he compiled it from those sources which he names.

Besides this work, Gariopontus also wrote the *Dynamidii*, a book treating of the virtues of remedies. De Renzi is of the opinion that two other treatises, attributed to Galen, are really due to Gariopontus, namely *De catharticis* and *De simplicibus medicaminibus ad Paternianum*. The first contains some of the principles of the Methodists, while the second is a catalogue arranged in alphabetical order of simple medicaments contained in the three kingdoms, with a short description of these medicaments and their therapeutical indications. This compilation is derived from Pliny, Galen, and Theodore Prisciani, and is dedicated to a certain Paternianus, whom he addresses as *carissime frater*.

No matter what has been said to the contrary, Gariopontus played an important part in the history of medicine by directly transmitting to the School of Salerno the writings of the Graeco-Latin authors before knowledge of the Islamic writers was introduced.

John Platearius the Elder, who flourished about the year 1050, was, if tradition be accepted, the husband of the celebrated Trotula, of whom we shall shortly speak, but we only know of him by his son, John Platearius II.

In his *Practica*, which is supposed to have been written between 1090 and 1100, Platearius the Younger frequently speaks of his father, who had then been dead some time. Thus he gives his father's treatment for lethargy and states that he resorted to every known remedy, but without success.

He also refers to the treatment of epilepsy according to his father's teachings.

In the *De aegritudinum curatione* the son again quotes his father. These chapters are in reality the same as those found in the *Practica brevis,* also by Platearius the Younger. In the chapter on hoarseness, he speaks of a certain electuary recommended by his father, and in the chapter on phthisis he refers to the diagnostic method which his father had developed after years of experience.

As has been said, it is by the *Practica brevis* that the doctrines of the elder Platearius have come down to us. It is also to a namesake, if not a relative, Cophon the Younger, that we owe our information respecting Cophon the Elder. It appears that the latter flourished at Salerno about 1050, before the arrival of Constantine, and that, as a teacher, he was very popular. In the introduction to his book, Cophon the Younger states that he will set out the precepts *ex Cophonis ore suisque et sociorum scriptis quae compendiose collegit.*

It is not known whether Cophon the Elder was the father or the master of the Younger, but it is certain that he preceded the latter by at least thirty years, and that he was a contemporary of Platearius the Elder. Of his writings we have only a few articles in the *De aegritudinum curatione.* His system is that of Galen, and no trace of Islamic influence is to be found. From what has been said it is clear that, during this first period of its existence, the School of Salerno possessed its own characteristics. The doctrines taught were taken from Greek and Latin writers and so the teaching was completely opposed to that of the Islamic school. It is perfectly true that the works of the masters of Salerno so far mentioned are entirely derived from Hippocrates, Galen, Pliny, and Dioscorides, as well as from Caelius Aurelianus and Theodore Prisciani. It is also to be pointed out that they were written in the form of lectures. As we shall see, some Islamic elements were little by little introduced into the teachings and the doctrines of the School. But it cannot be said that the masters borrowed from the Arabs. It was rather the latter who bowed to the medical teachings of this period of the school. Before we speak of Constantine the African we must, from the point of view of chronology, have something to say of the lady physicians of the School of Salerno.

From the writings of the masters we know that there were a great many women physicians who were held in high esteem and greatly sought after by patients. Thus, in the *Circa instans*, a treatise on materia medica, and in the *Practica*, by Platearius the Younger, mention is made of a great number of remedies that the lady physicians employed which were thought highly of by the school. To give an example of these a few quotations will suffice. In the first place here is an ointment which was a sovereign remedy for sunburn: *Nacta singulare unguentum valens ad solis adustionem, et quamlibet fissuram, maxime ex vento, et contra pustulas faciei ex aere, similiter contra maculas et excoriationes faciei, quo utuntur mulieres Salernitanae: Recipe: radicis lilii . . . cerusae . . . masticis . . . Olibani-camphorae . . . axungiae . . . aquae rosatae.*

Here is an excellent ointment to keep the hair soft: *Contra asperitatem capillorum, commisceatur pulvis terrae sigillatae cum aqua calida, et post lotionem capitis, hanc aquam infundatur et post paucum alia aqua tepida fiat lotura: sic operant mulieres Salernitanae.*

While the lady physicians prescribed pills for dysuria in women, for their noble clients they had, as may readily be imagined, a number of formulae for beautifying the person. Here is a prescription for haemorrhoids: *Quaedam autem mulier Salernitana probavit quod ad omnes hermorrhoidas ficus valet succus ejus.* They also employed astringent injections and fomentations for vaginal discharges: *Ad exsiccandam superfluiditatem matricis, fiat fomentum ex aqua decoctionis ejus (calamentum). Hoc, ut testantur mulieres Salernitanae, satis valet.*

In his commentaries on the Tables of Master Salernus, Bernard the Provincial also gives us some information in respect of the practice of the lady physicians. He refers to preparations composed of aloes macerated in rose water for swelling of the face; of fumigations of olive leaves in infantile paralysis, of vapours of antimony in cases of cough, of galbanum in suffocation, and so forth. Bernard also refers to certain superstitious practices that the ladies of Salerno resorted to. For example, to cure melancholia, betony was plucked on Ascension Day at about three o'clock in the morning, and at the same time a Paternoster was said.

Of the lady physicians whose names have come down to us we would mention Calenda, Abella, Mercuriade, Rebecca and Stephania. But we will only deal at length with the most famous of them all, namely Maestra Trotula, who has passed into literature as "Dame Trot" of the fairy-tales. According to tradition she flourished about the year 1050, and, as we have seen, was the wife of Platearius the Elder. Many documents attest the fact that this celebrated woman lived during the reign of the last Lombard princes, hence before the arrival of Constantine the African. Baccio says that she belonged to the family of the Ruggieri, and this opinion is accepted by a number of competent historians. On the other hand, there are those who, with Sudhoff and his pupils, refuse to accept her as an historical personage at all; maintaining that she arose out of a misunderstanding. According to this negative view, one Trottus, a doctor of Salerno, left compilations known as "the Trotula"—and rumour has done the rest. The matter is therefore still *sub judice*, and fortunately the decision is of no consequence for our present purpose.

The principal book attributed to Trotula is entitled: *De morbis mulierum et eorum cura.* In this treatise we would refer to the advice given to take sand baths on the sea shore in order to reduce flesh, this being accomplished by the perspiration produced by the heat. The chapter on the care of the newly born and the chapter on the choice of a nurse, as well as hygiene and the feeding of infants, are not to be despised. Trotula gives particular attention to dentition and teaching the child to speak.

There is also an interesting chapter on uterine polypi and their treatment, while another chapter has for title: *De modo coarctandi matricem ut etiam corrupta appareat.* In this she says: *Nisi de restrictione amplitudinis vulvae propter honestam causam liceret tractare, nullam de ea mentionem faceremus; sed quum per hanc impediatur aliquando conceptio, necesse est tali impedimento sic subvenire.*

When Trotula speaks of *cancro atque inflammatione virgae virilis et testiculorum foramina multa cum excoriatione*, it might at first sight appear as if she had a vague idea of syphilis, but if this passage is read with care, it at once becomes evident that she knew nothing of the aetiology or symptomatology of that disease.

The *De morbis mulierum* is written with a certain elegance and contains a number of judicious precepts, but there are also traces of superstition, as, for example, the following means of diagnosing the sex of the infant *in utero*: *ad cognoscendum utrum mulier gestet masculum vel feminam, accipe aquam de fonte, et mulier extrahat duas vel tres guttas sanguinis aut lactis de dextro latere, et infundentur in aquam: et si fundum petent, masculum gerit; si supernatent, feminam.* Trotula also advises the tying of the cord at a point three fingers' breadth from the umbilicus.

Trotula not only treats of diseases of women and labour, but also all other branches of medicine. She wrote on epilepsy, diseases of the eyes and ears, and those of the teeth and gums. Whatever view we take of her historicity, the doctrines of Trotula are rather more practical than theoretical and her general teachings accord with those of Galen.

With the arrival of Constantine the African the prestige and the reputation of this savant from the Orient necessarily attracted the attention of the physicians of Salerno, but it is also true that the School still adhered to its doctrines, which were purely Galenical, although they accepted the new knowledge brought by this monk.

Constantine arrived at Salerno about twenty or thirty years after Gariopontus had died. He was born at Carthage about the year 1015, some say 1010, but the story of his life is rather legendary than truly historical. Leo of Ostia says that Constantine left Carthage and wandered in distant countries for thirty-five years. In his intense desire to acquire knowledge he visited the Islamic schools at Bagdad, and travelled in India and Egypt, where he acquired medicine and other sciences. After his return to Carthage he was looked upon as a sorcerer, and it was decided to execute him for this reason. However, he was able to escape and, reaching Sicily by ship, from there he took refuge at Salerno. Thanks to support given him by the brother of the king of Babylonia, who at that time was at Salerno, and who recommended him to Duke Robert (Guiscard) as a man of great merit, he became secretary to this prince; but, soon becoming tired of the chicanery of the court, he withdrew first to the Convent of Aversa and afterwards to Monte Cassino, where he spent the remainder of his life in translating the writings of the Arabs into Latin, and where he died, probably in 1087.

It is very doubtful whether Constantine ever professed at the School of Salerno, for none of his disciples when speaking of him refers to the School.

The writings of Constantine are very numerous; Leo of Ostia has given what is probably a complete list and states that many have been lost. The following are those which were printed for the first time in 1536 or 1539, having the title: *Summi in omni philosophia viri Constantini Africani, medici, operum reliqua hactenus desiderata*—1. *Viaticum de morborum cognitione et curatione*; 2. *De remediorum et aegritudinum cognitione*; 3. *De urinis*; 4. *Opus Constantini proprium de stomachi affectionibus naturalibus et non naturalibus*; 5. *De melancholia*; 6. *De incantatione et adjuratione collique suspensione, epistola ad filium*; 7. *De mulierum morbis*; 8. *De chirurgia*; 9. *De gradibus simplicium.*

These various writings show that Constantine prefers Isaac and Ali Abbas among the Islamic writers, and he has given us a translation of Isaac's treatise on fevers and the latter's *Viaticum* and *Common Gods*. It is important to note that Constantine wrote nothing original, and that all his books are plagiarisms or skilfully disguised translations. He translated from Arabic instead of Greek, and this is the principal point to be remembered. It should also be added that he took special pains to eliminate in his translations anything that might identify the original book. He eliminates all proper names which are too Oriental and substitutes his own name in order to prevent, he says, any other writer from stealing the fruit of his work.

The writings of Constantine are less empirical than those of other writers of his day. His knowledge of anatomy is that of Galen, only far more gross, and the same may be said of his physiology, which is principally based on the doctrine of spirits or the forces of the body. These are of three kinds, namely vital, animal, and natural. The first reside in the heart, the second in the brain, and the third in the liver.

The vital force gives rise to the pulse by communicating to the arteries and heart, by means of the pneuma, the faculty of beating. The natural functions are carried out by the pneuma circulating in all the blood vessels of the body. Like Galen, Constantine places generation, nutrition, and growth in the latter class.

Constantine's pathology is also Galenical, but altered by Islamic subtleties and Aristotelian distinctions, and for him the vital spirits and the four humours of the body, when they have undergone changes, are the cause of disease.

As to therapeutics, Constantine gives us some very good advice. He especially warns the physician to observe the strength of the patient during the phase of full development of a disease and carefully to examine the nature of the latter. Although a follower of Galen's teachings, it is probable that Constantine was influenced by the School of Salerno, for he adopted some of the principles of Methodism, for example the use of relaxing medication, that is to say drugs which open the pores.

His pharmacy is more complicated than that of Gariopontus, but it is richer in tonics, sudorifics, and stimulants. His surgery is merely an abridged edition of Paulus Aeginata.

In his treatise on diseases of the stomach, dedicated to the celebrated Alphanus, he states that he has compiled this work from the ancient writers, in order " to be agreeable to him and also because he has not found the subject treated in a complete way by any author ".

Briefly, it can be said that Constantine was the first to introduce the Islamic writings into the western world, and he thus contributed to the preservation of much that might otherwise have been lost.

The School of Salerno, although it did not entirely adopt Islamic medicine, nevertheless felt its influence through Constantine. At this period of its growth, medicine had made such a great development at Salerno that the foundations upon which it was built were no longer strong enough to support it. The fountains of the material for Latin translations had become dry, so that it was necessary to find other and more complete works which would contain further medical knowledge. A few more books and the medicine of the School of Salerno would be quite self-sufficient, but the books were wanting, and after considerable effort it was necessary to resort to Syriac literature, which was itself composed of translations into Arabic from the Greek, so that the Latin translations made from the Arabic by Constantine helped to preserve medicine in the West. Therefore the introduction of the Islamic writers into the West had a great advantage, but, on the other hand, was the means of putting a stop to the originality which had so far been the mark of all Italy and especially Salerno. However, Constantine's influence on the latter was probably not so great as is generally believed, and, as we shall show, Galen's writings never enjoyed such influence as during the Islamic domination.

The principal masters of the school of Salerno during the XIIth century were: Archimathoeus, Nicholas Praepositus, Matthew Platearius the Younger, and Master Petrus Musandinus, but of these only Archimathoeus need detain us, as the writings of the others did not contribute to the advance of medical science.

Archimathoeus flourished about the year 1100. The first of his books to which we will refer is entitled: *De adventu medici ad aegrotum*, and describes the way in which a physician should behave towards his patients. It serves as an introduction to his second work on the practice of medicine. Henschel points out that this introduction is very similar to the Hippocratic books entitled the *Law*, *On the Physician*, the *Precepts*, and *On Decorum*, as well as some of the passages in Galen. The author almost exaggerates the dignity of the physician, and is careful to instruct the student as to the moral dangers of his profession. The Christian sentiment which gave rise to the exercise of charity is marked, because the writer instructs the physician to watch over the salvation of the soul as well as the salvation of the body. Archimathoeus also says that it is well for the patient to confess before the physician comes, or at least to promise to do so if it is advised on account of the gravity of the case.

In his treatise on *Medicine*, Archimathoeus begins by giving the same advice as in his *De adventu medici*, showing by his own experience how the physician should proceed, and also states that he has no pretension of composing a didactic work, his aim being to describe cases which, by the help of God, he was able to cure. Therefore we have a clinical treatise, probably the first of the kind written since the books of the *Epidemics* of the Hippocratic Collection. The diagnosis unquestionably leaves much to be desired, but shows at least that the writer was a good observer and an excellent therapeutist who did not hesitate to employ powerful remedies. For example, he advises arsenical fumigations in the treatment of chronic bronchial catarrh, but it must be remarked that in all his treatment he clings to the doctrines of Hippocrates and Galen. The observations made by the author offer nothing of interest, as far as medical ethics go ; he makes a distinction between true physicians and vulgar physicians, specialists and physician-druggists, the last three of whom, he says, are personages of mediocre instruction and with consciences still more mediocre. And at this point we might quote the very curious verses of the *Regimen* in respect of the medicaster :—

> *Fingit se medicum quivis idiota, profanus,*
> *Judaeus, monachus, histrio, rasor, anus ;*
> *Sicuti alchemista medicus fit aut saponista,*
> *Aut balneator, falsarius aut oculista.*
> *Hic dum lucra quaerit, virtus in arte perit.*

This shows that the physicians of the School of Salerno held the dignity of the profession in high esteem.

The most renowned work of the School of Salerno at this period is unquestionably the famous didatic poem known by the various names of *Regimen Sanitatis, Flos Medicinae, Regimen virile*, and *Schola Salernitana.* In fact if the merits of the work are to be judged by the number of editions, translations, and commentaries which have been made in all languages, there are few books that can be compared with this poem. Baudry de Balzac was able to find two hundred and forty editions of the *Regimen* between 1474 and 1846, while there are also a multitude of French, German, English, Italian, Spanish, and Polish translations, as well as some into Hebrew and Persian.

It would be idle to discuss all the opinions emitted in respect of the origin of this poem, which is quite as obscure as that of the School of Salerno itself. We do not know how this poem came to be written, who was its author, nor what was the precise date at which it appeared. However, there are some known facts which may throw a little light on the subject.

The dedication of the poem to the King of England has

led some to suppose that the *Regimen* dates from the year 1100. But this hypothesis has a weak point, in that there is a very old manuscript version in England, the dedication of which says *Francorum Regi* instead of *Anglorum Regi*, and there is even another at Paris which bears the title of *Roberto Regi*. As we do not know to what French or English king the poem could have been addressed, the date 1100 cannot be fully accepted and the most that can be said is that it appeared between the middle of the XIth and the commencement of the XIIth centuries, because the doctrines and the receipts contained recall those of Gariopontus and Trotula with some slight trace of Islamic influence. None of the names advanced as authors has been able to withstand historical criticism ; not that of John of Milan, still less that of Novoforo, and least of all that of Arnold of Villanova, can be accepted.

Whether the *Regimen* is considered as a medical consultation addressed to the King of England or to the King of France, or as a series of aphorisms, it is none the less true that its essential characteristic is exclusively dietetic and hygienic. It is a guide for the regulation of daily life and a well ordered use of all things necessary for preserving life in health and disease. The sources of the poem are Hippocrates and Galen, and what cannot be found in these two authors is supplied by Dioscorides and by Pliny. Besides the precepts laid down by science, the *Regimen* contains domestic rules of hygiene dictated by everyday experience. A few quotations from the poem will suffice to give the reader a general idea of it.

Pure air should be breathed and vitiated atmosphere avoided :—

*Aer sit purus, habitabilis et bene clarus*
*Nec sit infectus, nec olens faetore cloacae*
*Alteriusque rei corpus nimis inficientis.*

Be moderate in everything :—

*Esca, labor, potus, somnus, mediocria cuncta :*
*Peccat si quis in his, patitur natura molesta.*

When arising in the morning never forget to wash the face and hands, comb the hair and brush the teeth :—

*Lumina mane manus surgens gelida lavet unda,*
*Hac illac modicum pergat, modicum sua membra*

PLATE IV

A PHYSICIAN EXAMINING THE URINE

Engraving enlarged by A. Mittendorff from Fludd's *Integrum Morborum Mysterium*, 1632 *(Author's Collection)*

[ *face p. 224*

*Extendat, crines pectat, dentes fricet. Ista*
*Confortant cerebrum, confortant caetera membra.*

Never eat without hunger or drink without thirst :—

*Non bibe ni sitas, et non comedas saturatus.*

Never commence one meal before the preceding one has been digested :—

*Tu nunquam comedas, stomachum nisi noveris esse*
*Purgatum, vacuumque cibo quem sumpseris ante.*

In speaking of the predominance of the humours according to the season and the four ages of life, the School of Salerno emits a theory which dates back to Hippocrates :—

*Consona sunt aer, sanguis, pueritia, verque;*
*Conveniunt ignis, aestas, choleraque juventus ;*
*Autumnus, terra, melancholia, senectus ;*
*Decrepitus vel hiems, aqua, phlegmaque sociantur.*

The description of the temperaments is entirely derived from Galen. But for lack of space we cannot go into the detail of the rest of the poem, which deals with the choice of food and drink as well as with the therapeutic values of the simples. It is enough to say that their use is essentially based on the theory of the elementary qualities, namely heat, cold, dry, and moist.

To sum up, it may be said that the development of the School of Salerno remained practically stationary during the XIIth century. Semeiology was limited to the study of the pulse and especially to the examination of the urine, and these elements formed the basis of the practical teaching. The urine was examined in the morning; if it was of a lemon yellow colour, bile predominated, while if it was thick and red, blood predominated; phlegm predominated if it was thick and white, and *atrabile* if it was simply white. A urine which was in a medium condition between these four indicated a perfect state of health.

What is to be particularly noted during this period of the school's history is the beginning of a juridical and administrative organization. Up to this time the fame of the school had arisen without any privileges and without any favour of royalty, and empirics practised medicine side by side with the physicians of the school. But, from the year 1134, everything was changed, and in order to protect his subjects from the charlatans Roger II promulgated laws governing the practice of medicine. He decreed that all those wishing to practise the healing art in his states should come before the authorities in order to obtain permission, and in case of infraction of this law imprisonment and confiscation of their goods was the penalty. From this time on the School of Salerno acquired a celebrity which no other institution of the kind attained in early times.

From the end of the XIIth century to the middle of the XIIIth, medicine at Salerno was derived mostly from the Islamic physicians. The writings of the teachers were fewer and less important than is generally supposed and the school henceforth exercised but little influence on the progress of medicine other than by the great number of students who flocked there from Italy and other European countries.

The names of the most famous physicians, or rather the only names we know in this epoch are those of Gerard of Salerno, who popularized the Islamic works by his translations, and Roger the Surgeon, who, it would seem, remained faithful to the Latin translations from the Greek. John of Procida may be mentioned, although his name would have remained obscure had he not been the instigator of a political drama of a most bloodthirsty nature; and lastly mention should be made of the Four Masters, who commented on Roger's *Surgery* and made the last struggle to maintain the traditions of the school.

Many physicians of the Middle Ages bore the name of Gerard, among whom may be mentioned Gerard of Cremona, the famous translator of the Islamic physicians; then we have Gerard of Solo and Gerard Berturiensis. It has been proved, however, that there was a Gerard, who, if not of Salerno, at least belonged to the school and professed there. Master Gerard, who flourished about the year 1190, wrote a certain number of books that have been erroneously attributed to Gerard of Solo, who flourished at Montpellier at the commencement of the XIVth century. Peter of Spain, whose work entitled *Thesaurus Pauperum* did not appear later than 1275, refers several times to Gerard in respect of the latter's commentary *Super Viaticum Constantini;* this amply proves that it must have been written by Gerard of Salerno. Two other commentaries are attributed to him, one entitled *Super Macrum*, the other on the *Dynamidii* of Gariopontus. There are still three other works attributed to him which were in use during the XIVth century, namely *Introductorium juvenum, seu de regimine corporis humani in morbis, scilicet consimili, officiali et communi ; Libellus de febribus ;* and *Tractatus de gradibus medicinae.*

A large number of Italian surgeons were known by their writings during the XIIIth century, and were divided into two schools. The one, following Galen, maintained that relaxation and moisture were the natural state of the body rather than dryness ; hence they treated wounds and ulcers with poultices and moist dressings : the other sect employed a diametrically different method, inasmuch as they only used drying remedies, because Galen had also said somewhere in his writings that dryness was nearer the healthy state of the body than moisture.

Roger of Parma, his disciple Roland, and William of Salicet (1201–1277) belonged to the first school, while Bruno of Longoburgo (1252) and Theodoric of Cervia (1205–1298) belonged to the second. However, Henschel points out that Roger did not exclusively employ emollients and humectant applications, because he frequently used irritating fomentations according to indications, and, for that matter, the two surgical schools were not as exclusive in the applications of their methods as Guy de Chauliac maintains.

Roger of Parma, or more correctly Ruggero, flourished at Salerno at about the year 1230. He is the earliest of the Italian surgeons whom we know. It is said that some of the manuscripts of Roger's *De chirurgia* contained in the Bibliothèque Nationale of Paris mention that Roger had been the Chancellor of the University of Montpellier, and this mistake has frequently been repeated by writers on the history of medicine.

Roger's treatise on surgery is composed of four books : the first deals with diseases of the skull—fractures and wounds of the head ; the second deals with diseases of the neck ; the third with diseases of the upper limbs, chest and abdomen ; while the fourth treats of diseases of the lower limbs, the use of the cautery, and the treatment of leprosy and convulsions.

Roger's remarks on wounds of the head are worthy of notice. He especially recommends the surgeon to be suspicious of the slightest wound of the head. He describes fractures of the skull with great minuteness. Before withdrawing arrows from wounds the surgeon must ascertain whether or no the weapon is barbed, because in such case the wound is much more serious. In order to withdraw the weapon, Roger flattened the barb with forceps and afterwards withdrew it with great caution. If the nature of the wound prevented the carrying out of this manœuvre, Roger introduced an iron or copper canula, after which the arrow could be withdrawn without lacerating the tissues.

Roger has given a good definition of fistula, of which he describes several kinds. He used sea sponge internally in cases of scrofula, which was a perfectly rational practice because it contained iodine, although of course the surgeon was unaware of the fact. William of Salicet scoffs at Roger for his treatment of scrofula, although he treated his own cases in a most unscientific way in that he excited suppuration of the enlarged lymph-nodes by irritating applications and afterwards attempted to enucleate them. Roger's *Surgery* was commented on by one of his disciples, Roland of Parma, who was professor at Bologna. But the disciple did not follow the master's rules, for he tended to operate to excess. For example, he advised the removal of enlarged lymph-nodes and goitre by surgical procedures, rather than recourse to internal medication.

There is little to say of John of Procida, who was born about 1225 and flourished about 1260. He is better known in political life than as a physician, although it is said that the favours showered on him by Emperor Frederick II, Conrad IV and Manfred were due to his skill as a physician. As a reward for his medical care, Frederick II gave him the island of Procida, whose name he assumed. After the death of Conrad, John was stripped of his honours by Charles of Anjou, and determined to have the crown passed to Peter III, King of Arragon. With great skill he planned a vast conspiracy against Charles of Anjou which resulted in the massacre known as the Sicilian Vespers and the loss of Sicily to France. He afterwards became the faithful counsellor of the Arragon princes of Sicily, and died, it is said, at a very advanced age.

In Italy surgery continued to progress after the death of Roger and his disciple Roland. After him, in chronological order, come Bruno of Longoburgo, professor at Padua, whose surgical principles were directly opposed to those of Roger; Theodoric of Cervia, a disciple of Hugh of Lucca; William of Salicet, professor at Bologna and later at Verona; and Lanfranc of Milan, who was expelled from that city by Matthew Visconti. Lanfranc fled to France and came to Paris in 1295, where he gave lectures at the request of Passavant, Dean of the Faculty, and acquired an extraordinary celebrity. And lastly there are the Four Masters of Salerno, who commented on Roger's *Surgery.* Of these latter only mention will be made. Their names are unknown and only their manuscript works have come down to us. These are entitled *Expositio quator magistrorum Salerni super Chirurgiam Rogerii*, and *Glossula seu apparatus quator magistrorum super Chirurgiam Rolandi.*

The spirit in which these works are written clearly shows that the doctrines of the School of Salerno were still defended in the middle of the XIIIth century, and we also know that the Four Masters remained the principal authority in matters surgical because Guy de Chauliac, who came about eighty years after, refers to them frequently in his book on surgery, and contrasts their doctrines with those of Galen.

Although the Four Masters explained Roger's and Roland's surgery, they did not merely copy these two writers but put forward ideas and remarks of their own. Thus in the chapter on fractures of the skull, Roger remarks that the patient is in danger for one hundred days, while the Four Masters state that he is in a serious condition only for two weeks.

Following the example of the physicians of their day and of Roger and Roland who had gone before them, the Four Masters make a distinction between the medicine and surgery of the poor and of the rich, and give a large number of treatments for indigent patients on the one hand and for a rich clientele on the other.

As may be seen, the School of Salerno offers nothing of any particular note during the first part of the XIIIth century, and, as we have already said, the practice of medicine at Salerno during this long period depended almost entirely upon Islamic medicine, but surgery received a great impulse from the work of Roger, and he remained faithful to Graeco-Latin traditions. However, although the School of Salerno now began to lose its autonomy, it did not yet lose its importance or reputation; the ordinances of Emperor Frederick II in 1224, which were completed by Roger II's decree, gave it a celebrity which few institutions of the kind have ever attained.

THE FACULTY OF MEDICINE AT MONTPELLIER.—On account of the great influence exercised by the Faculty of Medicine at Montpellier it is necessary to say a few words as to its foundation. It received its statutes on August 17th, 1220, from Cardinal Conrad d'Hurach, Bishop of Porto and Sta. Rufina, the Legate of Pope Honorius III.

Sent to France to settle the affairs of the Church relating to the Crusade against the Albigenses, this high ecclesiastical dignitary stopped in the City, which had been papal territory since the year 1085, and the prelates of the region who came in his honour transmitted to him the complaints of the medical corps, since the latter were for the greater part recruited from among the clergy. By an unrestrained competition which there was no law to prevent, most regrettable abuses had arisen, resulting from the practice of empirics who had neither culture nor scruple, which injured the standing of conscientious practitioners. It was for this reason that, in the name of the undisputed authority he derived from the Apostolic See—council having been held by the Bishops of Maguelonne, Agde, Lodève, and Avignon and several other prelates, as well as some physicians, professors and students—Cardinal Conrad, with the formidable threat of spiritual punishment, issued the famous statutes whose essential provisions remained in vigour for over five and a half centuries until the legal death of the School by the Law of April 12th, 1792.

But it must be recalled that acknowledgment by the State does not mean creation. The high ecclesiastical person in question merely undertook to regulate the life of the School on account of its prosperity. Hence Cardinal Conrad only gave an official consecration to a learned body of very ancient repute. The " Narrative " of this act is the most solemn testimony that we have, because it states that "*for a very long time the profession of medical science has shone and blossomed with signal glory at Montpellier, whence have spread abroad all over the world its health-giving abundance and the life-giving diversity of its fruits*".

Forty years previously the public authorities had had to deal with the medical teaching at Montpellier. Requested by some to restrict the right of teaching to those who were competent, Guilhem VIII, who then governed the city, refused in his proclamation of January, 1180, to give anyone the monopoly of lecturing in the Faculty of Medicine. The name of " Faculty of Medicine " is used for the first time in this proclamation.

On the contrary, he proclaimed that, because there was no positive test of the personal capacity of each person who wished to teach, " *he would authorize any man, whoever he might be and from wherever he might come, to read and interpret* " treatises on medicine. It is of little importance whether this be regarded as liberality with regard to initiative or a desire not to interfere with the large following of the School. The fact remains that it is a recognition in an official document of the existence of the Faculty, which certainly was far older than this text, since it rejects the request made to change the regulations.

If one is to believe Rabbi Benjamin of Tudela, whose *Itinerary* gives essential details of the journey that he made in 1174 to the south of France, the Jewish colony of Montpellier was successfully cultivating medical sciences at this time. Secondly, a pupil of Abelard, John of Salisbury, Bishop of Chartres, whose death occurred in 1160, tells us that Montpellier and Salerno were rivals for the favour of medical students. He also states that students came away with their minds filled with barbarian ideas, the result of their contact with infidels.

Patients flocked to Montpellier long before this date in the hope of cure that they might receive from the physicians there, whose renown had extended throughout all Europe. Such was the case of Heraclius de Montboissier, Archbishop of Lyons, who, in a letter by St. Bernard of Menthon (*Epist.* 307) dated 1135, is stated to have turned aside from his journey "*ad limina*" to place himself in the care of the physicians of Montpellier, not without profit to his health, although with great loss to his pocket.

Still more positive is the declaration of Anselm of Havelberg, the biographer of Adalbert II, Archbishop of Mayence. According to him (in 1137), "*Montpellier offers to Medicine both a home and a temple. Here both doctrines and precepts are taught by physicians who, meditating upon the forces of things, teach hygiene to the healthy and obtain the cure of the sick.*" It would be hardly possible better to show the existing prosperity of this centre of learning and the success of the teachers there.

Lastly, before the death of Avicenna, the anonymous author of the celebrated *Book of Medicine*, who died in 1037, and who we know was a Jewish professor and had been instructed at the school of Rabbi Albon, of Narbonne, was one of the most popular teachers at the School of Montpellier. Beyond these documents we have no further data upon which to rely. It appears clear, however, that from the very beginnings of the city, on account of the trade of which it was the centre for the entire Mediterranean, the Jewish-Arabian physicians came there and, as we know, they upheld the Hippocratic doctrines, which, from these remote days, have remained in favour at this school. The arrival of these infidels seems to have been contemporary with the beginning of the reign of the Guilhems about 990. This explains the legend on an old seal of the Faculty which surrounds the effigy of the Father of Medicine and which may be translated:—"*Hippocrates of the School of Medicine of Montpellier, founded in the Xth century.*"

From what has been said there is no doubt but that the official constitution of this school dates from 1220, but it unquestionably existed long before even that of Paris, whose first diplomas, according to the statute of Robert de Courçon in 1215, only date from 1270, while Salerno did not confer diplomas until 1237.

At a later date Louis VIII sent to the episcopal palace the formula of an oath of fidelity to the laws of the kingdom with an express order to the professors to make both licentiates and doctors take oath before any diploma was conferred upon them. Finally, during the year 1289, the Faculties of Montpellier were united under a common rule and were made a university by Philip the Fair. The royal decree creating a university was immediately confirmed by a Bull of Pope Nicholas III. The staff of the Faculty of Medicine was at first small :—a chancellor and four doctors-regent. Gilles de Corbeil, physician to Philip Augustus, Henry de Guintonia (1239), Peter Gauzanhain (1260), Arnold of Villanova (1245–1310), and Gerard of Solo (1300) are the earliest known masters of this Faculty.

Soon, however, the professors rose against the claims of the clergy and, in order to counterbalance these, sought the influence of royal authority, demanding insistently a vindication of their rights and privileges. Philip VI of Valois gave them full justice, while King John decreed in their honour that a Beadle should carry a silver mace at the head of the Faculty as a sign of its power and rank.

It is well to recall that at this period the Faculty of Medicine at Montpellier furnished physicians to kings as well as to the Popes who resided at Avignon. Pope Urban V had a college built for the physicians, which he called the College of Twelve. He created two Chairs and gave the professors the right of wearing the red robe. Louis XII and Francis I further enlarged the privileges of the Faculty. Henry IV created two more Chairs, one of anatomy and one of botany, the first being filled by the celebrated anatomist, André du Laurens, and the other, for surgery and pharmacy, by François Ranchin. Furthermore, he ordered Richer de Belleval to lay out a botanical garden, which for many years was the finest in Europe.

During the XVIIth century a very serious quarrel arose between the physicians of Paris and those of Montpellier on account of a certain Renaudot, a doctor of the latter Faculty. Both sides defended the rights and prerogatives of their schools with great violence. Nevertheless, although a compatriot and friend of Cardinal de Richelieu, Renaudot lost his case and Parliament solemnly declared that one must be a doctor of the Faculty of Medicine of Paris in order to practise medicine in that city. This decision only resulted in an increase of the anger of both parties ; Courtaud, Magdelain and Isaac Carquet, physicians of Montpellier, entered into controversy with Guillemeau, Guy Patin, René Moreau and Riolan of Paris, which led to the publication of a vast number of pamphlets with obnoxious satire and threats. Nevertheless, and in spite of the famous decision of Parliament, there were always some physicians of Montpellier attached to the court. And, moreover, Louis XIV was very generous towards the School of Montpellier. He founded two new Chairs and also appointed a demonstrator of chemistry. He decreed that the professors and doctors of this School could unite to form a kind of University or Faculty entirely distinct from the other Faculties, although remaining under the academic discipline of the Bishop, who by right was Chancellor of all the Faculties. From this time on the Faculty of Medicine assumed the name of the University of Medicine of Montpellier, and at once made itself distinct from the other Faculties by formulating its own rules and discipline.

The principles of the School of Montpellier were merely the development of the great theories of the School of Cos. *Olim Cous, nunc Monspeliensis Hippocrates.*

The early teachers there were wise and more or less enlightened Empirics, who, always prudent in their practice, often obtained most fortunate results. Soon the combination of the doctrines of Hippocrates and Galen with the materia medica of the Islamic physicians resulted in the formulation by these early physicians of a code and religion which brought them back to the continual observation of Nature as taught by the Father of Medicine.

These early physicians gave particular care to the description of disease; the most famous among them, whose verbal and written teachings had great effect on the progress of medicine, are Gilles de Corbeil, who has left a much esteemed work entitled: *De virtutibus medicaminum*, as well as a poem on the diagnosis of disease by visual examination of the urine; Arnold of Villanova, whose pharmaceutical formulae and recipes were for long the Codex of the medical profession generally; Blaise Ermengaud, physician to Philip IV, who made a translation of Avicenna with the commentaries of Averroës, as well as a treatise on Asthma entitled: *Regimen de asthmate;* and Bernard of Gordon (1307) the author of several books, among others

FRANÇOIS RABELAIS
A painting in the Library of the University of Geneva
*(Reproduced by special permission)*

[ *face p. 234*

a treatise on crises and critical days entitled: *De crisi et criticis diebus atque prognosticandi ratione*, and another entitled: *Lilium medicinae*, which taught the treatment of all diseases. Gordon also wrote a treatise on therapeutics entitled: *De decem ingeniis seu indicationibus curandorum morborum*, and invented the lozenge which bears his name and which was used for years in cases of "ulcers of the kidney and bladder".

When Guy de Chauliac (1298–1368) appeared upon the scene, he it was who restored surgery to its former place. His books became classic and contained many excellent precepts; he also wrote a very detailed description of an epidemic of plague which wrought great havoc in the XIVth century.

Jacobus Sylvius, whose real name was Dubois, was first at Montpellier and then went to Paris, where he became the first demonstrator of anatomy. In 1566 Rondelet was renowned for his vast knowledge of natural history. In 1584 Laurent Joubert wrote with equal success on all branches of medicine, and we are also indebted to him for a very remarkable book entitled: *Erreurs populaires au fait de la médicine et du régime de santé*, which he dedicated to Marguerite of France, the first wife of Henri IV. This work was so popular that it was reprinted ten times in six years and there were in all at least fifteen editions, the best of which is that published at Rouen in 1601.

André du Laurens, whose remarkable treatise on anatomy contains a summary of all the anatomical writings of the ancient physicians of Montpellier, was also among the better-known professors at Montpellier, and we would again recall that Sylvius of Montpellier was the first to profess anatomy at Paris.

In 1655, Lazarus Rivière (Riverus) published a work on medicine, which for years enjoyed the greatest popularity, while the works of Richer de Belleval, Chicoyneau and Magnol on anatomy and botany had great success. Mention should be made of Chirac and Astruc (1684–1766), whose teachings on physiology, surgery and pharmacy had a European reputation.

François Rabelais (1494–1553), one of the master minds of the Renaissance, took his degree of M.D. at Montpellier, where he afterwards lectured on anatomy, demonstrating his lectures on the dissected body to crowded audiences. He was the first to translate from Greek into Latin and to comment upon the *Aphorisms* of Hippocrates, the first edition of this work being published at Lyons in 1532.

Many other illustrious physicians of Montpellier could be mentioned, but we will conclude with Raymond Vieussens (1641–1715), whose famous treatise on the anatomy of the nervous system is highly esteemed at the present day for the discoveries in that system which it sets forth.

## CHAPTER XV

### MEDICINE IN THE XVIth CENTURY

In dealing with the development of medicine during the XVIth century, we must in the first place distinguish three great currents of thought in relation to the principal medical doctrines. After this we shall speak of the most remarkable works accomplished in the various scientific branches belonging to the healing art.

During preceding centuries attempts had been made to translate and understand the writings of the ancients, but the XVIth century was no less eminent, both in its literary and in its scientific movements, and in medicine many distinguished men gave themselves up particularly to translation of the ancients and commented on their works. We will merely mention the principal of these who continued the work undertaken in the XVth. century by Nicolaus Leonicenus (1428–1524) and Thomas Linacre (1460–1524).

A physician of the Faculty of Paris, by name William Kock, translated several Greek works, while John Hagebut (Hagenpol, Cornarius) also made good translations of Hippocrates and Galen, Plato, Plutarch, Dioscorides and Aëtius.

John Günther of Andernach, also known as Winter (1487–1574), born in Germany, studied at the University of Louvain, where he became professor of the Greek language and where he had Vesalius as a student. He afterwards came to Paris and, after receiving his diplomas, soon became physician to the court of Francis I. As we shall see later on, he devoted himself to the study of anatomy, at the same time lecturing on the writings of Hippocrates, Aristotle and Galen, as well as of Demosthenes, one of his favourite authors. Having become a Protestant, he was obliged to flee to Metz, where he continued his work until he died, near Strasburg, of a serious form of fever. He translated into Latin nearly all of Galen, Oribasius, Paulus Aegineta, Alexander of Tralles and Caelius Aurelianus. He also published numerous commentaries on different works of the ancients.

Leonhard Fuchs (1501–1566) commented on Galen and Hippocrates and made a careful revision of their texts; he also wrote several volumes of commentaries and others on botany and materia medica. He wrote a book attacking the authority of the Islamic physicians and was one of the first to compile an "Institute of Medicine", to which we shall refer shortly.

Jean de Gorris, or Gorreus, was born in Paris in 1505 and became Dean of the Faculty of Medicine in 1548. He occupied a high position in medicine, was an intimate friend of de Thou the historian, and was universally esteemed for his great knowledge and urbanity. He has left several books of commentaries on Hippocrates and Galen, as well as on materia medica and blood-letting, but it is especially his *Dictionary of Medical Definitions* that is remembered and has remained the true picture of ancient medicine. This work is extremely rare, but even to-day, in spite of the many imitations that have appeared, it is that which gives the true interpretation of ancient science. Castelli, who lived at the end of this century, continued the work of de Gorris, and his *Lexicon* had far more success. In fact, it is more complete, but that of de Gorris in some respects is preferable.

The names of Louis Duret (1526–1586) and Jacques Houillier are inseparable, the latter being the pupil of the former, and both enjoyed great renown during the XVIth century. Houillier belonged to a rich family of Étampes; he became Dean of the Faculty of Paris in 1546, and practised in the capital up to the time of his death. Duret was born at Baugé in Bresse, of a gentle Piedmontese family. He devoted himself to the study of letters and ancient writers and became professor at the Royal College, or *Collège de France*. The books of these two physicians are principally concerned with commentaries on the *Prognostics* and *Aphorisms* of the School of Cos, and for years enjoyed an immense reputation.

Anutius Foës was born at Mayence in 1528 and died in 1591 or 1595. He came to Paris to follow Houillier's lectures and later returned to his native city. Besides several commentaries, he published a kind of dictionary, similar to that by de Gorris, entitled: *Economia Hippocratis alphabeti serie distincta.* But his great work was his edition of the first complete collection of the Hippocratic works, republished a great many times and probably still the best we have at the present day.

John Keys, or Caius (1510–1573) was a professor at Cambridge. He corrected the texts of Galen, Celsus and Scribonus Largus. Mercuriali (1530–1606) of Forli published a critical edition of the works of Hippocrates which is far inferior to that of Foës, as well as a book on the gymnastics of the ancients which is very erudite. Montanus of Padua published an edition of the works of Galen, while Christopher de Vega, professor in the University of Alcala, is known for his commentaries on Hippocrates and Galen.

Other physicians of this period attempted to reconcile the humoral doctrines of the Islamic physicians with those of Galen, and in this respect M. Sylvaticus is by far the most successful.

We must now refer to the writers of Institutes of Medicine, because they attempted in their writings to co-ordinate the various branches of medical science. These *Institutiones Medicae* originated during the XVIth century and were a new way of presenting the subject. Hippocrates had given his general ideas on the science in several of his books, but he gave no general systematic account comprising the principal branches of medicine, and essential definitions were wanting. Galen, however, understood the importance of this systematization and appears to have wished to develop it in several of his works, especially in *Ars medica, De Partibus artis medicae, De Optima secta,* and *Introductio, seu Medicus.* Oribasius had been the first to include under the name *Synopsis* all knowledge of medical science accumulated up to his time, arranged according to its various branches. He undertook this work at the time when the Emperor Justinian had had the *Corpus Juris* published, to which the name of Institutes was given, and the Synopsis represents, in medical science, the first application of the idea of "Institutes", which name was first used for a work on law. From this time on writers published their works under the titles of Synopses, Pandects, Canons, and Compendia. Thus

Aaron, a physician, who flourished at Alexandria in the year 622, wrote his Pandects as did Matthew Sylvaticus at a later date. Islamic physicians—Avicenna and Mesua the Elder—wrote Canons, which name literally translated means the teaching of general *rules.* Gilbertus Anglicus (1180–1250) wrote a work entitled *Compendium totius medicinae,* but it was not until the XVIth century that the idea of Institutes reached its full fruition.

We believe that Leonhard Fuchs was the first to publish an "Institutes of Medicine". His work appeared in 1530, and is a very incomplete production; but in 1544 and 1569 those of Fernel were published, which were far more complete and were epoch-making. Mercado's Institutes, which appeared soon after, were very much larger, but full of subtleties and ramblings, and should rather be regarded as an encyclopaedia than as a system. During the same century Heurn and Castelli also published Institutes, and the tradition continued in the centuries following.

A word must here be said in respect of Fuchs and Fernel. The former follows Galen very closely, or, at least, is inspired by that great Roman physician. His work is divided into five books, as follows: *Lib.* 1, *Medicina generalis, et res naturales; Lib.* 2, *Res non naturales; Lib.* 3, *De rebus praeter naturam; Lib.* 4, *De signis medicis, de indiciis, de urinis, de pulsibus; Lib.* 5, *De curandi ratione.*

The place and date of the birth of Jean Fernel have given rise in the past to much discussion, but the careful researches of Figard have settled this point, and we now know that he was born at Montdidier in 1497. He studied in Paris at the Faculty of Medicine, and afterwards became one of the most celebrated physicians of his century. He died in 1558. Fernel wrote on fevers, medicaments, and especially on pathology and philosophical subjects, to which we need not now refer. His chief work, entitled *Medicina,* appeared in 1544, and at a later date was republished with many additions on special diseases and bore the name of *Universa Medicina.*

The work, however, really contains three parts. Seven books treat of physiology, describing the parts and their use, the elements, temperaments, the spirits and innate heat, the faculties, functions and humours, and generation. The books on pathology, of which there are three, deal with

PLATE VI

JEAN FERNEL
*(Author's Collection)*

[*face p. 240*

diseases and their causes, their symptoms and signs, the pulse and the urine. Seven other books are devoted to therapeutics and to cures, blood-letting, purging and the action of medicaments as well as their use. It is clear that Fernel, although accepting the tradition of Galen, was desirous of reforming the study of pathology, in which he included the study of the causes and signs of disease. But it was only at a much later date—with Gaubius and Astruc—that semeiology really took its place in pathology, although it had been the subject of several works during the XVIth century. We shall refer to Fernel's pathology later on.

The physicians of this century were quite familiar with the two principal tendencies which divided the philosophical schools of the time, namely neo-Platonism and neo-peripateticism. They were divided as to the truth contained in these two currents of human thought, represented by the two great philosophers of antiquity, the one a philosophical idealist but a realist in the scholastic sense, the other an experimentalist and observer, although a nominalist logically, and therefore they were divided into two groups, the one of dreamers and idealistic speculators, the others observers and experimentalists who made discoveries to which we shall refer later. But the observers left the philosophy which they had adopted far behind, leaving discussions to the philosophers and devoting themselves to the study of facts. It is rather remarkable that the realistic party, which claimed to be that of reform, was triumphant only in appearance, while the philosophy which seemed to have been defeated triumphed in the end. The study of the XVIIIth century will reveal to us this astonishing result.

We will in the first place consider those who accepted the dream of neo-Platonism. The teachings of this neo-Platonic school were imported from Constantinople by Gemistus, Pomponius Laetus, and Marsilio Ficino, and in the west found a soil ready for their reception, having been cultivated by the Arabists during the XIIIth, XIVth, and XVth centuries. The neo-Platonists had the same idealistic dreams, the same doctrine of morbid realism, the same astrological conceptions, and the same opposition to peripateticism as had the Arabists. And, as a matter of fact, the two doctrines were derived from the same source, the ancient School of

Alexandria, one passing by way of the Grecians, the other by way of the Arabians, reaching the west and gaining fresh force by their union there. It was to this double current of thought that the reformers of the XVIth century owed their inspiration.

Giovanni Argenterio of Castel-Nuovo (1513–72) appears to have been the first to revolt openly against the teachings of Galen. But we would point out that he was quite different from the other reformers to whom we shall refer, because his doctrine tended towards Scholasticism. It is not strictly correct to place him at the head of the reformers, as many historians have done. These latter have had in mind his violent attacks upon Galen for having modified the Hippocratic tradition, and they have not taken his scholasticism sufficiently into consideration. He was, in fact, a nominalist and not a realist, like the other reformers of medicine. None of the theories of the physician of Pergamus were safe from his attacks; he objected to the large number of spirits that Galen admitted in order to explain the action of the faculties of man. He stated that these spirits were purely imaginary things, and that a single one was sufficient to explain the manifestations of life. He objected to the confusion between disease and the near cause. He maintained that diseases were not derived from the elementary qualities but represented a disharmony in the body, an *ametria* resulting from the complication of the parts of the body. The Galenists and humoralists attacked him, but he was supported by Laurent Joubert and Rondelet of Montpellier, Jerome Capivacci, professor at Padua, Dutith of Honkowicz, a Hungarian, and many others.

Cornelius Agrippa von Nettesheim followed another method. He attempted to make an alliance between medicine and the Kabbala. In this he was the forerunner of Paracelsus. He wished to do for medicine what Reuchlin and Pico della Mirandola were doing for philosophy. According to Agrippa there were three worlds, namely the intellectual, or the world of ideas, spirits, and demons; the celestial world, or the world of stars; and the elementary world, or the world of terrestrial bodies. These three worlds mutually corresponded, so that what took place in one influenced the other two. And it was the particles emanating from terrestrial

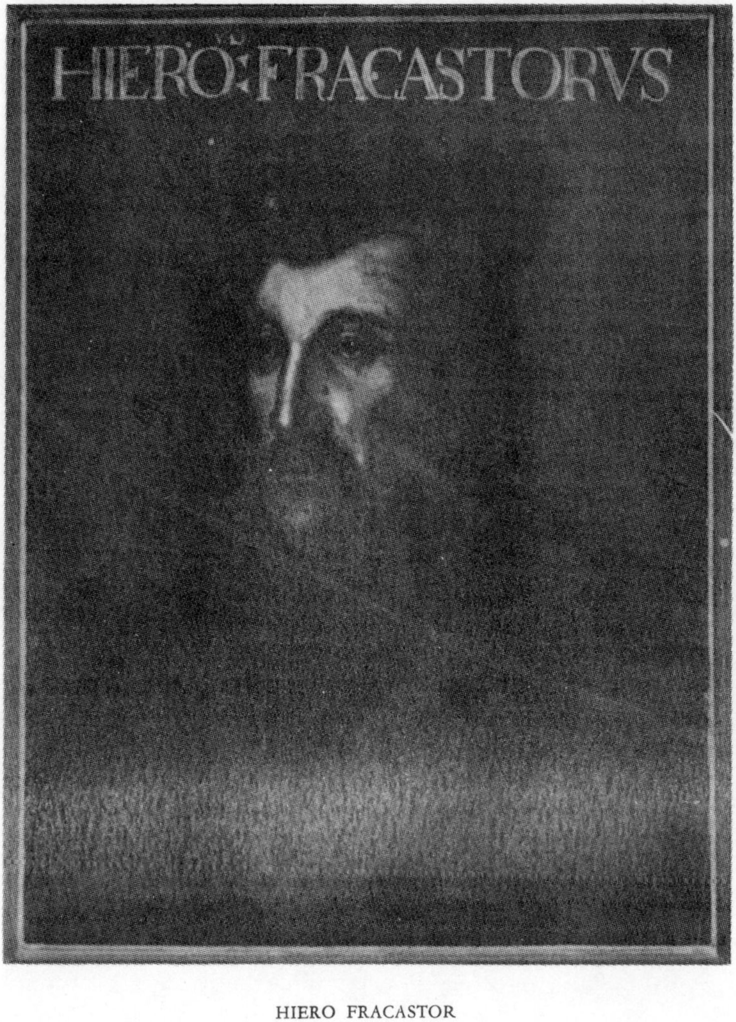


HIERO FRACASTOR
Pitti Gallery, Florence
*(Reproduced by special permission for the author by Brogi)*

[*face p. 242*

bodies which linked these all together. For that matter the substantial forms were the bases of occult qualities; the terrestial forms corresponded to celestial forms, while their exemplary forms or first ideas resided in the Archetype. The humours, the material particles, certain words and certain forms of speech and certain numbers, established the union between the three worlds, and the key to this union was possessed by the Magi. As may be seen, this is the Kabbala, magic, pure and simple; and Agrippa boasted that he could make gold.

This doctrine was attacked and defended with great violence. Weier vigorously opposed the Kabbala, the belief in demons and sorcery, while he was attacked by Wilhelm Adolf Scribonius, who upheld the existence of demons and their influence. Giambattista della Porta attempted to explain all supernatural things by sympathy and antipathy of the bodies depending upon the great soul of the world—it was Plato's soul of the world, of which he made a spiritual force animating all creation. Porta was the forerunner of Mesmer.

The result of all this discussion was the appearance of an enormous number of books on demonology, necromancy, astrology, and chiromancy. Among the writers of these books may be mentioned Bartolommeo Rocca, John of Endagina, and Andrea Corvi, who wrote on chiromancy. Horst wrote lengthily upon a miraculous golden tooth that he said grew in the mouth of a child of ten years living in Cilicia, and claimed to make divination by this tooth. The famous Michael Nostradamus, who was born in Provence and was M.D. of Montpellier, combined astrology with medicine. So, too, did Mizaud of Montluçon and J. Carvin of Montauban, as well as Bartisch, who wrote on diseases of the eye, and Settala, who discoursed on birth marks.

And now the great figure of Fracastor appears. He was born in 1484, at Verona, and died near his native city in 1553, so that it will be seen that he belonged rather to the XVIth than to the XVth century. His book, *De Contagionibus*, which had such an enormous influence, only appeared in 1526, and his famous poem on syphilis in 1530.

Alchemy developed with the Kabbala. Its initiates tried to make gold by transmuting metals. By the decomposition of one material they professed to make others, and, although they had many absurd ideas, their operations contained the embryo of modern chemistry. Basil Valentine, whom some have thought to be a German Benedictine monk, appears to have been the first writer on alchemy of this period, but some have supposed that he lived in the XIVth century, while others believe he lived in the XVIth. Following him may be mentioned Quirinus Apollinaris, physician to the Court of Beyrut; Nicholas Barnaud and Isaac Hollandus, not to mention others who were famous alchemists.

The alliance in medicine between the Kabbala and alchemy was completed by Paracelsus, who maintained that a physician should be alchemist, theosophist, and magician all in one. In other words, all these sciences were to be brought together in a single synthesis, and this synthesis was the work attempted by Paracelsus and his followers.

Paracelsus, otherwise Theophrastus Bombastus von Hohenheim, was born at Einsiedeln, Switzerland, in 1493. His father is said to have been a physician, but we know that he was an alchemist. The son was at first attracted by alchemy, and studied successively under several masters, including physicians, and then began his travels, which only ended at his death at Salzburg in 1541 at the age of 48.

For two years he was Professor of Medicine at Basel, in 1526–1527, but, on account of his radical teachings and certain difficulties that he had with the city authorities, he was obliged to leave.

It would seem that, after having studied alchemy, Paracelsus wished to study medicine in the works of Galen, but he found this means of acquiring medical knowledge too slow and, by the help of his imagination, built up a system of medicine of his own. At his first public lecture at Basel he publicly burned the books of Galen and Avicenna, violently attacked the ancient writers, respecting only Hippocrates, and boasted of his contempt for science, of which for that matter he was entirely ignorant. For him a single method was sufficient, namely a kind of theosophical intuition by means of which he said that man should come into intimate contact with God and all created things. In this intuition there is a mystic light which teaches all things to the human mind and gives it the strength to drive away demons; by it one communicates with God, from Whom all things are

PLATE VIII

PARACELSUS
*(Author's Collection)*

[*face p. 244*

received, because man creates nothing. Adam contained within him all the sciences because he contained the germs of all creatures, and it is by searching the Adamic man within oneself that one will discover science.

This process of intuition developed by Paracelsus was a fundamental principle of the Gnostic philosophy of the School of Alexandria, of which the theosophists of the XVIth century were merely the followers. According to Paracelsus a man who renounces all sensuality and blindly obeys the will of God will be able to identify himself with the acts of the celestial reason and thus will possess the philosophers' stone. These theories were simply words on the part of the gnostics and theosophists, so that Paracelsus' statements should not be taken too seriously. For him and his pupils, as for the gnostic school, to renounce all sensuality and obey the will of God was merely to fall into a state of ecstasy, as one of his celebrated followers, Jerome Cardan, declared when he claimed that he could at will fall into a state of ecstasy during which he could hear and see anything that he desired. By this means he could foretell the future, because the signs indicating forthcoming events became visible on that finger-nails.

Consequently, the contempt for all knowledge obtained by work and application and the pride in the belief that one can obtain wisdom from God directly, are qualities belonging to Paracelsus and to other fanatics, both ancient and modern. The true theosophy, as these people maintain, has at all times consisted in becoming intimately united with God, the Eternal Father of all good spirits. This union is attained by inward contemplation of the Supreme Being and the renunciation not only of all sensation but also of all the faculties of the mind. Therefore the theosophist has no need of devoting himself to difficult studies, since without them, his mind being kept in an entirely passive state, the Divinity itself, of which he is an emanation, will impart to him its light and its wisdom. Since thus he has absolute control of the demons they will obtain for him all that he desires. The theosophist who has thus made himself worthy to share the divine light has no further need of a positive religion or religious ceremonies. The inner light and the theophanies into which the Divinity absorbs him surpass these common usages and make them unnecessary. This gnostic system was handed down from the School of Alexandria to the Kabbala and from the Kabbala to the theosophy of the Xth century.

Man, said Paracelsus, is a microcosm, or little world, which corresponds to the whole universe or macrocosm, the great world; all the parts of the organism are spiritually contained in the macrocosm. In each body there are two essences, the one spiritual, the other material. The spiritual may also be called astral, because it possesses its Idea or paradigm in the celestial intelligences which reside in the stars. The material essence contains the signs or figures of the spiritual body, and all the art of the philosopher consists in finding out the signification of these signs. In order to find the spiritual essences belonging to the material bodies, man must renounce all sensuality and obey God's will, sinking his own intelligence in order to receive the celestial intelligences. Thus, as we have already said, he would possess the true philosophers' stone.

Paracelsus maintained that Galen, by basing his theories on the four qualities, was entirely mistaken, because these qualities are nothing. Only the essences are something—realities. All bodies contain three essential elementary principles, namely salt, sulphur and mercury. They may acquire different qualities from the action of heat, cold, dryness or moisture; they are dependent upon the astral body, which is a peculiar kind of vital force or Archeus, principally seated in the belly, but also distributed throughout the body. Diseases are neither changes arising in the primal bodies nor organic lesions, as Galen maintained; they are essences of real entities which enter into us, and are derived from five principal causes, namely the *ens asterum*, or astral entities, which stamp upon the body the changes caused by the stars; the *ens veneni*, which is the poisons contained in food; the *ens naturele*, which is natural entities controlled by the astral entities; the *ens spirituale*, or the spirits and the demons; the *ens deale*, or the immediate effects of the acts of God upon us. In the treatment of disease one must find remedies corresponding to each morbid entity, and to accomplish this one must follow the theosophic method. Plants possess, as all other created things, their astral paradigm, and the shapes that they represent are the figures or signs of this paradigm. Thus their anatomy, or the analytical and synthetic study of the signs, will allow of the recognition of their corresponding diseases; in other words, the form of a plant indicates the astral idea corresponding to its form or essence, and here Paracelsus merely develops the theory of signatures. Finally, as it is this essence which acts and not the quality of bodies, it is necessary to distil plants and make extracts and tinctures to obtain their active essence.

Paracelsus did help the advancement of medicine by popularizing the theory of morbid species, and credit must also be given him for introducing mineral substances into therapeutics.

Much has been said about the private life of Paracelsus that is largely legendary and need not concern us.

Jerome Cardan was born at Milan in 1501. He cynically relates the debauch of his parents to which he owed his birth. At first professor of mathematics and afterwards becoming a physician, he practised at Paris, Bologna, and lastly Berne, where he died at the age of seventy-five years. He was very learned and possessed a brilliant and penetrating, but also extremely extravagant mind, and, as Boerhaave has said, *sapientior nemo, ubi sapit, dementior nullus, ubi errat.* His philosophical method was the mystical ecstasy into which he could fall at will, and by which he could, as he says, enter into relation with " all beings and all things ".

Cardan taught that everything was derived from earth and water by the action of celestial heat. He taught that there were only two qualities, namely, heat which is the formal cause, and moisture which is the material cause. All organic bodies are animated; everything is born from putrefaction; everything is controlled by numbers which bring terrestrial things into touch with the constellations. Strictly speaking there is no general principle that can be called nature. Galen was entirely in error in everything, especially in his therapeutics, in which the principle *contraria contrariis curantur* is absolutely false. It is noteworthy that Cardan was always contradicting himself in turn affirming and denying the same thing. He dabbled in astrology, magic and all the extravagances of his time.

He had a very great opinion of himself and claimed that great physicians were only born once in a thousand years and that he was the seventh. Although he was an unceasing worker and learned far in advance of his time, and thoroughly well versed in mathematics and physics (in which he excelled), Cardan, as far as medicine was concerned, was only a reflection of Paracelsus.

Amongst other physicians who followed the teachings of Paracelsus and Cardan may be mentioned Thurmeyer of Basel, an alchemist of great repute, who was supposed to have manufactured gold for the King of England and the Margrave of Brandenburg. He made himself celebrated by some remarkable cures, accumulated an immense fortune, and died in poverty. Adam Rodenstein explained some obscurities of Paracelsus, but Peter Séverin is probably the most celebrated of that enthusiast's followers. He published an explanation of the doctrines of his master and developed the realist theory of morbid essences, which he called seeds—*semina morborum*—thus combining the doctrine of Paracelsus with that of Fracastor.

A certain number of physicians attempted to combine the doctrine of Paracelsus with that of Galen, but it is only in the following century that the notable representatives of this tendency are to be found. If we would fully understand the thoughts governing the reformers of medicine of whom we have spoken we must note that their true tendencies were realist, as we have already pointed out. That is to say, they wished to impart a concrete reality and substantial existence to medical abstractions. Disease, for them, was not merely a simple state of a sick person ; they became specific realists in Fracastor's sense. Disease for them had a real material and objective existence, so to speak, which was represented by contagion, a morbid ethereal vapour, a fifth essence of nature, a true seed or a kind of astral spirit.

Leonhard Fuchs maintained that disease is a substance and for this he was a century later attacked by Plempius. Many physicians of the XVIth century directed their thoughts toward this fifth essence, which they supposed entered into the make-up of all bodies. They pointed out that the ancient physicians admitted four essences, namely water, earth, fire, and spirit, and they maintained that a fifth must exist which would be between the spiritual essence and the three material essences. They supposed that this fifth essence existed in all bodies and all beings, and to it they attributed the principle of life existing between the soul and the body. They also believed that in this essence was a means of relationship between terrestrial bodies and the planetary beings. They also supposed that its perversion constituted morbid principles and lastly they attributed to it the action of drugs, which could be abstracted from material bodies. Hence the term "abstractors of quintessence", applied alike to alchemists, to theosophists, and to the followers of Paracelsus, and finally turned to ridicule by the laughter and satire of Rabelais.

# CHAPTER XVI

## PHYSIOLOGY, ANATOMY, PATHOLOGY, NOSOLOGY, THERAPEUTICS, AND SURGERY IN THE XVIth CENTURY

Until the middle of the XVIth century physiology and anatomy remained much as taught by Galen, an outline, or skeleton, unclothed by detail. Physicians studied in the works of the sage of Pergamus treatises on the faculties, on the mind, on the natural faculties, on the use of the parts and on anatomical subjects. To these they added the study of Aristotle's *De anima*, and also the theory of the Thomists and the Scotists concerning the soul. Indeed, they obtained knowledge wherever it could be found. The various compilers of Institutes (and Fernel especially, whose influence was so great) did an immense service to medicine by bringing together all this knowledge in one body. We must therefore now turn to the writings of Fernel, because they contain the best physiological knowledge of the time.

The books on physiology by Fernel are as follows: *De elementis ; De temperamentis ; De spiritibus et calido innato ; De facultatibus ; De functionibus et humoribus ; De hominis procreatione atque de semine.*

The science of medicine is thus sufficiently co-ordinated. It is of course only derived from Galen, but it is Galen put in order, made clear and popularized. Although anatomy is not given a distinct place by itself it is allotted much space in the first book, which treats of the parts, because it is, in fact, only a subdivision of physiology, and the study of the forces and functions should naturally follow it directly. But, while Fernel and the writers of Institutes gave shape to Galen's works, the ideas which they put in order had been much shaken. The doctrine of the elements had been severely attacked and manifestly was on the wane, while in its place that of Aristotle and the Scholastics in respect of substance had been frankly accepted, and it was currently laid down, as by Thomas Aquinas, that a body (or any being) was formed by a conjunction of a material and an active principle. Thus man was made up of a spiritual mind substantially united to a material body. Fernel was entirely aware of the adoption of these ideas and attempted to harmonize them as well as he could with the theory of the four elements. For that matter he accepted them frankly and in his curious treatise, entitled *De rerum abditis causis*, reveals himself as an accomplished Scholastic.

On the other hand, the alchemists had begun to demontrates that earth is not composed of a single element, but made up of several substances. The analysis of water, and afterwards of air, was to come two centuries later, when the theory of the four elements was to receive its death-blow. But as early as the XVIth century the theory had been shaken by the analysis made of earth, while the recognition of chemical principles, regarded as substances, had already confused it. And, still more, the supposed fifth essence was admitted, although regarded as abstract, and never referred to by Galen. It was looked upon as the vital principle, or the principle of the existence of man, but just what it was Fernel found difficult to decide. However, he came to the conclusion that this vital principle was a sort of third entity existing between the soul and the body, the idea of which he attributed to Alexander Aphrodisiensis (A.D. 200).

On the other hand, many of the reformers of medicine admitted two principles in man, namely a more or less materialized soul governing the functions of the body and a principle of intelligence, which some believed to be the true soul, while others, following the teachings of Paracelsus, called it the first Archeus. This was merely a reminiscence of the doctrine of the Albigenses. Still other physicians were divided, in that some followed the teachings of Averroës and others those of the School of Alexandria, but both contended that the spiritual principle was an emanation from God, a ray of the divine intelligence ; but while the former regarded the soul as a true material principle, the latter gave it pure form. Lastly, many Scholastic physicians adopted the doctrine of the philosophers of the XIIIth century, some explaining it, as did St. Thomas, by maintaining that individuation is purely material. Others upheld, with Duns Scotus and St. Bonaventura, the idea that each individuality possesses a principle of *haecceity*, a simple but entirely spiritual principle according to the followers of the Saint, a spiritual and material principle according to the Scotists.

It must be remembered that Galen admitted three kinds of principal faculties, namely the natural, the animal, and the vital; the latter was suggested to him by the Stoics, but in the XVIth century Aristotle's five faculties of the soul, reduced to three by the Scholastics, were taken into consideration. Fernel also thought that the moral faculties, which were admitted by some of the philosophers of his day, should also be taken into account, and he vainly attempted to reconcile these divergences, although he accepted Galen's teachings, and we shall see how Galen's classification triumphed in the XVIIth century and endured until modern times.

In other ways this classification was extremely weak. Several of the Scholastic physicians, for example, Joubert, questioned the reality of these supposed powers or faculties which formerly were admitted and, being determined Nominalists, treated all these conceptions by purely Nominalistic principles as having no real existence. They either maintained with the Scotists that the soul had not need for any adjuvant forces, and that it acted by itself, or they left aside these questions of doctrine and, by observation and experience, tried first to verify the teachings of Galen and then to overthrow them.

The renaissance of anatomy began as early as the XVth century. In the XVIth century it developed tremendously; two theatres for dissection were established, one in 1552 at Venice and the other in 1556 at Montpellier, although in the latter university dissections had been made for years, for we know that Rabelais dissected there in 1532. Anatomical discoveries became numerous through the work of Günther of Andernach, Fallopius (1523–1562), Michael Servetus (1509–1553), Andreas Vesalius (1514–1564), Gaspard Bauhin (1560–1624), Berenger of Carpi (1480–1550), Andreas Caesalpinus

(1524–1603), J. C. Arantius (1530–1589), Coiter, John Philip Ingrassias (1510–1580), Fabricius ab Aquapendente (1537–1619), Realdus Columbus (1516–1559), and Bartholomeus Eustachius (1520–1574).

The anatomy of Galen was overthrown or, perhaps, it would be better to say, replaced by a distinct science which tended to become separated from physiology. In order to offer the reader an idea of discoveries in anatomy, we will here give a few in chronological order. In 1532 Charles Étienne (1503–1564) discovered the veins of the liver, and in the same year the lymphatic vessels of the kidney were demonstrated by Nicholas Massa (1499–1569). In 1534 Sylvius and his pupil Vesalius discovered the valves of the veins; in 1546 Ingrassias studied the anatomy of the ear and described the stapes; in 1547 Cornarius described the valves of the azygos vein. The great Italian anatomist, Arantius, gave a description of the muscles of the upper eyelid in 1548, while in 1542 Eustachius published his celebrated anatomical tables. In 1553 Michael Servetus described the pulmonary circulation; in 1571 Caesalpinus studied the heart and lungs, as well as the arteries and veins, and apparently foresaw the discovery of the general circulation. In 1572 Fabricius ab Aquapendente described the valves of the veins and also showed that he had some knowledge of the general circulation. In 1579 Bauhin described the valve of the caecum which to-day bears his name, while in 1593 Casserius (1561–1616) described the anatomy of the ear and confirmed the findings of Ingrassias.

The result of these discoveries was considerable, and, coupled with those of physics and mathematics, led the majority of the learned to observation and experiment, thus turning their thoughts away from metaphysics. Consequently, from this time on. physiology and anatomy became almost exclusively the subjects of observation for the study of the organic functions. The science of the nature of man thereby abandoned the general consideration of life and the great philosophical studies, which up to that time had been considered as the foundation of medicine. Undoubtedly attempts were made to return to the older philosophy, but they were never successful. Observation and experiment were to make great progress, as we shall see.

Pathology made great advances in the XVIth century in all its branches, as well as in its doctrines. Although we have already spoken of the theories emitted by the reformers of medicine of this century, we must return to the consideration of the doctrine of disease, which is nothing but a doctrine of ætiology. Fracastor affirmed the specific nature of contagion by means of material particles. This theory was violently opposed by J. B. Montanus (1488-1550), Valleriola, and especially Facio, who absolutely denied contagion in his work published at Genoa in 1584 entitled *Paradossi della pestilenza.*

The propagation of disease by contact or from contagious matter became evident in variola, the bubonic plague, measles, and above all syphilis. All this undoubtedly did not prove that realist specificity was true as a doctrine, but its supporters maintained that the cause producing disease must be the real morbid factor.

Ambroise Paré attempted to show the difference between the propagation of variola, of measles, and of bubonic plague, and thus became the inventor of the theory of infection parallelly with that of contagion. But it was in Paracelsus that the theory of specificity was fully developed. We have already pointed out how Paracelsus developed this idea, supported by all the alchemists and astrologists, and how he attempted to show that disease was the result of five kinds of power. The *ens astrale* came from the constellations, and only produced disease in an indirect way by activating and infecting the atmosphere. The *ens veneni* was a matter born of the corruption of ingested food, and this became putrefied either locally in some part of the body, or in one of the emunctories, when this putrefied matter was retained within the organism and could not be expelled. The *ens naturale* contained the principle of what the ancients called the natural causes, upon which all others had an influence. The *ens spirituale* was a moral influence, while the *ens deale* was the influence of God derived from religion, and included all the immediate effects of divine predestination. This doctrine thus attributed various diseases to causes really subsisting in the patient, and, so to say, substantialized disease. It was specificity in its purest form and the disciples of Paracelsus (among others Peter Séverin), admitted a kind of germination of diseases, they having a development similar to that of plants and animals; hence the expression *semina morborum*, which they used. Thus disease was due either to an intoxication of the organism or else to a parasitism, a doctrine which had already been discussed by the ancients.

Many physicians did not accept these notions. A minority maintained the Scholastic theories, as did Mercado and even Fernel to a certain extent; they distinctly upheld that diseases are merely accidental forms without reality or substance. Other physicians remained faithful to Galen, maintaining that diseases are simply organic affections, a mere suffering of the parts diseased, or of their elements or humours. Among them Thomas Erastus (1523–1583), whose real name was Lieber, fought against Paracelsism with all his might in his *Disputationes*, from 1572–1573, and he was hardly more indulgent to the concessionary party, at the head of which he placed Fernel.

In speaking of the writers of the Institutes of Medicine we referred to Fernel, who was in truth disposed to certain concessions, as Erastus says, but with great reservations, for he rather accepted the general teachings of Galen and the Scholastics, while sometimes accepting the ideas of the reformers of medicine. Although it has been said that Fernel was the first of the classical writers who attempted to throw off the yoke of Galen, this is not quite the exact truth, because, although on certain subjects he does not agree with Galen, in others he closely follows him. Undoubtedly he felt the importance of the Scholastic doctrine of disease and was not ignorant of the fact that diseases are distinct from each other. Hippocrates had already developed this idea, which had been completely misunderstood by Galen, but had received confirmation from the development of new diseases. On the other hand, Fernel found in Galen a scientific systematization, the value of which he did not underestimate, as well as the commentaries of the physician of Pergamus, which he regarded as the legitimate expansion of the teachings of the School of Cos. Hence he took from Galen all that he could, although he profoundly modified his pathological doctrine. In the first place he defined disease as an 'affect' of the living body:

*morbus est affectus contra naturam corpori insidens.* He speaks, as does Galen, of diseases of the similar parts and those of the organic parts, but takes care to show that disease in the generic sense is an affection of the entire substance: *affectus totius substantiae.* Like the Scholastics, he says: *forma est morbi species in materiam impressa inductaque,* thus showing that according to his way of thinking the morbid species are forms without reality—simple impressions. He is thus able to make a definite distinction between the 'affect' *disease* and the 'affect' *symptom,* as had not been done by anyone up to that time. Disease is an 'affect' of the entire substance of the living body, while the local symptom or 'affect' is a disorder arising in a part of the body or of its functions.

In his curious little treatise entitled *De abditis rerum causis,* the second book of which treats of pathology, Fernel reviews the epidemic, endemic, virulent, and contagious diseases, and gives descriptions of syphilis, elephantiasis, and rabies, which had been neglected by other writers; he examines their causes and refutes the doctrine of materialistic specificity; he admits that everything coming from without may be the cause of disease, but that, according to the doctrine of Hippocrates, it is within the human body and of the corruption properly belonging to it that disease is born.

Thus he developed an ætiological doctrine, which is far removed from that of Galen, and clearly shows the influence of the Scholastics.

It was on the ætiological doctrine that the pathological doctrine of the XVIth century was based, and so it was on the right road. In Fernel's book the question is lengthily dealt with and he puts forward arguments which could reasonably be discussed to-day. Contagious, epidemic and poisonous diseases do not, in fact, spread unless there is a predisposition to the disease among the population and each person becomes infected according to his constitution. And lastly all so-called specific remedies are merely antidotes which bring about changes in the constitution. This doctrine endured for a very long time, but underwent successive modifications as time went on, and, as we shall show, it was made clearer in the XVIIth century, while in the XVIIIth century it became more enlightened still.

In addition to discussing these doctrines, the physicians of the XVIth century, following in the footsteps of those of the XVth, had to study the great epidemics, to combat which demanded all their skill. And we must now briefly consider these epidemic diseases and their history.

The French pox, which was not called syphilis till much later (although this term was given to it by Fracastor in his poem which appeared in 1530), made its first appearance in Europe in 1494. Brassavola is the only early syphilographer who gives 1485 as being the date of the first appearance of this terrible scourge. All other writers of the XVIth century adhere to the former date. It is not our intention to discuss the origins of syphilis, which for some historians date back to Roman or mediaeval times. What is perfectly clear is that its medical history only commenced at the end of the XVth century and that the first work devoted to this disease was one by Nicolaus Leonicenus (1428–1524), entitled *De epidemia, quam Itali morbum Gallicum, Galli vero Neapolitanum vocant,* which was published at Venice in 1497. A year later Lopez de Villalobos published his little work on what he calls the accursed Bubas, which was published at Salamanca in 1498, and five years later Joseph Grünbeck wrote on the *Mentulagrum,* or corruption of the male member. The disease in the first place was regarded as an epidemic and, as it first appeared during the siege of Naples and as both the French and the Neapolitans were attacked, the latter called it the French Disease while the French called it the Neapolitan Disease. It was also called venereal disease, or *lues venerea.* Such were the various names given to this new disease.

Leonicenus especially describes the eruption, which had no resemblance whatever to any eruptions described by the ancients, Galen or Avicenna, and he regards it without qualification as a new disease. In speaking of the eruption he says: *Pustulae in obscenis partibus orientes quae postea per totum corpus ac praecipue in facie cum dolore se dispergunt.* Thus from its very appearance syphilis was regarded as a dermatosis and the patients were treated with inunctions of mercurial ointment. This treatment, which was entirely empirical, was successful, and it was not long before it was regarded as the only medication for the disease.

Alexander Benedictus, who accompanied the Venetian troops to the battle of Fornovo, where he was able to observe the disease closely, refers to its genital origin and says that " this virus of prostitutes will soon infect the entire universe ". He is also one of the first to speak of virulent gonorrhoea, but he does not appear to regard this as being among the symptoms of syphilis, as was done later. He had the opportunity of performing autopsies, and in one performed on a woman he found periostitis and osteitis. As to treatment, he refers to mercurial inunctions and describes the accidents to which they give rise, such as tremor, paralysis and falling out of the teeth.

Gaspar Torella, in his treatise entitled *De Pudendagra sive Morbo Gallico*, dedicated to Caesar Borgia, which was published at Rome in 1497, gives the first clinical history of the disease, which we will give in full. *Æger I. Morbum contraxerat quis de mense Augusti* 1497 ; *rem habuerat cum muliere habente pudendagram. Illi aderat ulcus in virga cum quadam duritie, longe tendente versus inguina ad modum radii cum sorditie et virulentia. Post sex dies, ulcere semisanato, arreptus fuit ab intensissimis doloribus capitis, colli, spatularum, brachiorum, tibiarum et costarum. Elapsis postea decem diebus apparuerunt multae pustulae in capite, facie et collo.*

Torella gives the symptomatic picture of the disease as it is given to-day, but he is not an advocate of mercurial treatment, which appears to have been without effect in the cases of Alphonso and John Borgia, while it caused the Cardinal of Segovia to develop a very severe form of cachexia. He especially proposes prophylactic measures to prevent the spread of this " horrible and contagious disease ", and asks the Pope and Emperor, King and Lords to appoint matrons to examine the public women, and when they are found to be infected to send them to a special hospital, where they may be treated by a physician or a surgeon appointed for this special purpose.

In his treatise on surgery (1514) John of Vigo (1460–1520) treats of this new disease at length. He advises mercurial treatment by inunction or plasters applied to the arms and legs until salivation occurs. He states that when the disease is confirmed it has periods of recurrence, "*per intervalla annorum et mensium,*" and that it is difficult to obtain a cure. He was one of the first to give mercury in pill form, using the red precipitate for this purpose.

As the inunctions then used frequently resulted in very severe complications, the bark of guaiacum came into use. It was given either in decoction or maceration. The famous Knight Ulrich von Hutten had related the history of his cure by means of this treatment in his tract entitled *De Guaiaci Medicina et Morbo Gallico,* published at Mayence in 1519.

For some time it had generally been thought that syphilis had been imported into Europe by the companions of Christopher Columbus and, as this disease was extremely common among the inhabitants of the island they first discovered—Hispaniola—and the usual treatment there was with the wood of guaiacum, it was logical to try the same treatment in the Old World.

In 1527, Jacques de Béthencourt, of Rouen, in his *Nouveau Carême de Pénitence,* refers to visceral complications of the disease, especially of the liver. He seems to prefer treatment by mercury to that by guaiacum, when properly given. In 1532 Nicholas Massa of Venice was the first to describe gummata in the dead body, calling them *materiae albae viscosae.* In 1546 Fracastor, who in 1530 had written his famous poem entitled *Syphilis, sive Morbo Gallico,* took up the clinical study of the malady in his treatise on contagious diseases. He regarded it as a contagious affection contracted during coitus, and he states that it begins with small ulcers on the genital organs, soon followed by a generalized eruption of pustules, including the scalp. He refers to the disastrous effects occurring in the mouth and pharynx, as well as to gummata, exostoses, osteitis, nocturnal periarticular pains and loss of the hair, eyebrows and beard. He also makes mention of fever, syphilitic cachexia and congenital syphilis. Fernel was the first to show that infection of syphilis could only occur if a solution of continuity of the mucous membrane or skin was present and that it was at the point of inoculation that the primary sore occurred.

According to Franck there was no year during the entire XVIth century in which the bubonic plague did not rage in some district of Europe, and this would certainly seem to be the case, when we consider the enormous bibliography of this disease during the period. The physicians were able to study this disease carefully, and the result of their observations was the separation of bubonic plague from other pestilential fevers, and the description of the so-called lenticular fever, which is perhaps nothing else than typhus fever, or else cerebro-spinal meningitis.

The first description of bubonic plague is supposed to have been given by Rufus of Ephesus. Procopius, in the VIth century, refers to the bubo in the great plague of Constantinople in 543. At about the same time Gregory of Tours mentions a very contagious and murderous disease, which he calls *lues inguinaria*, occurring in France and especially at Marseilles. Guy de Chauliac has left us a description of two epidemics occurring at Avignon in 1348 and 1360, but the history of bubonic plague was not really undertaken from the viewpoint of nosology and pathogenesis until Fracastor took it up in the XVIth century, and Mercuriali studied its symptomatology and prophylaxis.

At this period all continued malignant fevers were comprised under the name of pestilential fevers, having a contagious character and usually ending in death. For example, *sudor Anglicus* was a pestilential fever. Fracastor began by separating these fevers into two distinctly different types, which for a long time had been confused; firstly true pestilential fever, namely bubonic plague, and secondly the non-pestilential fevers, the most serious of which and the most easily mistaken for plague was what was called lenticular fever, in reality the typhus of the present day. Lenticular fever appeared for the first time in 1505 in Italy and again in 1528. It received its name because those who were stricken by it presented an eruption of spots resembling flea bites, having a dark red hue, appearing on the fourth to the seventh day of the disease. These spots appeared on the arms, back and chest; the disease subsided at the end of the seventh to the fourteenth day. It was a serious disease, although less so than the plague. It is the same disease as that described by Jourdan under the name

A MEDICAL CONSULTATION IN THE XVIth CENTURY

Engraving enlarged by A. Mittendorff from Facinus' *De epidemiæ Morbo*, 1518 (*Author's Collection*)

[*face p. 260*

of *Morbus Hungaricus*, and it developed more particularly in armies.

The true bubonic plague was especially well described at the end of the XVIth century by Mercuriali, who was officially delegated to study the two epidemics which raged in Venice and Padua in 1575 and 1576 respectively. The affection was characterized by a continued fever with restlessness, delirium, ataxy, a rapid and unequal pulse, epistaxis, bilious vomiting and fetid diarrhoea. At the end of the second, third or fourth day tumours of various sizes, painful or not, developed in the groins and in the axillae and mastoid regions. These bubos were either single or developed in clusters. They formed small tumours with a red base, while their centre was dark with a vesicular surface. Reddish, purple, or black spots, varying in size, and usually fairly numerous, appeared and exhaled a fearful stench. This description, given by Mercuriali, quite fits the bubonic plague of to-day. There were overwhelming forms and Günther of Andernach states that in the Paris epidemic of 1545 people fell dead in the streets and public places.

The statistics of the early years of the XVIth century are, from the viewpoint of mortality, terrific. Paulmier says that he only saved one patient out of a thousand, while at the end of this century Mercuriali states that the mortality was ninety-nine per cent. It is possible that the virulence had somewhat abated, but it is also true that prophylactic measures had been adopted. Patients were isolated, and likewise doubtful cases, even healthy people being separated if they were in any way suspected. Plague hospitals were established and physicians and surgeons were appointed to attend them, and could not visit any other patients. As a sign of their office they carried a small white stick in the hand: *virgulam quamdam albam gestant.* The isolation lasted for forty days. Hence the modern word of *quarantine.* Günther of Andernach says: *Venetiis extra muros omnes ejusdem modi aegros emigrare cogunt . . . ad quadraginta dies manere.* People could not travel from one country to another unless they possessed a health certificate.

Other hygienic and prophylactic measures were recommended, such as sufficient and healthy food and good water. The dead were buried outside the cities and disinfection of the houses and objects used by the patients was accomplished by the vapour of sulphur, by air and by sunlight.

Scurvy also appeared upon the scene in the XVIth century and has had several historians, John Weier being the most important. He published his observations on the disease in 1557. He states that Olaus Magnus, a Swedish writer, was the first to mention this disease, which he regarded as one belonging to armies and probably the same as that described by the ancients under the name of *scelotyrbe* and also *stomacace*. The Danes and North Germans called it *schorbuyck*, which corresponds to the word scorbutus.

At the beginning of the disease the patients complain of a feeling of heaviness and prostration with precardiac distress, weakness in the limbs, redness and painful swelling of the gums, soon followed by bleeding, and a yellow tint of the face. The haemorrhagic inflammation of the gums increases and the teeth begin to loosen. Then red spots appear on the limbs similar to flea bites and soon turn to large, livid, violet-red areas. As the disease progresses the legs become stiff and contracted, making walking impossible. Then either atrophy or swelling occurs in them, while occasionally ulcers develop which resist treatment. There is also difficulty of respiration. In serious cases death results from epistaxis which nothing can control. This disease was supposed to be contagious, and especially met with among sailors, soldiers, and populations of besieged cities.

Weier believed that the cause of the disease is defective diet, such as one finds on board ship, consisting of badly cooked pork and bacon, tainted preserved fish, old bread and bad water. As treatment he advised feeding with various kinds of flour and watercress. The gums should be treated with the juice of cochlearia.

*Sudor Anglicus* is also called ephemeral pestilential fever by Fracastor, because the patient may either recover or die in twenty-four hours. The subject is suddenly seized by an intense fever and one should favour the sweating and if it has no tendency to appear it should be provoked by suitable medication. This contagious disease appeared for the first time in England, in the year 1486, and recurred four times towards the middle of the XVIth century. It also made its appearance in Belgium, since when it has never been recorded as such, though in modern times identified with the Picardy Sweat and considered by Hamer and Crookshank to have been a form of Influenza.

Under the name of *cephalalgia seu catarrhus epidemicus* or of *catarrhus cum cephalalgia, gravedine anhelosa et tussi epidemica,* Valleriola describes a contagious disease which certainly was influenza. It spread over Germany in 1507, while it attacked France in 1510. The cough accompanying it was spasmodic in nature: *tussisque adeo valida, ut in praefocationis periculum deducerentur.* There was anorexia and great lassitude of the entire body.

It would seem that the epidemic of 1510 was not very serious, for the patients were allowed to walk out, but in order to avoid taking cold they covered their heads with a hood or *cuculiones.* Therefore, it is said, the disease was called *cuculuche,* and hence the modern French word *coqueluche.* This disease was also described by Fernel, Gesner and Mercuriali.

As to what the French call to-day coqueluche, this was described for the first time by Guillaume Baillou, in 1578, by the name of *tussis quinta* or *quintana.* He states that it preferably attacks infants between the ages of four and ten months, but older children may also contract the disease. He well describes the character of the cough as follows: *intumescere videtur et quasi strangulabundus aeger mediis faucibus haerentes spiritus habet.* He also reports the case of a little girl who developed phthisis following whooping cough. "*M. Sulpitii filiola tussim quintanam patiebatur cum febre. Destillatio in pulmones ab co tempore ita vi destillationis et febris exarcuit, ut tabida evaserit.*"

Baillou was one of the first to distinguish measles from variola, which from the time of Rhazes had been confused; he described the differential characters of the eruption and also the symptoms occurring at the onset of measles, such as lacrymation and inflammation of the pharynx and larynx, causing hoarseness and occasionally suffocation.

An epidemic of pneumonia appeared in Venice and its suburbs in 1535, and another at Brescia and throughout all Lombardy in 1537.

An epidemic of pleurisy raged throughout Switzerland and Upper Italy in 1555, and in England in 1557, and from here spread over the Netherlands and into Switzerland. It was extremely deadly.

Cerebro-spinal fever or ' brain typhus ', or, as it was called, *Morbus Hungaricus*, appeared in 1566 in the armies of Emperor Maximilian II, and spread along the banks of the Rhine. The epidemic nervous disease later called Raphania appeared epidemically for the first time in the XVIth century; in 1588 and 1593 in Silesia and in 1596 in Bohemia. It has lately been identified with epidemic encephalitis.

A petechial fever appeared in 1505 in Northern Italy and again in 1527 and 1528. It was described by Fracastor, and a similar epidemic appeared in 1557 at Poitiers, La Rochelle, Angoulême, and Bordeaux, which Coiter has described. A similar epidemic occurred in Lombardy in 1587 and had as its historian Andrea Treviso de Fontano; and lastly another epidemic of this disease, which developed at Trent, in 1591, has been described by Roberti.

Baillou (1538–1616) is probably the most remarkable writer of this century for the description of diseases; he was to the XVIth century what Sydenham was to the XVIIth. He was the first since Hippocrates to draw attention to epidemiology, and showed the inflammatory, bilious, and mucous elements predominating, according to the epidemic constitution.

During all this time, leprosy (elephantiasis Graecorum) was on the wane.

It was during the XVIth century that semeiology was given its name, though not a place in medical science. This branch should include all that is to be found in Hippocrates and Galen relating to prognosis. But, during the XVIth century, it was still buried in the commentaries on these writers, and it was Duret, Houillier, and Christopher de Vega who first took it up. Nevertheless Fernel, Lommius, Lemos, Fontanus, and especially Prosper Alpinus (1553–1617) wrote upon it.

As we have seen, Fernel may be regarded as the classical guide of his century. The second book of his *Pathology* is entitled *De symptomatis atque signis*. In it he explains that the symptom is different from the disease and the cause, and here again we have the traditional doctrine. He then goes on to describe the three kinds of symptoms according to Galen. Next he divides the signs into prognostic and demonstrative; the former are of three kinds: *alia coctionis vel cruditatis, alia salutis vel mortis, alia decretoria;* the latter are: *salubres, insalubres,* or *neutres.* In the third book he especially treats of the signs derived from the pulse and urine. It is evident that Fernel follows Avicenna in making this distinction between symptoms and signs.

Lommius wrote a work which may perhaps be regarded as the first general treatise on semeiology: *Observationum medicinalium, libri tres* (Antwerp, 1560). This is divided into three books: the first treats of diseases which attack the human body in general, the second describes the signs and results of diseases belonging to each part of the body, while the third is devoted to prognosis of general diseases and special affections. This little book contains many excellent precepts and shows that the author was a good observer.

The treatise by Lemos, *De optima praedicendi ratione, lib. IV* (Venice, 1592), and that of Fontanus, *Pronosticarum ad artem medicam spectantium perioche ex Hippocrato et Galeno collecta* (Turin, 1597), are of far less value.

Uroscopy, which had been enriched by the Islamic physicians, was written upon by Clement Clementinus, W. A. Scribonius, Hercules Sassonia, and Thomas Fyens. On the other hand, its abuses were condemned by J. Lange, Forestus, and Sigismund Kaehenter. Joseph Struthius and Leo Rognani wrote on the pulse.

The work *De praesagienda vita et morte* by Prosper Alpinus, and the book already referred to by Lommius are the two best works on semeiology of the XVIth century, and they may be read even to-day with profit.

The treatise by Prosper Alpinus is really remarkable and may be regarded as a classic. It is divided into seven books. In the first the writer deals with the prognostic signs in fevers; the second describes delirium, the senses, deafness, tinnitus aurium, heat and cold, pain, sleeping and waking; in the third is given the prognosis derived from the motor faculties, distress and anxiety, palpitations and convulsions; in the fourth book we have prognosis as derived from the vital faculties, the pulse, respiration, and natural faculties; the fifth book is devoted to the state of the different parts, while the sixth deals with crises and the seventh with the excretions.

It is clear that Alpinus had a very distinct idea of his subject, which in principle was that the morbid phenomena should be classified into genera. No subtle distinctions are made between the signs and symptoms, and the author takes phenomena one after the other and shows what signs may be derived in such or such circumstances. This is the Hippocratic idea in all its purity and distinctness. But it must be admitted that Alpinus neglected diagnosis; in speaking of each phenomenon he certainly did indicate the prognostic value that might be derived from it, but he did not refer to its diagnostic value, which is a regrettable omission. Although his classification is not perfect, the book nevertheless is far in advance of the time.

At the beginning of the XVIth century Anthony Benivieni published a work entitled *De abditis nonnullis ac mirandis morborum et sanationum causis* (Florence, 1507), which treated of a new branch, namely the records of autopsies. In this the author noted organic lesions, which had always been considered from the time of Galen as the cause of diseases: of course, a great mistake. As we know to-day, organic changes are not the causes, but the effects of disease; they are manifestations of the morbid process and, like all pathological phenomena, they represent signs by which a disease may be judged. With the writings of Benivieni one must also include the observations made by Marcellus Donatus, Schenck, Forestus, and Dodoens, who followed in his footsteps and enriched pathological anatomy.

It is clear that the therapeutics of the XVIth century must have been affected by the divergences of opinion in the domain of pathology. Some physicians simply upheld the therapeutics of Galen. Others took up the work of Dioscorides or the pharmacopoeia of the Islamic physicians. The alchemists had begun to introduce chemicals into medicine as well as essences of various bodies, as we have already pointed out. Travels, works on natural history, and the necessity of dealing with new diseases greatly stimulated therapeutics. Paracelsus and Cardan violently attacked the Galenic dogma of *contraria contrariis curantur* and substituted the doctrine of similars.

With the specificity of disease the ancient idea of antidotes was developed, and under the strong influence of the teachings of the Paracelsus specific medication became the principal aim of physicians who desired to discover specifics for every new disease, and especially for syphilis. Others sought for panaceas. Alchemy lent itself to the composition of medicaments and introduced mercury, sulphur, antimony, gold, and so forth, into the composition of tinctures and elixirs. At the instigation of Paracelsus an attempt was made to discover the essence of medicaments in order to combat the essence of disease. The systems of Paracelsus and Cardan brought forward the doctrine of signatures, according to which a medicament or any agent of nature showed by its external forms the qualities with which it was endowed. At the end of the century Porta was one of the principal promoters of this theory. By it, digitalis was tried in diseases of the heart, figwort in scrofula and hepatica in diseases of the liver.

Medical botany was considerably enriched, especially by the celebrated work of Conrad Gesner, whom we believe to have been the first great naturalist of Western Europe.

The study of materia medica, including chemistry, and the many travels which were undertaken, resulted in increasing a large number of new remedies. Brassavola popularized the use of guaiacum and China-root, which were brought from America about 1509. Sarsaparilla was introduced into Europe in 1530, smilax aspera in 1535, and sassafras in 1580. Jalap was introduced from Mexico about 1550, while the balsams of Peru and Tolu were respectively made known to us in 1565 and 1574. Ipececuanha was added to the new remedies in 1570.

The treatises on therapeutics published during this century either were compilations from the Greek and Islamic physicians, or else dealt with chemical preparations and popularized new remedies.

Brissot and Botalli wrote upon the use of blood-letting and, as this is important, we shall briefly refer to these two eminent men.

Pierre Brissot was born at Fontenay-le-Comte in 1478.

He first studied the Islamic physicians and at the time accepted their ideas, but he afterwards gave them up for those of the Greek physicians. Consequently he combatted the method of blood-letting introduced by the Arabs, extremely popular at the time, which was based on the notion that its action was derivative rather than revulsive, and that therefore blood should be let from the point of the body the farthest possible from the seat of the disease. Brissot, taking up Galen's opinion, regarded blood-letting as revulsive rather than derivative, and therefore considered that blood should be let at the point of the body nearest to the seat of the disease. For example, in pleurisy, blood should be let from the arm on the affected side. His book appeared after his death in 1525, and caused much sensation, but during his life he was the object of severe censure on the part of some of his confrères, who persecuted him to such an extent that he was obliged to leave for foreign lands. He went to Spain and then to Portugal, where he gave himself up to the study of botany, and there died. Although Brissot was supported by other physicians, among whom was René Moreau, the quarrel lasted for some time and finally became involved with a dispute raised in connexion with Botalli, of whom we shall now speak.

Lionardo Botalli, who was born about 1530 and died at a date unknown, came from Asti in Piedmont, and flourished about the middle of the XVIth century. He came to France and was physician to Charles IX and Henri III. It was a time when only new remedies and specifics were talked about, but a certain number of physicians still clung to purgatives, especially antimony, while others discussed the position taken by Brissot respecting revulsion and derivation. Botalli or Botal made a reputation by proclaiming blood-letting to be an heroic remedy in all diseases. He opposed all those who discussed revulsion and derivation, as well as the choice of veins, saying that all these were secondary in importance, and that it made very little difference from what part blood was let. His practice was above all to bleed copiously, resorting to it four or five times in succession.

Botalli was the forerunner of Broussais. He had many adversaries and consequently was persecuted. He even went before the Parliament of Paris and, although his procedures were condemned by this body, they nevertheless developed in France and Spain. Like many others who have attempted to develop new ideas in medicine, he died miserably in exile.

Surgery made great progress during the XVIth century in spite of the continual dissensions between the physicians and the surgeons. Gunshot wounds were carefully studied. J. de Romaris described the technique of the major apparatus for stone in 1525. Amatus Lusitanus introduced the use of bougies for stricture of the urethra in 1541. Franco performed suprapubic cystotomy for stone in the bladder in 1560, while the Caesarian operation was performed on the living for the first time by a butcher by the name of Nufer, who operated on his wife. But the foundations of modern surgery were laid in this century by Ambroise Paré of Paris and Felix Würtz of Basel. These two great surgeons began their career in the army, and, as they followed many wars, they accumulated a vast amount of material and developed extraordinary surgical skill. Strange to say, their works were independently written and it would seem that they never knew of each other. Paré was born in 1509 and died in 1590, while Würtz saw the light of day in 1518 and died in 1575, the year that the first complete edition of the works of Paré appeared.

Other surgeons of this century to be mentioned are Berenger of Carpi, who wrote remarkably well on wounds of the head and fractures of the skull; Mariano Santo de Barletta, a noted lithotomist, who commented upon the works of Avicenna; Francis of Arcé, born at Seville, who was celebrated for his cures of fistula; Jacques Guillemeau, surgeon to Henri IV, who was a very celebrated surgeon and obstetrician; John Philip Ingrassias, who wrote on tumours; Jerome Mercurii of Rome, who wrote one of the best works on obstetrics up to that date; George Bartisch of Königsbrück, who was a famous oculist, while François Roussel, physician to the Duke of Savoy, wrote his renowned treatise on the Caesarian operation.

Before closing this chapter it is necessary briefly to refer to the revival of Galenism, as its influence on the history of medicine was important. In so far as science was concerned, the Middle Ages depended entirely upon antiquity, but the knowledge obtained was acquired only through inexact translations which greatly disfigured the true sense of the writings. The preponderating influence of Islamic medicine had substituted for the rational spirit of Greek medicine a mass of dialectical subtleties and especially astrological and cabbalistic tendencies. In spite of attempts on the part of certain physicians to go back to the original sources and to observe nature directly, the XIIIth and XIVth centuries were dominated by the School of Salerno and Graeco-Islamic medicine. In the XVth century the political events of which the Orient was the scene and the invention of the printing press greatly favoured learning, by giving to the world a large number of Greek works up to then unknown or misunderstood.

The revival of Galen's dogmatism at this period was certainly a fortunate occurrence for science, but none the less it had disadvantages. It is difficult to realize to-day the absolute power which Galenism held for several centuries. Although Aristotle's authority lay heavy upon the entire Middle Ages and a part of modern times, it had had its vicissitudes. Even in the most glorious days of the Scholastics, Aristotle had his detractors, and the Platonists of all times sharply opposed him. In the end, his authority had for a long time been more nominal than real and it was only at a late date that the true Aristotle overthrew the fantastic doctrines with which his commentators had overloaded his writings. Platonism, Stoicism, and Epicureanism, each in turn held sway, and, although the fortune of Peripateticism in the Middle Ages seems to have been more startling, it was perhaps, among other reasons, because under the name of Aristotle there were comprised a number of theories which in no way belonged to him.

The influence of Galen on thought and science was far more considerable, and this is all the more important to note because he was not invariably devoted to abstract speculation. In his works are often found exact facts, easy to observe and to verify. He exercised such influence over the minds of the men of the XVIth century that it never occurred to them to make this verification. It is astonishing to notice how the anatomists and the learned men studied living things and the human body with the preconceived intention of finding there the confirmation of Galen's theories. Dissections of the human body, the study of therapeutics and experience derived from daily practice; all these effected no progress. This fixed idea of the infallibility of the master narrowed the horizon and closed eyes to such an extent that the most important discoveries were allowed to pass by without recognition, and if one was forced upon the attention of men they refused to believe what they saw. It is probable that such blind belief has never been paralleled in history. The physicians of the Renaissance, and even those of the XVIIth century, were Galen's slaves, and in following him saw what did not exist and did not see what was before them. Among many instances we will give the following. Galen taught that there was in the septum, which separates the ventricles of the heart, an orifice through which food and air became mixed. The belief in this fantastic orifice is not one of the least curious in the works of Galen. The septum separating the ventricles has normally no pore or orifice, but nevertheless on the authority of Galen, up to the time of Michael Servetus, the existence of such pores was admitted. Mundinus said that the septum was pierced; Le Vasseur maintained the teaching of Mundinus and twenty others said the same thing. Berenger of Carpi was the first to confess that these pores were not very visible in man. Vesalius himself, in the first edition of his work on anatomy, does not speak of imperforations of the septum, and it is only in the second edition, which appeared in 1555, two years after the publication of Servetus's *Christianismi restitutio*—which he is careful not to mention—that he refers briefly to this subject. For a man with the courage to question Galen, the world had to wait for Servetus. Yet these anatomists were really talented men; they had dissected many dead bodies and should have seen that the intraventricular septum is not pierced and that the pores described by Galen are an absolute impossibility.

Here is another example. Galen had found in an elephant a small, lyre-shaped bone in the intraventricular septum of the heart, and he gave it the name of the "incorruptible bone". He affirmed that it was present in the hearts of animals and man, although he had never seen it except in the elephant, and in this circumstance he resorted to his procedure of ordinary induction from animals to man, for, as we have said, it is an absolute fact that Galen never dissected the human body. Vesalius was the first to demonstrate that this bone did not exist in man.

It is a remarkable fact that those of the alchemists who were the most infatuated with their own fantastic ideas, nevertheless had some sane theories in respect of medicine. In the days when the schools were steeped in the scientific prejudices of Galenism and medical Peripateticism, the alchemists, driven on by a bold spirit and an insatiable curiosity, began to foresee the truth about the living economy. They had already surmised that it was necessary to separate the study of living from that of dead matter, and that all sentient and living things were governed by other laws than those that rule inanimate bodies. Arnold of Villanova, Raymond Lully, Isaac Hollandus, and Paracelsus were in the stream of Hippocratic medicine.

## CHAPTER XVII

### THE PRINCIPAL DOCTRINES GOVERNING MEDICINE IN THE XVIIth CENTURY.

Metaphysics may be said to have been the foundation of the sciences up to the XVIIth century, but the time then came when they were to be overthrown by the experimental method. Two currents of thought then developed. In the first an attempt was made to test the new causal theories by new facts, and it was thus that various medical doctrines had their birth. In the second all discussion of causes was rejected, and the only thing desired in physics and mathematics was the knowledge of the laws governing phenomena. Descartes denied the formal, efficient and final causes of Aristotle, and only recognized matter and movement. Bacon rejected the ancient doctrine of causes and professed only to accept laws derived from induction, but as a matter of fact made no difficulty of accepting various forms and causes from his own point of view. Gassendi, however, proclaimed that atoms were the principle of all things, and, although Descartes seems to refute this opinion, he uses it for his own theory of vortices; this was merely the ancient doctrine of Epicurus renewed.

Descartes felt the necessity of replacing the doctrine of final causes and therefore developed the theory of occasional causes, which was upheld by Malebranche and others, while he accepted the theory of the vital spirits—a reminiscence of Galenism.

In his turn Leibnitz developed the theory of the monad, which was to supersede everything—shape, matter, force, movement and extent. In his old age he regretted this, for he wrote to Arnaud a letter in which he confessed that it was wrong to reject the ancient Scholastic doctrine and that it should be re-adopted.

Then Newton appeared upon the scene and was, so to speak, a link between the XVIIth and XVIIIth centuries. He maintained that matter alone cannot explain everything, that it is moved by various forces which give to it a kind of vitality, weight, light, affinity and repelling qualities. At the same time Stahl proclaimed that heat is a peculiar principle.

In medicine, which has for its end the knowledge of living man in health and disease, there was a certain sluggishness of the scientific mind with regard to these two currents of thought. It should be understood that there was no intention of applying ancient metaphysics to medicine; Scholasticism, Hippocraticism, and Galenism were alike rejected, except by some few, who still devoted themselves to commenting on the ancients, although only on the finer points, making a last attempt at reconciliation with modern thought. Specificity, which was born of the great theosophical revolt of the XVth and XVIth centuries, was to end in a sort of Kabbalism or in union with chemistry or physics (both of which were new sciences), and, from the latter, were soon to develop the new systems of Iatro-chemistry and Iatro-mechanics. Finally, there was to be a renewal of the idea of force combined with the idea of matter, a kind of vitalism at first badly defined and multiple in its aspects, which was to prepare for the transition from the XVIIth to the XVIIIth century. XVIIth century thought is, in fact, the continuation of that of the XVIth, of the error made in rejecting metaphysics, the necessary foundation of all general scientific doctrine.

We will now attempt to explain the five schools of thought which divided the medical profession in the XVIIth century. These schools were the Hippocratico-Galenic, the Iatro-theosophical, the Iatro-chemical, the Iatro-mechanical and the Iatro-vitalist. As it is practically impossible to understand the three last without having some idea of the teachings of Van Helmont, Descartes and Leibnitz, we must briefly refer to these three great men.

A few physicians, as we have said, attempted to revive the ancient doctrines. Sanctorius (1561–1636) wrote a large work on the elementary theory of the ancients. He spent forty years of his life in weighing himself three or four times a day, and wrote a curious and interesting tract on the statics of the human body. Ponce de Santa Cruz of Valladolid upheld Galenism, while Stupani. G. Hoffmann, Marinelli and

DANIEL LE CLERC
*(Author's Collection)*

[face p. 274

Schelhammer rallied more especially round Aristotelianism. Zacutus Lusitanus, a Portuguese Jew (1575–1642), practised at Amsterdam. His two works, *De medicorum principium historia* and *Praxis medica admiranda*, were highly esteemed. The first of these was one of the first essays on the history of medicine, while Van der Linden's *De scriptis medicis*, published in 1637, is another partial contribution to the subject. The history of the healing art is to be found in embryo in the writings of Strobelberger, Barchausen, Meibomius, and Rivinus, forerunners of Daniel Le Clerc, who was born at Geneva on February 4th, 1652, and died on June 8th, 1728. The last writer's *Histoire de la Médecine* was first published in 1696; it is the first real history of medicine, and is written with scrupulous accuracy and in elegant Latin. Unfortunately it ends with Galen. In many respects it is far superior to any other work ever written on the subject, although the ancient doctrines are not always sufficiently explained.

Strangely enough, it was also during this century of attacks upon antiquity that René Chartier (1572–1654) published his great collection of the works of Hippocrates and Galen, which for a long time was considered the best edition of any. Chartier died before the completion of his work, but the Faculty of Medicine of Paris undertook to finish it at its own expense.

Among those who still clung to the ancients, although making concession to some of the new ideas, may be mentioned Sala, of Vienna, who tried to purge the theories of Paracelsus of their errors; H. Lavater, who attempted to prove that the Galenists had employed chemical remedies for a long time; and J. Hartmann, who was a Paracelsist, but united Galenic explanations with his theories. A number of other well-known physicians united the doctrines of Paracelsus and Galen and used chemical remedies in their practice. Varandé, Sennert, and Lazarus Rivière were more particularly attached to the ancient doctrines, although they tried to reconcile them with the newer theories. And lastly, Baglivi, of whom we shall have more to say, maintained the ancient doctrines, attempting to reconcile them with chemistry. He belongs to the transitional period from the XVIIth to the XVIIIth century.

The writers of the Institutes of Medicine of this period followed in the steps of their forerunners of the XVIth century and undertook to demonstrate synthetically the general constitution of Medicine. Of these there are seven whose names should be mentioned, Varandé, Sennert, Lazarus Rivière, Beverovicius, Plempius, Ettmüller, and Waldschmidt.

J. Varandé, or Varandeus, was born at Nîmes and studied at Montpellier, afterwards becoming professor there. He was born about 1560 and died in 1617. His principal work appears to have been published after his death, in 1620, and has for title : *Physiologia et pathologia, quibus accesserunt tractatus prognosticus et tractatus de indicationibus curativis.* It is a perfect example of the Institutes of Medicine and follows Fernel's teaching.

Sennert was born at Wittemberg in 1572 and died in 1637. His book *De consensu et dissensu galenicorum et peripateticorum cum chimicis*, which made a great sensation in Germany, appeared in 1619, while in 1611 he published his *Institutiones medicae et de origine animarum in brutis*, which had an immense success and went through many editions.

Lazarus Rivière (1589–1655) of Montpellier succeeded Varandé as professor. He derived his inspiration from Sennert, whose teachings he popularized in France. In 1640 he published his *Praxis Medica*, which is a kind of nosography divided into eighteen books and had tremendous success. His *Institutiones medicae* (reprinted in his *Opera omnia*) was held in high esteem because it gave an elegantly expressed and at the same time simplified summary of Sennert's writings. He divides medicine into five parts, namely physiology, pathology, semeiology, hygiene, and therapeutics.

J. Beverovicius was professor at Leyden and published his *Idea medicinae* in 1620. This little book is well written and in it the ancient writers are appreciated at their full value. It begins with a preliminary discourse on the origin and divisions of medicine and shows that the author was very familiar with ancient medical literature. He then goes on to treat the five branches of medicine in a charming way.

Plempius (1601–1671) was born at Amsterdam; he studied at Louvain and Leyden, then returned to Holland, and finally settled at Louvain, where he died. He is celebrated for having ardently defended Harvey's work on the circulation. In 1638 he published his *Institutiones, seu Fundamenta medicinae*, a curious treatise which reveals the attempt of the author to reconcile ancient medicine with the new ideas on the circulation. The first two books treat of physiology; the second is particularly interesting and when compared with Rivière's, Varandé's, or Sennert's, it is astonishing to see what enormous progress this branch of medicine had made in a few years. The third book, on hygiene, is very short; the fourth, on pathology, contains the teachings of Fernel, but is full of subtleties. The fifth book is on semeiology, while the sixth, which is very brief, deals with the therapeutics of Galen.

Waldschmidt published his *Fundamenta medicinae* in 1685. From his writings it is evident that he was a follower of Cartesianism.

J. Ettmüller was born at Leipzig in 1644 and died there in 1683. After having visited most of the European countries for instruction, he returned to practise, and his *Medicus theoria et praxi instructus* was published in 1685. This work was the one which gave him the greatest reputation, although he was a very extensive writer. His Institutes of Medicine are an elegant summary of the medicine of his day, but it is evident that he was influenced by de la Boë and Van Helmont. The work is divided into three parts, namely physiology, pathology, and therapeutics, and, what is most important, dietetics, a branch that had been very much neglected, is included in the latter. He includes semeiology in pathology, which is also as it should be.

Briefly put, the objectives of study in the XVIIth century were principally five: namely, physiology, of which anatomy formed a distinct division; pathology, which included a general study of diseases and their causes; nosography, which formed a distinct branch; semeiology, which had not as yet been included in pathology; and lastly therapeutics, which included dietetics, although some writers made this a separate branch.

The teachings of Paracelsus in the XVIth century were

a rather curious amalgamation of various opinions; with the medical theory of specificity were included the cabbalistic ideas of Cornelius Agrippa and others, as well as magic and astrology imported from the Orient. The followers of these teachings were divided by two currents of thought. Some devoted themselves entirely to chemistry, while others formed themselves into a sort of Kabbalistic sect and finally founded the order of the Rosicrucians. It is certain that during the XVIth and XVIIth centuries a great deal of time was given to magic and sorcery, and many books were written on these subjects. Among the principal writers on this subject were Jerome Menghi who, in 1550, published his book entitled *Compendio dell' arte essorcistica, et possibilita delle mirabili operazioni delle demoni et dei malefici; con i remedii opportuni all' infirmità maleficiale*; and John Weier who published his famous treatise entitled *De praestigiis daemonum et incantationibus ac veneficiis libri VI*, in 1564. This is unquestionably the most important book of those denying the reality of magic and sorcery. Frederick Spee published his *Cautio criminalis* in 1630; wherein he exposed the abuses of sorcery, showing that in most instances sorcerers were victims of hallucination rather than actuated by malice, and this had a very beneficial effect on the criminal courts, which became far more lenient in their judgments.

We must now turn our attention to three great minds of the XVIIth century—Van Helmont, Descartes and Leibnitz.

Jean-Baptiste van Helmont was born at Brussels in 1577. He studied at the University of Louvain and became Doctor in Medicine in 1599. He travelled much in France, Italy, and Germany, after which he returned to Belgium and there remained until his death in 1644. During his lifetime he was little known, because he published few books and it remained for his son, François van Helmont, to publish his complete works in 1667, under the title of *Ortus medicinae, id est initia physicae inaudita, progressus medicinae novus in morborum ultionem ad vitam longam.*

The *Ortus medicinae* is in reality a general consideration of man and of the cosmos from the point of view of medicine. The writer, after treating of what we may call method, deals with the first principles of human being and of life, the elements and matter, the cosmos, stars, and meteors.

Next he takes up general pathology in great detail and deals with the origin and development of disease. This is followed by therapeutics, the work ending with monographs on lithiasis and fevers.

Van Helmont has often been placed side by side with Paracelsus or Cardan, but we believe that this is a mistake and that his theories are quite distinct from theirs. It is clear that he takes the general idea of an Archeus from Paracelsus, but his Archeus is entirely his own and on almost every page he contradicts his celebrated predecessor. He accepts the three elements of the alchemists, namely sulphur, salt, and mercury, but it is evident that he inclines to chemistry and not to alchemy. Briefly, he is an original thinker who is conversant with all the current ideas, even those of Scholasticism, who borrows something from everyone, but who fundamentally shows a definite tendency towards Christian philosophy. He states that it was during sleep that his method was first revealed to him and that he learned to contemplate his soul. This is merely the theory of Aristotle and the Scholastics—sensibility serving the intelligence. Van Helmont has been accused of a mysticism similar to that of Paracelsus and Cardan, but here again a mistake has been made. He clearly states in his writings, in explanation of his intellectual procedure, that what he especially condemns is discursive or syllogistic reasoning which avoids the contemplation of things. Whoever has read the third book of Aristotle's *De anima* will find more than one reminiscence in Van Helmont's remarks, and yet the latter condemns the Peripatetic. In point of fact Aristotle holds the same doctrine but more as a Platonist, because his 'intellect agent' itself assumes the form of intelligible essences and is a kind of emanation from the divinity and appears to escape from human personality, while for Van Helmont the intelligence properly belongs to man, and so the essences proceed from ourselves and not from the divinity which is within us. It is quite true that Aristotle may not have said that his 'intellect agent' was a part of divinity, but this was the sense in which it was understood by his commentators, Alexander Aphrodisiensis and Averroës. For Van Helmont the efficient power is the ferment governing all the acts of living beings. The material elements are the principles *ex quibus* living bodies are produced; the ferment is the principle *per quod.* Now, this ferment is a formally created being which has neither substance nor accident, but is something quite particular like light, fire, or sound.

As to the question of the elements Van Helmont rejects the ancient doctrine; air is not an element; earth is compound; fire is not an element; water can only contain the elements, but is not an element itself. As the alchemists maintained, there are only three elements, namely, sulphur, salt, and mercury. In a way, there may be only two, the heavens and the earth, but on the earth there are three, for this very important reason, derived from experience, that they are indivisible: *manere semper indivisa.* One could almost believe that Van Helmont was giving the modern chemical reason for elementary substances!

But these are not the only material elements; there are the gases and the Blases. The gases result from ebullition caused within matter by the ferment. The gas of water is water vaporized, but these vapours are not all gases, because there is the sylvester gas which comes out of wood and also develops during the fermentation of wine. Here Van Helmont teaches modern chemistry; he shows the difference between air and vapours and really discovered carbonic acid. The Blases are impetuous movements such as earthquakes, thunder, movements within living bodies and emanations from stars or bodies. We have the idea of electricity that Gilbert put forward while recalling the electron of the Greeks, which was studied under the name of the magnet, and which soon would appear as a condensed force in Gouricke's electric apparatus. The *Blas humanum* was soon to be the nervous element, the vital spirit of Descartes, the nervous current of the physiologists of the XVIIIth century, as well as the animal magnetism of Mesmer.

Let us now return to the Archeus. In his treatise entitled *Custos errans*, Van Helmont shows that this ferment exists everywhere in the body. According to him the Archeus is like a *siliqua* which encloses the sensitive soul, while the sensitive soul contains the intelligent soul, so that all actions of life and of the body, as well as diseases, depend upon the sensitive soul, while the action of the mind is dependent upon the intelligent soul. Therefore in man there are two ruling elements closely linked together, and here we have the commencement of the doctrine of duo-dynamism in man, a doctrine which was to be more fully developed by Descartes and then in a more confused way by Stahl; and, still nearer to us, it was to become the modern vitalism of Barthez.

We cannot further analyse Van Helmont's teachings, but we shall refer to them again in speaking of the pathology and the therapeutics of this century. We wish only at this point to show the superiority of his conceptions. Those from which others will be derived and which reveal his general doctrine as original are different from those of his contemporaries. We believe enough has been said for the reader to understand the capital thought of his work, which derives the Archeus from physics and chemistry, and bases the science of life on the knowledge of its movements, due to a special cause which is the Archeus. Modern vitalism may, therefore, be said to have been founded by this great man, and it is by this vitalism that physics and chemistry became allied with medicine. In physiology Van Helmont was the first to describe two factors in gastric digestion, namely an acid and a ferment. He made chemical analyses of the blood, in which he found salt. He analysed urine and there found both salt and carbonate of ammonia, and it is not too much to say that Van Helmont may be considered the father of biological chemistry. We also believe that he was the greatest initiator of science in his time and his work dominated his century and those to follow, and that although he was not understood by his contemporaries. In spite of certain regrettable errors contained in his work, he unquestionably is one of the greatest masters of Medicine.

René Descartes was born in Touraine in 1596 and, after studying in a Jesuit college and having passed a few years in solitude, engaged himself in the service of Holland under Maurice of Nassau. He afterwards entered the service of Bavaria and went through the war against Hungary. He then left the Army, travelled through Germany and Holland, and returned to France after nine years' absence, only to recommence his peregrinations almost at once. In 1630 he returned to Holland, remaining there until 1649, and then started off to Stockholm to join Christina of Sweden. At Stockholm he founded an academy of science and died a few months later in 1650. It was during his voluntary exile in Holland that he wrote his principal works.

Descartes, as did all good humanists of his day, studied both the Scholastics and the Peripatetics. But he also, like all thinkers of the time and perhaps more than any other, had developed the spirit of revolt against the ancients and the desire to change the doctrine of causes. Hence he wished to regard the world differently from others and conceived it as being composed of matter in movement. This matter, which had been discussed so much in previous centuries, had been regarded by some as in essence a mere receptacle of form. Others had attributed to it an existence of its own. But Descartes considered that its only property was extension, and supposed it had been primordially put in movement by a single primal impulse, so that all ulterior phenomena which were produced, continued to be produced, and would continue to be produced to infinity, and were simply the result of mathematical laws acting upon a movement which had begun as a vortex. Although in the first place he was not inclined to admit the atomic theory, he was inevitably led to it by the teachings of Gassendi and had to accept the rehabilitation of the atomism of Democritus and Epicurus. He therefore conceived that all things in nature, including animals, were machines composed of substances in movement, and laid down the theory that science should only consist of the knowledge of the mathematical laws followed by these machines. Only man appeared to him as endowed with a soul, and this was the intelligent soul which was directly related with the vital mechanics of the body, receiving impressions from this body and being able to control certain of its movements. He considered that the soul was seated in the pineal gland of the brain, where it caused movement in the body by stirring up the brain, thus engendering the vital spirits in the cerebral ventricles, whence they spread throughout the organism. He supposed that these vital spirits caused ebullition of the blood and of the material atoms, thus developing heat; and that the cause of this ebullition or fermentation was a kind of subtle matter or ether, which he considered as the common substratum of all things in nature.

It is clear that Descartes was greatly influenced by the ideas of Van Helmont. Matter and movement is matter and the Archeus; the vital spirits are the Blases produced by fermentation; the spirit, as Van Helmont thought, is distinct from vital movement. Descartes says nothing as to where he got his inspiration, but one may easily surmise the source. According to him the union of the soul with the body, upon which there had been so much discussion, was a kind of adhesion, and not a substantial one as Aristotle and the Scholastics had taught, not that of a motor and a mobile, as Plato had maintained, but merely one of occasion, so that the soul did not exactly move the body, nor the body the soul, but whatever took place in one resulted in movements in the other, reciprocally. Thus from this was derived the great theory of the occasional cause, which is one of the foundation stones of Cartesianism and was afterwards upheld by Malebranche and others, although they did not always realise that the *occasion* taken as a *cause* inevitably presupposes an *action*, that is to say, a transmission from the motor to the mobile.

Thus Cartesianism overthrew all science based on the substantial union of matter and its active principle, the form of entelechy. Descartes forced the learned to leave aside all former metaphysical conceptions and only to take into consideration the movements of nature, or life explained by mathematical, mechanical, physical or chemical laws. Taken as a whole this conception is less vitalist and less medical than that of Van Helmont.

Leibnitz is a third powerful product of the philosophical thought of the XVIIth century. He was born at Leipzig in 1646 and studied there, having among his teachers one Thomasius who was extremely well versed in Scholasticism. Although he took up the study of law he none the less pursued studies in all the sciences cultivated in his day. He went to Paris and there met Huygens who instructed him in all the mathematical and physical researches of the time; for several years he was in touch with François Van Helmont; he travelled in England and Holland and finally settled down in Hanover, where he wrote all his works, and died in 1716. As is known, he shared with Newton the honour of the discovery of the differential calculus.

Leibnitz seems to have dabbled in Cartesianism. He was more eclectic than many thinkers of his time, having a great fund of Scholastic learning. Matter, as Descartes understood it, did not seem to him to be the exact representation of the truth; he understood that purely mathematical and mechanical laws could not explain what appeared to him to be everywhere and to be both logical and moral, or dependent, as he said, upon ethico-logical laws. Briefly put, metaphysics governed the world. Descartes only saw bodies and movement in nature and these, according to Leibnitz, are simple phenomena. The body is merely the image of substance and movement is only the image of action. Mathematics only explain the abstract laws of possibility; they teach nothing real. Beside them is the metaphysical calculation of contingency and finality which alone explains the realisation of the intelligible world. A step further and his disciple, Wolf, would lay down the theory of reality in the sufficient reason, which is merely a consequence of these principles, and brings us back to the great Scholastic argument of the *convenientia*.

Nevertheless, Leibnitz returned to his first idea that matter can only be conceived as a phenomenon, and its movements likewise; that these are extensions of an indivisible cause, just like a mathematical point, and it is to this metaphysical point—which is a true primal substance composed of possible matter and force—that all concrete elements of nature must be referred. This is what Leibnitz calls a monad. In this conception the soul is a point, the monad is the human being. It is true that there still remained to be explained the union and relationship between the soul and the body, the spirit and matter. These Leibnitz can only understand as the effect of a pre-established harmony, and thus our intellectual ideas are not derived from sentient ideas, are not the effects of an impression (as Locke maintains), but develop in the soul from a pre-established harmony when the senses are impressed. This theory recalls that of the occasional cause of Cartesianism. Towards the end of his life Leibnitz, as we have already pointed out, came back to the doctrine of substance according to the Scholastic school.

It was to these three great philosophers, Van Helmont,

FRANCISCUS SYLVIUS
*(Author's Collection)*

[*face p. 284*

Descartes and Leibnitz, that the three great schools of medicine of the XVIIth century owed their formation, continuing into the XVIIIth and XIXth centuries—we refer to the Iatro-chemical, the Iatro-mechanical, and the Vitalistic and Animistic Schools. We shall now consider the first of these.

Franciscus Sylvius, or de la Boë, was born in 1614 and died in 1672; he was the chief founder of the Iatro-chemical school, in that he was the first to develop an entire system of medicine based on chemistry. It must, however, be recognized that the adhesion of Sennert, Willis and other great physicians to these chemical explanations singularly favoured the spread of the system.

Like Paracelsus and the chemists of the XVIth century, Sylvius admitted the three primal elements of all bodies, namely mercury, sulphur and salt, but he also included the ferments discovered by Van Helmont and made them the basis of his medical conceptions. According to his way of thinking, therefore, all the phenomena of life, both in health and in disease, could be explained by chemical ferments contained in the fluids of the economy. The blood was the depository of the alkaline, sulphurous and acid bodies, in which they counterbalanced each other, but the purpose of the secretions was to separate them and it was thus that digestion took place by means of the ferments contained in the saliva, bile and pancreatic juice. The chyle was merely the volatile spirit of the food, also containing a subtle or volatile oil and an alkali neutralized by a weak acid. The entire physiological system of Sylvius is based on this model. Diseases result from an acrid alkalinity or acidity of the humours; the morbid causes simply increase the alkalinity or acidity in various ways; thence all diseases arise. The aim of therapeutics, therefore, is merely to correct these morbid corruptions, to neutralize the acridity by dulcification or oleaginous drugs; the acidities by alkalies, and the acrid-alkaline diseases with acids and volatile salts. Purgatives expel acridities. Diaphoretics expel acids, while opium and narcotics correct acridity of the bile and so forth.

It is quite unnecessary to go further into detail because the reader will have obtained a general idea of these theories from what has been said. Sylvius was first professor at Amsterdam and returned there after having had enormous success at Leyden. He was the first of the moderns to rehabilitate clinical teaching at the bedside. The immense reputation that he enjoyed greatly increased the fame of the Iatro-chemical school, in which Boerhaave was soon to be a shining light.

Thus launched, Iatro-chemistry soon had many adherents, but also many variations because each wished to interpret it in his own way. It spread throughout Germany and England, but its introduction into France was slower, because the Cartesian school had brought Iatro-mechanics into favour; it had less success in Italy and none at all in Spain. A representative man of this school was Thomas Willis, of England, who was born in 1621 and died in 1675. His system was rather nearer that of Paracelsus in that he admitted the three elements of the alchemists, namely salt, sulphur and mercury. But he also adopted the theory of the ferments, considering them generally acid, according to Van Helmont's ideas, and declared that some were malignant and derived from outside the body, thus explaining certain diseases, particularly malignant fevers, which were frequent in his day. Willis also admitted the Cartesian theory of the vital spirits and supposed that they were secreted in the brain by a kind of process of distillation. As a result of this belief he attributed great importance to the nervous system. His therapeutics were based on similar explanations, but, unlike the chemists, he resorted to blood-letting. Willis had a very great influence over Sydenham, who adopted many of his ideas.

Many adherents to this school could be mentioned, but we will merely refer to one or two. William Croone (1633–1684), a physician of London, explained the movements of the muscles by the effervescence of a nervous fluid. This was the beginning of *neurosism*, which, as we shall see, developed during the following century. Martin Kerger, of Germany, claimed that he could cure all diseases by chemical drugs only. Otto Tachenius, of Westphalia, was an ardent advocate of Iatro-chemical theories and introduced them into Italy during a long stay he made there. Charles Barbeyrac attempted to reconcile the ideas of Sylvius with those of Descartes, while J. Minot, of Paris, was the best writer on this system, which he applied to the study of fever. The Iatro-chemical system was opposed, as may be readily understood, to others; but became combined with the Iatro-mechanical doctrine, especially in the XVIIIth century. Its greatest adversary was Robert Boyle, who was somewhat of a partisan of the Iatro-mechanical school and came to Paris especially to oppose the Iatro-chemical school.

The considerable development of mathematical and physical sciences at this time naturally could not continue without tempting physicians to make use of them in their medical theories, because it is a fact one should never lose sight of, that in all times medicine has been influenced by the philosophical and scientific systems in vogue. There is in the general development of the sciences a sort of unity from which one cannot escape, and from the moment that some progress has been made in one of them by a system or a procedure, it goes without saying that others will attempt to apply in their domain what has been successful in another. Now, Descartes and Pascal, and Newton later, had far too much success with their philosophical and scientific systematizations for medicine not to be tempted by them and to try to explain life and disease by means of mechanical theories.

Descartes had startled thinking men by teaching that the soul in man is merely a motor, that even animals are only machines and that in all living bodies movement can be explained by mechanism.

Giovanni Alfonso Borelli (1608–1679) seems to have been the first seriously to apply mathematics and mechanics to medicine. Born at Naples in 1608, he came to Pisa, where he devoted himself intensely to dissection, less for the anatomy itself than to explain the mechanical play of the organs. He was also the first to study the muscular fibres of the heart. He then went to Florence and afterwards withdrew to Rome during the last few years of his life, where he died in 1679 at the age of seventy-one. His great work was *De motu animalium* (*Pars prima*, 1680; *Pars altera*, 1681) and was not published until two years after his death. In the first part he notes the shortening of the muscles during contraction, measures their strength at their points of insertion as well as the resistance of the bone, and compares them to mechanical levers. He also applies mechanical theories to locomotion and the flight of birds. In the second part he treats of the movements of the heart and lungs, and the respiration ; he also deals with the liver, kidneys, and brain and with nutrition.

Many Italian physicians took up this doctrine and developed it in different respects, often also bringing chemistry to their aid, because nearly all of them admitted the vital spirits and the ferments. But it should also be pointed out that most of them were, at the same time, attached to Hippocraticism and it is thus that Lancisi, Bellini, and above all Baglivi, were quite as much Hippocratico-Galenists as Iatro-chemists.

Laurence Bellini (1643–1703) was the most brilliant disciple of Borelli, whose lectures he had attended at Pisa. It was he who compared the secretions with filtrates, and from this very fact and contrary to the truth he pretended that the fluids secreted were all prepared in the blood. He also invented the theory of obstruction of the blood vessels in the explanation of fever, and maintained that blood-letting acted by aiding the circulation and by re-establishing the elasticity of the vessels. His best known disciple was J. de Sandri, a professor at Padua.

Donzellini, of Venice, wrote an elegant treatise on the application of mathematics to medicine. Gulielmini and Lancisi explained the phenomena of life by hydrostatics. Bazzicaluve attributed the development of heat and the fermentation of blood to the friction arising between the corpuscles of the blood. Michelotti attempted to demonstrate that the flow of liquids is in direct relation to the density of the humours and the diameter of the blood vessels. On account of his treatise on the motor fibres, Baglivi belongs to the XVIIth century, but his great work appeared in the XVIIIth.

In France, Chirac combined Iatro-mechanics with chemistry. He was probably the first clinician to draw attention to inflammation of the intestine in serious types of fever and so was perhaps the first to describe typhoid clinically.

William Cole (1635–1716) of London combined chemistry with Iatro-mechanics. He studied the circulation and explained the occurrence of fever by tension of the nervous system, this theory, with that of William Croone, being a forerunner of the *neurosism* of the XVIIIth century.

Many physicians, while accepting all that physical, mathematical, mechanical and chemical science gave to medicine, thought that the vivifying principle of the *being* was made too little of. Some (like Pitcairn and Claude Perrault) upheld the importance of the soul, and thus prepared the way for the animism that was soon to be developed by Stahl. In going through the principal writers of the XVIIth century one perceives the preparation for the great vitalist reaction of the XVIIIth century, more particularly in the writings of Van Helmont, Plempius, Ettmüller, Sylvius, Riolan and many others.

In this respect particular mention should be made of Francis Glisson (1597–1677). He is especially known for his treatise on rickets and his work on the anatomy of the liver, as well as for his *Tractatus de natura substantiae energetica, seu de vita naturae, ejusque tribus primis facultatibus*, published in 1672. In this work Glisson shows (contrary to Cartesianism) that all bodies and beings which move themselves must possess an internal principle or fundamental force, to which are added a second energy which is the faculty of movement and communication with the interior, and, lastly, a principle of consciousness which procures the accidental qualities of the being. It is, says Glisson, a very serious mistake to admit, as do the Cartesians, that everything moves from outside, because the outside only procures the occasion for desires and movements. An internal principle alone can explain the activity properly belonging to beings and bodies. There are vital spirits, as the Cartesians maintain, and the irritable fibres develop action under the influence of the innervation that they receive from the brain ; it may even be said that all the parts possess a kind of vital or animal irritability, but, as the mechanism of a machine only explains the working of the machine and not its action, so the soul alone is capable of explaining life. There are many reminiscences of Scholasticism in Glisson's writings, but they were presented in a new light. Still it is probable that they were not understood in his day. They unquestionably, however, prepared the way for the vitalist reaction which was to come.

Viewed as a whole, the doctrinal movement of the XVIIth century may be briefly described as an incomplete triumph of the Baconian school and Cartesianism. There remained merely a ghost of the past, but it was a healthy ghost, which had its influence upon the rise of animism with Stahl and of the new vitalism. The old doctrine of the four causes—the formal, the material, the efficient and the final—which had been a particular subject of Greek philosophy, became completely discredited. The new science had made a clean sweep of the ancient metaphysics, while in medicine the ætiological doctrine of Galen had become obsolete, and was superseded by the mechanical and chemical theories. What predominated was really the basis of the Cartesian doctrine, that in nature there existed only matter and movement, and that all causes could be reduced to the external conditions of action. The study of the movements of nature and of life in their succession, the discovery of the laws governing these movements in their mathematical moments and the conditions of their production, would henceforth constitute science. This doctrine triumphed at the end of the XVIIth century and dominated the XVIIIth, but it was not an absolute triumph, because vitalism and specificity clung to it. As to the Baconian theory which eliminated all causality and accepted only laws deduced from observation and experiment, it was supported by the Cartesians, but only in so far as it was favourable to their doctrines. The union of the Baconian and Cartesiae doctrines disturbed men's minds, because it had no serious theory of causation and resulted in a kind of sceptic eclecticism in respect of the sciences, whence arose much confusion in the theories which were to be developed.

# CHAPTER XVIII

## THE ANATOMY, PHYSIOLOGY, PATHOLOGY, NOSOGRAPHY AND THERAPEUTICS OF THE XVIITH CENTURY.

We have shown that anatomy and physiology tended to separate during the XVIth century, although they did not become entirely distinct branches of science. Anatomy was especially brilliant during the XVIth century, while physiology emerged in the XVIIth and then made rapid strides, developing into a distinct branch of science. It is clear that the general idea of the science of man was not then distinctly formulated, but three main methods of investigation may be noted. The first was that of anatomy or simple dissection of the body, which came rather more within the domain of surgery. The second was that of experimental physiology and properly speaking belonged to medicine. The third was that of science in general, which tended to be given over to natural philosophy, as it was called.

Of the anatomists and physiologists of the XVIIth century particular attention must be given to Harvey, Achillini, Séverin, Malpighi, Riolan, Ruysch, Verting, Vieussens, Habicot, Pecquet, Duverney, Valsalva, Bauhin, G. Bidlov, and Bartholinus.

The principal treatises on anatomy are *La Pratique anatomique* (Paris, 1631) by Nicholas Habicot ; *Theatrum anatomicum* (1605) by Bauhin ; Vol. III of *Ars medicinalis*, by Vidus Vidius (1611), containing seven books of anatomy ; Riolan's *Anthropographia* (1618) and his *Opera anatomica* (1649), Wesling's *Syntagma anatomicum* (1641) ; Bartholinus's *Anatomia* (1651), followed by many editions ; Fabricius ab Aquapendente's *Opera anatomica* (1625). And lastly Hoffmann's *De partibus similaribus liber singularis* (1667) must be mentioned, as it is the first treatise published on general anatomy. The writer again takes up the ancient doctrines of Aristotle.

Physiology was still included in works on the Institutes of Medicine and few books were devoted only to it.

In the writings of Varandeus the subject of physiology is very little considered and as much may be said of the works of Lazarus Rivière and Plempius, but the latter's consideration of the subject is the richer in ancient and modern science and is the more important. With regard to the elements, Plempius accepts some of the doctrines of the chemists; in respect of the substance, the soul and the faculties he clearly supports, and very capably, the Scholastic doctrines. On the special functions of the organs he leaves Galen entirely and shows that he is completely informed as to all that the experimental researches of his day were able to furnish. Plempius was at first an opponent of Harvey, but later accepted the truth of his teachings. As to the circulation, the secretions, the glands, and organic movements, he was *the* authority of the time, and for this reason his book gives an admirable picture of the physiology of the XVIIth century.

At the end of the XVIIth century Ettmüller's writings show the still greater progress made since Plempius. In Plempius, physiology was in transition, while in Ettmüller the transition is an accomplished fact. His physiology is entirely outside the limits set by Fernel, within which all previous writers of Institutes of Medicine had kept. He presents the subject in twenty-six chapters, of which the first three are given up to the history of medicine and a study of the natural principles of the human body and the vital principle. Following chapters successively treat of nutrition and growth, hunger and thirst, mastication and deglutition, chylification and the change of chyle into blood, the circulation and the principal uses of the organs. He then considers the senses and movements of the parts, and lastly generation. From all this it is clearly evident that the science of physiology had become completely changed. Hardly two chapters are given up to general questions, and the remainder of the treatise is, so to speak, devoted to the science of organs in function or organic functions. Thus were laid the foundations of modern

GOVARD BIDLOO
*(Author's Collection)*

physiology; the general questions of the science of man are henceforth only a sort of introduction to physiology, while physiology properly speaking consists of the study of the functions of sanguification, of relation and of generation, and anatomy is given up to the study of the parts by dissection.

As to the general synthesis of the science—the idea which Medicine should have of the nature of Man—it will be the outcome of the doctrinal movement we have considered and the medical doctrines we have outlined. The doctrine of substance, that ancient and respected conception which had been developing since Plato and Aristotle up to the XVth century, was no longer generally understood; it was a matter of history lost in discussions on mechanics, forces, atoms, ferments and chemical elements. Many physicans still admitted the theory of the soul. Others accepted the Cartesian theory that the soul was the primal motor or simply an intellectual force; others admitted a kind of innate heat, the *impetum faciens* of Hippocrates; others again rallied round the Archeus of Paracelsus and Van Helmont, or the energetic of Glisson. The *flammula cordis*, the *ignis animalium*, the lamp of life, the implanted spirit, the animal spirits and the vital principle, were terms much in use. As to the faculties, or forces of action, which were five in number according to Aristotle, eight according to the Stoics, and three according to Galen and the Scholastics, they were no longer comprehended and their study was given up.

Briefly put, only the organs, and the humours in movement according to the physical and chemical laws under the direction of a vital principle or external forces were studied. The relationship between physiology and philosophy was given up, the former progressed by observation and experiment, and discoveries were both numerous and important.

The discoveries made in physiology during the XVIIth century may be considered in respect of the circulation, respiration, lymphatic and nervous systems, and organs of sense and generation.

*The circulation.*—In the preceding century, Michael Servetus had discovered the pulmonary circulation, while

Fabricius ab Aquapendente had foreshadowed knowledge of the general circulation and described the valves of the veins. But the importance of these discoveries was overlooked or not understood. William Harvey was born at Folkestone in 1578. After studying at Cambridge he went to France and then to Padua, where he followed the teachings of the Italian anatomists. He then returned to London and became physician to James I, and afterwards to his unfortunate son, Charles I, to whom he remained faithful during the Civil War. As a result of this his house was pillaged and his papers burned. Disillusioned, he retired to Lambeth, where he died in 1657 at the age of eighty. His work on the circulation is a simple dissertation of seventy-two pages entitled : *Exercitatio anatomica de motu cordis et sanguinis in animalibus* (Frankfort, 1628), dedicated to the unfortunate Charles I. In 1659 Harvey published a fuller work on the same subject : *Exercitationes anatomicae tres de motu cordis et sanguinis circulatione.* Just a little before this he published his *Exercitationes de generatione* (London, 1651), which in many respects is very remarkable and contains references to all discoveries made upon the subject. His writings show great patience and perseverance, while his style is that of a man of letters.

It would seem that he began to study his great subject about 1602, and by 1615 caught a glimpse of what he was seeking, namely how the blood was distributed to the different organs. By 1619 he had already discovered the movements of the heart and the blood, but it was only after having very carefully verified his findings that he published his little book in 1628. In the first place he showed that the pulse was not absolutely under the influence of the respiration (as had been maintained from the time of Galen) ; that the arteries contained neither air nor ethereal spirit, as had been said, but blood coming from the heart, forced into the aorta by the systole. This blood, he shewed, when forced out of the right ventricle through the pulmonary artery, returned into the left auricle by way of the pulmonary veins, and from thence passed into the left ventricle. He shewed that the right side of the heart was quite distinct from the left, that both ventricles contracted at the same time, that the blood was not merely kept in suspension in the blood vessels, but flowed through them; that when life had ceased the left ventricle first stopped beating, then the left auricle, next the right ventricle and lastly the right auricle, and that thus, after death, all the blood was contained in the venous system. He estimated the quantity of blood contained in the body as weighing fifteen pounds. He shewed that the heart beats about one thousand times an hour and that, during this time, it forces out some eighty-three pounds of blood and that such a quantity of blood could not be supplied by the liver in this space of time if the blood were exhausted in the other parts of the body. By ligating the vessels he demonstrated that the flow of blood was centripetal in the veins and centrifugal in the arteries. By analogy with the pulmonary circulation (which was already known), he demonstrated the general circulation.

This great discovery was naturally at first not accepted. It was violently attacked by Parisani, Primerose, and Plempius—who afterwards recanted—and especially by Riolan and Guy Patin of Paris, while Harvey was defended by his friend, Sir George Ent (1604–1689). In reply to Riolan he published a dissertation entitled *Exercitationes duae anatomicae de circulatione sanguinis ad Joannem Riolanum filium* (Rotterdam, 1649). As might be expected, the bigoted Faculty of Medicine of Paris of that day, urged on by the biting sarcasm of Patin, violently attacked those who accepted this new doctrine, and it required the interference of Boileau and Molière to cool the ardour of its learned members. Finally the Cartesians lent their aid to the recognition of the discovery and truth prevailed.

Soon other discoveries confirmed that of Harvey. In 1661 Malpighi demonstrated microscopically the flow of blood through the capillary vessels, while in 1663 Nicholas Stensen (1638–1686) described the true structure of the heart. In 1664 Maurocordatus experimented on the course of the blood through the lungs, while in 1669 Richard Lower (1631–1691) published his classical work on the heart. In 1681 William Cole showed that, viewed as a whole, the arterial system formed a cone, whose base was in the lower limbs and whose apex was in the aorta. The anastomosis between the arteries and veins was demonstrated by

E. Blancard, while Leeuwenhoek (1632–1723) microscopically demonstrated the blood cells and their movements in the capillaries. Fredrik Ruysch (1638–1731) exactly described the bronchial arterial tree and made himself celebrated by his anatomical injections, which showed the complete permeability of the circulatory system. And lastly Vieussens (1641–1715), at the end of this century, published his remarkable works on the structure and movements of the heart and the circulation in the capillaries.

This great discovery was enough to overthrow the physiology of Galen. It gave a new understanding of the respiration, the functions of the liver and kidneys and other glands. The part played by the humours in the body could no longer be the same; bile became known as a secretion, while phlegm (lymph) was known as white blood, mixed with red blood but contained in distinct vessels, and the 'black bile' was realized to be a myth. The reader will perceive how this discovery caused the ancients to be forgotten—nay, even discredited in greater measure than should have been the case.

*The lungs and respiration.*—In 1624 a German-Italian physician, John Faber, proved by insufflation that the air did not pass from the lungs into the vessels, and this discovery was of use to Harvey. Van Helmont had already upheld this theory and pointed out that air passed through the lungs as if they were a sieve and that the pulmonary cells were endowed with a motor force, although the act of respiration was above all accomplished by the muscles of the abdomen.

In 1654 two English physicians, Bathurst and Heurshaw, took up Van Helmont's experiments concerning the principal constituents of the air and found oxygen to be the 'principle of life'. Shortly after them Robert Hooke showed that animals died in air which had been deprived of oxygen. In 1661, Malpighi (1628–1694) published his work on the lungs, in which he stated that they were composed of lobules intercommunicating as well as communicating with the trachea and that they were surrounded by a vascular network. In 1667 Swammerdam (1637–1686) emitted a theory of respiration known by the name of the Cartesian Circle, because Descartes was the first to suggest it. He attempted to show that air entered the lungs because it became rarefied in the mouth and that the atmosphere became condensed within the chest when it expanded. In 1668 John Mayow (1643–1679) compared respiration with combustion, in which oxygen was the flame of life; it alone became mixed with blood, reached the heart and there represented the principle of fermentation; when it penetrated the organism in too great an amount it gave rise to fever. In 1667 Thomas Willis (1621–1675) demonstrated the presence of contractile muscular fibres in the smallest ramifications of the bronchial tubes and finally Borelli, (1608–1679) gave the true mechanism of respiration. Bellini (1643–1703) regarded the diaphragm as the principal organ of respiration, believing that its function was to force the blood into the capillary vessels.

*The lymphatic system.*—Erasistratus, it will be recalled, had seen the chyliferous vessels; in the XVIth century Fallopius had described the lymphatics of the liver; Eustachius had described the thoracic duct; and yet the lymphatic system was still unknown. The honour of the discovery is due to Aselli (1581–1626), who published his researches in 1622. In 1628 Pauli made a public demonstration of these at Copenhagen. In 1634 J. Wesling published drawings of the lymphatics in his works. Thomas Bartholinus (1616–1680) and Sylvius de la Boë (1614–1672) later on discovered their true functions. In 1647 J. Pecquet (1624–1674), as well as Wesling, discovered the cisterna chyli, which still bears the name of the former, and the ductus thoracicus. In 1641 Maurice Hoffmann (1653–1727) and J. G. Wirsung (died 1641 or 1643), a student of Wesling's, discovered the excretory duct of the pancreas, the true use of which was later on demonstrated by Bartholinus.

Olaus Rudbeck (1630–1702), in 1651, and Bartholinus, in 1652, made a distinction between the chyliferous vessels and the lymphatics, and this gave rise to a long discussion as to the priority of the discovery. J. Riolan (1577–1657) attacked Pecquet's discovery, just as he had attacked Harvey's demonstration of the circulation. At about this time Glisson's work on the structure of the liver appeared and, as we have said, contained an exact description of the lymphatic system of this gland. In 1651 Thomas Wharton

(1614–1656) gave to the world his celebrated work on adenography. G. Needham (died 1667) gave a description of the parotid duct in 1655 and five years later Stensen (1638–1686) did the same. The latter anatomist published remarkable works on the salivary and lacrymal glands, and described the excretory ducts of the latter. In about 1659 Swammerdam and Blacks discovered the valves of the lacteal vessels.

In 1664 Schneider (1614–1680) published seven large volumes on the nasal membranes, as well as on the mucous secretions of the nose (which until this time had been supposed to come directly from the brain), and at the same time described the anatomical changes arising in the nasal mucosa due to coryza.

In 1681 de Peyer (1653–1712), and in 1687 Brunner (1653–1727), demonstrated the mucous glands of the intestine which to-day bear the name of the former anatomist. In 1679 Rivinus (1652–1723) discovered the excretory duct of the sublingual gland and in 1691 Anton Nuck (1650–1692) published his classical work on the lymphatics and their glands. Duverney (1648–1730) made a still closer study of the chyliferous ducts and the lymphatics. Pacchioni (1664–1726) discovered the lymphatics of the dura-mater and those of the choroid and optic nerve were discovered by Valsalva (1666–1723).

In 1684 Méry (1645–1722) perceived the glands of the bulb of the urethra, which in 1700 were fully described by William Cowper (1666–1709).

*The nervous system.*—As the writer believes that Charles Lepois's writings on hysteria form the basis of modern neurology, some little detail will here be given of these. Charles Lepois—Carolus Pisc -(1563–1633) was consulting physician to Duke Charles III of Lorraine, in 1593, and in 1617 became physician to King Henri II of France. Some time afterward Henri II founded a Faculty of Medicine at Pont-à-Mousson and Lepois was made dean and first professor. He was a physician who, possessing great erudition, had at the same time a very observing mind. One of the most important of his works—he wrote several—is: *Selectiorum observationum et consiliorum de praetervisis hactenus morbis affectibusque praeter naturam ab aqua*

PLATE XIII

WILLIAM COWPER
*(Author's Collection)*

[ *face p. 298*

*seu serosa colluvie et diluvie ortis, liber singularis, etc. Ponte ad Monticulum, op. Carol. Mercatorem. MDCXVIII.* This work went through several editions and Boerhaave edited one, with a preface, in 1733.

The chapter in which Lepois deals with hysteria is entitled *Morbi capitis a colluvie serosa.*

In the part entitled *Consilium de epilepsia quo symptomata hysterica quidem vulgo dicta ad epilepsiam referuntur*, Lepois unhesitatingly shows the mistaken theories of the ancient writers, his statements being based on experience. In principle, he expounds this opinion, *Hysterica symptomata vulgo dicta, omnia fere viris cum mulieribus communia sunt.* (The symptoms ordinarily called hysterical are almost all common to both men and women.)

This opinion clearly eliminates the uterus as the site of hysteria and according to the author the nerves play the most important part in this psychosis. *Quoniam igitur, in hysterica suffocatione, totum convellitur et rigescit corpus, principium sane nervorum patiatur necesse est.* (Since in hysterical suffocation the entire body is seized with convulsions and stiffens, the principle of the nerves is necessarily diseased.)

Unlike Galen, Lepois does not admit that hysteria results from retention of the menstrual blood. He refers to a *nobilissima virgo* who had a most stubborn hysteria and whose menstruation was perfect. Further, he points out that the psychosis occurs in little girls, in women past the menopause, in those having profuse menses and finally, that hysteria occurs in males.

Our author also differs from Hippocrates. It is neither the uterus nor the stomach, nor any other viscus, which causes hysteria—it is the head: *itaque concludamus, tot tantarumque symptomatum quae falso hysterica creduntur, parum justis de causis uterum, ventriculum, aut aliud ex visceribus accusari, sed eorum omnium unum caput esse parentem, idque non per sympathiam, sed per idiopathiam, affectum male et perculsum eos motus universum corpus concutientes ciere.* (Boerhaave's edition).

Hysteria hardly differs from epilepsy. The starting point of the attack is in the central nervous system, and if the entire body stiffens, distends and is convulsed, it is not because the head becomes involved in the process, but because the principle of the nerves is involved and the cerebral meninges, of which the nerves are but an extension, are themselves shaken and rendered rigid.

Lepois attempts to explain physiologically the accidents of hysteria and he reaches this conclusion, which is remarkably correct, although absolutely false in theory : *Certe sensorium commune sive principium sensuum omnium in his affectibus laedi necesse est.* (It must be the *sensorium commune*, the principle of all the senses, that is injured in these affections.) He then adds that it has been demonstrated (*sic*) that the organ of the *sensorium commune* is the animal spirit which is seated in the ventricles of the brain. The brain contracts and expels the fluid—*colluvies serosa*—into the hollows of the nerves, hence first provoking restlessness, afterwards rigidity.

*Jam animi perturbationes sive terror, sive laetitia ex inopinato suborta evidente sane ex causa hystericos cient affectus ; videlicet per haec animi pathemata membranae cerebri nunc contrahunter comprimunturque, nunc explicantur et dilatantur ; his autem sive contractis, sive explicatis, aquam residem necesse est commoveri et in cava nervorum aut sponte exundare, aut veluti exprimi.* (Disturbances of the soul, sudden fear or joy, provoke the development of hysteria, because the emotions of the soul submit the membranes of the brain to alternations of contraction and compression on the one hand, on the other to extension and dilation ; now, in the movements of contraction or extension, the water contained in the membranes must be agitated, and so flow spontaneously into the cavities of the nerves or else be expressed into them.)

Lepois records the case of a young noblewoman which would to-day be called one of hysteria pure and simple, and he then goes on to demonstrate that this affection is not due either to retention of the menses in the uterus or to corrupted uterine fluid—whether it be the female seminal fluid or any other similar liquid—nor to affections of the viscera, for example, the liver or stomach, but clearly to a fluid collection which, accumulated in the posterior part of the head and there becoming amassed, swells and distends the origin of all the nerves, so as to set up convulsions in all parts, not merely external, but internal; then, seizing upon the consciousness, this fluid mass changes the parts where it is retained; it comes from the viscera, principally from the spleen, as well as from all other parts of the body. Thus as a river results from the concurrence of a number of small streams which unite to form it, likewise in the sinuses which are upon the surface of the brain and end at the posterior part of the head the fluid becomes amassed, not merely because there are empty spaces through which it can accumulate there, but on account of the declivous position of the head. The heat of the parts warms this fluid, it reaches the origin of the nerves and ends by distending them, rather more in the upper than in the lower part; then, progressively extending, it distends and involves the nerve ramuscles, then the muscles, and finally carries its ravages into all the organs, both external and internal.

Elsewhere (p. 103 of the *editio princeps*) Lepois says that he does not know whether this affection inspires, even in physicians versed in practice, greater terror or astonishment, because it paralyses both sentiment and movement. Sight and hearing are abolished and nothing arouses the patient from his torpor.

From the clinical viewpoint our author also refers to cutaneous anaesthesia, deafness, cecity and aphonia. He relates the case-history of a noble abbess who for one or two days preceding the hysterical attack lost her hearing, was seized by aphonia, then blindness, and finally became practically inanimate. A little further on in the text the case-history of a young girl is given, who was about to be buried and would have been had she not awakened in time. He also writes: *Et in famosa illa virgine Galla Maturina, quae, pro mortua medicis etiam habita, hujus lapidis primo olfacto e lecto restituta, alacris extemplo praeter spem ad mensam aleamque cucurrit* (. . . the famous case of Mathurine, the French girl, who was supposed by all the physicians to be dead, and as soon as she inhaled the odour of this stone, arose from her bed, quite well and happy, and against all hope started to eat and play).

During the XVIth and XVIIth centuries there were many

instances of hysterical sleep, such as were recorded in the many epidemics of demonopathy occurring during these eventful epochs, but until the advent of Charles Lepois, no physician had ever traced them to their true cause.

Lepois also speaks of paralysis of the upper and lower limbs and he is the first writer to refer to hysterical tremor preceding paralysis. *Sed et annotavi, hoc anno, in altera ingenua vicina nostra, de qua ante, quae, a secundo paroxysmo, tremorem brachiorum insignem passa est, tertio tandem in paralysim eorumdem incidit.* (I noticed this year in another woman, a neighbour of mine, that after a second paroxysm she presented a remarkable tremor in the arms which ended in a paralysis with the development of the third paroxysm.)

He also notes the occurrence of salivation, both in the male and female, at the end of the paroxysm. He also states that he has seen hysteria in men and children. He compares hysteria with epilepsy, from which one may suppose that he had met with cases of hystero-epilepsy.

At a later epoch Thomas Willis maintained and developed the ideas emitted by Lepois, which resulted in the famous polemic between him and Highmore.

It may be justly said that Charles Lepois was the first writer to reject the erroneous opinion which had reigned for centuries, namely, that the seat of hysteria was in the uterus. The work of Willis is undoubtedly remarkable in that, while upholding Lepois' opinion, he still further elucidated it by the vigorous discussions to be expected from an anatomist and a savant of the first rank.

Sydenham made an epoch in the history of hysteria by his wonderful clinical descriptions and observation.

J. Casserius was the first to make any real progress in the anatomy of the brain; he described the arachnoid, the corpus callosum, the cul-de-sac of the lateral ventricles, the pineal gland, the aqueduct of Sylvius and the optic thalamus. J. Wesling supposed that the vital spirits were secreted by the choroid plexus, and, as we have already pointed out, Descartes placed the seat of the conjunction of soul and body in the pineal gland. Sylvius de la Boë described the sinuses of the dura mater, the shape of the lateral ventricles, the corpora quadrigemina and their union with the pineal gland. J. J. Wepfer (1620–1695), noted for his writings on pathological anatomy, was the first to differentiate between rupture and occlusion of cerebral arteries. Thomas Willis was the first to publish (in 1664) a really complete treatise on the nervous system. In 1665 Swammerdam and Blacks described the arachnoid, which had already been done by Casserius. In 1669 Burrhus made a chemical analysis of the cerebral substance and at about the same time Leeuwenhoek discovered the vascular supply of the cortical layer of the convolutions. In 1684 Vieussens described the elliptical sinuses of the sella turcica, the sphenoid and the cavernous sinus. He also described the medullary centre of the brain and much more of the minute anatomy of the brain and spinal cord, while his description of the nerves was very exact. In 1695 Ridley published a remarkable book on the brain describing the dura mater of the nerves and the nerve fibres, from which arose Pacchioni's theory of the movements of the brain, which at the time had a great success. In 1697 Ruysch (1638–1731) gave an excellent description of the arachnoid and pia-mater.

*The organs of sense.*—The celebrated mathematician Kepler, showed how the crystalline lens refracted light, how the retina presented images, and how the ciliary processes withdrew from and approached the crystalline. But the most important observations on vision were made by a Jesuit of the name of Scheiner, who demonstrated the functions of the retina, the vitreous body, the lens and pupil. He calculated mathematically the cone of the light rays. Descartes compared the eye to a dark room. Towards 1672 Newton developed his theory of light, while Briggs applied the theory of colours to vision. Ruysch and Leeuwenhoek wrote on the structure of the eye, the former describing the choroid, while the second demonstrated the fibres of the crystalline lens.

The first discoveries in the anatomy of the ear were made by J. Casserius (1561–1616). He described the chord and membrane of the tympanum, the two apophyses of the malleus, the structure of the cochlea and the muscles of the ossicles of the tympanum. In 1640 Sylvius de la Boë found the prolongation of the incus, and in 1644 Follius (1615 ?) described the semi-circular canals, the handle of the malleus and the branches of the incus. Claude Perrault attributed hearing to atmospheric vibration, which was perceived only by the spiral lamina of the cochlea. In 1683 Duverney published his classical work on the subject. Schelhammer's (1649–1716) appeared about the same time. In 1689 Rivinus saw the fissure on the tympanic membrane which had already been noted by Glaser (1629–1675).

*Generation.*—At the commencement of the XVIIth century Fyens rehabilitated the ideas of Aristotle on generation. In 1649 Riolan described the texture of the epididymis and Highmore's body. Faber showed that the shell of the egg was the last part to form. In his work on generation, which appeared in 1651, William Harvey laid down the law *Omne vivum ex ovo*, and created the foundations of the theory of evolution. In the same year Highmore (1613–1685) described the windings of the spermatic vessels in the epididymis and their reunion in the body which bears his name. De Graaf (1641–1673) described the structure of the prostate gland and seminal vesicles and also gave the name of ovary to what had in women up to that time been called testicles. He described the changes taking place in the various organs after conception and spoke of the descent of the ovum in the Fallopian tubes. Swammerdam also wrote on the theory of evolution, while in 1668 Malpighi wrote on the incubation of the egg and the punctum saliens. Redi (1626–1697) wrote on evolution and opposed spontaneous generation, in which some still maintained belief. In 1675, Hoboken wrote on the placenta and the membranes of the ovum. Stensen followed the various phases of incubation of the ovum and confirmed Malpighi's teachings. In 1677, Bartholinus wrote a treatise on the ovaries and refuted the idea that a seminal fluid existed in the female. In 1677, Leeuwenhoek discovered microscopically the spermatozoids, although a young physician of Danzig, Louis von Hommen, had already described them. In 1681, des Noues discovered the glands which later on would be known as Naboth's bodies. The XVIIth century closed with a heated discussion on the theory of evolution.

Anatomy and physiology, now completely distinct

PLATE XIV

NICOLAS STENSEN
Pitti Gallery, Florence
*(Reproduced by special permission for the author by Brogi)*

[*face p. 304*

branches, tended to become perfected by experimentation and the general consensus of opinion was that study should be concentrated on the analysis of the parts, attempting to distinguish them from each other so as to discover their peculiar functions. A very distinguished group of men lived at this time, at the head of whom was William Harvey, among them being Bartholinus, Duverney, Vieussens, Aselli, Rivinus, Stensen, Swammerdam and Malpighi. Swammerdam was the inventor of the wax injections which Ruysch so greatly perfected and caused great strides to be made in minute anatomy. And lastly Leeuwenhoek discovered the blood corpuscles and rotifers, so opening the way to the knowledge of the infusoria, this constituting one of the greatest discoveries in natural science and medicine.

*Pathology.*—The reader will perhaps recall that in the XVIth century specific distinction had been made between different diseases, that 'real' species had been described and that the development of 'new diseases' gave great impetus to nosology and nosography, while semeiology was also regarded as a branch distinct from pathology. In the XVIIth century pathology remained much as during the preceding century, but towards the end a new systematization could be perceived with Ettmüller as the prime mover. Semeiology was included in pathology, so that a general science was developed which treated of the nature, the causes and the differences of disease. Finally there was a branch that Ettmüller had not foreseen, namely, pathological anatomy or the study of morbid lesions.

So far we have only considered the doctrines of the XVIIth century in outline, but if we do not carefully examine the ideas that the profession held of disease the subject will not have been sufficiently treated. It is all the more important to examine this question in detail because it represents a really critical phase in the medicine of the XVIIth century. It was on this point that the Galenic doctrine still held, and it may be said that it was the only one still remaining, to be finally conquered in the XVIIIth century. As we have seen, Galenism was the heir of Hippocraticism, but in point of fact had changed the pathological dogma on two points—by confusing the 'proximate' cause with 'disease' and by substituting artificial morbid species for natural species.

Galenism was confronted by Scholastics, who maintained that disease had no substance properly belonging to it, and for this very reason could have no ' conjoint cause ' ; but the development of new diseases showed of what a natural species consisted. Yet at the same time specificity, which had been born of the alliance of Islamic doctrines with neo-Platonism, admitted the natural species and substantialized them in the morbific causes of contagion. Fuchs, Fernel, and the Scholastics had seen the difficulty, and in his Institutes of Medicine Fernel, although he remained a Galenist, had already pointed it out.

The medical mind had become so thoroughly infected by Galenism, that, while trying to throw off the yoke, physicians slipped back into it while accepting Iatro-chemistry and Iatro-mechanics, and if they tried to escape it in another direction they drifted into specificity.

Van Helmont perceived that disease had no substance properly belonging to it and that it was only a form of life, and therefore he made it an ' idea ' of the Archeus. Of course the Archeus was superfluous, as we hold man to be composed only of a soul and a body. Secondly, by referring everything to the Archeus the body would be abolished, or one would be led on (as was he) to invent an imbroglio of powers concentrically placed—wheels within wheels. The soul contained a sentient soul, which in turn contained the Archeus, and this contained the aura vitalis. The soul and the body being substantially united, life was an act resulting from this union, and it was quite enough to say that life possessed its formula of normal expression as well as its formulae of morbid expression. Disease became a form of life and there the matter ended. Van Helmont conceived that life, viewed as a whole, was a kind of manifestation, an idea of the Archeus, and he compared this idea of life to an aura vitalis which was a kind of emanation, the idea of which can be fairly well understood because it has been given the name of aura epileptica. Disease is the result of a similar aura.

This doctrine of Van Helmont was evidently a Scholastic formula, with the addition of the idea of the Archeus, and represented the doctrine of essentiality or formal essences of diseases, while specificity, substantializing the morbid essence,

PLATE XV

THOMAS SYDENHAM
*(Author's Collection)*

[*face p.* **306**

gave to it a matter properly belonging to it by incorporating in it the material contagium coming from without. The formula of 'essentiality' is manifestly connected with the thought of Hippocrates, while that of 'specificity' took up the ancient idea of comparing the disease to a poisoning.

Sydenham is the greatest advocate of specificity in the XVIIth century, and in his writings we find this theory reduced to its simplest expression, for this great physician shines especially in observation, and he only takes from system just what is necessary to serve him as a guide. Now, the day of the first supporters of specificity had gone by; the search for the nature of morbid causes, which escaped both physics and chemistry, was unpopular; satisfaction was felt in regarding the morbid cause as a fact, and from all sides came the cry that further search for their nature should be given up. Thomas Sydenham (1624–1689) studied at Oxford and at Cambridge, taking his degree of doctor of medicine at the latter university in 1676. He established himself in London, where he enjoyed a great reputation as a practitioner both at home and abroad.

In order to give an idea of Sydenham's teachings, we can do no better than quote the first few paragraphs of Chapter I of his book entitled: *Medical Observations concerning the History and Cure of Acute Diseases.*

"A disease, in my opinion, how prejudicial soever its causes may be to the body, is no more than a vigorous effort of Nature to throw off the morbific matter, and thus recover the patient. For as God has been pleased so to create mankind, that they should be fitted to receive various impressions from without, they could not, upon this account, but be liable to different disorders; which arise (1) either from such particles of the air, as having a disagreement with the juices, insinuate themselves into the body, and mixing with the blood, taint the whole frame; or (2) from different kinds of fermentations and putrefactions of humours detained too long in the body, for want of its being able to digest, and discharge them, on account of their too large bulk or unsuitable nature.

"These circumstances being so closely interwoven with our constitutions that no man can be entirely free from them, Nature provides such a method, and train of symptoms, as may expel the peccant matter that would otherwise destroy the human fabric. And though this end would be more frequently obtained by these disagreeable means, were not her method obstructed through unskilfulness; yet, when left to herself, either by endeavouring too much, or not enough, the patient pays the debt of mortality; for it is an immutable law that no generated being can always continue.

"A little to exemplify this doctrine: What is the *plague* but a complication of symptoms to throw out the morbific particles (taken in with the air we breathe) through the proper emunctories, by way of external abcess, or other eruptions? What is the *gout*, but the contrivance of Nature to purify the blood of aged persons, and, as Hippocrates phrases it, to purge the recesses of the body? And the same may be said of many other diseases, when they are perfectly formed.

"But Nature performs this office, quicker or slower according to the different methods she takes to expel the morbific cause. For when a fever is required to loosen the morbid particles from the blood, to promote their separation, and at length discharge them by sweat, a looseness, eruptions, or other similar evacuation; as this effect is produced in the mass of blood, with a violent motion of the parts, it follows that the change, to recovery or death, must be sudden (according as Nature can conquer the morbific matter by a crisis, or is forced to submit) and that these efforts must be joined with violent and dangerous symptoms. And of this kind are all *acute diseases*, which come to their state with rapidity, violence and danger. Now, in this way of speaking, all those diseases may be esteemed *acute*, which, with respect to their fits taken together, go on slowly, but with respect to a single fit are soon terminated *critically*, of which kind are all intermittent fevers.

"But where the matter of the disease is such that it cannot raise the assistance of a fever, for its thorough discharge, or is fixed upon a particular part too weak to expel it, either on account of the peculiar structure of that part (as in the palsy, where the morbific matter is fixed in the nerves, and an empyema, where it is discharged into the cavity of the chest) or through a want of natural heat and spirits (as when phlegm falls upon the lungs weakened by age, or an habitual cough) or lastly, from a continual afflux of new matter, whereby the blood becomes vitiated, and by its vigorous endeavours to throw it off overpowers and oppresses the part affected; in all these cases the matter is slowly brought to concoction or not at all; and therefore diseases proceeding from such indigestible matter are what we properly term *chronic.* And from these two contrary principles, acute and chronic diseases respectively arise.

"As to acute diseases, of which I now design to treat, some of them proceed from a latent and inexplicable alteration of the air, infecting the bodies of men, and not from any peculiar state or disposition of the blood and juices, any further than an occult influence of the air may communicate this to the body. These continue only during this one secret state or constitution of the air, and, raging at no other time, are called *epidemic distempers.*

"There are other acute diseases arising from some peculiar indispositions of particular persons; but as these are not produced by a general cause, few are seized with them at once. These also appear in all years, and at any time of the year, indifferently, some exceptions admitted, which I shall hereafter mention in treating of this kind particularly. These I call *intercurrent* or *sporadic* acute diseases, because they happen at all times when epidemics rage. I will begin with epidemics, and chiefly propose to give a general history thereof."

From this quotation, the reader will perceive that the specificity of Sydenham was very attractive, because it took into account the causes of contagion of disease and linked up with the Hippocratic doctrine of crises and coction, besides justifying the new theory of the morbid species which were raging at the time. Thus specificity reached what might be called its classical period, in which its theories were linked up with the observation of facts and the teachings of tradition. Sydenham and his followers were excellent nosographers; they clearly distinguished between the various morbid species and their forms, and followed with great attention all morbid phenomena and their evolution, and it is not too much to say that the main point of Sydenham's pathology was the distinction made between the morbid species.

But it is not enough to be a good observer and to classify

facts derived from observation, and this is really all that one can find in Sydenham's specificity which, as we have said, is classical to the highest degree. Besides observation and classification it is essential to find the key to these laws, that is to say their *raison d'être*. It was clearly impossible not to see the lack of cohesion in this theory of Sydenham's. To declare that disease is a state of nature developing to overcome morbid matter coming from particles contained in the atmosphere, and then to say that this can be explained because the Sovereign Master has willed that the humours be subjected to impressions derived from external things, clearly exposes one to the question whether the morbid matter itself, or the impression produced by it, is the disease, and this is not an easy question to answer. Then, afterwards, to maintain that the various putrefactive matters retained within the body are the cause of disease, is to suggest that the first explanation has not been understood and introduces another which is equally doubtful; for why should this retained matter be retained?

This idea of the retention of putrid humour, which is pathological simply because it is retained, would seem to show that Sydenham did not think it was the humour itself which was the cause, but the retention. And after having so carefully dwelt on the infection from the atmosphere due to putrid matter, as to state (as Sydenham does further on in the texts) that he has never been able to understand the cause he invokes, seems to be somewhat unreasonable. In fact Sydenham shows the inanity of his elaborations on the subject in a passage, in which he says that, although he has observed with every possible care the epidemic constitution of various years in respect of the manifest quality of the atmosphere, in order to discover the causes of so great a variety of epidemic diseases, he has never been able to come to any conclusion. And then, further on, he goes on to say that there are in some years various epidemic constitutions which are derived from neither heat nor cold, dryness nor moisture, but rather from an inexplicable change which occurs in the bowels of the earth.

No one can deny that the atmosphere may be corrupted by putrid matter held in suspension, and that this may be the cause of disease. But from this fact to the theory of specificity the distance is great. In order to establish his theory, Sydenham should have been able to show that there are as many species of putrid matter as there are species of disease. Since he cannot show this, the putrid matter he invokes is nothing more than a cause of impression like the impression of cold or heat, dryness or moisture, or any other cause. And it is consequently this variable impression made upon each individual that becomes the true cause of the morbid species, and it therefore becomes clear that we return to the doctrine of morbid forms, as understood by the Scholastics, Fernel, and Van Helmont, and to the teachings of the School of Cos.

It would be a great mistake to suppose that the medical profession of the XVIIth century was unable to understand these difficulties, when we see that, shortly after Hippocrates, the Dogmatists raised them against the supporters of the theories of morbid poisons. Like the rest of the advocates of the specificity which issued from Arabism, Sydenham merely returned to this ancient theory of disease as a poison which had been long since discarded.

Although admitting the very clever observations of the followers of specificity, a large number of Galenists would have nothing to do with their theories and replied that changes of the atmosphere, contagion (by Fracastor's theory), or any other cause, merely altered the organic constitution, and it was in this change that disease resided. Hence many Galenists adopted the chemical or mechanical theories which laid it down that disease must be a fermentation or an obstruction or some similar condition.

If the reader would realize to what extent Galenism held the mind of the XVIIth century, he need merely turn to this characteristic passage in Ettmüller, "The entire body is the subject of health and consequently that of disease." One would suppose that the author would develop his subject as Hippocrates or Van Helmont would have done and go on to say that disease was a kind of diathesis, an infection involving the entire body, but such is not the case, for he continues: "But diversely, according to the parts, the contained parts, namely the blood and the spirits, which are the nearest to the root of life, are the principal subjects involved. The solid, or containing parts, are less involved. Life radically and fundamentally exists in the blood and spirits, while in the solid parts it is only by derivation, that is to say that these live only as long as they are irrigated by the blood and the spirits." Let it be here remarked that this distinction between the contained parts and the solid parts is the starting point of the great division made by the solidists and humoralists in the following century. But special stress should be laid on the way Ettmüller regards the change of the humours and spirits, which is the first effect of the disease and even its cause, because this change is already the disease. This is what Galen called the conjoint cause and this is what was supposed to cause the disease. All this represents a peculiarly vicious circle, which in reality makes a disease and even the cause of a disease that which is only an effect of disease.

Ettmüller takes Van Helmont's theory as a starting point, and regards disease as a simple idea or a simple form, as the Scholastics would do. But the further he goes, the further he gets from his starting point, and gradually inclines towards Galenism, almost to the point of accepting the conjoint cause. A step further and he would accept the conjoint cause as a continent cause, and so arrive at specificity!

Ettmüller next declares, in a chapter entitled "On Different Diseases", that there are three essential differences in diseases, namely diseases of the spirit, diseases of the contained humours and diseases of the containing solid parts. So, from here on, he has adopted Galenism and the knowledge of the morbid species escapes him, as it did Galen, although he recognizes, as also did Galen, that diseases are divided into species. Hence these Galenists could not understand these naturally distinct diseases, as they observed them and as they presented themselves.

*Nosography.*—Among the principal nosographers of the XVIIth century should be especially mentioned Charles Lepois, Sydenham and Morton (1635–1698). The last was Sydenham's rival and blamed him for his antiphlogistic medication, while he himself lauded the use of cinchona. Morton's descriptions of rheumatism and gout, as well as of fevers, are well done, but do not equal those of Sydenham, who was one of the most acute observers of his century. The latter's description of acute diseases and his observations on epidemics, especially their influence upon intercurrent diseases, his pictures of eruptive fevers, particularly of smallpox, and his studies on gout and dysentery can be read to-day with profit.

During the XVIIth century the following diseases are to be particularly noted. From 1610 to 1620 an epidemic of what appears to have been a kind of gangrenous sore throat raged at Naples and in Castile. It was described by F. Nola, de Villareal, P. Caseles, A. de Fontseca, Scombati and several others. Purpura was mentioned for the first time in 1650 at Leipzig by J. Lange. Sennert appears to have been the first to observe scarlet fever, but he mistook it for a form of measles. It was very prevalent in England and both Sydenham and Morton described it as a distinct disease.

In about 1650, a so-called croupal or 'polypous' sore throat was described, which was epidemic in France and in England. The first descriptions of it were given by Christopher Bennet (1656) and by Nicholas Tulp (1685). A cerebral affection with convulsions developed in 1658 in Vogtland, and in France and in England in 1650, 1674, and 1675. It was described by Thomas Willis and by Brunner. In 1665 and 1666 forms of petechial fevers were prevalent in England, a description of which has been left us by Sydenham and Morton, who also gave good accounts of smallpox, measles, dysentery, intermittent fever and an affection that was called epidemic apoplexy, which was probably one form of what we now call encephalitis lethargica.

Rickets was first described in Holland and afterwards in England and in Switzerland: in the latter country by Reusner, in 1582. Later on the disease was described by Boot under the name of *tabes pictava*, and then in 1682 by Glisson, who gave it the name of *rachitis*.

Cretinism was first mentioned by Haefers about 1675, while J. Bontius was among the first to give a good description of the skin lesions of leprosy as met with in India and was the first to write on beri-beri. And lastly, J. Floyer wrote an excellent treatise on asthma, published in 1698.

Pathological anatomy had during this century drawn the attention of physicians, especially when the great work of Theophilus Bonet, to which we have already referred, appeared in 1674. It was the starting point for the future development of this important branch, although mention should be made of a few minor works on the subject which preceded it. These are as follows: N. Fonteyn's *Responsionum et curationum medicinalium*, 1637, and *Observationum anatomicarum*, 1654; P. Salmutz's *Observationum medicarum*, 1648; J. D. Horst's *Decas observationum epistolarum anatomicarum*, 1656; R. Salzmann's *Varia observata anatomica*, 1669; Wepfer's *Historia apoplecticorum*, 1667; Schrader's *Observat. anatom. medicor.*, 1674; E. Blancard's *Anatomica practica rationalis*, 1688.

*Therapeutics.*—We have pointed out the revolt against Galenism during the XVIth century and how Paracelsus wished to substitute *Similia similibus curantur* for *Contraria contrariis curantur*. The doctrine that diseases were true morbid essences and that drugs contained essences which acted as antidotes to the poisons of disease was considerably extended and, as new medicaments were discovered, only one thing was looked for, namely, to find specifics for each disease or even to find a universal specific or panacea. But searches in this direction proved fruitless. Mercury, guaiacum, ipecacuanha, cinchona, gold and antimony were valuable acquisitions, but none of them was a specific. The theory of signatures, as taught by Paracelsus, was enthusiastically taken up by G. della Porta. Hepatica was given in diseases of the liver, pulmonaria in diseases of the lungs, digitalis in diseases of the heart and figwort in diseases of the glands, but generally speaking little satisfaction was obtained from their use.

During this time the new pathological theories based on chemistry and physics engaged the attention of physicians. Attempts were made to neutralize the alkalis of the blood and humours with acids and to control acidity of the humours with alkalis. Deobstruents were given to dilute the blood, while resins and balsams were given to thicken it. It should be added that blood-letting was brought back into fashion and was regarded as the most potent antiphlogistic, because it was about this time that the word "phlogistic", which had been borrowed from the alchemists, had been adopted by Stahl.

The doctrine of the indications for treatment as laid down

by Hippocrates was practically unknown; the theory of the conjoint cause was alone accepted. Some attributed disease to acidity and therefore employed alkaline treatment; some regarded disease as an obstruction of the vessels and therefore used deobstruent remedies. Others only saw in disease a poisoning of the body and searched for specifics or antidotes. The theory of vitiated humours also held sway; these were treated by drugs which removed the 'peccant' humour from the body by means of purgatives, diuretics or sudorifics. Even the great Sydenham said that the old method of treating disease was founded on the knowledge of the conjoint causes and so went ahead in the treatment of disease with purging blood-letting and sweating.

Although Galen came to be despised in the XVIIth century, the foundations of therapeutics remained Galenical and the aim was to treat the conjoint cause of the disease on the principle of *contraria contrariis curantur*.

Antimony was not only a new remedy, but a chemical product and for this reason the Galenists of Paris—and they were numerous—were naturally its enemies. As a purgative and emetic it took the place of hellebore which had been used by the ancients, and of senna which was employed by the Arabs. Consequently the Galenists proscribed the use of tartar emetic.

In 1657, Sir Christopher Wren proposed introducing medicaments into the veins in order to obtain a more prompt and decisive action, and this method was essayed the same year by Clarke, Robert Boyle and Heurshaw. In 1665 Richard Lower, who had tried it, proposed transfusion of blood in very debilitated patients. At first attempts were made with transfusion of blood from animals and afterwards from young people. Denys, of Paris, introduced this method the next year into France, and from here it was carried into Germany, while J. Riva introduced it into Italy. On every side transfusion was acclaimed, and this resulted in continued quarreling among the profession.

New drugs were abundant, in the form of either chemical preparations or exotic plants. Paracelsus had praised opium and made a sort of specific of it in cases of fever. Lime, in the form of powdered oyster shells, had also been greatly lauded for cases of lithiasis by Paracelsus and its use greatly extended.

Of course, acid and alkaline preparations were everywhere used. Sydenham introduced powdered deer-horn in dysentery, which was merely lime in another form. Peruvian bark was introduced into Europe through Spain in 1640, although its use met with much opposition in France, Belgium and England. Very sharp quarrels arose in respect of its value as a panacea for fever. It was also prescribed by Sydenham in gout and dysentery, as well as in smallpox, suppuration and gangrene, but its correct use in cases of malaria only came in the XVIIIth century, when Torti laid down proper instructions for its use.

Ipecacuanha was greatly lauded by Helvetius, a famous physician and courtier of Paris. Louis XIV, having been cured of a dysentery by this remedy, whose nature had been kept secret, bought the secret and gave it to the public. This drug was first used for dysentery, diarrhoea and haemorrhages and afterwards as an emetic, antispasmodic and sudorific in cases of asthma, constipation and pulmonary tuberculosis. Arnica, which had been introduced by Paracelsus, continued to be used as an application to bruises, as well as to haemorrhoids. Valerian, which had been used during the previous century, was again brought into favour by Rivière, Panaroli and Wepfer. Belladonna, which Conrad Gesner had used in dysentery, came into fashion in the XVIIth century for the treatment of rabies and cancer. Towards the end of this century the use of digitalis in scrofula was advocated in England.

In 1694 a great treatise on botany in three volumes was published by Tournefort and was the commencement of botanical classification, soon to be followed by Linnaeus and Buffon.

To have a clear idea of therapeutics during the XVIIth century, one should read Ettmüller's book entitled: *The Proper Choice of Medicaments*, for it was published towards the middle of this century. Medicaments are dealt with under the following headings:—purgatives, laxatives, emetics; mineral purgatives; diaphoretics from the animal, vegetable and mineral kingdoms; vegetable, animal and mineral lithotriptic diuretics; incisive and detersive remedies for the spleen, liver, uterus, stomach and chest, derived from the vegetable, animal and mineral kingdoms. There were

COUNT de BUFFON
*(Author's Collection)*

[*face p. 316*

PLATE XVII

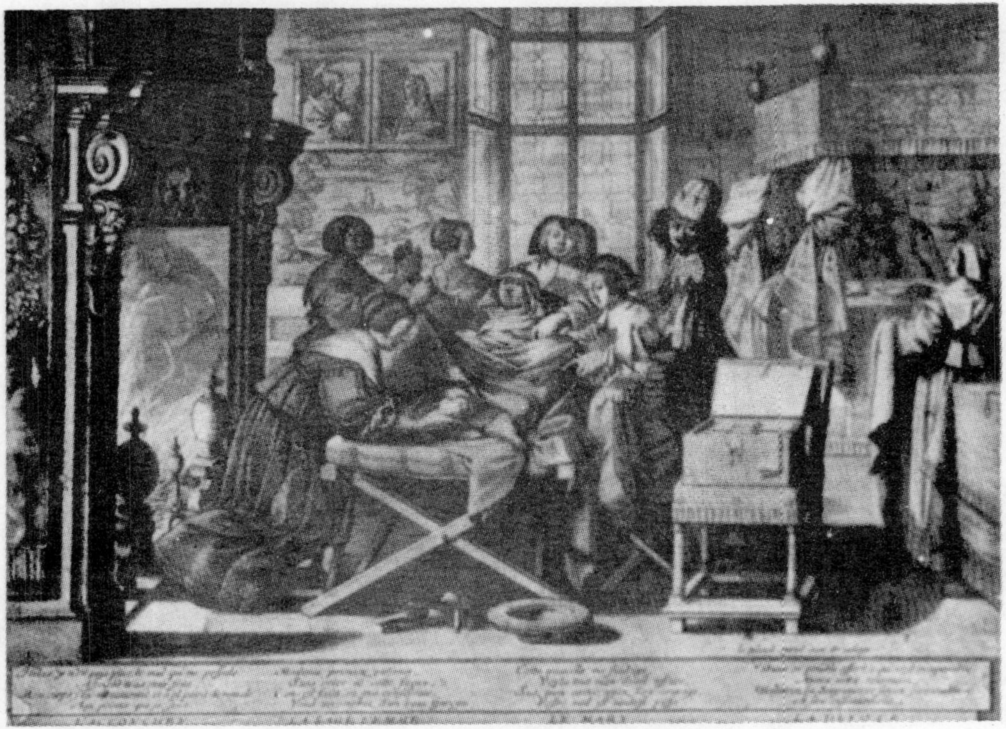

A LABOUR IN THE XVIIth CENTURY

After A. Bosse *(Author's Collection)*

[face p. 317

also what were called nervine cephalic remedies and anti-epileptic drugs, not to speak of hypnotics and astringent and detersive external applications. This gives a general idea of the indications which particularly occupied the minds of the profession of the time.

Other writers divided up medicaments into arthritic, ophthalmic, and hysteric remedies, phlegmagogues, cholagogues and so forth, which shows that they classified them according to the use made of them for the various viscera of the body and the different humours.

Ludovicus and Ettmüller inaugurated several excellent ideas, in that they condemned the over-abundance of Greek and Arabian medicaments, and maintained that one hundred drugs in all were quite sufficient for medical art. They rightly condemned the filthy compositions that had been used since the time of Galen and tried to reduce the number of formulae for pills, electuaries and other mixtures, and showed that simple infusions and decoctions of plants were far preferable.

*Surgery.*—There is little to say of surgery during the XVIIth century. It was greatly neglected during the first half, but later on there were a certain number of men who attained some little fame. Foremost amongst these is Richard Wiseman (1625–1680) whose principal merit is to have been the first to give a good description of tuberculosis of the joints. John Woodall (1556–1643) although he lived in the first half of the century, is deserving of mention because he is the author of *The Surgeon's Mate* (published in 1617), the *Viaticum* (published in 1628), and other treatises on surgery. Others to be mentioned are Habicot (died 1624), Bowister who operated cataract, Thomas Bartholinus, and Glandorp (died 1640), although these were little known. Jacques Beaulieu or Frere Jacques, as he was called, attained considerable fame as a lithotomist.

The science of obstetrics was more favoured and was greatly advanced by the writings of Mauriceau (1637–1709), Paul Portal and Molinetti (born 1675); mention may also be made of Thévinin, Calfin and, towards the end of the century, Lamotte (1655–1737), Belloste (1654–1730), Saviard and Maréchal.

In this century forensic medicine was founded by Zachias and by Devaux. The first medical congress with which we are familiar was held at Rome and lasted from March 10, 1681, to June 8, 1682. From three to four meetings were held monthly, the total number of physicians taking part being forty-six.

# CATALOGO DEL CONGRESSO MEDICO ROMANO.

Oue ſono deſcritti i Nomi degli Autori, e le Materie da loro trattate ogni Lunedì.

*Dal* 10. *Giorno di Marzo* 1681. *ſino all'* 8. *di Giugno* 1682.

*ALL' EMINENTISS. E REVERENDISS. PRENCIPI*

IL SIG. CARD. CARLO PIO.

IL SIG. CARD. DECIO AZZOLINI.

IL SIG. CARD. PALVZZO ALTIERI.

IL SIG. CARD. FEDERICO COLONNA.

IL SIG. CARD. FLAMINIO DEL TAIA.

IL SIG. CARD. GIO: BATTISTA DE LVCA.

IL SIG. CARD. FELICE ROSPIGLIOSI.

IL SIG. CARD. BENEDETTO PANFILIO.

IN ROMA. Per Felice Ceſaretti 1682.
All' Inſegna della *Regina*.

*Con licenza de' Superiori.*

Front page of the cover of the programme of the Medical Congress held at Rome in 1681-1682. An extremely rare document

*(Author's Collection)*

## CHAPTER XIX

## THE PRINCIPAL MEDICAL DOCTRINES OF THE XVIIIth CENTURY

During the XVIIIth century systems and medical doctrines became so very numerous that it is rather a difficult matter to co-ordinate them. For example, at the very beginning of the century, three men appeared who may be regarded as forming a distinct group and as the forerunners of organicism. We refer to Lancisi, Hecquet and Baglivi. Organicism appeared with Lancisi at the very beginning of the century and later on it had as supporters Sénac and Morgagni, but its greatest light was Bordeu, who emerged somewhat after 1750. After them Stahl, Frederick Hoffmann and Boerhaave, though contemporaries, had no doctrinal unity, but nevertheless they represent an historical group.

Manget, Friend, Astruc and Hazon, at the beginning of the XVIIIth century, formed a group of excellent historians of medicine and although Bordeu and Zimmermann belonged to a later generation, we feel that they too should be included with this group.

The humoral school developed almost at the very beginning of the XVIIIth century and continued to exist to its end, but its most brilliant exponents only came after Boerhaave towards the middle of the century, and, although there are from twenty to thirty years between them, we believe that Gaubius, Stoll and Pringle may be taken as a group.

Then towards the middle of the century von Haller appeared, developing his theory of irritability and the "neurosism" of his forerunners, especially that of Charles Lepois; Cullen of Edinburgh with his theory of spasm; and John Brown with his theory of excitability. These men also, we believe, form an historical group distinctly defined in so far as doctrines are concerned, which follows chronologically the preceding groups. Next we have the naturalist school composed of Buffon, Charles Bonnet, Linnaeus and Spallanzani. The latter is particularly noted for his discussions on generation.

And lastly the school of vitalism, with all its modalities, developed from the impetus given it by Barthez, Erasmus Darwin, John Hunter and Bichat, and this brings us to the end of the XVIIIth century.

*Lancisi, Hecquet and Baglivi.*—These three names are those of the leaders of organicism at the beginning of the XVIIIth century. It is not clear how they reached this theory, because its doctrines had not as yet been formulated. They were supposed to be Iatro-mechanicians with a smattering of Hippocraticism and Galenism. We have attempted to show in what way organic diseases were explained in Galenism—that thay depended more particularly upon abnormal organic functioning. It must also be recalled that, according to Galen, a disease was a lesion of the parts of the living body. This idea was revived by Fernel, in spite of his leaning towards Scholasticism, and had continued to be in favour with many physicians. It became flourishing at the end of the XVIIth century in the hands of Ettmüller. The Iatro-mechanicians rallied to it, because it sustained their hypotheses.

Giovanni Maria Lancisi (1654–1720) was commissioned by Pope Clement XI to study carefully the causes of sudden deaths, which were extremely frequent at Rome at the end of 1705 and the beginning of 1706. This was the starting point of his book which appeared in February, 1708. It is a little work which to-day would be called a pamphlet, merely containing the records of several cases with autopsy. But it is especially the first part which is interesting, because in it the author considers the question rather from the physiological than from the pathological point of view, and there develops his ideas of life and death, which, a little less than a hundred years later, were to be taken up by Bichat.

In the first chapter he attempts to show that life depends upon a movement of the solids combined with the liquids

PLATE XIX

CHARLES BONNET
*(Author's Collection)*

[*face p. 320*

under the guidance of the soul, and that this movement is triple; the blood is put in motion by the heart, the air is put in motion by the lungs, and the nervous fluid is put in motion by the brain. From all this, Lancisi, in his third chapter, comes to the conclusion that death results from the cessation of the movement of the air, blood and nervous fluid in and by the organs. Briefly put, as the author shows in his fifth chapter, life and death depend upon a good or deteriorated state of the three principal organs, namely, the brain, heart and lungs.

The importance of this little volume was very great at the time when it appeared. Lancisi discredited the claims of chemiatry and pointed out that one of the most important things in physiology and in medicine is to study thoroughly the *mechanism* of phenomena. This was one of the finest applications that Cartesianism had so far inspired and it gave a very considerable impulse to the movement that pathological anatomy was already experiencing, which soon was to have Sénac and Morgagni as its immortal exponents. Nevertheless, it must be admitted that it contained certain errors. The fact that an organ accomplishes an act or that an instrument performs work does not imply that all the action can be explained by the organ or the instrument, because the peculiar action depends upon all the things which govern it, and merely to understand the working of a machine does not explain the action of the machine as a whole. Therefore Lancisi falls into error. From the fact that the brain, the lungs and the heart cannot cease functioning without life becoming extinct, he makes out that life is dependent upon their functions. As we shall see later on, Bordeu developed organicism more correctly, although he did not arrive at the truth, and it was only in the XIXth century, under the influence of Bichat and Laënnec, that organicism was freed from its early errors.

Lancisi was born at Rome in 1654 and was first physician and confidential chamberlain of Popes Innocent XI, Clement XI and Innocent XII. He made a great reputation in science and, in spite of an extremely large practice, continued his reading and writing. He published a large number of books up to the time of his death in 1720 at the age of sixty-five. He published many dissertations upon various subjects, but his most famous work is the one we have mentioned entitled: *De subitaneis mortibus*, which went through several editions. Starting from the ideas of the chemiaters, he at length, as we have seen, embraced solidism, a system which had already commenced in the time of Ettmüller and was to continue.

Phillippe Hecquet (1661-1737) was one of the first to perceive the reaction against chemistry and frankly to enter into it. He was born at Abbeville and, after studying medicine and taking his diplomas at Rheims, returned to his native town to practise. But he soon afterwards went to Paris in order to increase his learning and there received the M.D. In 1710 he was appointed physician to the Charité Hospital and two years later was elected Dean of the Faculty of Medicine. He passed the last ten years of his life, partially paralysed, with the Carmelites, whose physician he was, in the Faubourg St. Jacques.

His writings, which to-day are quite forgotten, and were never very popular, had nevertheless a very great influence on the medicine of his day. He maintained that digestion took place by trituration and he vigorously attacked the abuse of laxatives for correcting or evacuating the so-called "peccant" humours. He greatly lauded the use of opium calmatives and narcotics, and above all the use of blood-letting and water, exposing himself to the biting criticism of Le Sage, who turned him to ridicule in his novel, *Gil Blas*, under the name of Dr. Sangrado. His medical doctrine is more particularly given in his book, entitled: *La Médecine théologique, ou la médecine créée telle qu'elle se fait voir ici sortie des mains de la Nature* (1733) which was republished in 1736, under the title of *La Médecine naturelle vue dans la pathologie vivante.* Written in a very animated style and with reasoning not always exempt from exaggeration, Hecquet's book regards the blood and movement of the solids as the mechanical cause of disease, and explains all by too much or too little tension of the solid organs. He thus approached the ancient theory of Themison and prepared the way for Hoffmann, Cullen and Brown. Unquestionably Hecquet did much damage to his reputation by his exaggerated ideas and the violence of his language; he was also unfortunate in not understanding the value of inoculation and, consequently, in opposing it.

George Baglivi (1668-1707) was merely a passing light, as he died at the age of thirty-eight, but for all that he left his mark on the medicine of the XVIIIth century. He studied medicine at Naples and at Padua, and then came to Rome, where he attended the lectures of Malpighi. He has left two works which had an immense celebrity and caused solidism to progress greatly, although he declares in several places therein that he is an advocate of chemiatry. The first work is entitled: *De Praxi Medicae, libri IV* (Rome, 1696); the second is: *Tractatus de fibra motrice et morbosa* (Perugia, 1700).

Baglivi was twenty-eight years old when he published his *De Praxi Medicae* and thirty-two when he published his treatise on the motor fibres. These two works are the effusions of youth, but their importance calls for an examination, because the ideas contained clearly show the state of medical opinion at this time. A few passages taken from his practice of physic will suffice to give the reader an idea of the doctrines contained therein.

"A Physician is the Minister and Interpreter of Nature: let him contrive or do what he will, unless he obeys Nature, he cannot govern her: For the Springs and Causes of Diseases lie far beyond the reach of human reason; and oftentimes Nature commences a new Work, when our efforts are at an end.

"*Hippocrates*, the Prince of Physicians, speaks in the Words of Nature, rather than those of Man. His Perfection in the way of Physick was such, that the Ages of Antiquity have not produced his Equal, and in succeeding Ages he will not be parallel'd; unless Physicians return to their Understanding, and being rous'd, as it were, from a deep Sleep, perceive what a vast difference there is between the Historical and Masculine Physick of the *Grecians*, and the speculative sorry Advances of later Upstarts; unless they give less Credit to imaginary Opinions, and conclude, that *Medicine* ought not to be confin'd to the Limits of our Reason; but, on the contrary, ought to be recall'd from those Streights, to the open field of Nature.

"Whatever it is that distinguishes the modern Theory

from the ancient Ignorance, 'tis all owing to the Experimental Philosophy of this Age. But in order to enlarge the publick Good, by vertue of the Labours of private Men; the Men of this Age ought to use their utmost Efforts in the same way to arrive at a perfect Knowledge of Practice, which is the capital Thing of the whole Art. By this means, we shall not only lay aside the Opinions and Prejudices that have been long settled in our Minds, but likewise carry the Art of *Medicine*, from a state of Infancy and Ignorance, to an adult and wise Constitution.

"There's nothing that takes the Mind more off from the Knowledge of Diseases, than the boundless pursuit of Speculation and Disputes, that the *Arabian* Physicians, and the *Galenists* that came after 'em, have so licentiously Encouraged even in the Practice itself. They over-look'd the fertile and far extended Fields of Nature, where such eminent Genius's might have had a freer range, and chose rather to throw themselves among the Thorns and Trifles of the Dialecticks; in which, being long entangled, they never rais'd their Mind to the hopes of new Inventions.

"The two chief Pillars of Physick are *Reason* and *Observation*: But Observation is the Thread to which Reason must point. Every Disease has, not a fictitious, but a certain and peculiar Nature, as well as certain and peculiar Principles, Increase, State and Declination. Now, as all these are brought about independantly of the Mind, so in tracing their Nature we have no occasion for a subtile and disguis'd way of Disputing, but only for a repeated and diligent Observation of what happens to the several sick Persons, and such an acuteness of Mind as is conformable and obedient to Nature's Measures.

"If we compare *Hippocrates's* Aphorisms, Prognosticks *&c.* with the Observations of later Authors, we shall plainly see that the Nature of Diseases is the same now as it was in the former Ages, and that their Periods observe the same order as formerly. From all these Premisses we may justly conclude, that Physick is not so uncertain, nor grounded upon a slight Foundation, as 'tis commonly thought; but built upon certain Rules, confirm'd by repeated Experience: For the Observations which make the principal part of the Art, have the human Body for their Subject; the Motions of which, whether Natural or Sickly, have a stable Spring, and regular and constant Periods: So that the Advances of Medicine, being grounded upon such Observations, cannot but be certain and perpetual.

"Thou' we are altogether ignorant, wherein the disorder of every Part and the Nature of every Disease consists; yet we observe that each of 'em has its own form, *i.e.* certain measures of Decreasing and Increasing, or constant and determin'd Periods. That 'tis so, will manifestly appear, if we allow Nature to act of her own accord, and do not interrupt her by improper Administrations. When it happens otherwise, 'tis the Method of Cure and not Nature that causes it. For two Patients seiz'd with a Plurisie (for instance) and treated different ways, by two different Physicians, will likewise have different Symptoms: So that if there be an Error in the Method of Cure, the Physician, and not the Disease, will be the Author of many Symptoms.

"Many things that surpass our Comprehension are not to be contemn'd; but 'twould be a piece of Wisdom, while we cannot canvass their true Nature by Reasoning, diligently to take notice of the effects that appear outwardly, and from thence to form Precepts in order to Practice. For when the Human Reason Despairs, or is not sufficient for the unravelling of Difficulties, it uses to waste itself in giving a probable Reason for 'em, and spend its strength upon superfluous Things: Or, to speak in the Words of *Sir Franc. Bac.*, *Fol.* 293, 'When once Men despair of finding the Truth, everything about 'em Languishes; whence it comes to pass that they rather turn aside to pleasant Disputations, and some superficial Views of things, than stand up in the way of a severe Enquiry.' When Reason therefore is Blind in such difficult Matters, we ought to make Observations, and propose 'em to the Reader without any Disguises of Speculation; as *Asclepiadorus* in former times is said to have Painted happily without Colours.

"I reckon it necessary to divide Physick into the first and second Species. By the first I understand a pure History of Diseases, obtained by sole Observation at the sick Man's Bed, and related by the Patients themselves.

In order to compass this History, there's no Occasion for other Sciences, or the Reading of Books; for in regard it makes a Science or Fund of Knowledge by itself, and depends upon Observation, and the Narratives of sick People, whatever Accession it receives from without must needs confound it, and render it uncertain; and from thence sprung the Errors I have so often hinted at. Upon this Head a Physician ought to act the Part of a Witness, that barely relates without passing any Judgment, and to set down distinctly the minutest Circumstances: For some of 'em are no sooner perceiv'd than they point to the right Method of Cure; and others afford such Light as facilitates an Enquiry into the Nature of more difficult things; so that Observations may justly be divided into the *Luciferae*, which afford an useful Light, and the *Fructiferae*, which are attended with a real and immediate Fruit. In compiling therefore this History of Diseases, we must not fly off from the Coherence of things, and give our Minds a loose at every turn, as the Poets do; but submit our Wit to the real Appearance of things, conquer Nature by Obedience; and learn the peculiar Language in which it speaks.

"Many Diseases spring from a trifling Cause, and thereupon mustering up a dismal Train of Symptoms, are cured without any sensible Evacuation; such are the Bite of a Viper, the violent Disorders occasioned by the Smell of a Ship or the Sea Air, and sometimes reaching the very Agony of Death, the dismal Distempers occasioned by looking upon the Object of one's Hatred, the Diseases arising from passionate Commotions of the Mind, and an innumerable Train of such like Disorders; which are produced in the human Body without the Ingress or Egress of any visible Matter to foster them, merely by the Impulse of external Bodies, or a violent Sally of Imagination. As many heavy Diseases depend upon a trifling Cause, that sometimes is invisible, and not introduc'd within the Body; so a great many considerable Distempers are cured in a minute, not by any sensible Evacuation, but by the Production of some new Change in the Position, Texture, Figure and other qualities of the Humours that gave the Disease a Being. Such are the Cures of Quartan Fevers, or other Diseases accomplished by a sudden Fright, by the Application of specifick Remedies to the external Parts without any sensible Evacuation, by the Change of the Air from one Climate to another, &c."

In his book *De Fibra Motrice*, Baglivi's solidism becomes more manifest. He points out that there should be an equilibrium existing between the fluids and the solids, but that it is the motor fibres of the heart and blood vessels that give rise to the movement of the blood and the fluids; and that the movement of the nervous fluid proceeds from the motor fibres of the dura mater. It is the state of the fibre—the most interesting point in the question of vitality—which is to be considered in health and disease. This book is more curious than useful to read, but it nevertheless contains some very judicious remarks and, with that of Lancisi, was the starting point for the return of solidism, which later on became organicism.

We now come to another group of men, certainly more important than the preceding—we refer to Stahl, Hoffmann and Boerhaave. These three men dominated the end of the XVIIth and beginning of the XVIIIth century; they lived at the same time, but this is their only point in common, for their characters and geniuses were as distinctly different as were their doctrines. They may be characterized by saying that Stahl was a man of doctrines, Hoffmann a man of systems and Boerhaave an eclectic; the first was above all a master, the second rather more a practitioner, while the third was a professor. The first left a reputation for his works, the second for his practice and the third for his teaching. Stahl was the chief of modern vitalism, Hoffman that of solidism, preparing the way for the school of irritability and spasms, while Boerhaave was the chief of the humoral school. None of them produced anything original, for Stahl was a direct descendent of the animists of the XVIIth century, Hoffmann's teachings were derived directly from Glisson and Baglivi, while those of Boerhaave came directly from Ettmüller and Sennert.

George Ernest Stahl was born at Ansbach in 1660. He became physician to the Duke of Saxe-Weimar and later on was made professor at the University of Halle at the request of his former fellow-student, Frederick Hoffmann, who wished him to help in the foundation of this university. He died at Berlin in 1734.

Stahl has left a large number of works, among them a collection of dissertations ; his *Theoria medica vera* contains chapters on physiology and pathology, while his *Negotium otiosum* is an attack upon Leibnitz and his principles. In another tract he devotes himself more particularly to the two departments of activity of the soul. The *Collegium casuale* is devoted to clinical medicine, while there exist other tracts devoted to chemistry and one on phlogistics.

Stahl is an author who must be read to be understood. His thoughts are usually extremely obscure, while his style is dry and lengthy ; hence the difficulty of properly summarizing his theories.

According to Stahl, man is a material mixture put into activity by an immaterial and immortal soul. The soul is united with the body in a sort of combination, just as fire may be combined with matter, so that it acts only by itself without any intermediary. There are no forces, faculties, or vital spirits—all these are pure hypotheses—but the soul has, so to speak, two departments of action ; one animates the body and directs its functions ; the other is that of reasoning, intelligence, and voluntary action. It is the movement produced by the soul which is the intermediary between it and the body. Stahl recognizes the objection that it is difficult to understand how a spiritual and immaterial principle can be united with a gross and material substance. But he himself does not find it difficult to understand. What he above all denies and opposes are the intermediaries supposed to exist between the soul and the body. Stahl's doctrine has been called ' animism ', or, that of autocracy of the soul. It is absolutely different from the Scholastic doctrine of substance, according to which the soul is united to the body like a motor to a *mobile*. We shall see later on how Barthez, by straining Stahl's doctrine, developed vital 'duo-dynamism', and at a still later date we shall see how Bichat exploited the same ideas.

In order to judge Stahl's physiological doctrine correctly, all questions of psychology should be left aside, because this unquestionably is his weak point, and attention should be concentrated upon what he especially wished to demonstrate. namely movement produced by the soul. It is on this idea of *movement*, ever present in his mind, that are based all his explanations of the nature of man. This *movement* may be voluntary, but beside it there is the instinctive and local movement of the parts—the vital movement—which becomes particularized in the tonicity of the directing vessels of the blood and humours. It is upon this tonic movement that the circulation, secretions, excretions and other unconscious actions of life depend. If this idea is not clearly understood, it is quite impossible to comprehend a single word of Stahl's pathology.

Stahl refutes the Galenist theories and specificity, which, as we know, regarded disease as being the result of a dyscrasia of the blood and humours, a morbid material born within us or else a pathogenic poison entering the body, which had to be expelled. Stahl severely criticises these hypotheses, and tries to show that man becomes diseased on account of his disposition to become morbidly changed, but as it is the vital movement that gives rise to this disposition it is by a change of this movement that disease is caused. Therefore, a material change does not produce disease, but is produced by it. Disease is the morbid change of the vital movement, or, as he says : " We are led to the conclusion that the most general cause of disease is a disturbed condition that nature develops in respect of the control of the animal economy." This recalls the teachings of Van Helmont ; eliminate the Archeus and in its place put the movement of the soul and the two doctrines are the same. It is also the same doctrine as that of the Scholastics when they interpret Hippocrates by saying that diseases are morbid forms of vitality and not concrete realities.

Thus Stahl enters into the purest of medical traditions. He concentrates his thought on morbid movement, which is merely vital movement having undergone changes. He studies the causes which engender it, the effects produced by it, as well as their types, and it is by the state of the tonicity of the parts and the blood vessels that he more particularly estimates the morbid condition present. The movement is produced in each disease according to a type properly belonging to it, and hence gives rise to immutable morbid species unless they are disturbed by a meddlesome treatment on the part of the practitioner. They end either by critical evacuations or else by an imperceptible change of the morbid movement to the normal. For Stahl a crisis is a violent movement of nature attempting to rid itself of morbid matter and viewed as a whole disease is a struggle of nature against a morbid cause. A morbid movement appears to him violent only because it is disturbed and not regular as in the normal state, and the evacuations take place imperfectly or irregularly. Only the critical evacuation can be judged because all movement of nature has its natural result in an excretion, which is derived from food absorbed. This idea was, as we shall see, taken up by Bordeu. The conservative energy of health is, therefore, an effort of nature, or, better still, an effort of the soul to triumph over movement which is improperly carried out and to bring it back into its normal course.

Then, entering into what may be called the genesis of disease, Stahl shows that plethora and thickening of the blood are the starting points of three principal kinds of inflammation, that is to say, of effusion, stasis and corruption, in which tonicity is the most important ætiological factor. The movements necessary for preventing or overcoming these accidents constitute crises according to the regions of the body where these accidents occur, as well as the synergies which are in play and also the type of the disease. From this Stahl can easily deduce his system of therapeutics, in which he discountenances any imprudent interference on the part of the physician by the use of disturbing medication which would prevent the movement from re-establishing itself. Sanguineous evacuations have a moderating effect on movement and dissipate both plethora and thickening of the blood, so that the physician should have the greatest confidence in expectant treatment and beware of violent remedies.

We will not refer to Stahl's writings on chemistry, but it must not be forgotten that, in pathology, credit is due to him for laying stress on haemorrhoidal flux and showing the great influence played by gout in disease. Stahl can be regarded as a true follower of Hippocratic Medicine at its best. From the point of view of philosophy he is, like all of the German schools, pretentious and vague, but he is endowed with practical tradition, and would have been a genius if only he had propounded his views less confusedly. Amongst the immediate disciples who popularized Stahl's doctrines,

FRIEDRICH HOFFMAN
*(Author's Collection)*

[*face p. 330*

may be mentioned Gohl, Michael Alberti, and especially Juncker. The writings of the two last physicians had a great success. Among others who were more or less enthusiastic followers may be mentioned Tabor, Porterfield, Whytt, Hartley, Goddard, Bonnet and Platner, who admitted the existence of a nervous fluid depending upon the soul.

*Frederick Hoffmann* was born at Halle in 1660 and died in 1742. He studied at Jena at the same time as Stahl. He possessed those qualities which are essential to make a distinguished practitioner, and consequently he had a large practice from the beginning of his career to the end of his life.

Hoffmann was a ceaseless writer and has left many works, of which the most voluminous is the *Medicina rationalis systematica*, a work in nine volumes, but of only mediocre value, written at the age of sixty. A number of curious cases are recorded in the *Centuria consultationum et responsionum medicinalium*, but of all his books the one to be read is *Medicus politicus, sive Regulae prudentiae secundum quas medicus juvenis se dirigere debet.*

Like all practical minds, Hoffmann left aside the great questions arising from the point of view of animism as upheld by his friend Stahl. He maintained that it was useless to think deeply and adopted all theories that fitted in with his ideas, especially those which appeared to him most generally accepted, for he was extremely avid of success and honours. Inspired by the mechanical school, by Baglivi's notion of the motor fibre and by Stahl's theory of tonicity, he admitted the theory of spasm and relaxation of the fibres; with Hippocrates and Galen he admitted the autocracy of nature and the theory of crises and critical days. He also accepted the theory of plethora and flux as formulated by Stahl and, following Sydenham, adopted the theory of vitiation of the humours and the material causes of epidemics. And yet lastly, strange to relate, he did not refuse to accept the action of the heavenly bodies in disease, as taught by Paracelsus and Fracastor. This jumble of theories made Hoffmann's system lack unity. It was a mere eclecticism that attempted to co-ordinate truths picked up by Hoffmann here and there. But it was a useful eclecticism which aimed above all at helping to advance the theories of the time and at getting the most out of them. It is perfectly true that Hoffmann had his little secret prescriptions which he surrounded with mystery, thus enhancing his reputation as a skilful physician : Hoffmann's anodyne is still official.

All things considered, Hoffmann did little to advance medicine ; he preceded Cullen and Brown and perhaps inspired them, especially the latter, who rehabilitated the *strictum* and *laxum* of Themison. In his writings one finds a little of everything but without co-ordination, and he certainly adopted Stahl's theory of morbid movement, which is the culminating point of his pathology. Credit should be given him, however, for popularizing the use of mineral waters, and this may perhaps be the only real benefit that posterity owes to him.

Buchner, Nicolaï, Eberhard, Riga, Rosetti and von Gorter were physicians of talent and more or less the partisans of Hoffmann. They discussed among themselves whether the vital spirits and the nervous spirits were the same things. Von Gorter maintained that the vital spirits existed in all parts of the body, and that the nervous spirits existed only in the nerves. The latter theory was finally accepted.

*Hermann Boerhaave*, who flourished at the same time as Stahl and Hoffmann, represents the most perfect type of clinical professor. He was born in 1668 at Voorhout, a small town near Leyden. When Boerhaave was sixteen years of age his father died and he then gave himself up to the study of mathematics in order to make a living by giving private lessons. At the same time he studied Oriental languages and, after obtaining the degree of doctor of philosophy at the age of twenty-two, began to study theology, continuing all the while mathematics, by which he earned his living.

He was then advised to study medicine, which he did, taking his degree in 1693. In 1701 he was appointed to the Chair of Theoretical Medicine at the University of Leyden, succeeding the celebrated Drelincourt, and from this time until his death he devoted himself entirely to teaching. After 1722 he suffered from gout ; he died in 1738.

Boerhaave began the study of medicine rather late in life, his favourite authors being Hippocrates and Sydenham. From his very careful classical education and his study of mathematics he was equipped with all the requisites for a

HERMANN BOERHAAVE
A rare colour print. *(Author's Collection)*

professorship and he also possessed a great gift for speaking. As a teacher he had an immense success, but this was all, for he really produced nothing by which posterity could benefit. His doctrine was a mixture of Iatro-mechanics and Iatro-chemistry, to which was added a small dose of Galenism. It was eclecticism made easy, and nothing more.

Boerhaave wrote extensively. A few years after his death only three or four of his works were still in use and to-day enter into the domain of history. And, what is more, of these works only one, namely his *Institutiones medicae*, had any really durable success, and this only because it was a clear and concise summary of the science of medicine in his day. His *Methodus discendi medicinam* was greatly over-estimated by von Haller, who even took the trouble to comment on it (the cause of its temporary success), a piece of work which he afterwards regretted. Boerhaave's *Aphorisms* are a feeble imitation of the *Aphorisms* of Hippocrates and would soon have been forgotten had it not been for the very practical commentaries by which they were enriched by his pupil, Van Swieten (1700--72). His *De Viribus medicamentorum* hardly requires mention, as it is composed of notes of his lectures taken by his students, yet it gives a very good summary of the state of materia medica in his day.

Unquestionably Boerhaave was an excellent observer and a good clinician, and his doctrine is a very good combination of the mechanical and the chemical theories. Still he was but a passing light, and after his death soon forgotten.

*The Historical School.*—The disparagement of antiquity which was the fashion during much of the XVIIth century, did not prevent some from still studying the ancients. The humanists had opened the door to the commentators, who in turn opened it to historians. The greatest minds of the XVIIth century proclaimed Hippocrates as the greatest genius of medicine, and, in spite of the new theories of Iatro-mechanics and Iatro-chemistry, as well as specificity, the writings of the great master of Cos were still read. At the end of the XVIIth century and the beginning of the XVIIIth a certain number of works on the history of medicine appeared.

John Freind (1675–1728) wrote a *History of Medicine*, which was a continuation of the one by Daniel Le Clerc of Geneva. The history of Islamic medicine is the most reliable part of this book, although Arabian philosophy is ignored and for a discussion of this we must turn to Casiri's writings.

J. Astruc (1684–1766) of Montpellier, who later became professor at Paris, published an interesting work entitled *Mémoires pour servir à l'histoire de la Faculté de médecine de Montpellier.* Hebenstreit (1702–57), a professor at Leipzig. wrote an interesting study on the therapeutics of the ancients. Piquier (1711–72), of Valencia, Spain, published an excellent work on the *Prognostics,* and the first book of the *Epidemics,* of Hippocrates. Ackermann (1756–1801) wrote his *Institutiones historiae medicinae,* which still is one of the best manuals on the subject. N. Eloy (1714–88), of Louvain, wrote a *Dictionary of the History of Medicine* which was the first collection of medical biographies written and has formed the basis of all which have appeared since. Bordeu (1722–76) wrote his *Histoire de la Médecine* with the intention of popularizing inoculation. The writer regrets that space forbids giving extracts from this admirable work, which he considers one of the finest literary productions of the XVIIIth century. Towards the end of this century Kurt Sprengel (born 1766) gave the world his great *History of Medicine* in nine volumes, which was not completed until the beginning of the XIXth century. Sprengel was an extensive writer and his Institutes of Medicine was one of the last works representing this tradition.

Many physicians who had adopted particular theories, or were given to eclecticism, at the same time held medical tradition in the back of their minds and regarded respect for the ancient dogmas and precepts as the foundation of medical science. Those who especially maintained tradition were von Haën, Van Swieten, Gaubius, Huxham, Bordeu (in spite of his organicism), Stoll and a host of others, and it is to this current of thought that are due the excellent writings on nosography which appeared during the XVIIIth century.

*The School of Humoralism.*—The school of humoralism is the direct continuation of the chemical school, or perhaps it were better to say one of its offshoots. It had its beginnings in Leyden among the followers of Boerhaave, who laid stress on the importance of the humours and more or less put aside the part played by the solids. But they still clung to Galenism which confused disease with its phenomena. The doctrine was the result of distinguishing between diseases of the humours and diseases of the solids, a separation which had been made before and which had become accentuated at the end of the XVIth century, as is evidenced by Ettmüller's writings.

Nicolas Falconnet (1644–1734) and Dippel are perhaps the only real chemists of the XVIIIth century, for Nicolas Andry and Astruc—who upheld the part played by ferments in digestion—were thoroughly saturated with humoralism, which regarded disease as a peculiar morbid condition of the humours. Floyer, Pringle, Gaubius, Vogel, Selle, Huxham, Roederer, Wagler, Stoll, von Haën and Van Swieten, are representatives of this doctrine and had for the most part been students at Leyden. Their common merit is to have studied disease by careful observation and thus to have enriched nosology. But from the standpoint of general doctrines they returned to Sydenham's fundamental idea of morbid changes in the humours, thus following the teachings which so greatly influenced the eminent professor of Leyden.

In order to understand this school, Floyer's book on asthma, Pringle's on diseases of armies, Van Swieten's commentaries on Boerhaave, Huxham on fevers, and Roederer and Wagler on the mucous disease should be discussed here, although a very good idea of the doctrine may be obtained from the writings of Gaubius and Stoll, which alone we shall here consider.

Gaubius, whose name is still known in posology, was born at Heidelberg in 1705 and studied at Leyden, where he later on became professor of medicine and chemistry, and died in 1780. His work on pathology is rather more notable for the sensation with which it was greeted than for its real value. Like the works of Boerhaave, it contains a singular mixture of classical ideas and theories. At the beginning the writer tells us "*melius est sistere gradu quam progredi per tenebras*", but he by no means follows his own precept. He divides medicine into two parts; the first deals with all natural things in man; and the second with what may be called preternatural things; he points out that, on account of their final objects, the former may be called the art of preserving health and the latter the art of curing disease.

The first part is divided into three sections, namely

physiology, which deals with the human economy, and the nature, causes, and effects of life and of health ; secondly, physiological semeiology, which comprises the signs that reveal life and health in their different degrees or states ; thirdly, dietetics, which ordain the rules for preserving health.

The second part of the book comprises pathology, pathological semeiology, and therapeutics. This general survey at once reveals the system adopted, which seems hardly to trouble itself whether its conception is practical or not. Undoubtedly Gaubius must have realized that health can only be understood by the disturbances that it undergoes, that there are no ' signs ' of health, but only those of disease, and that dietetic measures can only be studied from the viewpoint of diseases to be avoided. Now, here is a quotation giving the classical idea in which truth can be recognized : "But it is in the very nature of man that the principal foundation of all medicine is placed. Nature, alone, acting by her own forces and without the help of the physician, preserves health in the greater number of men and also cures their diseases. When her action ceases or is opposed to art, all efforts are vain ; it is to scrupulous observation of nature and the attempt to imitate her that medical art owes its origin and afterwards its development."

Gaubius says that physicians are the ministers of nature. He distinguishes different diseases of the body, and elsewhere recognizes a principle of life, when he says : "Not only because disease is an affection of life and without it can no more be conceived than can health, but also because there is an active principle in diseases quite distinct from the diseases themselves." However, clarity of ideas is not always obvious, as for example, when he says : "It is evident that the general nature of disease consists of unhealthy states of the living body which have this peculiar property, that they partly contribute to the functions of the body, while diseases, both in general and in particular, have this in common, that they have their seat in the faculties of the body." It is evident that Gaubius here confuses diseases with their symptoms. Disease is the general condition of disturbed life, while the symptom is the pathological function of a diseased organ.

Elsewhere Gaubius explains that one should not define

disease as a struggle of nature for her preservation, because it is not the struggle which is the disease, and he points out that the adversary is the disease. Thus he returns to the idea which considers disease as having a material being, yet it is clear that he does not understand the subject. Like all Galenists he studies in the action of the causes those effects produced in the living being, and it is these effects that he looks upon as diseases. In his study of causes, however, Gaubius certainly does accept the classical distinction between internal and external causes and quite correctly recognizes that the former are predisposing only. He quite justly remarks: "The detrimental influence has no effect if it does not act on a body disposed to receive its impression," and further on says: "there is no universal predisposition for all kinds of disease, and even the most perfect state of health is unable to defend itself with equal strength against all harmful causes in general, or against any one in particular." Therefore, according to Gaubius, there are as many particular predispositions as there are possible diseases, and this is what he calls "morbific seeds". "I call morbific seeds every disposition peculiar to the body which favours the production of disease when a detrimental and analogous force unites with it; they are also called predisposing seeds".

Entering into the study of the effects produced in the solid parts by the causes, he particularly stresses those which the fluids suffer, such as defective cohesion or thickening and above all acrimony of the humours, which is the result of an acid or an alkaline vitiation, or a fixed volatile one.

The detrimental forces of the atmosphere also produce poisons or a chemical acridity, because they contain vitiated or acrid principles. This likewise applies to miasmas. Decay comes from an alkaline principle, as von Haën also maintained, but Pringle upheld the theory that the principle was acid, because alkaline treatment was successful.

After all this Gaubius returns to the question of morbific seeds which are attached to the vital principle contained in the nature of man, and are existent throughout the economy and only develop under the influence of detrimental causes. All this is a mere repetition of what has been said, without adding anything, but it is clear that Gaubius intends to convey the idea of innate morbid predispositions.

*Maximilian Stoll* was born at Erzingen in 1742. After having lectured on ancient literature, he decided to study medicine in 1767. He went to Strasburg, and afterwards to Vienna, where he attended the lectures of the celebrated von Haën, whom later on he was to succeed as professor. He died in 1788.

Stoll is the genuine type of an upright, learned and modest physician, thoroughly attached to his art and to his duty. From the doctrinal point of view his value is secondary. To understand his teachings, his work on the practice of medicine (of which the first three parts only were published during his life) must be read carefully. His aphorisms on fevers and their cure are also worthy of note.

Stoll follows the Hippocratic tradition, as did Pringle and Sydenham. He is both a conscientious and an attentive observer, so that his works are more useful than interesting. Although we cannot adopt the theories dominant in his days, we cannot but admire his rare sagacity in observation and analysis of diseases. He clearly shows the conduct the physician should follow in the treatment of disease and his appreciation of the incessant variations of morbid movement. His errors, like those of all who followed his doctrine, are in always mistaking the effects for the causes. For him the morbid matter is invariably bile, pituit, phlegm, or acrid serosities; he always sees these agglutinated in the organs or absorbed and infecting the economy, so that he judges all morbid movement of diseases by the movement of the principal humours. It is chiefly in such theories that that humoralism persists which is the result of a too commonplace appreciation of the Hippocratic writings and of bad doctrinal reasoning, for here again the effect is invariably taken for the cause and the disease is regarded as a being materially represented in the morbid matter. Yet, Stoll and his followers had rare sagacity and prudence in the treatment of disease, especially of fevers in general, dysentery, pneumonia, and smallpox. On the subject of the malignancy of diseases, both Stoll and Selle were singularly proficient. Pringle, who preceded Stoll, was unquestionably a very excellent practitioner, but we cannot consider his writings here, and it may be said that in many ways the professor of Vienna was his superior.

## CHAPTER XX

## THE DOCTRINE OF IRRITABILITY, THE BRUNONIAN THEORY AND NATURALISM

Under one and the same heading we must here consider certain theories which seem to differ, but in reality have a common basis. Descartes, by reviving the Galenic theory of the vital spirits, which he understood in his own particular way, had unintentionally dealt a severe blow to Iatro-mechanics, for he thus brought back into science the *idea* or *force* which he had tried to exclude from his own mechanical theory. The discovery of electricity just at the time when Willis and Lower were tracing disease to the nervous system, when Croone was explaining muscular movement by the effervescence of a nervous fluid and Cole was talking of nervous tension and Glisson of irritability or a principle of energy, created a current of opinion in favour of a particular nervous force. This idea was strengthened by the publication at the beginning of the XVIIIth century of Newton's theories, which admitted distinct forces in nature under the names of attraction, gravity and light. At the same time Stahl's theories of tonicity and phlogistics, von Gorter's and Whytt's (his disciples) attribution of the movements of the body to the stimulation of Baglivi's motor fibre, and Hoffmann's opinion as to the spasm of the fibres and vessels, caused a tendency towards 'neurosism'.

Boerhaave taught that the nerves formed a weft for all solid organs and Sprengel states that in 1721 Boetticher, of Berlin, proclaimed the existence of a nervous fluid, while Stuard attempted to demonstrate this experimentally in 1732. Afterwards came the writings of Blaine in 1738, von Haller in 1752, Bertin in 1759, Rose in 1762, and Lecat in 1765. A weekly publication was started by Unzer of Hamburg, which was devoted to the subject of 'neurosism' and to explaining all phenomena by irritability. The idea of a nervous fluid principle, or nervous force, had sprung up in consequence of the writings of Descartes and Willis in the XVIIth century, and, after having taken various forms, ended with the work of von Haller, which, as a matter of fact, settled the physiological question and formed the basis of all future work in this direction. This occurred about the time when Cullen was applying to pathology his theory of spasm, adapted from the teachings of Baglivi, Stahl and Frederick Hoffmann. Haller in physiology, and Cullen and Brown in pathology formed the two culminating points of the doctrine of irritability and neurosism. Haller's experiments were repeated by his pupils, Krannermann, Winter, Bicker, Van der Bos, Eoder, and P. Castelli ; these were attacked by Robert Whytt, Brause and Bianchi, and even by Lecat, who stressed the existence of nervous fluid. In brief, it was thanks to von Haller, Cullen and Brown that the doctrines of irritability and neurosism were developed towards the middle and end of the XVIIIth century. These were, in another form, tentatively revived by the late Sir James Mackenzie in his doctrine of reflex actions in disease.

*Albert von Haller* was born at Berne in Switzerland on October 16th, 1708, and there died on December 12th, 1777. He studied under Boerhaave at Leyden and received his M.D. at the age of nineteen. He then returned to his native town and built up a large practice. From 1736 to 1753 he was professor at Göttingen, where he gave himself up almost entirely to experimental research work. He then returned to Berne and continued his physiological experiments.

*Von Haller* was more of a savant than a practitioner, in spite of his early success as a physician. With knowledge more extensive than deep and with a constant desire to learn, he also wrote on botany and even composed poetry and attempted novel-writing. He was instrumental in the production of many theses by his students, and during his life he wrote more than two hundred works. His collections of writings on medicine, surgery and materia medica, all of which are voluminous productions, are derived from his personal notes taken from his readings, and are extremely useful for the history of medicine. They include notes taken by his students. His writings on botany have long since

PLATE XXII

ALBERT VON HALLER
*(Author's Collection)*

[*face p. 340*

fallen into oblivion, as have his poetry and his unfinished novels, though his *Elementa physiologiae* is one of the greatest books of the century, Lastly we must mention his *Artis medicae principes*, which is an edition of the works of Hippocrates, Aretaeus, Alexander of Tralles, Celsus and Rhazes.

On account of his learning and character as well as his writings, von Haller has left a great name in medical history, but he must also be judged by the results of his work. In this respect it is certain that he stimulated the evolution of the science of physiology which had been prepared as far back as the XVIth century by Descartes.

On 22nd April, and again on 6th May, 1752, von Haller read his essay on sensibility and irritability before the Academy of Science at Göttingen, and from this time dates the great revolution that he accomplished. This memoir is curious in more respects than one, and we make some extracts from it in order fully to expose the theories of its author.

" I call an irritable part of the human body that which becomes shorter (contracts) when it comes into contact with a foreign body.

" I call a sensitive fibre in man that which, being touched, transmits the impression of this contact to the brain ; in animals, in whom we have no certitude in respect of the soul, one may call a sensitive fibre that which by irritation will set up evident signs of pain in them.

" When Boerhaave had established that the nerves were the basis of all solids, he went on to argue that there was no part of the human body which was not sensitive and capable of movement properly belonging to it, and this theory, which I have proven to be inexact, has been generally accepted."

" The epidermis is insensitive, as are fat and cellular tissue, while the skin is sensitive." " The muscles are sensitive and this is due to the nerves which they receive." " Tendons are insensitive, but this is because nerves supply the muscles but not the tendons." " Since then, in man it is only the nerves which are sensitive, it is very natural that the tendons which are not supplied with them are deprived of sensitiveness."

Von Haller then shows that the ligaments and the capsules of the joints are insensitive. "It is not to the capsules of the joints, in which it is so difficult to find nerves and which therefore are insensitive, that the acute pain in gout is to be attributed; the real seat of the pain is in the skin and the nerves which spread over their internal aspect. Nature has properly willed that parts exposed to continued friction should be devoid of any feeling." The periosteum and bones are insensitive. "I have never been able to find any nerve accompanying the artery and vein at their point of entrance into the bone." "Deventer, Ambroise Paré, Duverney and nearly all writers state that the bone marrow can give rise to severe pain; this statement seems unfounded, because the bone marrow is fatty in nature and receives no nerve. I have had no experience in this matter, however."

"The dura mater is insensitive and without movement, and it cannot be believed, as has been said, that it sends the animal spirits of the brain throughout the body. The brain certainly has alternating movements, as Schilckting has observed, but they correspond with the respiration and in all my experiments the brain rose up during expiration and fell back during inspiration." "This phenomenon is not peculiar to the brain; it entirely depends upon the faculty that the blood of the right ventricle of the heart has of filling the lungs during inspiration, and that of the large venous vessels of emptying into this ventricle, and so forth." "The Italians and those who deny the existence of animal spirits conceive the nerves to be like tense cords; besides the arguments which refute this opinion, it is also necessary to point out that the pia mater, which envelopes even the finest nerves, is itself insensitive." "Sensitiveness belongs to the medullary substance of the nerves." "The pleura is insensitive; pleuretic pain resides in the intercostal nerves; this also applies to the mediastinum. The arteries and veins do not seem to give rise to pain." "The heart is a muscle supplied with nerves." "I have assured myself by a large number of experiments that the viscera, namely the lungs, liver, spleen and kidneys, are without sensibility or only have it to a very slight degree. . . . If it is objected that there are nerves supplying these organs, I will reply by saying that I do not maintain that they are without all sensation, but that they possess it only in a very slight degree." "The glands are supplied with a few nerves which give them a very weak sensitiveness " "The breasts, penis, and tongue have a large nerve supply and are very sensitive." In summing up, von Haller says, "The sensitive parts of the body are those which are supplied with nerves, and the nerves themselves; there are only, therefore, nerves which are in themselves sensitive and their sensitiveness resides in their medullary part, which is the same as the internal substance of the brain, the pia mater being its envelope."

Such is the general summary of the first part of von Haller's essay, and we will now briefly sum up the second part, which is even more important than the first.

"I now come to irritability, which is different from sensitiveness; the most irritable parts are not sensitive,and the most sensitive parts are not irritable. I will prove both these propositions by facts, and I shall show at the same time that irritability is not dependent upon the nerves, but on the primordial fibres of the parts which are susceptible to irritability."

Von Haller goes on to say that nerves are not irritable and do not present any of the oscillations or vibrations that have been attributed to them. He then enters into details respecting parts which are very sensitive, but not irritable. He opposes the opinions of Stahl and his followers (and of Whytt in particular) who maintained that all movements of living beings depend upon the soul, and he recalls Baglivi's argument (which led Baglivi to attribute irritability to solids) that the heart when separated from the body continues to beat.

"The soul is sentient, it represents its body (that is to say the body containing it) and by means of the body the entire universality of things. I am myself, and nobody else, because that which is called the ego undergoes changes in all variations arising in the body. In a muscle or intestine whose changes make an impression on another soul than my own and not upon my own, the soul of this muscle is not mine and does not belong to me. But, if one of my fingers is cut off, or if a piece of the flesh of my leg is removed and therefore has no longer any connexion with me, I do not follow any of these changes, and they cannot cause me to experience any idea or sensation. . . . The amputation of my leg in no way involves my will, which remains complete; my soul has in no way lost any of its force, but it no longer has any control over this leg, yet, nevertheless, this leg continues to be irritable; hence irritability is quite independent of the soul and of the will."

"These experiments also prove that all muscular force does not depend upon the nerves, because after these have been divided the muscular fibres are still capable of irritability and contraction."

We will now leave aside numerous details and come to the doctrinal conclusions.

"From all these experiments it would appear that in the human body only the muscular fibre is irritable and has the faculty of shortening (contracting) when it is touched by a foreign body. It also results from this that the vital parts are the most irritable. . . . This differentiates the vital organs from the others. The former, being extremely irritable, only have need of a very weak stimulus to put them into play; one such stimulus, for example, is the blood or the humour which passes into their cavities. The latter, which have little irritability, are only moved by the power of the will, or by very strong stimuli, the application of which causes violent movement known under the name of convulsions."

Von Haller says that irritability is dependent upon the gelatinous mucosity of the muscles. "This idea is strengthened because children, in whom gelatinosity predominates, are far more irritable than adults."

Irritability continues after death and in parts separated from the body; it is also present in muscles whose nerves have been destroyed; it is only destroyed by drying or freezing, while in living parts it can be destroyed by opium, except in the heart.

As to the practical results derived by medicine from his work, von Haller has been modest enough to say little, but it is clear that from this time on medicine was entirely changed. Life was explained by irritability and disease depended upon this wonderful property, while therapeutics had it alone to deal with. Von Haller did not invent the idea of irritability and he made the great mistake of giving this name to the phenomenon of contractility. But he drew attention to this property of the muscle and clearly distinguished between it and nerve impulse of the sensibility; he showed that this latter depended upon the nerves and only existed where they were. From this point of view the revolution in physiology produced by Haller is considerable. But this is where his work ends. He did not follow up the distinction between motility and sensibility of the nerves, and it was not until sixty years later that Sir Charles Bell made this important demonstration. Unquestionably von Haller was very learned and in many ways rendered great service to medicine, and especially to physiology, because he introduced experimental work. He laid too much stress on the multiplication of experiments as constituting science, while his doctrine gave rise to many researches and discussions and at the same time inspired in others the theory of spasm and stimulus. Numerous were the discussions as to which were the irritable parts and whether or not irritablity depended upon nervous force. Some writers used irritability in order to develop a theory of fever ; Fabre used it to explain the phenomenon of inflammation and rejected the mechanical theory, and he was followed in this respect by L. Hoffmann and later by Borsieri, Van der Hennel and Berlinghieri.

William Cullen was born in Lanarkshire, Scotland, in 1710. He studied medicine at Glasgow and after much travel became professor successively at Glasgow and Edinburgh. He died at the latter city in 1790, having won an immense reputation. His principal works are his *Materia medica,* his *Synopsis nosologiae methodicae* and his *Elements of Practical Medicine.* It is in this latter work that we shall find the teachings of this celebrated physician. No writer, not excepting Sydenham or Stoll, has ever taken greater pains to give an exact description of disease. Cullen was an observer of the first order who understood how to combine method and clearness with great precision, a rare accomplishment. His descriptions of fevers and gout are remarkable in the highest degree, and, with Sydenham, he is one of the very first nosographers.

At first blush his doctrine does not seem to be more neurosist than that of Willis ; it even has such close relationship with that of Frederick Hoffmann that one might feel inclined to say that it was based upon it, and consequently had some colouring of chemiatry. Spasm, atony and acrimony are three terms that constantly recur in his writings. Although Cullen claims that he is a solidist, he nevertheless professes a great esteem for Gaubius, but when one reads his works it will be perceived that in general it is to spasm and to atony of the elementary fibres and capillary vessels that he most often reverts, while the concession he makes to the notion of acrimony of the humours is a reminiscence of his youth, and spasm and debility preoccupy him above all.

There is a point upon which we wish particularly to insist, namely the new form which he gives to his explanations. While for his predecessor, Hoffmann, as well as for Sydenham, an acrid humour of organic disturbance is the conjoint cause of disease, for Cullen it is merely a mechanism. Hence for him it results that a meticulous study of disease does not consist in a search for the conjoint cause, but for the physiological mechanism of the morbid acts. He studies the mechanism of movement, and in this respect Cullen is more Cartesian than one at first might suppose. But in justice to Cullen it may be said that he was one of the first exponents of physiological medicine. In other words he explained morbid acts by physiological acts.

Cullen has also been considered as the chief of the school of neurosism, and his doctrines were accepted by Gregory, Macbride, Schoeffer and many others.

The writer, not being of a puritanical mind, will not harp upon the private life of the unfortunate John Brown; it is sufficient to say that his doctrine—the Brunonian theory—governed the practice of medicine in most countries for over a quarter of a century, and therefore is important from the viewpoint of the history of medicine. He was born in great poverty in 1735 at Bunkle, Scotland. His life was one long struggle for livelihood, and should inspire one with commiseration. He died in 1788.

His doctrine is the basis of many modern ideas. Man and all living beings cannot exist by themselves; an external stimulus is necessary. Man does not in himself possess a secret power, a principle whose nature escapes our means of investigation, which at times increases and at others languishes. It is excitability which is the force, a power varying according to the individual and to the different states of health. It has no special seat in the body, but is spread throughout the organism because the being represents a whole and a perfect unity, so that possible changes at any given spot in the body are merely relative effects of degree. Brown stresses this doctrine of the being (which is at once ancient and quite true) and even goes so far as to say that excitability (which for him is the vital force) cannot really be increased in any part of the economy if it is decreased in the system taken as a whole. In other words, he wishes to imply that from the moment the bodily activity languishes as a whole, it also languishes in all the parts.

Excitability put in action by a stimulus keeps up the regular working of life upon the condition that the stimulus is properly adapted to it. But if this stimulus is too strong or too weak the excitability, or action of life, becomes changed, because excitability has become exhausted. It is exhausted if the stimulus is too strong, hence giving rise to direct weakness. It will languish if the stimulus does not sufficiently excite it, and hence an indirect weakness ensues. All causes acting upon the human being which have the power of causing disease will operate in the same way. If excitation is too strong there is exhaustion or direct weakness, but if at the same time the reaction is very sharp, then the disease is called sthenic. If the excitation is too weak, languishing occurs with indirect weakness, and the disease is then called asthenic. But Brown maintains that there are very few sthenic affections and that man has constant need of stimulus. He can never be excited too much if one understands how to produce excitation by carefully husbanding excitability, because this power increases by stimulus. Yet Brown points out one should take into consideration opportunity in life—what Hippocrates called the *occasion*—because, to become ill, it is not enough merely to be excited too much or too little. The excitement must be contrary to nature. For Brown, opportunity is a kind of predisposition. Of this he has rather a confused idea, but does make it clear that there is a pre-existing state of disease in it.

Brown does not admit genders or species of diseases; for him there are only general and local diseases. General diseases result from a shock of the entire system, but occasionally may become local diseases. Local diseases result from a local lesion and only exceptionally do they become general.

Brown's treatment essentially consists in the proper exhibition of stimulants, because these only exist in nature. In sthenic diseases, one must be moderate in their use, while in asthenic affections mild stimulants are first to be used and their strength should be gradually increased in order to renew and develop excitability by excitation. Opium he considered the strongest stimulant.

This system was very fascinating because it looked so like the truth. Hence it had tremendous success. Girtanner appropriated it and introduced it into Germany in about 1772; Locatelli and Moscati introduced it into Italy; Weikard in his turn introduced it into Germany and unmasked Girtanner's claims. The system was introduced into Russia, and soon the Brunonian theory was exploited in various ways all over the continent. Rasori and Broussais practically adopted the Brunonian theory for their systems, but reversed Brown's teachings, holding that sthenic diseases were common and asthenic maladies infrequent; hence their therapeutic consisted of contra-stimulants and antiphlogistics.

Brown certainly showed clearly that living beings have need of external surroundings for living, and that their force can only exercise itself provided that it is brought into action by external solicitation. It is evident from this that Brown adopted the ancient doctrines which he undoubtedly derived from his theological studies. Instead of regarding the external surroundings as the object of the act, and instead of saying that the vital force has need of an objective in order to act and that the external surroundings give it this objective, creating an outlet for it, he says that the external surroundings act as a stimulant for the creation of the force. Brown came very near the truth, and yet the essential point escaped him, for, by saying that external causes stimulate, he admitted that the action is always the same and simply varies according to the intensity of the stimulant. If the external circumstances are an objective of the act, it necessarily results that the force must vary its act according to the objective, and therefore an action which varies in its forms and in its modes according to the objective

PLATE XXIII

ERASMUS DARWIN
*(Author's Collection)*

[ *face p. 348*

to which it is adapted must be studied, because it is not merely an action increased or diminished according to the stimulus.

*Naturalism.*—We must now briefly consider the part played in medicine by the naturalists during the XVIIIth century. The celebrated English botanist, John Ray, died at the beginning of this century and the works of Malpighi, Swammerdam, Redi, Lancisi and Leeuwehoek had appeared. Then came Tournefort, Trembley, Buffon and Daubenton, Linnaeus and Charles Bonnet. Réaumur was to give up mathematics and physics and devote himself to the study of insects, while Camper, directly following Buffon in the study of man, would have as followers Blumenbach, Spallanzani, de Jussieu, Meckel, Erasmus Darwin and John Hunter. At the end of the XVIIIth century came von Humboldt, Lamarck, Geoffroy Saint-Hilaire, and Cuvier.

The works of these learned men cannot be examined here. Our only object is to show their influence on medical doctrines. In the first place they classified diseases as natural species. Undoubtedly this idea had already been admitted by Sydenham and others, but it had remained sterile, and what had been accomplished by Felix Plater and attempted by Stahl was not further developed. In reality it was John Ray and Tournefort who gave the impetus and Selle and Linnaeus, continuing the work of the latter, were the first to make such pathological classifications as were later elaborated by Pinel and de Sauvages.

The idea of *morbid entity* was one rooted in medical tradition, but the species was always difficult to identify, and it was only after the writings of Tournefort, Buffon and Camper that the idea of species—so important in natural history—was finally applied in medicine.

The naturalists also gave a vigorous impulse to experimental science and it even may be said that they founded it. It had already been commenced in the previous century by Harvey, Malpighi, Swammerdam and Winslow, but Buffon, Haller and others greatly developed experimental science as applied to physiology by their writings on artificial generation, irritability, regeneration of tissues and the experimental study of digestion. Thus the naturalists, by their experimental work, adopted the ideas of organicism, but on the other hand they reacted against the too materialistic and mechanical theories of this system by constituting a general science of man alongside of purely organic physiology. In the XVIIth century physiology had occupied itself with general questions on the nature of man, as had been done by the ancient medical philosophers, but with Boerhaave and Haller this science threw off all alliance with philosophy and became simply a mechanical science of organic functions, as the Cartesian school required. Bonnet, Buffon and Blumenbach returned to the study of the general science of man, and it was to this current of thought that Barthez and Bichat became adherents.

And lastly, the foundations of comparative anatomy were laid by the naturalists. This science, it is true, had been foreseen by Aristotle and for a short time it had been understood by the great philosophers of the XIIIth century, but its real founder was Daubenton, who was followed by Vicq d'Azyr, Réaumur, Blumenbach, Erasmus Darwin, Meckel and John Hunter.

## CHAPTER XXI

## ORGANICISM AND VITALISM

Towards the end of the XVIIth century Iatro-mechanism so completely counterbalanced Iatro-chemistry that the mechanics of the living being rather than the composition of the humours became the object of study. This undoubtedly resulted in the tendency towards solidism, of which the first signs are to be found in Ettmüller and which became more accentuated in Baglivi, Lancisi and Hecquet. While the chemical school became blended with the humoral, the Iatro-mechanical school drifted from solidism into organicism. From the idea that solids were the principal conditions of life there was only one step to the idea that vital movement was all important in organic functions.

Morgagni (1682–1771) in his book entitled *De Sedibus et causis morborum*, published in 1760; Sénac (1693–1770) in his treatise on diseases of the heart, which appeared in 1749; Lieutaud (1703–80) in his work on medical anatomy which was issued during the years 1749 to 1766 (and later on in his *Practical Medicine* and his *Materia Medica*); and Auenbrugger in his treatise on percussion entitled *Inventum novum ex percussione thoracis humani, ut signo, abstrusos interni pectoris morbos detegendi*, published at Vienna in 1761; all strengthened the movement which sought to understand life, disease and health by the working of the organs. Bordeu was the first exactly to describe the play of the organs. Two divergent currents of thought, one towards materialism, the other towards vitalism, succeeded in influencing this movement each in its own direction.

Théophile de Bordeu (born at Izeste, France, on 21st February, 1722, died at Paris 23rd November, 1776) is one of the most illustrious figures in medicine. Space forbids referring to all his important works; but it is necessary to review them as a whole in order that we understand his general doctrine. When Bordeu developed his system, it was a reaction against the materialism of the Iatro-chemical and Iatro-mechanical schools. Bordeu let no opportunity pass for affirming and demonstrating that life cannot be explained without a principle of being and laws of vitality entirely different from what is purely mechanical and chemical. Briefly put, it was the matter composing the organ that was everything, and the life of the organ was a function of the being. Hence Bordeu cast aside all occult forces and thought that consideration of the theories of dynamics, although not false, was at least useless. We will now examine the subject of his writings.

"Up till now we have supposed that the humours are really contained in the blood; this opinion seems nearer the truth than that of those to maintain the contrary. But we cannot lose sight of the fact that there are many objections to be made to it. . . .

"Let us first see if it can really influence the practice of medicine. A practitioner who believes that the various humours are really contained in the fluids, as soon as he finds some one of the emunctories defective, cannot avoid blaming this sort of bad mixture of the fluids, or cacochemy, the result of a superabundance of retained humour, and therefore he must act accordingly. On the other hand, he who believes that the emunctories are made for forming the humour which later on they will eliminate from the body, will only fear the plethora resulting from suspended excretion; he cannot have the same views as the other and the difference of opinion will turn upon the question to which we are now referring." (*Recherches anat. sur les glandes*, CXIV.)

This dilemma is well put and is the most weighty that the XVIIIth century had to solve in medical science. It meant, if Bordeu's opinions triumphed, the absolute end of humoralism, but he saw the importance of its solution and did not under-estimate the objections that might be raised to his theories. For example, he questions whether bile is really urine and he says: "The chemists who admit that a peculiar ferment exists which manufactures humour to repair (organic losses) may be mistaken, but there is some truth on their side; after all it would be useful to settle these questions once and for all and to study them more thoroughly. At the same time it can be decided whether or not drugs can change the mass of humours in the living subject or alter or suspend movements that are called spontaneous; whether one can count, and how far, on this sort of remedy; whether or not there is any one of them that can make bile, and so forth." (*Ibid.*)

Bordeu then goes into this question of medicaments. "There are perhaps medicines which can evacuate a humour by increasing its quantity in the blood or rendering the humours more or less mobile or thick. Others produce evacuations by acting directly upon a glandular organ. Indeed, there are many things to examine. They are essential and should be regarded as the foundation of true materia medica." (*Ibid.*, CXV.)

He then questions whether or no drugs may act on a single organ, which in turn will depress the functions of all the organs—a reminiscence of Paracelsus and van Helmont, which gives him the key to the riddle. In order to demonstrate his point he stresses the action of mercury on glands, and shows that the drug is eliminated by them, and he asks whether or no there are similar actions produced by morbid matter or by other drugs. Next he establishes the difference between secretion and excretion, a difference that had been too difficult to recognize, and which was in fact the clue to the problem of glandular activities.

It was in 1752 that Bordeu for the first time proclaimed this proposition, thus formulating the doctrine of organicism, which regarded life as the sum total of the lives of each particular organ. In this theory, certainly, the unity of the being was overlooked as well as the general co-ordination of all the actions peculiar to the being. But the exaggeration of the theory of organic functions to the point of error was perhaps a condition without which the truth it contained would have been allowed to pass unnoticed.

We will now examine the second formula, which Bordeu gave at the end of his life and which is to be found in the first part of his book entitled *Recherches sur les Maladies Chroniques.* Twenty-three years had elapsed since he had formulated the first proposition; so that his mind had become more matured and his ideas were clearer.

"By disease one should understand a disturbance of the functions dependent upon some organic vitiation, or proceeding form an increased or decreased action of some part; for it has been said that we are only ill when our functions are disturbed or when the energy or tonus of the parts is destroyed. In the writings of Aretaeus and other physicians of his time traces can be found of organicism, which was then better developed and better understood than it has been until now. As it is upon this well-conceived organicism that the knowledge of health and disease depends it will be extremely useful to link up with it the observations we are going to make. Thus we require for the exercise of health a series of regulated and determined organic movements. When their harmony does not exist an indisposition or disease arises in the body.

"Each disease has its own course and evolution and period of time it takes to run its course; it has its phases of violence and of duration, which, so to say, are impossible to alter. An attentive observer will note, in the excretion of a gland or during the process of digestion, first, a certain change in the body which announces the approach of disease or repair (of the body), secondly, the phenomena indicating its presence or formation, thirdly, the combined effort of all the organs to terminate the disease, either by eradicating it completely and bringing the body back to health or by changing it into another (disease)—an effort which may collapse before the violence of the disease and become extinguished with the life of the patient. This order of changes, which is common to all diseases, seems to establish a resemblance of form between them, as Hippocrates has pointed out, which their severity or mildness, slowness or rapidity (of development) and so forth are unable to remove from them.

"As to miasmas and noxious corpuscles, poisons and virus of all kinds, which are known to be the material cause of many ills, and against which many specifics are vaunted, it is very certain that miasmas do exist, but, firstly, their nature is absolutely unknown and perhaps always will be; secondly, experience has proved that these miasmas affect the body only in proportion to the dispositions contained in it, so that—a noteworthy fact—what injures one part is often salutary to another; thirdly, the cure of a body infected by these miasmas, whether this be obtained by specific treatment or otherwise, is always subordinated—as are the phenomena accompanying it—to the laws of life or to the movement and sensibility of the parts and to the order of their functions. Hence it follows that: firstly, the nature of the miasmas being absolutely unknown to us, the means for combating them are beyond us and reason cannot furnish us with them; secondly, the object of the physician in respect of these pernicious substances is to attempt to understand those temperaments and idiosyncrasies which they may affect; thirdly, it is of especial importance to know by what movements art or nature can succeed in destroying the miasma so as to regulate these movements.

"Take, for example, the virus of smallpox. . . . One must suppose that if it does not act it is because it does not find a favourable disposition in the body, a disposition which has been destroyed in those who have already had the disease. Hence this same disposition is partially the principal cause of the disease; so that the readiness to receive the impression of the miasma of variola and the various phenomena or effects that it produces are what the physician should especially study. All the rest is merely accessory and far beyond his capacity.

"As the disposition of the body is the cause of sterility or fecundity in women, so is it in the case of the miasma of variola. One can very well compare the accidents arising at the beginning of a disease with the phenomena of generation, because in each case there is, so to speak, a sudden upheaval, the order of the movements becomes changed and that which becomes established only disappears when an excretion takes place. If there are temperaments which readily fecundate the germs of disease; if there are those which convert everything into that which properly belongs to them (meaning their own idiosyncrasies and predispositions) as, for example, is seen in asthmatics, gouty subjects and many other sickly individuals, who in an epidemic become afflicted with asthma, gout, and so forth, or when pleurisy or sore throats are prevalent, so are there temperaments so strong that they resist the action of the greater part of the miasma and even become immune to the poisons. The temperament and idiosyncrasy are therefore the real fields for the diseases spread by air, water and other non-natural things. The duty of the physician . . . consists in skilfully keeping away all that is injurious and removing from the germs the ailment which fertilizes them, by changing the disposition of the body. It is the natural constitution which makes the Turks susceptible to the plague, the English to the sweating sickness, and so forth . . . What is the disposition of the body which can resist these bad influences? This is the chief thing that we must know."

Bordeu believed in the soul as well as in a principle of life in man, as is shown in several places in his *Histoire de la Medecine.* He was thoroughly conversant with the Hippocratic writings and he was far from ignoring the affinity of diseases and morbid movement—a theory revived by Stahl—as well as the crises and critical evacuations. Right or wrong, he felt compelled to fit all these theories in with his conception of organicism. He wished to reconcile this organicism with the doctrine of predisposition, which he had developed better than any before him, and in which it will be seen that he was influenced by the arguments of Fernel in respect of contagion. But unfortunately he failed in his attempt at reconciliation and we must admit the inconsistency of this great mind.

Bordeu's object was to show that the entire being possesses its proper function as such and that each organ is a physiological element possessing its own special function, and when one perceives how greatly he insists upon the relationship between the functions and the attention that should be given to the vital movement which flows at times in one function and at others in another, it is evident that he implies more than appears on the surface.

*Vitalism.*—There is no doubt that vitalism was in the minds of many at this time and the expression "vital principle" was being used when Barthez appeared upon the scene. He was born at Montpellier on 11th December, 1734, and died on 15th October, 1806. The principal work in which he exposed his theory appeared in 1798, and is entitled *Nouvelle mécanique des mouvements de l'homme et des animaux.* During his life Barthez had no great influence on medicine, but it would be a mistake to overlook the great impetus that he gave to the doctrine of vitalism. He undertook to show that there was a principle of *life*, something other than mere mechanics or chemistry, upon which depended the phenomena of vitality and which was distinct from the soul. A few quotations from his writings will suffice to give the reader an idea of his doctrine.

"Facts do not show that the movements executed in the living body are due to the same thinking being whose influence determines voluntary movement.

"In the present state of our knowledge in respect of man the various movements occurring in the human body are due to two different principles, the nature of which is unknown, but whose action is not mechanical. One is the thinking soul, the other the principle of life."

Barthez understood the necessity of thoroughly comprehending the unity governing the various phenomena of the body, and in respect of this he says: "The proper method of philosophy in the science of man requires that the iving forces residing in each organ which produce both general functions, such as sensibility, nutrition and so forth, and special functions, such as digestion, menstruation and so forth, shall be regarded as due to a single principle of life." He also states: "I call the vital principle of man the cause which produces all the phenomena of life in the human body. The name of this cause is an indifferent matter . . . if I prefer that of vital principle it is because it presents a less limited idea than the term *impetum faciens* of Hippocrates, and other names by which the cause of the functions of life have been designated."

Barthez insists upon the difference between the vital principle and the soul, because the functions of the body are independent of the will and also because of the multiplicity of movements and of sentiments opposed to each other in man, and because these contradictory conditions can only be explained by two principles. And he concludes: "Given these proofs, it seems to me that we cannot avoid making a distinction between the vital principle of man and his thinking soul."

He seems to maintain that the vital principle and the thinking soul are two absolutely distinct principles; hence the term "human duo-dynamism" given to his doctrine. But in concluding Barthez seems to infer that we may have to do with two forces belonging to the one and same principle. This principle of life exists from the very commencement of the formation of the being and engenders both life and its functions.

Having developed the doctrine of a vital principle, Barthez takes up the study of the phenomena of life from the view-point of their synergies and their sympathies, and it may be said that this is really the most original part of his book. "I designate by the word synergy a concourse of simultaneous or successive actions of the forces of the various organs, a concourse such that its actions constitute by their harmonious order or succession the form properly belonging to a function in a state of health or of a species of disease."

Barthez defines three kinds of synergy: firstly, the synergy dependent upon an analogy of structure, for example all the muscular tissues; secondly, a synergy resulting from the combined function of several organs for the development of a given action or for a succession of actions, controlled by the nerves or by the blood vessels; and thirdly, the synergy resulting from two organs having peculiar connexion with each other and depending upon an individual idiosyncrasy or constitution.

Barthez built up his pathology and therapeutics on these general physiological data. "According to my theory diseases are essentially the results of affections of the principle of life in man. . . . Or else they are the necessary results of primary physical lesions in the organization of the different parts of the body. But, according to the same theory, the diseases are in general automatically produced by the action of either external or internal morbid causes in conformity with the laws established by the vital principle, which are neither mechanical nor arbitrary."

All this, of course, clearly lacks precision, and in this respect Barthez certainly hesitates and is forced to borrow from physical and chemical theories. The perusal of his *Traité des maladies goutteuses*, which is his most important work on pathology and therapeutics, gives one this impression. He accepts Sydenham's specificity, maintaining that there is a specific state in gout, and yet this does not prevent him from saying, like Cullen, that it is a diathesis. As to the cause of the gouty principle, he supposes it to be a retention of calcareous matter within the body.

But from the theoretical point of view, the most interesting part of this work is the system of *pathological elements* which is given as the basis for therapeutical indications. Barthez teaches that diseases are composed of simple morbid elements, as in rheumatism, fever, pain or the calcareous diathesis, and he tries to show that therapeutics should have as an end the combating of these various elements of the disease. It is clear from this that Barthez had a glimpse of something which was really valuable, and that he wished to make more importance of the syndromes of disease, which had always been neglected.

To sum up it can be said that Barthez gave an impulse to vitalism without having clearly formulated it as a doctrine.

*John Hunter* was born in 1728 and died in 1793. He is one of the greatest physicians that Great Britain ever possessed, and although he is far better known as an anatomist and surgeon, it is really in the domain of general physiology and general medicine that he is most illustrious. His *Lectures on the Principles of Surgery* and his treatises on blood and inflammation, are works that are to be read to-day with the greatest interest. He frankly admits the doctrine of the vital principle. He says that animal matter is endowed with a principle that in ordinary language can be called life, but this principle is perhaps the most difficult to conceive in all nature, because there is no other principle so complex in its effects. He shows that this principle does not result from the peculiar change which properly belongs to animal matter, because this same change occurs in the cadaver when the principle no longer exists. He thinks that there is a certain analogy between this principle and the magnetic force of a magnet, and attributes two properties to it, namely preservation and action. The most simple idea of life is that which consists in regarding it as the principle of preservation which prevents dissolution of animal matter, a process which occurs as soon as matter is deprived of it. Another point of view is that which supposes it to be the principle of action. Now, here are two very different properties, although they proceed from the same principle, because the first may exist independently of the second. In point of fact, it is to be noticed that it is not necessary for the preservation of animal matter for the action to exist in all parts of the body; there are many parts in an animal which appear to be possessed of little action, and yet they enjoy life quite as much as the more active parts. As another proof of this Hunter refers to the life of an egg, which, living, is more resistant to freezing than when dead.

Hunter shows how all things in the being are alive, even the blood, and how everything lives in unity on account of the harmonious way in which solids and liquids are combined. He thus ends the dispute between the humoralists and solidists. His pathological doctrine accords with his physiological doctrine. Disease is not for him a change of the humours and solids, as the Galenists had had it, but is a morbid action which causes these changes. He points out that disease can hardly be supposed to be a natural state in animals, and that it can only be the result of an abnormal impression which disturbs the natural actions of the body. This abnormal impression may act at the time of the formation of the animal, thus giving it (the animal) a permanent abnormal action ; or it may occur later during intra-uterine life. But it is more prone to manifest itself after birth, because an animal is exposed to many and varied influences which represent just so many impressions which are contrary to his natural actions. Hunter believes that it is very probable that the morbid actions repose practically upon the same principles as do the natural actions. Like the latter they cause certain dispositions of the parts to appear and bring about the formation of certain morbid products.

Hunter points out that the simplest idea that he can formulate of the generation of disease is that every animal is endowed with the faculty of contracting an action and a susceptibility for receiving impressions. Every impression produces a disposition, this disposition may give rise to an action, and this action constitutes the immediate sign of the disease. Disposition and action are always in relation with the nature of the impression and that of the part receiving the impression. He also believes that every action, be it natural or morbid, has its primal source in that susceptibility of impression which exists independently of any disposition or action (provided that no impression or stimulus comes into play) because the disposition only occurs as a result of an impression and the action is only produced when the disposition is sufficiently intense for the part to have a greater tendency towards action than toward resolution. The actions of the body are exactly similar to those of the mind, and this also applies to the causes and the effects of these actions.

Hunter shows that all animals are endowed with a certain number of predispositions which render them susceptible to a certain number of impressions, each one of which may give rise to a disposition properly belonging to it. Certain predispositions are stronger than others, and this explains the immense variety of disease. Strictly speaking, Hunter does not believe that there is anything that one can call a predisposing *cause.* What is commonly designated by this expression is merely an increase of the predisposition for the disposition of such or such an action.

In considering the great work accomplished by Hunter there are two things which strike us as astonishing. One is how he could attain such a high conception of medical tradition, and the other is the little influence that he had upon British medicine of his day. It is probable that the influence of Brown and Cullen prevented Hunter's teachings from being readily accepted, and on the other hand it must not be forgotten that Hunter followed the teachings of Percival Pott, who, although known as a surgeon, was in reality a much better physician. It was undoubtedly by Pott that Hunter was taught the elements of traditional medicine, which, at bottom free of all science foreign to medicine, was admirably developed by him in spite of his being overlooked by his contemporaries. But at the end of the XVIIIth century and at the beginning of the XIXth century, Hunter's teachings played an immense part in the reform of therapeutics.

Bichat forms the link between the XVIIIth and the XIXth centuries, as Baglivi had done between the XVIIth and XVIIIth. He was born in 1771 and died in 1802, a little less than thirty-one years of age. In order correctly to estimate his importance, we would point out that he was representative of the vitalist opinions of his time. A few quotations from his work entitled *Recherches sur la vie et la mort* will suffice to give an idea of his teachings. He opens by saying that " the definition of life is looked for in abstract considerations ; I believe that it can be found in this general expression : Life is the sum total of the functions which resist death. . . . Such is the existence of living bodies, which everything surrounding them tends to destroy. . . . Had they not a permanent principle of reaction they would soon die. This principle is that of life, unknown in its nature ; it can only be realized by its phenomena, because the most general of these is this usual alternation of action on the part of external bodies and of reaction on the part of the living body."

Bichat's doctrines of general anatomy are the same. He says : " There are two classes of beings in nature, two classes of properties and two classes of science. Bodies are organic or inorganic, properties are vital or non-vital, the sciences are physiology and physics. Animals and vegetables are organic, minerals are inorganic. The vital properties are sensibility and contractility. The non-vital properties are gravity, affinity, elasticity, and so forth. Animal and vegetable physiology and medicine compose physiological sciences ; astronomy, physics and chemistry and so forth are physical sciences." Further on he adds : " The (vital) properties whose influence we have analysed are not precisely inherent in the molecules of matter, which is their seat. In point of fact they disappear as soon as these molecules have lost their organic arrangement. It is to this arrangement that they exclusively belong." This idea was borrowed from Von Haller, who thus explained sensibility and irritability. Bichat restricts the vital properties to sensibility and contractility and this might lead one to suppose that he misunderstood vegetative phenomena, and yet he admits that there is an organic or vegetative life alongside of animal life.

At the same time he threw himself into organicism, following in the steps of Bordeu, whom, in fact, he imitates. From this standpoint one might say that his *Traité des membranes* and his *Anatomie générale* are merely a continuation of Bordeu's writings, but he parts company with Bordeu and, instead of regarding the functions in the play of an organ, makes life dependent on the sum total of the functions of the life of each organ in particular. To make his thoughts clear we will quote the two following paragraphs from his *Anatomie générale*.

"All animals are a collection of different organs, each one of which performs a function peculiar to itself for the preservation of all (the entire body). They are just so many machines belonging to the general machine which constitutes the individual. Now, these individual machines are themselves composed of several tissues of very different nature, which truly form the elements of these organs. Chemistry possesses its simple bodies, which, by various combinations, form compound bodies . . . likewise anatomy has its simple tissues, which by combining four and four, six and six, eight and eight, and so forth, compose the organs.

"Since Bordeu much has been said about the individual life of each organ, which is nothing else than the peculiar character which distinguishes the sum total of the vital properties of one organ from the sum total of vital properties of another. Before these properties had been analysed with precision it was clearly impossible to form an exact idea of this individual life, and, according to the idea that I advance, it is evident that, the majority of organs being composed of very different simple tissues, the idea of individual life can only be applied to these simple tissues and not to the organs themselves. A few examples will make this doctrine clear. The stomach is composed of serous and mucous tissues, as well as of all the common tissues, such as the arteries, veins and so forth, which latter need not be taken into consideration. Now, if one considers the life of the stomach in a general way, it is clear that it will be impossible to form a precise idea. In point of fact the mucous tissue is so different from the serous, and each so completely different from the muscular tissue, that to consider them as a whole is to create confusion. This applies to the intestine, bladder, uterus and so forth; if one does not make a distinction between the tissues belonging to these composite organs, the expression *individual life* is indefinite."

If we take Bichat's doctrine literally, the life of the stomach would result from the life of each of its component tissues, which would be absurd. But if, on the contrary, we understand what he really means, namely, that in order to comprehend the function of an organ the functions of each of its tissues must be taken into account, then everything is explained and is perfectly consistent. Now, this very simple idea had to be understood by the men of his time in order that an end might be put to the disputes of the solidists and the humoralists, and it is for this reason that organicism marked a real advance beyond the stage of the rival Iatro-chemical and Iatro-mechanical doctrines. By demonstrating that the life of the entire human organism was made up of particular organs Bichat established the truth. The doctrine of organicism reacted forcibly upon pathology, and the study of disease was put upon a solid basis.

In his *Recherches sur la vie et la mort* Bichat was unquestionably singularly inspired by the work of Lancisi, but it may be affirmed that in his writings he revived the general science of Man which since the time of Boerhaave had been completely neglected.

In order to understand the progress made in anatomy and physiology during the XVIIIth century, it will be well to divide that time into three periods. The first period is that of direct continuation of the researches carried out during the XVIIth century and is quite fertile in discoveries. The second period is practically represented by Haller, while the third comprises many discoveries of the highest importance.

*First period.*—Discussions on the circulation continued at the end of the XVIIth and the beginning of the XVIIIth centuries. Harvey's doctrine was fiercely attacked by Méry and Littré, but it at last triumphed, thanks to the researches of Duverney, Silvestro, Verheyen, and especially Winslow and Sénac, who described the muscular fibres and the valves of the heart.

Stroem, in 1707, explained the necessity of expiration as an obligatory act following inspiration. Méry was the first to show that the air becomes mixed with the blood in the lung, and following this Helvetius studied the structure of the lungs and maintained that the blood was thickened by the addition of air. Lieberkühn experimentally proved that air did not enter into the pleural cavity, while Hamberger and Haller discussed the part played by the intercostal muscles and diaphragm in respiration, a question which also occupied the minds of Sénac, Brémont and others.

Ramby showed that what Valsalva had taken for the

excretory ducts of the suprarenal capsules were in reality arteries. Duverney described the lacteal vessels and their origin.

Littré described the nasal mucosa in greater detail than had been done by Schneider. Pourfour du Petit attempted to show that the nerve fibres cross each other in the cerebral substance and medulla oblongata, and this discovery was the foundation of all modern researches on the minute anatomy of the nervous system. He also described the septum lucidum and refuted the opinion that the cerebellum was the seat of sentiment. Among others who studied the nervous system mention should be made of Lecat, Meckel and Huber.

Pemberton showed that the processus ciliaris caused the lens to change its shape. Morgagni studied the lacrymal ducts, while Saint Yves showed that the choroid and not the retina was sensitive. Pourfour du Petit described the changes occurring in the eye at different ages of life. Dumours showed that the cornea was quite distinct from the sclerotic and maintained that the fibres of the iris were elastic and not muscular. And lastly Zinn studied the movements of the eye and the structure of the ciliary process. The minute anatomy of the ear was advanced by Valsalva, Morgagni and Cassebohm.

In 1700 Andry's work on generation appeared, in which he explained this act by spermatozoids and maintained that worms developing in man were derived from eggs which filled the atmosphere. Duverney and Breudel showed the existence of the ovum and its passage from the ovary into the uterus. Lister, Nigrisoli and others discussed the part played by the spermatozoids. Hale demonstrated the existence of the allantoid and Santorini studied the muscular structure of the uterus and the corpus luteum. Haller studied the incubation of the ovum, while Monro followed the development of the foetus in animals and described the muscular fibres of the uterus. His son studied the seminiferous canals and William Hunter made injections of them and also the lymphatics of the testicle. John Hunter made injections in the placenta and demonstrated its finer anatomy. And lastly, C. F. Wolff developed his theory of epigenesis and Buffon published his researches on generation.

*The Second Period.*—In 1752 Haller published his work on sensibility and irritability and in the same year Bordeu published his epoch-making work on the glands. Haller's erudition was unquestionably great, but his discoveries may be summed up in his work on irritability and sensibility and his researches on the circulation in the foetus. He in himself represents a period of the XVIIIth century, for not only does he sum up the work done before him but also personifies the aspirations of the physicians of his day. It is not too much to say that with Haller anatomical physiology was founded. Unquestionably much detail remained to be studied, but he laid the foundations of this science.

*The Third Period.*—This covers the last twenty-five years of the XVIIIth century. In 1774, with the publication of *Les Nouveaux Eléments de la Science de l'Homme* by Barthez, vitalism came out in great vigour, and if this remarkable physician had had the courage of his opinions would have triumphed during many years. Barthez' theory of the principle of life composed of a soul and a vital principle could not stand the test of the critics of his day and was doomed to failure.

In 1777 Lavoisier gave to the world his theory of respiration by combustion, a theory already prepared for by the discovery of oxygen. In 1780 Spallanzani published his researches on digestion and artificial fecundation and thus definitely settled the much discussed question of the ovum and spermatozoid.

In 1785 and 1787 Michaelis and Ackermann respectively published their researches on regeneration of the nerves and Fontana took up the question of irritability. In 1788 Soemmering published his classic treatise on the brain and cord, while in 1791 he began his publications on monstrosities.

In 1789 Cruikshank and Mascagni demonstrated that all the lymphatic vessels ended in the lymph-nodes and that the whole lymphatic system communicated with the thoracic duct. In the same year Crawford completed the work of Lavoisier in his essay on animal heat. In 1790 Priestley calculated the quantity of oxygen which passed into the blood, and Ackermann showed the relationship existing between cretinism and the development and shape of the brain.

In 1791 Fischer described the lumbar nerves and Galvani demonstrated muscular response to electricity. Gall published his work on the nature of man and admitted the existence of a vital force quite independent of the soul. Fordyce published a study on digestion in which he attempted to prove that albumen was the nutritive substance *par excellence*.

In 1792 Danz described the anatomy of the foetus at different stages of pregnancy. Vauquelin published his researches on the respiration of worms and insects, while Autenrieth analysed blood. In 1793 Gerlach described the synovial bursae ; Peipers described the third and fourth cervical nerves ; and Volta gave to the world the construction of his battery. Abernethy published his researches on the composition of animal matter.

In 1794 Fourcroy and Vauquelin published their work on animal chemistry and the former declared that chemistry can in no way explain the phenomena of life.

In 1797 Monro published his work on the brain and the ear ; Rosenmüller wrote on the lacrymal glands, and Andersh on the nerves of the heart. Von Humboldt wrote on galvanism of the muscular fibres and nerves, and Roose on vital force. And lastly, in 1799, Bichat published his two epoch-making works on general anatomy and on life and death.

The XVIIIth century was a brilliant one for surgery, particularly in France and Britain. Among the most noted surgeons of the former country should be mentioned J.-L. Petit, especially noted for his work on diseases of the bones. Others who contributed greatly to the advance of surgery are Garengeot (1688–1759), Le Dran (1770), de Lamotte (1655–1737), Morand (1697–1773), A. Louis (1723–1792), de la Faye (1781), Quesnay (1694–1794). Mention should be made of P.-J. Desault (1744–1795) for his writings on surgical anatomy, as well as of Frère Cosme, noted for his skill in operations for stone of the bladder.

The great surgical names in Britain are William Cheselde (1688–1752), Alexander Monro of Edinburgh, Percival Pott, and John and William Hunter (the latter an obstetrician), all of whom contributed to the progress of this branch of the healing art.

# CONCLUDING CHAPTER

## A BRIEF SURVEY OF THE EVOLUTION OF THERAPEUTICS

As the fundamental aim of medicine is the treatment of disease, it seems proper that a brief summary should be given of the evolution of therapeutics during the period that we have now traversed.

Immediately after its birth, treatment of disease was entirely empirical, but its practice was gradually enriched by experience that had been found fruitful. The Babylonians placed their sick in the public places and highways and sought advice from passers-by who might have seen similar cases or know of some remedy that might bring relief. The Egyptians, to whom the earliest organized medical science must be attributed, were also the creators of pharmacy; they employed liniments, tonic potions and plasters, and used laxatives and enemata, but to this form of treatment they added the use of sacred ceremonies, incantations and magic, a fact which proves that suggestion has been found of value in all times and in all places.

The Greeks began by resorting to suggestion; they treated internal diseases by prayers, charms and votive offerings, limiting medical practice to the dressing of ulcers and wounds. But hydrotherapy lent its aid to suggestion, and it is said that Melampus restored to sanity the daughters of Proetus, afflicted by mental disease, by means of sacred ablutions and purging with hemlock.

In the temples, which began to be erected about the XIIth century B.C. in different parts of Greece, such as those at Cos, Cnidus, Rhodes, Epidaurus and Pergamos, the Asclepiads preserved therapeutic secrets richer in dreams and visions than in medicaments. They took oath never to reveal their knowledge, but, as the practice of the healing art gradually became more rational, secrecy was relaxed, and in the VIth century B.C. Pythagoras wrote a book on the properties of plants and on the use of squills. At this time hygienic measures, diet and gymnastics were more especially employed, but later on they were eliminated from treatment, to be again employed in our day.

A century later Hippocrates brought together all the books pertaining to the medical knowledge acquired before his time, thus erecting a monument which after twenty-four centuries is still the admiration of all who know it. But it was not Hippocrates who enriched therapeutics; he himself gave us no new medicaments, though he founded the science of dietetics, and from the very start he brought it to such perfection that even to-day there is little to be added. His medical system (which in respect of the cause is *vitalism*, and in respect of the effect is *humoralism*) should not allow us to forget that he was the first to invite us to Empiricism, when he says: "In medicine we do not think that it is proper to have recourse to hypotheses; the unknown should be reached from the known; teaching should be accepted from the most simple men if they appear to know something decisive in respect of a given thing. It is thus, I believe, that our art has developed. Great attention should be given to what happens by chance, if the phenomenon can be confirmed upon several occasions."

Yet two centuries passed by before Philinus of Cos and Serapion of Alexandria formulated the laws of Empiricism. They recognized three sources of study, namely, chance which furnishes the facts, experiments which make it known if it is possible to reproduce these facts, and lastly analogy by which recognized procedures found useful in the two former cases may be applied to similar cases. Archagathus (219 B.C.) introduced Greek medicine into Rome, but his popularity failed on account of his brutal methods of treatment. In the following century Themison developed Methodism, in which treatment was very limited. He attributed all disease to *strictum* or *laxum*, but this did not prevent him from practising Empiricism like his predecessors, in every case where he could not classify a disease in the too narrow limitations of his doctrine, as must have very frequently happened.

Athenaeus (69 B.C.) founded the Pneumatic sect, of which Plato and Aristotle had been forerunners, and had as disciple Aretaeus. Pneumatism passed like a breath of wind over Empiricism, which was in no way shaken, and was itself extinguished, only to reappear with Stahl towards the end of the XVIIth century under the name of animism.

During this time pharmacy prospered at Rome and materia medica was enriched by new acquisitions. Its very varied pharmacopoeia included aconite, poppy, henbane, hemlock, hellebore, and many other plants. From the mineral kingdom it took arsenic, antimony, iron, sulphate and acetate of copper, the carbonates of sodium and potassium, nitrate of potassium, alum, calcium, gold and silver. The animal kingdom furnished cantharides, salamanders, and vipers, as well as the mineral waters classified as sulphurous, aluminous, saline and bituminous. It is, however, only right to say that aconite, arsenic, the solanaceae and vipers were first employed as poisons before becoming remedies, and that physicians received them directly from the hands of the magicians and sorcerers.

Encouraged by the exigencies of a rich clientele, who wished only to take expensive remedies, polypharmacy set itself no limits, and he had most success who could invent the most extraordinary medicaments. Andromachus of Crete, physician to Nero, compounded a remedy composed of seventy-eight different ingredients, in fact all the materia medica of his time, and called it *theriaca,* which we may rightly assume to be the masterpiece of Empiricism. Be this as it may, the *theriaca* was employed throughout the ages, even unto the middle of the last century, while the great Trousseau himself advised its exhibition in confluent smallpox, in serious types of measles and in other forms of malignant fever.

Galen appeared to put a little order into the progress of medical science, which was then going astray in the realms of fantasy. He revived the doctrine of Hippocrates, namely, that of the four cardinal humours—blood, pituit, bile and atrabile. When blood was in excess plethora developed, and when either one of the remaining three was in too great abundance cacochymy ensued. To revive the doctrine of Hippocrates merely meant that Empiricism was given new impetus. Galen's therapeutics were in no way original and, although he certainly deserves his reputation as a skilful and lucky physician in the treatment of his patients, his success was due to the fact that he had good judgment in the use of medicaments approved before his time.

After Galen, and during the decadence of the Roman Empire, therapeutics fell to a low level, and the reader will probably remember that Aëtius of Amida (502–575 A.D.) treated his patients by incantations. At about the same period Alexander of Tralles (525–605 A.D.) went to the opposite extreme and invented a treatment consisting of three hundred and sixty-five potions that were to be taken by the patient during a period of two years. During the long night of the Dark Ages, Arabia was the only refuge offered to the luminaries of intellectual life, and, as we have pointed out, the Islamic physicians contributed largely to the progress of pharmacy, or it may not be too much to say, they created it in the scientific sense. It may unhesitatingly be said that they perfected it to such a degree that the discoveries of modern organic and inorganic chemistry were necessary to bring it back to the level to which they had raised it.

We know that Avicenna gilded and silvered his pills, that he made extracts, syrups, and electuaries, requiring delicate manipulations that would have delighted the pharmacists of only thirty years ago. The Islamic physicians were familiar with the alembic, and Abulcasis by its use discovered spirits of wine. Without referring to the many substances derived from the mineral kingdom which were unknown up to their time, we will simply say that the Islamic physicians published a codex which regulated the use of medicaments and no new product could be prescribed without the permission of the government authorities.

But the mysterious, the inexplicable and the impossible attracted them. Abulcasis attempted the transmutation of metals and, although his researches and those of other alchemists have largely contributed to the discoveries and the progress of chemistry, the same cannot be said of the labour expended in the search for the elixir of life, a quest that excited the enthusiasm and ardour of this learned man and his many disciples. These researches absorbed considerable intellectual force which, rationally directed, would have certainly aided the progress of therapeutics, then still in their infancy.

We will not stop to examine the *Code of Health* in which the precepts of the School of Salerno were set forth in Leonine verse. Leaving aside the stagnant treatments of the Middle Ages, and coming to the Renaissance, dominated by that impetuous individual, the "destroyer of genius", namely Paracelsus, we may say at once that the glory of Paracelsus is a result rather of his genius than of his destructive brutality, for the edifice built by Hippocrates and Galen still remains almost intact in spite of his attacks upon it, while the building of which he himself laid the foundation has endured through centuries and is added to every day. He sowed the first seeds of medical chemistry, which had no existence before him; he strongly advocated the use of antimony, iron, lead, arsenic and mercury—the specific of syphilis—which still survives, and will probably exist for a long time to come as the last trench of empiricism to be taken.

Paracelsus tells us that "experience has shown that mercury is the sovereign and only remedy for the cure of all ulcers tainted with the great pox. Sublimated mercury has been retained in this business as a general remedy because its great virtue has been known to everybody. It is given by mouth, and cures by inducing abundant expectoration of saliva, not because the saliva is the cause of the disease but because it is mixed with it".

Paracelsus also referred to the extraction of the quintessence of plants, but this was only accomplished at the beginning of the XIXth century when P. J. Pelletier and his collaborator, Caventou, prepared sulphate of quinine and afterwards proceeded to the extraction of vegetable alkaloids.

Paracelsus even foresaw the practice of asepsis, for he says: "Do not touch wounds, as they cure themselves; it is the external agents which militate against the process of cicatrisation." He inaugurated an ingenious diagnostic method still used to-day for the diagnosis of indefinite syphilitic manifestations, and he affirmed that by the nature of the remedy one might determine the nature of the disease. Although it must be admitted that the mental equilibrium of Paracelsus was far from perfect, he certainly gave a great impetus to the progress of medicine. He was led astray by his love for the occult sciences, delved deep in the Arcana and dallied with researches for the discovery of mysterious panaceas complicated with astral influences, but on the other hand he foresaw with marvellous lucidity of intelligence explanations of things still hidden in obscurity. As he says : " Before the end of the world a large number of supernatural things will be explained by physical causes."

While anatomy and surgery—the despised legacy of Herophilus and Erasistratus—progressed by the work of Vesalius, Eustachius and Fallopius, therapeutics lay dormant as if exhausted by the sudden impulse given by Paracelsus. We will now go on to the XVIIth century, when, under the fertile influence of the philosophy of Descartes, new doctrines sprang to life. Empiricism had continually progressed since the days of Hippocrates and experimental science had likewise been considerably enriched. The number of known diseases had been increased and with them both medicaments and medications. Having nothing to guide them, having no positive method, ignorant of pathogenesis, deprived of experimental physiology upon which certitude could be based, physicians of those days had only their memory to resort to, and therefore filled their minds with as many facts as possible so as to be able to find them again should similar cases occur. Certain partial theories existed as well as some special opinions relating to a given organ or a given viscus, and from these theories a logical medication could be derived without resorting to empiricism.

But these theories and opinions were fantastic, and reference to a single one will be quite sufficient as an example. In the days of Hippocrates the uterus was regarded as an animal which could be flattered and attracted by pleasant odours, while it disliked fetid odours extremely and attempted to escape from them, so that in the middle of the XVIth century we find Amatus Lusitanus treating a uterine prolapsus, as he thought, with considerable ingenuity, by causing his patient to inhale musk and pleasant-scented herbs in order to attract the uterus upwards, while the vulva was exposed to the stench given off by galbanum and the smoke of burning feathers in order to cause the displaced organ to recede. As is seen, empiricism at this time was preferable to the therapeutics of sophism, which had commenced to become burdensome, and the medical profession, wearied of always referring to memory, felt the necessity for a method which would have really rational treatment as a starting point.

It was then that Borelli developed the Iatro-mechanical doctrine, according to which all physiological and pathological acts could be reduced to a system of movement (or shock), balancing, pressure and relaxation. During this time Sylvius founded chemiatry, in which chemical agents were preferably employed. This doctrine, the germs of which had been planted by Rhazes and developed by Paracelsus and the "Stagyrists," attributed disease to acridity. This acridity could be either acid or alkaline, and was treated by contrary chemical medication; a system that singularly simplified therapeutics, but was, of course, absolutely insufficient, or nearly so.

A little later Baglivi attempted to resuscitate the *strictum* and *laxum* of the Methodists, but does not appear to have been very convinced, for he says that many different theories respecting diseases and their treatment can be put forward, and that if any one of these theories represented all the known facts, any one of them would be able to produce cure. As can be seen, this merely complicated the question in attempting to simplify it. Baglivi studied the question of revulsion with the cantharides that even the prudent Hippocrates had given internally in cases of hydropsy, but was fearful of the use of cinchona in cases of malaria and preferred sal ammoniac and camomile. This man, who wished to overthrow Empiricism, was in reality a retrograde empiricist, in therapeutics.

His contemporary, Boerhaave, became the apostle to the Iatro-mechanical theory to which we have just referred. In his youth he suffered from an ulcer of the thigh, for which treatment, carried out for four years, had proved fruitless. As a last resort he decided to treat his ulcer with urine, because it contained salts in solution. For all this Boerhaave became a renowned practitioner and inaugurated clinical teaching by the bedside.

Boerhaave taught that there were salt, putrid, and oily

temperaments. These temperaments in reality represent what to-day we call diatheses, the oily temperament being arthritism, in other words a general condition in which the functions of the organism work imperfectly. His treatments, which, it appears, ought to have been tonic and stimulant, were rather depleting and debilitating, and were selected from among purgatives, alkalines and sudorifics, dietetics and blood-letting, with a good dose of suggestion added.

In order to oppose the Iatro-mechanical system, G. Stahl created animism, which was merely a perfected pneumatism. He admitted three movements in the body; the circulatory, secretory and excretory. The soul presided over these movements for the regulation of the equilibrium in health and to correct this equilibrium in disease. This theory would seem to imply a psychical or suggestive treatment, but such was far from the case. Stahl's therapeutics were those of the empirics of his time, although he was very moderate in the use of remedies and it is only just to say that in cases of fever he did not exhibit cinchona bark but followed an expectant plan.

And lastly, when organic dynamism, developed by Frederick Hoffmann, has been mentioned, it will be seen that, although the XVIIth century did not bring forth the doctrine which might have been expected, it at least attempted to produce it upon several occasions.

Bordeu gives an excellent outline of the condition of Empiricism during this time when he says: "The king appointed a royal commission with the king's physician as its chief. This commission was intended to collect and examine the empirical remedies and then to select the most useful among them. It was from this school, or rather court, that the majority of remedies employed to-day (XVIIIth century), such as mercury, tartar emetic, various neutral salts, cinchona, ipecacuanha, kermes and so many others are derived, which finally oblige the Dogmatics to remain in their entrenchments."

Inoculation of smallpox, soon to be succeeded by the vaccination we owe to Jenner, had been transmitted throughout the ages among various peoples, and Lady Mary Wortley Montagu, having had her son inoculated at Constantinople, introduced the practice into England. Thus was confirmed the aphorism of Hippocrates: "The medical art is formed little by little and daily becomes enriched by new discoveries; it cannot arrive at the highest point of its perfection until a great number of generations have come and gone."

Two medicaments are to be particularly noted in the therapeutics of the XVIIth century, namely antimony (or rather tartar emetic), which, after savage attacks and passionate eulogies, was at last admitted into the materia medica and continued to render great service in the treatment of disease, and cinchona, which was introduced into France and Spain in 1679. This specific for paludism took its place beside the specific for syphilis, thus enlarging the field of Empiricism, and continued to be one of the great glories of Empiricism up to the year 1882, when Richard demonstrated the parasitic nature of intermittent fever, and Laveran distinctly established its pathogenesis, hence transplanting the Jesuit's powder from the domain of Empiricism into that of pathogenic therapeutics, which were beginning to develop.

As may be seen, the struggle against Empiricism in the XVIIth century was not very successful; the Iatro-mechanists, the chemiaters, the animists and the dynamicists had completely failed in their attempt at substitution. The XVIIIth century gave evidence of greater prudence. It produced no colossus and even seemed resigned to accept the domination of the past; but beneath the silence it was forging invincible weapons which would be used by the XIXth century to assure the triumph of the new therapeutics.

Leeuwenhoek had created micrography, which was soon to be used by Bichat for opening up the road to an unknown science, namely histology. During this time von Haller laid the foundations of physiology and Lavoisier placed chemistry on the solid and unshakable basis which Paracelsus had foreseen rather as a therapeutist than as a scientist. The ideas of Paracelsus had brought forth fruits to be plucked in the XVIIIth century, for at the time when Lavoisier formulated the laws of chemistry, a physician brought back into favour a form of medication which had been created by Paracelsus—this physician was Mesmer, and his agent was animai magnetism.

PLATE XXIV

FREDERICK DEKKER
*(Author's Collection)*

[*face p. 376*

However, the end of the century was to be marked by a discovery of the highest importance, namely vaccination, performed by Jenner for the first time on May 14, 1796. The youngest daughter and the greatest glory of Empiricism, vaccination took its place at the head of specific remedies, while at the same time it opened up the road to an entirely new medication, namely prophylactic therapeutics. Later on, we shall see how under the influence of the discoveries at the end of the XIXth century, it overthrew the very doctrine to which it owed its birth.

From the very beginning of the XIXth century advantage was taken of the work of the preceding centuries. Clinical observation, systematically established by Boerhaave, developed greatly and increased its means of investigation; as early as 1674 Thomas Willis had noted the presence of sugar in the urine of diabetic patients, while in 1673 Dekkers discovered albumen in the urine. But it was Laënnec who, by his discovery of auscultation, brought clinical medicine up to its present level. His precision in investigation limited the field of Empiricism.

Then Broussais appeared upon the scene with his theory of excitation. According to him there was but one pathogenic agent, namely excitation. This could show itself in two ways; if the excitation was too weak, debility ensued, while if too strong irritation resulted. In his therapeutics it would seem that Broussais neglected debility and directed his attention especially to irritation, which he treated by depressing remedies derived from Empiricism. In opposition to the doctrine of excitation a new doctrine was developed by Samuel Hahnemann, the essence of which was conveyed in the phrase *similia similibus curantur*—we refer to homoeopathy.

From this time on therapeutics gave rise to specialism. Mesmer's successes tempted certain practitioners, who carefully sought among forgotten medications for those that might lend themselves to greater development and a more complete systematization; thus were created hypnotism, metallotherapy, electro-therapy, gymnastics, hydrotherapy and many others now brought to a high degree of perfection. Then came the great discovery of general anaesthesia by ether, made by Morton in 1846, while a year later Simpson discovered the anaesthetic use of chloroform.

As the story of the first use of ether has often been incorrectly reported, perhaps the writer may be excused if he gives the true facts in detail. The facts are taken from the Biographical Notes of John Collins Warren, of Boston (*The Life of John Collins Warren, M.D.*, by Edward Warren, M.D., Boston, 1860). The first operation under the influence of ether was performed on the 16th October, 1846.

"The introduction of ether into surgical operations was done by my hands. Mr. W. T. G. Morton, a dentist, of Boston, called on me to say he had found the means of preventing pain in surgical operations; and he was so sanguine in regard to his new application, that I agreed to employ it on the first opportunity.

"The prevention of pain in surgical operations had been a subject I had discussed almost annually in my lectures. I had tried many experiments myself, and had allowed mesmerists and magnetizers to make their trials.

"Nothing, however, had the desired effect, in any degree, but opium; and in cases which threatened to be very painful, as in a case of lithotomy, if I saw no objection, I was in the habit of giving to grown males eight or ten grains, with some degree of effect in obtunding the pain.

"The use of ether, after a few trials, became quite satisfactory; and, from that time, few surgical operations were performed in Boston without it. Many hundred operations have been done by Dr. Mason Warren and myself with ether; and, considering the great power of this agent, it is wonderful we are able to say, that no important ill consequence at any time has occurred.

"A little more than a year after the introduction of ether, Dr. Simpson, of Edinburgh, very unluckily introduced chloroform as a substitute. Chloroform was already known to chemists, and had been used as an anaesthetic by Mr. Bell, of London, the previous summer. Soon after, a series of deaths from this substance began to take place, and continued, till in about two years, twenty deaths had occurred. Having previously published *Ether, with Surgical Remarks*, containing an account of ether, and of a number of surgical cases and new operations in which it had been happily employed, I felt myself bound to show the dangerous effects of chloroform, and to warn surgeons against the use of it.

Moreover, I thought it best to recommend ether in the place of it, or, what I particularly preferred, 'strong chloric ether,' which I had directed to be prepared as a substitute. This is preferable to the other, with the exception that it makes the face smart; an inconvenience which can be avoided by rubbing the face with ointment.

"The first publication I ever made on ether was a newspaper article soon after its introduction. I also wrote letters to the South, recommending it; and to the *British and Foreign Medical Review* in London, and the Paris *Medical Gazette*. In the latter part of 1847, I published *Etherization, with Surgical Remarks*, and, in the year after, *Objections to Chloroform* (effects of chloroform and strong chloric ether as narcotic agents). I should also mention, that, as much as forty years ago, I recommended and employed sulphuric ether in alleviating the last pains, particularly from pulmonary diseases. In such a way I employed it for Thomas Davis, Esq., at that time Treasurer of the State; also for my sister, Mrs. Brown, to relieve pain.

"About two years before Morton made his application to me, Dr. Wells, of Connecticut, applied for leave to introduce the nitrous oxide, or exhilarating gas, in the Massachusetts Medical College. I agreed to it, and he made the trial, but not with such success as to command attention. I have seen it used, however, since, with a decided anaesthetic effect. But it is not so convenient as ether, and not so safe; for it prevents the oxygenation of the blood to an alarming degree.

"It was not until some time after I had used ether, that, in a conversation between Dr. Charles T. Jackson, Dr. Gould and myself, I learned that it was on the suggestion of Dr. Jackson that Mr. Morton was first led to use ether to prevent pain. A violent controversy subsequently took place between Drs. Jackson and Morton, and I was frequently appealed to for evidence on the subject. The amount of what I know may be comprised in few words. Dr. Jackson suggested the use of ether to Morton, and Dr. Morton first employed it to prevent pain in the extraction of teeth; and, at his request, I first used it in a surgical operation. Dr. Jackson has also stated to me, that he advised Mr. Morton to apply to me to use it in a surgical operation."

In 1845 Rynd invented the subcutaneous method of introducing drugs into the organism, a method popularized by Pravaz, which rendered incalculable service to empirical therapeutics.

In 1866 Guérin invented absorbent cotton dressings, which, to a certain extent, formed a barrier to infection, while two years later the great Lister gave to the world his methods of antisepsis, for the immortal Pasteur had already shown how frequently infection was due to bacterial invasion. The discoveries of Pasteur completely resurrected surgery and transformed therapeutics. By the discovery of specific bacteria Pasteur created pathogenesis and by experimenting with attenuated virus he founded pathogenic therapeutics. From this time on Empiricism has taken a secondary place in the healing art, while pathogenic therapeutics with pharmacotherapy, serotherapy and opotherapy are developing every day to the great benefit of humanity.

That great mind of the Renaissance, whose satirical utterances had so profound a psychical influence on the reform of medicine, religion and law in the years to follow—we refer to François Rabelais—once said that the practice of medicine is but a farce played by three actors; the physician, the patient and the disease.

It may have been so once; to-day, the practice of medicine is an Empiricism tempered by science, but an Empiricism that will become more and more scientific if only the enthusiasms of the moment are corrected by the philosophy and judgment that nothing but a knowledge of the History of Medicine can supply.

# INDEX

Mediaeval persons known only by their Christian name and their place of origin are indexed under the latter, e.g., Milan (John of). French names beginning with a separate Le, La, Du, or Des, are indexed under L or D; in all others the preposition or article is disregarded. In German names the Umlaut is replaced by *e*.